Functional Skills in Language and Literature

Functional Skills in Language and Literature

Dr. Richa Dewani

RANDOM PUBLICATIONS
NEW DELHI (INDIA)

Functional Skills in Language and Literature

ISBN 978-93-5111-960-9

Published in 2016 in India by

RANDOM PUBLICATIONS

4376-A/4B, Gali Murari Lal, Ansari Road
New Delhi-110 002
Phone : +9111-43580356, 011-23289044, 011-43142548
e-mail: sales@randompublications.com,
info@randompublications.com, randomexports@gmail.com

Reprinted 2026

Type Setting by : Friends Media, Delhi-110089

Preface

By function is meant intralinguistically the role individual linguistic items play within an overall linguistic system, and-and this is an extension of traditional usage, although quite commonplace in sociolinguistic literature- also extra linguistically the role linguistic systems play in society. By form is meant the various linguistic items themselves.

It is held in this book that the functions of language, both intralinguistic and extralinguistic, are crucial in accounting for linguistic change. To dismiss functional pressure as being at all influential in the direction of linguistic development would be extreme. To take a simple example: the history of the English pronouns shows a steady replacement of many less distinctive native h-types by markedly distinctive forms borrowed from or influenced by Scandinavian (e.g. they, their, them and, probably, she).

The shift from native to Scandinavian forms seems to coincide with the rise in importance of pronouns as grammatical 'tracking-devices' as the older inflectional mechanisms fell into decay; and there are therefore both intralinguistic (system-based) and extralinguistic (contact-based) issues involved in explaining the change.

Language proficiency tests and diagnostic tests are not specific to any one curriculum, but on the other hand, progress assessments should evaluate students' ability to implement the language knowledge and skills that they have learned through their studies in a particular course, and placement assessment seeks to determine the level of students' knowledge/skill with reference to placement within a particular curriculum.

Literature moves in language as a medium, but that medium comprises two layers, the latent content of language — our intuitive record of experience — and the particular conformation of a given language — the specific how of our record of experience. Literature that draws its sustenance mainly — never entirely — from the lower level, say a play of Shakespeare's, is translatable without too great a loss of character. If it moves in the upper rather than in the lower level — a fair example is a lyric of Swinburne's — it is as good as untranslatable. Both types of literary expression may be great or mediocre.

The book functional skills emphasis more on the self assessment and easy user-friendly language. They will also count towards other qualifications, including diplomas and apprenticeships.

– Author

Contents

1

Function and Role of English Teaching

ENGLISH LESSON PLAN FOR BEGINNERS

Teaching English has been an incredible learning experience for us. It studied Japanese in Colleges including Kansai Gaidai so He has some idea what it's like to work towards not only grammatical understanding, but actual functional mastery of a foreign language. It had the chance to experience the frustrations, the triumphs, and all the emotions that come in between. He had no formal TESL training before coming to Japan, so It was relieved to find that Smith's provided full, intensive training courses designed to suit even someone with as little experience. It was nervous at first, but I had the full support of the training staff and fellow coaches (as we call ourselves) here at Smith's. Two years later, I'm still here and It welcome the challenge that each individual class brings.

At Smith's Kyobashi we have a large percentage of beginner level students, so I'm never at a loss for chances to perfect my beginner level lesson techniques. I've heard teachers at ordinary schools complain that beginner level lessons can be challenging because the students have such underdeveloped listening skills. In addition, I've heard those same teachers claim that a beginner level student's limited vocabulary makes them unable to sustain extended conversations. When I hear things like that, I can't help but breathe a sigh of relief that I joined a school like Smith's.

At Smith's we have a standard target balance for Student-Talk-Time and Coach-Talk-Time. That balance is STT 70 per cent, CTT 30 per cent. I take great comfort in knowing that every time I reach this ratio in class he has truly helped my student improve his or her skills. As a student of foreign language myself, It can understand why having that much talking time is crucial. Like many Japanese studying at English schools in Japan today,

It was chock full of book knowledge with no chance to practice using it. It wasn't until I joined some conversation focused classes with low student to teacher ratio that It was forced to actually put that knowledge to the test. I was forced to simply speak. If the student is speaking for 70 per cent of the class time, It can spend that much more time focusing on the student's needs rather than wondering if what I'm saying is being comprehended in full or not. At Smith's we say: keep it simple and let the student practice. After all, that's the reason the student is coming to class in the first place.

As for concerns as to whether a beginner level student can sustain extended conversation or not, I let the Smith's curriculum handle that. By simply following the lesson plans step by step, even from my very first week, I was able to provide a full array of exercises that keep students of any level practicing and taking up lesson time with what a good conversation lesson should be full of: The student speaking English. Please note: not static listening, not reading, not thinking about; actually speaking.

In my typical Beginner level class It welcome the student into my classroom and get seated by 0 minutes on the hour. At Smith's most students tend to filter into the lobby about 10 minutes before their scheduled time slot. The curriculum has been so easy to use that, after some initial study to familiarize myself with the notations and lesson plan content, it takes me no more than a few minutes to select a student's lesson. This leaves me with plenty of time to relax, take a break, grab a coffee or tea, and chat with students and other coaches in the lobby area. Since things run so smoothly, I've never had a problem starting a lesson at the top of the hour.

ET

It's winter time, so the students are generally burdened with heavy coats, bags, or shopping parcels. It take this opportunity to establish trust with the student right from the start. There are two empty seats available for this one-to-one class so It casually ask the student "Which seat do you want?" indicating both seats in turn. On average, the student looks a little confused at this point. I always imagine: He must be wondering why It asked such a silly question.

It's at that point the student's expression changes from confusion to one of surprise and understanding. Even before sitting down, he whips out his note book and hurriedly flips through the pages to double check. Sure enough, this is the exact same grammatical situation that he had finished his previous lesson with. Slapping the note book shut and straightening up with pride, the student triumphantly says "Either will do!" It say "Well then, please take a seat!" and we share a laugh as he sits down comfortably.

This simple technique of reviewing and important point from the previous lesson reassures the student that It know exactly who he is and what he's studying. This is important whether the previous class was taught by me or another coach on staff. My favourite part about establishing this trust right off the bat if watching the students shoulders relax afterwards, showing their level of comfort. What's more, the shoulders snap back to attention as soon as It start to speak again. There's something about getting that review in within the first minute that really lets the student know that class has begun and, even if it may sound like it, we're not just chatting; it's practice time.

ROUTINE

After establishing trust with the student and warming up just a bit by asking them about their work day or recent weekend I transit into the new material which I've selected to have the student work through. In this case, I choose our Question and Answer routine number two called "To the Station". I always start by scrawling "Routine" in bold letters across the top of the board and announcing the word so that the student knows what type of lesson to be ready for. At Smith's we have three major lesson styles, each with multiple sub categories.

If I do a good job of being clear and consistent in my transitions, the student will be ready for the style of practice coming up next. Upon announcing the lesson type, I often see students pulling out colour coded notebooks or flipping to a certain section of a larger notebook. When I see this I know the student and I are on the same page right from the start.

Smith's Question and Answer (Q and A) routines are great for beginner level students. They focus on strengthening confidence in grammar, responding to common questions, and stringing short simple ideas into longer, fluent, compound sentences. I choose to work the student on Q and A questions 1 through 3, 6, 7, and 10. For this student, questions 3, 6 and 7 are being presented as new material. I start by tying the new routine into the previous routines the student is already familiar with. Smith's Q and A routines are sequential and build upon one another, so with less than a minute review or Routine 1 (using only the hint bar) I can move directly into Routine 2 using the new question number 7.

I draw out the second sentence using question 2 and then introduce new question 3 to complete the thought. In comparing sentences one and two, the student notes that the verbs "get on" and "ride" are typically expressed using only a single verb in Japanese. I quickly demonstrate the difference between the two. The student gives a long "Ooooh" and nods his head as he notes this point into his book.

The format is familiar to the student, but the material is new so of course there are some times where he's going to need some help. This is where I see some doubt in the student's face. It's that same look of doubt that I saw during the student's first trial lesson. I use board work to help the student along. I ask him questions and give visual hints as to the answer I'm looking for. If the student gives a partial answer, I lock it onto the white board (leaving blank underlines for missing words to be filled in later). The student takes comfort in knowing that he's gotten 80 per cent of the sentence correct on his own and is happy to receive and extra hint in order to finish it off. At sentence 6 we come to an impasse where the student is having a vocabulary problem. He's completed the target sentence with the exception of a single word and is repeating out-loud the Japanese word "kaisatsu... kaisatsu". It's at times like this that the student's eyes practically scream "Please! Help me! Get me out of this hole!" The student and I both know what he's trying to say but he just needs a slight push to get there. I put my marker to the white board before the student begins to feel too frustrated and scrawl "ticket gate" onto the section of my board reserved for new vocabulary.

We had a few sentences that needed worked on, and there are a few new words in the "vocab box" but we worked through all 11 sentences in this routine.

The next thing I do is a pronunciation check. To the student I simply say "Ok! Hatsuon check!" Hatsuon is the Japanese word for pronunciation. I often use Japanese when speaking directly about parts of speech or classroom-based grammatical terms. I don't see a need to confuse students with technical terms for grammar that they don't need to carry on a conversation. We're a conversation school after all, right?

The student repeats the sentences he's just formed (mostly of his own effort, I offered only hints or support when needed). This time, although the student is focused on their pronunciation, I note a definite change in body language from being uncertain and possible defensive to leaning forward, into the classroom, exuding confidence. It's as though their thinking "Round two is mine." As the student goes through each sentence, I listen for possibly damaging pronunciation errors at the same time as writing an abbreviated hint version of all 11 sentences horizontally across the lower part of the board.

Now it's time for the true test. I erase the full sentences leaving only the one word hints at the bottom. I ask all the same questions again, and the student answers in full, with very few mistakes if any. The student often seems surprised and relieved at this point, but it comes as no surprise to me anymore. Through the design of the lesson, the student has already practiced each individual sentence five times or more without even realizing it.

Furthermore, each routine is designed specifically to reinforce the students existing knowledge and give him the confidence he needs to speak fluently. I don't necessarily have to understand the mechanics of the lesson to that level of detail, I just know it works! After completing the entire routine using the hint bar only, I congratulate the student with a hearty hand shake and the student exhales loudly. He understands that the workout is over and slumps back into his chair but noticeably has a smile on his face. I imagine he's feeling the weight of his accomplishment at this time. After double checking with the student, I clear the entire board outside of the "new vocab" box and write up the heading for the next segment of my four step lesson plan process.

As I mentioned, at Smith's we have three major lesson styles. Those lesson styles are transitioned between using a 4 step process that we call "the Loop".

By using this 4 step process in every lesson we ensure a great number of things to both ourselves and the students. Not the least of which is a consistent easily identifiable direction of study that the students can feel.

ITEM

Since the student has already worked through some new material in the Routine, the next step is to cover something for review. Thanks to the Loop, I can guarantee my students that every single lesson will contain some form of review to ensure they maintain everything they've worked for so far. This student's review comes in the form of the basic level Item lesson plan, Past 1. The student has already completed this lesson once, so I can jump right into to Presentation section of the lesson. I write the example dialog up on the white board as the lesson plan describes and proceed to practice it with the student. The student plays the part of A and I am B. We use the Smith's cards corresponding to this lesson to which makes sure the student can focus on making natural sounding sentences without wracking their brains for subject matter. We focus more on creativity with higher level students, once the basics are locked down. Comparatively, this part of the lesson is much less intense but still focused. The student and I share a laugh when I answer "Yes, I did." To a question like: "Did you go to the beach yesterday?" It is the middle of December after all.

After a nice ten minutes of review I move into my fourth and final step of the Loop: the One Point. I transit again by simply asking the student if I can wipe the board. This time the student realizes there's something he hasn't noted yet and says "Oh! Oh! Wait!" while he scribbles down a few more crucial notes. After the student finishes, I clear the board and write One Point as the new heading. I always enjoy the unique way students express themselves when it comes to One Points. The firs thing they do is look at the clock. If a Smith's coach says "Ok, One Point." The student knows the lesson is over, usually before they realise it. Some write a simple heading, some draw stars, some make a cloud to write the one point into. I've see some students who switch to coloured markers and draw little hearts next to where they will put the One Point into their notes. Let's just say that they are a popular favourite.

ONE POINT

Today's one point is A 3.24. We've had a great lesson and I'm actually a little light on CTT so I let go a little and tell the student to imagine we had a promise to meet, but I am late. We do a little roll play back and forth until the student is comfortable with how and when to use the One Point phrase. The students all seem to enjoy pretending to be mad at me for being late for some reason. We have another good laugh. With that, my Loop is complete so I clear the board again. After checking the student's notes to make sure none of the new vocabulary has been overlooked I clear the "vocab box" as well and thank the student for another great lesson. We walk back out to the lobby together and say a cheerful goodbye and see you next week. I grab a hot tea and head back to fill in extra details on the student's lesson report. I've got a good fifteen minutes to relax before my next lesson so I chat with another coach about something interesting that happened during her lesson. We head out and take a seat in the lobby together to wait for the next set of students. They should be coming in anytime now.

ENGLISH LANGUAGE LEARNERS

The everyday demands of classroom instruction increase in complexity from year to year—with respect to curricular demands, accountability, and the diversity of the student population. New state frameworks and instructional trends require grade-level curricular standards to continually change. The demands of accountability vis-à-vis state standards and student performance on standardized tests influence district policies regarding instructional practices and how to best address the needs of the burgeoning numbers of English language learners. In addition, the linguistic diversity of English language learners has im-portant implications for the design of programmes intended to address the range of levels of English language learners' oral fluency, literacy skills, and cognitive growth. A variety of materials can be used to engage learners in English lan-guage content instruction; however, if these students are to attain grade-level standards in English language subject matter instruction, they must master communicative and cognitive skills as well as master strategies for reading and learning from expository text, the staple of content instruction and the domi-nant type of text included in materials employed to teach content. This formi-dable mix of demands requires an answer to these two questions:

- How can teachers effectively manage the complexity of skill, content, and English language development instruction and also make this instruction accessible to English language learners?
- What are the implications for determining appropriate instructional materials?

This chapter will present ideas and strategies to help teachers optimize the education of English language learners in subject matter instruction. The potential to teach language and to enable access to learning across content areas will be addressed through four key instructional dimensions: communication-based instruction, content-based instruction, cognitive development, and study skills. Implications for appropriate instructional materials will also be addressed.

COMMUNICATION-BASED INSTRUCTION FOR ENGLISH LEARNERS

Communication-based instruction can be an effective tool for providing English language learners access to content area learning. Communication-based instruction is designed to parallel the way children acquire their first lan-guage. Krashen's acquisition-learning hypothesis holds that infants acquire language subconsciously rather than cognitively learning the language. When learning content in a second language, students need instructional approaches that allow them to interact with and construct meaning from lessons present-ed in class. Language is the medium for learning and communicating impor-tant subject matter. For students learning *in* the language rather than *about* the language, effective communication is interactive, authentic, and meaning-ful, with ample opportunities to hear and respond in the target language and to get feedback from native speakers, the teacher, instructional assistants, vol-unteers, and other English language learners.

Direct and indirect modeling of English language structures and conven-tions with corrective feedback can and should be included in communication-based instruction through directed lessons according to Fillmore and Snow. Gersten and Baker also believe that English learners need for-mal feedback if they are to learn the language; however, they point out that merging content instruction with English language development usually trun-cates the amount of time devoted to learning the second language. They be-lieve that sheltered instruction (instruction designed for making sure English language learners understand content instruction) usually does not include adequate English language development in the context of writing. Like Snow and Fillmore, they believe that this phenomenon has a deleterious effect on student writing.

The written conventions of the target language should be linked to oral communication and content through daily language lessons in writing, spelling, and grammar that are connected to the related readings of the con-tent curriculum, not taught as isolated and unrelated skills. Connecting daily language lessons to related reading succeeds in linking written language con-ventions to oral communication and content by demonstrating for English language learners the ways in which writers use literary devices such as figures of speech, similes, idiomatic expressions, metaphors, imagery, analogies, and the prosodic features (rhythm, intonation, and phrasing) of the dialect. The readings help demonstrate the use of grammatical structures and spelling con-ventions across genres of literature and expose English language learners to new vocabulary development in context rather than in isolated word lists that have no meaning or connections to their world.

In content instruction, it is important for students to learn the structures of the English language in order to interpret the work of related readings across subject matter instruction. The ability of English language learners to suc-ceed in "content" learning has to do with how well they can infer meaning, draw conclusions, learn terminology, analyze problems, and synthesize infor-mation from various sources, which means they need to transfer and apply reading and language conventions across the curriculum. Students make gains in language acquisition by interacting with speakers of the English language in meaningful contexts, and their English language oral fluency increases as they begin to respond and sustain communication in the target language— just as accuracy in reading and writing develops with daily involvement in pur-poseful application. When language is regarded as a medium of learning, it offers a context for communicating the thinking process in the subject matter without the need to translate content.

The Benefits of Sheltered Language Strategies

Sheltered language strategies allow students to develop knowledge of subject matter areas through their English language. Through these strategies, teachers ensure that lessons are comprehensible to learners of different English lan-guage proficiency levels and also provide English language development.

An effective sheltered instruction technique is to draw from the learners' background knowledge in the area of study. Relating the subject matter to the students can involve not only asking questions regarding what they have learned in school about the content but also eliciting what students know about the topic from their own life experiences and personal connections. If the teacher observes that students lack sufficient background or personal information or connections about the subject, then lesson planning needs to present basic foundations of the subject matter through the use of visuals, realia, hands-on experiences, guest speakers, field trips, or related readings. During content instruction, complex concepts and information can be clarified through demonstrations and experimentation. Lesson delivery should include simplification of explanations and vocabulary development by means of showing examples, demonstrating differences and similarities, and speaking with simpler syntax and added gestures. As the students acquire more oral fluency and comprehension, the complexity of content that they can handle can increase gradually as a result of their more frequent communication in context-reduced discourse. It is important to maintain a comfortable participatory learn-ing environment that allows students to practice their English language with-out fear of making errors, seeking clarification, or taking linguistic risks.

Giving students an amount of "wait time" to interpret information or to process questions related to content is encouraged before demanding a response. Students learning content via a new language may have difficulties with cognitively demanding tasks or with discussions presented in context-reduced situations with few external supports for meaning.

Students may want to par-ticipate, but they may have difficulty formulating a response or incorporating appropriate content vocabulary learned in class. It is important for the teacher to frequently check learners' comprehension by collecting and evaluating stu-dent work samples in the subject area. Monitoring a student's degree of com-plexity in the use of the English language is another way of measuring progress in English language acquisition through communication-based instruction. In addition to the sheltered strategies presented for communication and comprehension of content learning, there are other approaches to stimulate a communicative setting in the classroom.

The Benefits of Student Interaction

English language learners benefit from language modeling and reinforcement of linguistic structures through peer interaction in the classroom. Students then have the opportunity to learn the target language in a natural communicative setting through the use of authentic and meaningful language. Providing an op-portunity for daily peer interaction in the classroom allows for the academic and language success of the students. The interaction gives students a chance to develop an understanding of one another's culture. This enables positive cross-cultural attitudes to develop among the learners because the diverse languages and cultures represented in the classroom are assigned equal status.

There are programmes that tend to group students in separate classrooms by language dominance; native speakers are grouped together for their daily pro-gram, while English language learners are assigned to other classrooms. If at all possible, native speakers and English language learners need the opportunity to participate jointly in content learning through team teaching situations in which student groups are integrated for instruction. According to Cummins (1981), children best learn the English language when they are actively involved in the process of communicating with one another. Therefore, activities should include the integration and joint participation of speakers of the target language with English learners when-ever possible.

Peer participation incorporates collaborative learning through mixed groupings comprised of various levels of language production and content expertise. A variety of groupings—pairs, triads, and small groups—can facilitate learning and meet the linguistic and instructional demands of all learners. Students in such settings have the opportunity to gain insights on how others access curricular knowledge and process information in their English language. Social learning theorists have shown that students learn and are motivated by observing others' actions and their consequences—for example, by observing someone persist in a task and achieve suc-cess. Student motivation can, therefore, be strongly influenced by the study behaviours modeled in class: They can observe how other learners manipulate the expository material contained in textbooks, handouts, computer-generated printouts, or library references. There is no better way to learn reading strate-gies for non-fiction material than to see other students infer meaning from a text. Interaction encourages students to become educational and social partners in the process of learning. Such partnerships lower the anxiety attached to seeking necessary assistance when presented with new concepts or difficult content materials in class. The resulting opportunities to verbalize content knowledge open doors for authentic peer dialogue.

The Benefits of Teacher-Student Interaction

Equally important for English language learning is modeling by and interaction with the teacher. Teachers must provide students with modeling of the strate-gies needed to comprehend content material and content instruction. Teachers can, for example, model active listening skills by maintaining eye contact with a speaker and watching his or her gestures. Teachers can direct students how to use textbooks, reference materials, or environmental print in the classroom to enhance understanding of the subject matter. Learning to take notes, make an outline, pose a question, or otherwise seek help can also be demonstrated.

Effective teacher-student interaction involves interacting equally with all students during whole-class or small-group instruction. Providing students with equal access to the curriculum may require certain academic interventions, me-diated structures, or other additional assistance. It may be necessary to prompt or give additional response time to newcomers or beginning-proficiency students who are in need of teacher guidance and reassurance.

A critical aspect of the development of language and content learning is providing a setting for English language learners to negotiate meaning in daily instructional interactions. *Negotiation of meaning*, a term coined by immersion experts, is the process by which participants arrive at un-derstanding one another. It is the collaboration needed in conversations or discussions to express needs, ideas, thoughts, and intentions; it also involves helping others extend and refine their communication skills. The strategies used in the negotiation of meaning are both verbal and non-verbal. A verbal strategy might involve expanding answers to refine the language with the use of semantics, settling on an appropriate rate of speech or providing simplified vocabulary, paraphrasing, or sentence structure to clarify meaning. A nonver-bal strategy might incorporate facial expressions and gestures to match what students hear with what they see or do.

As students begin to acquire higher proficiencies in the English language, teacher-student interactions need to gradually model more complexities in language structure. According to the input hypothesis of Krashen, input promotes progress when it is more advanced than the learner's level of profi-ciency. The learner acquires the ability to function in a new language by listening to input a little more sophisticated than his or her actual level of lan-guage production. Vygotsky's theory of the Zone of Proximal Development is another way to view this means of language learning. According to Vygotsky, children can learn within a range: tasks children can complete independently are at one end of the range, and tasks they cannot complete, even with assistance, are at the other end. The zone most productive for children is between these extremes, where there are tasks children can com-plete when assisted by a knowledgeable or more competent other.

Face-to-face interaction with the teacher tends to provide useful visual cues and non-verbal language to augment comprehension of subject material presented in the lesson. This provides the opportunity for English language learners to engage in content learning through the process of creative con-struction. The teacher has an opportunity in the classroom to model correct language use and to provide indirect and direct error correction. He or she can provide optimal language input and allow for maximum student output by utilizing higher-order thinking and questioning skills.

METHODS AND APPROACHES OF TEACHING ENGLISH

SCOPE

Many children learn several languages at a very young age. Language teaching involves many methods. All the available methods may be appropriate to different contexts. There is no one single method strongly recommended in the teaching of English since the level of the learners differ from one anothers. So, it becomes inevitable for a teacher to know the different methods of teaching and learning Awareness of variety of methods help him to apply the relevant method in his classroom successfully.

ACQUISITION	LEARNING
1. Acquisition is an act of gaining knowledge and skill by your own.	Learning is the act of gaining knowledge and skill by study and from experience etc.,
1. It is an active process by which mother tongue capability develops in a human	
1. It is done in a very early stage with in 5 years.	It is done in a later stage.
1. It is an unconscious process	
1. It is an active process and by taking clues (hints) children construct on their own.	Language learning is a conscious process
1. The main focus is on Communication or reception and of a message. In language learning the thrust is on Syntax and grammar	It involves the skills of reading, speaking and writing.
1. The context is usually crucial and meaningful.	It need not be important in language learning.
1. Motivation is a necessary for acquisition.	Learning does not need motivation.
1. The outcome of acquisition is fluency.	In learning, fluency is not guaranteed.
1. Acquisition is a subconscious process in acquiring mother tongue.	Learning is a conscious process in knowing the rules of the language.

As a teacher the objective of teaching English must be achieved. Many children learn several languages at a very young age but some fail to learn even the basic English. A child acquires all the necessary skills in his mother tongue easily whereas it fails in the second language. The salient features which affect the learning of second language among the students are discussed above:

JIM CUMMINS' INTER DEPENDENCE HYPOTHESIS

According to Jim Cummins' a firm foundation in L1 is essential to master L2. Learning of mother tongue is a natural process. This natural process should be adopted in learning English as second language. L1 learning takes place in the early stages. So, the same process can be adopted in L2.

- Due attention on correct pronunciation and accent.
- Formation of speech habits should be paramount. (important)
- Formal Loud Reading.
- Avoid teaching of grammar.
- Life related words are introduced.
- Create exposure to language (L2) for communication.
- Create informal atmosphere in L2 classroom.
- Build up efforts for real life communication.
- Encourage learners to focus on the meaning or message, not on form.
- Be tolerant to errors. If correction is needed, do it incidentally.

METHOD, APPROACH, DESIGN AND PROCEDURE

What is a Method?

A method refers to the overall plan for the proper presentation of language material. It is based on selected approach and procedure. It include three parts

1. Approach
2. Design
3. Procedure.

What is an Approach?

An approach is concerned with the theory of the Nature of Language and Language Learning.

What is a Design?

- A Design concerns with the general specific objective of the course.
- A syllabus model
- Types of learning and learning tasks.
- Role of learners and teachers
- Role of learning materials.

What is a Procedure?

A procedure is the actual happening of the classroom techniques, practices and behaviours.

GLOBAL ISSUES AND ENGLISH TEACHING

The last ten years have seen an explosion of interest in global issues and global education by the international English teaching profession. This can be documented in the journals and conference programmes of international English teaching organizations such as TESOL (Teachers of English to Speakers of Other Languages) and IATEFL (the International Association of Teachers of English as a Foreign Language), as well as in the pages of the *Global Issues in Language Education Newsletter* of JALT's Global Issues Special Interest Group.

While this new interest in global education has manifested itself in a number of ways, I'd like to focus on five specific areas where the influence of global education has made itself felt:

- New thinking about the aims and mission of the English teaching profession;
- New ideas about the content of English language teaching (ELT);
- Out-reach efforts by ELT associations to global issue speakers and organizations;
- The growing emphasis in ELT conferences on global issue themes; and (5) the formation of global issue interest groups within the English teaching profession.

RETHINKING AIMS

One key trend in the English teaching profession linked to the growing interest in global education is a rethinking of basic educational goals, the "why" of English education. Perhaps most people know the old joke about English teaching acronyms which says that, of all the different types of English teaching — TEFL (Teaching English as a Foreign Language), TESL (Teaching English as a Second Language), TESOL (Teaching English to Speakers of Other Languages) and so on, the most common type of English taught in classrooms round the world is TENOR (Teaching English for No Obvious Reason). In other words, English has always been on the syllabus, so that is why we teach it. Because it is so common to get tied up with the teaching of grammar, literature and communication or with the daily routine of classrooms, textbooks and tests, it is all too easy for English teachers to forget fundamental questions of purpose — the question "What's it all for?"

A growing number of educators are now beginning to discuss what the aims of English language teaching should be — given the serious global issues that face our world. The American educator H. D. Brown (1990), for example, phrases this in terms of the mission of the profession:

What are we doing for the Earth? What are we doing to save it? What are the issues? And what on earth does this have to do with you as an ESL teacher? It has everything to do with you as an ESL teacher. Global, peace and environmental issues intrinsically affect every human being on earth. These issues provide content for your content-based humanized teaching of the 90's. We teachers have a mission, a mission of helping everyone in this world communicate with each other to prevent the global disaster ahead. The 90's are in your hands.

Other educators prefer to talk about the moral dimension of English teaching and the need for an approach to language education which aims at fostering a sense of social responsibility in students. This idea was discussed in a keynote speech by William Kirby, Commissioner of the Texas Education Agency, at the 1989 international convention of the English teaching organization TESOL:

What good is it to teach our students to read if they only read degrading pornography? What good is it to teach students to write if they use their knowledge to write racist graffiti? What good is it to teach students arithmetic if they use their skills only to embezzle others?

The implication here is that we can't call our English teaching successful if our students, however fluent, are ignorant of world problems, have no social conscience or use their communication skills for international crime, exploitation, oppression or environmental destruction.

INTERNATIONAL CONTENT

In addition to a rethinking of goals, the "why" of English teaching, the new interest in global issues has also led to a rethinking of content, the "what" of education. This is related to the growing interest of the profession in content-based language teaching. Content-based teaching argues that language is most effectively learned in the context of relevant, meaningful, motivating content which stimulates students to think and learn through the use of the target language. Content educators such as Brinton, Snow and Wesche (1989) and Mohan (1986) stress that language is a means of learning about the world and recommend the use of motivating themes and authentic materials in classroom teaching.

If one accepts this thesis of content language teaching, then the next question that arises is "What content is worth teaching?" A growing number of educators are proposing world problems or "global issues" as subject matter which can both meet the need for more meaningful content, and address the lack of educational relevance of much of the general English education in schools around the world. This view has been voiced, among others, by the British educator Alan Maley (1992):

Global issues are real issues: the spoliation of the rain-forests, the thinning of the ozone layer, acid rain, nuclear waste disposal, exponential population growth, the spread of AIDS, state violence and genocide in Kurdistan, Tibet and Bosnia, ecological disaster compounded by war in Ethiopia and Somalia... the list is depressingly long.

What has this to do with the teaching of EFL? English language teaching (ELT) has been bedeviled with three perennial problems: the gulf between classroom

activities and real life; the separation of ELT from the main stream of educational ideas; the lack of a content as its subject matter. By making Global Issues a central core of EFL, these problems would be to some extent resolved. (p. 73)

GLOBAL OUTREACH

In order to bring real world content into the classroom, teachers must step outside the field of English language teaching to access materials and information from outside sources. A further trend related to the growing interest in global education, therefore, concerns the efforts by English teaching associations to reach out to global issue experts and organizations for ideas, stimulation and resources. This outreach has taken a number of forms.

The English teaching organization TESOL, for example, has appointed an official liaison to the United Nations who writes articles on the UN and the global issues it deals with for the TESOL newsletter and its 20,000 subscribers worldwide.

TESOL has further shown its commitment to promoting global education through a series of conference workshops which introduce English teachers to experts, resources and ideas from global issue fields. These have included "TESOL Day at the United Nations" at which UN personnel instructed English teachers on how to integrate global issues into their teaching; "TESOL Day at the Carter Center" where teachers attended workshops on conflict resolution by peace experts from former President Jimmy Carter's staff; and "TESOL Day at the Rainforest" at which English teachers were shown how to integrate ecology themes into their lessons by environmental experts. Similar initiatives have taken place in Japan where experts in areas such as peace education, human rights issues and environmental problems have addressed English teachers at JALT conferences about how best to teach these global issues in their classrooms.

This outreach can also be seen in the kinds of featured speakers invited to international conferences. JALT's recent 1996 international conference in Hiroshima, for example, featured UNESCO expert Felix Marti speaking on Linguapax, language teaching, and world peace.

Featured speakers at other international conferences have included US civil rights leader Andrew Young, international educator and human rights advocate Mary Hatwood Futrell, Vietnamese peace activist Le Ly Hayslip, and cross-cultural expert Milton Bennett speaking on tolerance and intercultural understanding.

The invitation of outside speakers such as these to international ELT conferences underscores the commitment of English teaching organizations to link English education to the outside world, raise awareness of global issues, strengthen commitment to socially responsible teaching and remind teachers of the wider social context of their classroom work.

CONFERENCE SESSIONS

English teaching organizations around the world are increasingly featuring global education and global issues in their conferences. One way this can be seen is through the conference themes being chosen. Examples include conference themes such as "Language and Social Justice", "Global Age: Issues in Language Education", "Bridges to Better Understanding", and "World Peace and English Education". That this trend is not limited to English education can be seen in the organization of an entire conference on the theme "Global Issues in Foreign Language Education" by the Modern Language Association of Poland.

Over the past decade, there has also been an explosion of conference presentations focusing on global education themes at ELT conferences round the world. JALT's 1986 conference handbook, for example, reveals no presentations at all on global issue themes, yet its JALT'96 Hiroshima conference ten years later featured over 50 such sessions. These included presentations on such themes as international awareness through video, global education and the Internet, AIDS awareness activities, and teaching about human rights. JALT's annual conference now regularly features conference colloquia, roundtable discussions, and workshops featuring English educators from countries such as Russia, Germany, Thailand, and Australia speaking on topics such as global issues, peace education, environmental awareness, and international understanding as they relate to teaching methods, textbooks, and curriculum design.

The same trend can be seen at other international ELT conferences around the world. IATEFL's 1996 conference, for example, featured a first-ever global issues conference strand with presentations on global issues: these included project work in Brazil, a One World Week event in Portugal, peace studies in Hong Kong, and ESL for international understanding in California. TESOL's 1996 conference in Chicago featured a peace education breakfast seminar, plenary talks on social responsibility and "subversive teaching" for a better world, an academic session on peace education and materials writing, and over 100 presentations by teachers from countries as varied as Poland, Canada, France and Korea with titles such as *Global Issues E-mail Projects, Social Issues and the Language Class, Teaching Strategies for Reducing Prejudice, and Integrating Global Cultures into EFL Materials.*

SPECIAL INTEREST GROUPS

A final trend within the profession is the formation of global issue special interest groups within major international organizations. The first such group to form was JALT's "Global Issues in Language Education" National Special Interest Group (N-SIG) in 1991. Its aims were defined as; To promote the integration of global issues, global awareness and social responsibility into foreign language teaching; To promote networking and support among educators dealing with global issues in language teaching; and To promote awareness among language teachers of developments in global education and the related fields of environmental education, human rights education, peace education, and development education.

Since then, similar groups have been formed in other organizations around the world. These include a Peace and Health Education Interest Group in TESOL Italy (1994), a Global Issues SIG within the Korea TESOL organization, a Global Issues SIG in the UK-based IATEFL association, a Global Education Study Group in the Japan Association of College English Teachers, plus ongoing efforts to establish a Global/Peace Education interest group within the US-based TESOL organization.

The establishment of these groups has enabled English teachers around the world who are involved with global, peace and environmental education to receive funds, begin projects, issue newsletters, hold workshops, obtain conference time to share their research and teaching experience, and to further promote global education within their organizations. The existence of these groups serves to validate global education as a legitimate goal of English teaching and to highlight the social responsibility of the profession.

THE DIAGNOSTIC ASSESSMENT TOOLS IN ENGLISH

The Diagnostic Assessment Tools in English project has been developed in consultation with leading academics and in consideration of current national and international research in the area of early years literacy. As this literature review indicates, the tools developed for this project reflect recent developments in early years teaching and assessment practices, and in some instances offer innovative examples of testing materials that could guide future research. This review will situate the Diagnostic Assessment Tools in English project within current research, focusing on the domains of early literacy, reading, and speaking and listening, to highlight the project's importance within the growing field of early years literacy studies.

Research has recently focused on the importance of early intervention and diagnosis for those students struggling with literacy, and those surpassing expectations. According to Raban (1997), studies have indicated "that children who start school with less knowledge about literacy than others can soon begin to experience a sense of failure, especially as they are presented with increasingly difficult texts". Raban and Ure suggest that research has also identified the need to capture a wide range of abilities in those early years so that curriculums can be adjusted accordingly and no-one is left behind. Bailey and Drummond, in their study of early literacy intervention in the United States, write of one group of students for whom early diagnosis is essential, a group who "may be low-achieving and who may benefit from specific attention".

"These students likely do not have the most dramatic difficulties in the class, but without receiving monitoring and modification to instruction, they may continue to struggle and eventually fall into a higher risk group".

The Diagnostic Assessment Tools in English have been developed in response to the identified need for early intervention and diagnosis in both low and high-achieving students. Such a diagnosis can provide essential information that will help prevent students from falling into higher risk groups, and enable further progress for those students already excelling.

As current research suggests, assessment has an important role to play in this early intervention. Wheldall and Madelaine argue that "effective intervention for children struggling to learn to read and to spell is predicated upon accurate and meaningful assessment". Westwood similarly suggests that, "the role of assessment in literacy during the early years of schooling continues to receive increasing attention in the field of educational research. Assessment, it is now commonly argued, is essential to the practice of effective teaching of literacy".

Raban and Ure also argue that, "some children's needs and difficulties may be easy to overlook and other children's special talents and interests may remain hidden. However, careful observation and assessment will reveal these differences".

A recent United States study into the response-to-intervention (RTI) framework found that for those children who have difficulty learning "small-group intervention, additional assessment to determine precise intervention targets, teacher professional development, or targeted individual intervention might be initiated". Yet, as this study also suggests, the application of RTI is complicated by "the relative paucity of adequate progress-monitoring measures that are sensitive to the short-term skill development that occurs as a result of specific support or intervention". Bailey and Drummond write of the difficulty of developing "carefully tailored instruction". This difficulty is due to the fact that interventions need to diagnose students both accurately and effectively, and to be based on more than teachers' perceptions of at-risk students – a perception that "can have long-term negative effects on student performances in some instances". The tool suite provided by the Diagnostic Assessment Tools in English provides a highly useful addition to teachers' nedgement, thereby helping teachers to avoid the damaging effects of misdiagnosis.

Although recent research has stressed the importance of teaching early literacy authentically and in context, there is a general acknowledgement of the need for simple, directed assessment tasks that allow for easy and accurate diagnosis of student abilities. There is value, in a "simple view of reading", where emphasis is placed on the over-arching skills of decoding and comprehension. Scull similarly argues for "the importance of both decoding and comprehension in primary school curricula". According to Westwood, it is essential to concentrate on these central reading skills because they provide teachers with more accurate data. He states that "by focusing directly on these key processes and skills and by using tests and tasks specifically designed to reveal competence or lack of competence in fundamental skills, teachers can gain much more accurate information than they would obtain from informal holistic observation of students at work on so-called 'authentic' tasks".

For these skill areas to be assessed successfully, particularly in the early stages of development, there must be a focus on oracy. As McCabe writes, "much research finds that reading problems derive from problems in oral language acquisition". Current research has proposed effective ways to improve oral language and emergent literacy skills through what McCabe describes as "various interventions on distinct aspects of literacy-related oral language". Westwood divides these literacy-related oral skills into the following areas: phonic knowledge and skills (such as knowledge of simple letter-to-sound correspondences, recognition of orthographic units), phonological subskills (such as segmentation and sound blending) and vocabulary. The Diagnostic Assessment Tools in English have been designed for the purpose of simple and direct diagnosis in all these skill areas. In their coverage of AusVELS Foundation to Level 4, these tools focus on the decoding and comprehension skills required for successful reading practices, as well as the phonic and phonological skills required for literacy development more generally, and in both oral and written formats as appropriate.

Although simple and direct, these tools also reflect the importance of what Raban describes as "interacting with print in meaningful contexts". Such interaction requires assessment tasks that arc both culturally inclusive and relevant to students, which has been an aim in both the design and selection of material for this project. Meaningful interaction also requires an approach to literacy that is "more inclusive of children's experiences of the world and their ability to make meaning from their environment". The project tools try to reflect these experiences, notably through the inclusion of tasks assessing students' knowledge of 'environmental print' and 'concepts of print'. As Raban argues, establishing students' awareness of the concepts of print is particularly important when considering the "differences in the way that literacy is organised in different cultures and communities" as well as the way "literacy has different values and functions in people's daily lives". McCabe highlights the value in tasks focusing on concepts of print when she states that "although preschool children seldom pay attention to print in various types of storybook reading, *explicit referencing of print* is one way to significantly increase such attention".

All early literacy, early reading, and speaking and listening tasks developed for this project are delivered one-to-one. Raban and Ure suggest that one-to-one assessments have the added advantage of helping to address parents' concerns about assessment procedures and to reassure them "that we have realistically and systematically appraised their child's progress and learning style". Perhaps the most significant value offered by individual assessment tasks is the way they prioritise the role of oracy in comprehension. As Scull writes, in recent research "comprehension instruction is described as best achieved through collaborative, conversational approaches... that support a flexible, opportunistic use of strategies". Scull categorises these strategies as follows: literal, inference, reaction/evaluation, child's experiences and extending knowledge. When discussing comprehension monitoring, Scull writes that "students' ability to recall and summarise information - as well as to infer from texts they have read, evaluate information and identify the important from the unimportant - is central to this process".

The comprehension skills mentioned by Scull closely resemble those used in the Diagnostic Assessment Tools in English reading set (both oral and written): retrieving information, linking information across the text, inference, demonstrating a global understanding, and reflecting on the text (which includes justifying personal opinions and expanding on prior knowledge). The speaking and listening tasks also require students to recall and summarise the information they have heard. In the setting up of most of the tasks, in particular oral reading and writing, teachers are directed to spend time discussing the topic and establishing prior knowledge. Prediction questions are also asked in several of the oral reading tasks, and where possible in the written tasks. Through her research, Scull found that "through prediction, teachers encouraged students to use their prior knowledge to facilitate their understanding of new ideas encountered in the text", and further that her results "indicate higher levels of performance when students were required to insert prior knowledge or draw on personal experiences". These tools have forged more innovative ground by modeling positive methods of interaction for teachers and foregrounding those reading skills that may receive less attention in some classrooms. By covering an array of important reading skills, these tools guide teachers towards targeted and thoughtful interactions with their students. Furthermore, because of the variety of reflective questions that require students to evaluate their ideas and build on prior knowledge, these tools may even help to prepare "the young reader to challenge the monologic concept of text meanings and shift towards 'polysemic' readings [as well as the] 'difficult task of struggling to come to an active, personal and individual interpretation of meaning, and to engage in a personal search for unification".

Current research has also highlighted the importance of assessing the metacognitive skills of their students, those skills that enable students "to see and hear enactments of those inner mental processes that are the essence of literate behaviour so they can appropriate them and deploy them for themselves". Because written assessment tasks complicate the teacher's ability to assess these skills, questions relating to the metacognitive process were taken up more appropriately in the Speaking and Listening Tools for this project, and will be discussed further on in relation to these tools.

The innovative Speaking and Listening Tool suite developed for this project assesses students in the areas of both conversation and presentation. These tools consist of video footage of pair discussions and presentations, from which students are asked a series of questions. These questions have been developed to prioritise listening skills. In this way, these tools reflect a growing field of study, which argues that listening skills are being neglected in classroom contexts. In the *International Journal of Listening*, Beall et al. write that "although listening skills have been linked to literacy at an early age and long-term academic success" listening instruction is scarce in primary and secondary education. Jalongo states that "despite the fact that listening is the language skill that hearing children and adults use most, it is the one that is taught the least – an inverse relationship between the real world and the classroom". She also argues that this neglect is being reflected in assessment, further undermining the importance of these skills in the classroom. "Even when listening is part of the written and taught curriculum, it sometimes is neglected in assessment, and this tends to diminish its relative importance in today's test-driven curriculum". The lack of interest in teaching and assessing listening skills is derived from the belief that interactive skills do not need to be taught. According to UK academic Jones, there is a general assumption "that because talk is interwoven into the fabric of the classroom and daily life in general, competency develops 'naturally' and without the need for explicit teaching". To address this, Jones argues for "the importance of rigourous planning for speaking and listening and the need to plan in specific and regular opportunities for assessing this area".

The Diagnostic Assessment Tools in English Speaking and Listening Tools promote the importance of teaching and assessing these skills. More specifically, they highlight the particular skills needed to interact successfully and model how these interactions could take place in a classroom setting. As Beall et al. suggest, teaching students how to communicate effectively is not an easy task: " ... the ability for teachers to elicit effective listening from their students is vital, yet it is one of the more difficult tasks that teachers face on a daily basis", partly because "students bring a variety of listening and learning styles into the classroom". Jones gives credit to Professor Robin Alexander's recommendations for improving students' interactive skills through dialogic teaching, which are conveyed in four key areas: *collective*, *reciprocal*, *cumulative* and *supportive*.

Although a formal assessment cannot easily model successful interaction in all these areas, it can prioritise dialogic teaching in both the setting up and format of the task. The Speaking and Listening Tools, for example, encourage a *collective* approach in that they involve a dialogue between teacher and student, in preparation of and during the assessment. This is particularly the case with the pair discussion tasks, which are also *reciprocal* in approach; that is, they require the teacher to listen to the ideas and alternative viewpoints of their student. These tasks are also *cumulative* in that they highlight the importance for the student of building on the ideas of their peers. Video format, as "visible listening", is an important pedagogical component because it uses the "documentation of experiences ... as the basis for discussion and interpretation".

The video footage provided for these tasks is both 'authentic', in that it is a largely unrehearsed video of students discussing a topic, and 'successful', in that the students are interacting well together. Such modeling is useful to teachers and students; it allows both to evaluate those skills enabling positive interaction in an assessment context, as well as to question what improvements could be made. These benefits also apply to the video footage of the presentations. The metacognitive focus of these tasks could usefully be used as part of a broader teaching programme in which students are encouraged "to learn about the social elements of talk, the expression of feelings, the development of relationships and how additional aspects, such as body language, work together with talk in order to develop such relationships and affect or sharpen communication".

Metacognitive awareness, as suggested earlier, is a growing field in early literacy studies because it enables students "to evaluate progress and set targets for improvement". Jones argues that talk is fundamental to the idea, as promoted by Vygotsky, "that when the process of learning is brought to a conscious level, children become aware of their own thought processes that helps them gain control over *how* they learn". These Speaking and Listening Tools, by making an analysis of communication skills part of assessment tasks themselves, encourage students "to think about their thinking and to articulate thoughts about their learning". Indeed, such an approach addresses the ongoing issue, as found in a 1998 German study, that "many students do not have a clear concept of listening as an active process that they can control". This study further found that "students report greater listening comprehension when they use metacognitive strategies such as asking questions prior to listening, managing interest in the subject, and using elaboration strategies to apply the information".

Effective speaking and listening is more likely, as Jones argues, when children know "what kind of talk [is] required" and when there is "an appropriate selection of topic, which allow[s] children to build on their previous knowledge and understanding". Scull also argues the value in setting up the task, in creating "opportunities for students to discuss topics at length using spoken language in which all contextual details are supplied, where information is sequenced and temporal, and where everything is made clear to the listener". Framing is used in the Speaking and Listening Tools where a discussion of the subject would not interfere with the task items. Furthermore, the "kind of talk" required for these tasks is, to some extent, modeled in the videos themselves.

Topics were selected on the basis that they were relevant and interesting to students, and would therefore be likely to inspire discussion. As Scull writes, "speaking and listening is best taught when teachers engage students in talk that is purposeful and meaningful to the students themselves".

The Diagnostic Assessment Tools in English project makes a valuable contribution to early years literacy, as is evident from the way it reflects current national and international trends in the field of early years research. The project tools foreground the importance of directed assessment for diagnosing specific areas of difficulty for low-achieving students, and excellence in high-achieving students.

The Reading Tools address the array of skill areas encomp-assed in decoding and comprehension. Although directed, these tools encourage student engagement with the selection of relevant topics, and by contextualizing print and literacy within wider social and environmental contexts. The Reading, Writing and Early Literacy Tools draw on prediction and students' prior knowledge, a technique shown to produce "higher levels of performance". The focus on oracy in one-to-one assessments not only allows teachers to engage more attentively with each student, it promotes collaborative approaches to learning.

The Speaking and Listening Tools address the lack of attention commonly given to interactive skills in the classroom, encouraging *collective, reciprocal* and *cumulative* approaches to learning. The video format of these tools, along with the task items, models successful teaching and learning practices. By drawing on metacognitive skills, these tools further allow students to gain control over their learning.

ROLE OF ENGLISH IN NEO-LIBERAL INDIA

As far as Indian students are concerned the importance and pressures the students encounter are really unique. Due to globalization of Indian economy the country has become one of the fastest growing economies in the world. The economy is open to every competent person. The unemployment in India is not linked with lack of job opportunities in the country. But it is linked with the lack of competency among the prospective candidates. In the process of developing core competencies, the knowledge of English language is *sine qua non*--. Even though the economy is developing the environment around the learner is not conducive to develop competency in English language. The environment around the student is a stumbling block to acquire language abilities. At home they have the heavy influence of mother tongue and whatever English they learn, they learn either in a passive lecture method or in translation method without having a chance to learn in an interactive way.

SOCIO-ECONOMIC BACKGROUND

India is a country in which the society is well-knit with complex admixture of various castes, creeds, religions and different socio- economic backgrounds. The learning of English language as second language is highly influenced by the social background of an individual. Due to its agrarian background, majority of learners come from rural background. As a result, the students in rural schools have limited exposure towards language learning. The reason behind their low level of competency in English can be linked with two reasons: first, lack of environment that encourages the students to learn the language, secondly, they have the teachers who do not have sufficient exposure to teaching English in a scientific way.

As a result they resort to teach English either by teacher-centered method or translation method. Moreover, the students learn all other subjects in their regional language by which, they do not have any need to gain mastery over English language.

STUDENTS' PROBLEMS IN LEARNING

The students with different abilities and students with under privileged backgrounds have peculiar problems to deal with in learning English language. It is to be noted that the socio economic back drop of the student cannot be altered by an English teacher. He is limited to the extent of imparting available student friendly technique to induce interest among the students. In the traditional teacher centered teaching methodology, the under privileged students have been deprived of getting the benefit of modern technical know-how that is used in teaching English. The rural students are not exposed to language laboratory, they do not hear of collaborative learning, peer teaching and they are always at home with lecture method and rot memory method of learning the language. As a result they are not able to gain mastery over the language learning. In this connection it is to be remembered that a suitable method should be devised or designed to meet the needs of the student in learning language skills. Here we discuss some innovative methods which can be proved as student friendly in helping the students to acquire the basic language skills.

METHODS OF TEACHING ENGLISH

As the English teacher has to inculcate the basic LSRW skills as a first step to help students acquire competency in English language he has to follow various methods in teaching of English as second language. He has to mix up both traditional and modern methods of teaching and evolve a method that is suitable to the students. The following are some of the methods that can be both innovative and student friendly in teaching English in an interactive way.

ENRICHING VOCABULARY METHOD

As the students have the rural background and they are habituated to lecture method, the teacher should start teaching in lecture method and translation method initially and try to inculcate direct method of teaching English via grammar translation method. The teacher has to reschedule the entire syllabi of English into thoroughly manageable units or modules and add vocabulary that is necessary for students to understand the background of lesson. The teacher has to take live examples and the English words which are equal to colloquial language words and make the student understand and use the words thoroughly. The teacher has to engage the students with remedial work and corrective assignments in the field of grammar and vocabulary building. The teacher should talk English in natural way within the purview of their limited vocabulary giving those speaking exercises on the objects and events of their surroundings, so that they try their level best to express themselves. For example, the teacher can give exercises on local festivals, favourite dishes, favourite movies, etc.

JUMBLING METHOD

The one of the best methods to be followed by the teacher in teaching of English is jumbling method. In this method the teacher divides a task into different small tasks which are mutually related and independent. The class is divided into groups and each group is given a segment of task. Then the members of the groups are interchanged and made into different groups again. Then the students are encouraged to talk and present their work. No student is exempted to talk. The teacher further has to encourage the student to follow reversal of roles which means that the teacher gives the tasks to the students on selected topics and they are expected to prepare the topic and present before the class as a teacher. In that way the student is able to develop not only the competence on the subject but also develop the basic life skills like problem solving and thinking. Further the teacher has to divide the class into different groups with not more than five students a group and should give them an assignment of telling the story before the class or reading news in the prayer.

SYNTAX RESTRUCTURE METHOD

The teacher should reconstruct the syntax in a manageable and an understandable way. For example in the teaching of Active Passive voice, the following method should be followed. First, the student should understand that in active to passive voice they are subject, verb and object. When subject is active it is an active voice. When subject is silent or passive it is a passive voice. The verb with an object is called transitive verb and a verb without an object is called intransitive verb. When we ask a question to verb with what, whom, if there is an answer it is an object. All sentences in all tenses with general syntax can be regarded as in active voice.

PICTORIAL METHOD

Pictorial method is the other method through which students can develop their speaking skills fastly. In this method the teacher draws a picture and every student is encouraged to describe the picture in his own words irrespective of grammatical errors. Further the teacher draw a table with data and asks the students to write in a paragraph format and further encourage the students to speak on that topic.

CREATIVE-POETIC METHOD

In this method every student is encouraged to listen to popular movie songs in their regional language. They are encouraged to observe the vocabulary and the situation of the songs. They are given simpler day to day English vocabulary and its colloquial equivalent words.

Then they are given some controlled situations. They are encouraged to write poem irrespective of meter or rhythm. This method helps them understand the situation and develop explanatory power especially in writing in the short run and speaking in the long run.

MATERIAL CREATION METHOD

In this method each and every student should be given a concept and they are encouraged to write a thought provoking caption or placard sounding the entire concept in few words and after all the students prepare their captions, the material is jumbled among the students and they are encouraged to write on the concept. This method encourages the students to develop comprehension and creative skills.

ENGLISH EXAMPLE

In Middle English phonological studies, the evidence of rhymes has long been used as a primary source of information. Comparison of rhyming forms with distinct etymologies enables the investigator to reconstruct authorial pronunciation as well as localise the place of origin for the text. Of course, this procedure depends on an assumption: that Middle English authors attempted exact rhyme.

Although this assumption has sometimes been challenged, it is nevertheless plausible in medieval conditions. Middle English poets were closer to oral traditions of verse than those of the present day; verse was, we know, commonly rather than rarely read aloud; and thus a forced rhyme would be stylistically foregrounded more obviously than would now be the case.

In the postmedieval centuries, however, a practice of 'conventional' rhymes developed, whereby poets rhymed forms which had once been entirely acceptable acoustically but which sound-change had made no longer current. Thus, for instance, William Blake rhymes mine: join in a poem of 1783, even though these words (as in most varieties of Present-Day English) almost certainly no longer contained the same vowel in his variety.

Similarly, the practice of 'eye'-rhyme, whereby written similarity outweighs spoken distinction, seems to have become common from approximately the same date; thus Robert Burns, in his Augustan (as opposed to Scots) verse, can make play with the similar visual appearance of rough and plough/bough, even though the rhyming elements of the three words were differently pronounced in the incipient standardised forms of spoken English (both English and Scottish) at the time.

The simple Bard, rough at the rustic plough, Learning his tuneful trade from ev'ry bough. In these lines there is an ironic contrast between the Augustan register of language (in which the three words are eye-rhymes but not ear-rhymes) which 'linguistic acceptability...is...increasingly vested in the visual rather than the aural', reflecting a shift from the world of orality to that of the literary poet with a literate reading public. Burns, of course, a man keenly conscious of the interaction of social settings, is playing on this historical development in The Brigs of Ayr, contrasting the oral and quasi-mythical Scots world of the 'simple Bard' with the literate, Augustan English of the opening of the poem.

The problem of conventionality in rhyming practice, and what that means for the phonological interpretation of poetic usage, is acutely presented by the rhyming practice of John Keats. Keats suffered at the hands of his first reviewers, and one of the grounds of their criticism was his habit of rhyming such pairs as higher: Thalia, thorns: fawns, thoughts: sorts, indicating that his accent was non-rhotic (*i.e.,* 'non r-pronouncing'; cf. Southern English beside Scottish and some US pronunciations of bar).

In Present-Day English, of course, non-rhotic accents are (in the United Kingdom, if not invariably in the United States) prestigious, being associated with Received Pronunciation, but at the beginning of the nineteenth century such rhymes were regarded by many people as 'Cockney', and therefore inappropriate for serious literary discourse. Thus John Lockhart in Blackwood's Edinburgh Review criticised Keats as without 'learning enough to distinguish between the written language of Englishmen and the spoken jargon of Cockneys'.

It is significant that Lockhart criticises Keats for deviance from a norm derived from written usage. And as late as 1877, Thomas Hood the younger considered that 'such atrocities as "morn" and "dawn", ..."fought" and "sort", are fatal to the success of verse'.

It has been shown, however, that Keats's lack of rhoticity was not wholly stigmatised by contemporaries. B.H. Smart, for instance, in his prescriptivist A Grammar of English Sounds, comments that 'the smooth R, is often pronounced with so little force, as to be, in fact, nothing more than the vowel sound AH'. Although in his earlier A Practical Grammar of English Pronunciation (1810) Smart seems to have regarded non-rhoticity as something Londoners were 'too liable' to exhibit-since the written mode was seen by him as offering a guide to correct pronunciation-nevertheless he seems to accept it as characteristic of quite large numbers of persons whose social status is not in doubt.

And an analysis of the rhymes of, for example, P.B. Shelley shows that poets of impeccably upper-class descent were fully capable of using non-rhotic rhymes without receiving any comparable attack from contemporaries. L. Mugglestone has pointed out that part of Lockhart's venom may be due to his Scottish origins; the accents of Present-Day Scots and Scottish English are still rhotic, and Lockhart's attack on Keats's usage may have been an assertion of the value of a Scottish accent as well as of the primacy of writing over speech.

Vocalisation of r may have been sporadically stigmatised, as a failure to pronounce a letter sanctioned in writing; but, in general, the disappearance of postvocalic r in upper-class nineteenth-century speech, and not just in that of Cockneys, is clearly attested.

Thus the attack on Keats by Lockhart and others is not a simple attack on some linguistic deficit; it is rather the use of any tool to hand to aid a knocking review. The three examples discussed above-Farman, the Chetham Gower, Keats-all demonstrate how textual analysis and an understanding of context help our understanding of linguistic output. A theme of this study is that an understanding of texts in relation to their contexts is essential to an adequate theory of diachronic linguistics; thus philology and linguistics are ideally complementary disciplines for students of the history of a language, and not competitive paradig m, a theoretical paradigm for the historical study of English will be sketched in, based upon a linking of philological and linguistic traditions.

FUTURE OF ENGLISH

Had English evolved a new future on the model of the synthetic future in French or had it borrowed from Latin and Greek their employment of reduplication as a functional device (Latin tango: tetigi; Greek leipo: leloipa), we should have the right to speak of true morphological influence. But such far-reaching influences are not demonstrable. Within the whole course of the history of the English language we can hardly point to one important morphological change that was not determined by the native drift, though here and there we may surmise that this drift was hastened a little by the suggestive influence of French forms.

It is important to realise the continuous, self-contained morphological development of English and the very modest extent to which its fundamental build has been affected by influences from without. The history of the English language has sometimes been represented as though it relapsed into a kind of chaos on the arrival of the Normans, who proceeded to play nine-pins with the Anglo-Saxon tradition.

Students are more conservative today. That a far-reaching analytic development may take place without such external foreign influence as English was subjected to is clear from the history of Danish, which has gone even further than English in certain leveling tendencies. English may be conveniently used as an a fortiori test. It was flooded with French loan-words during the later Middle Ages, at a time when its drift towards the analytic type was especially strong. It was therefore changing rapidly both within and on the surface.

The wonder, then, is not that it took on a number of external morphological features, mere accretions on its concrete inventory, but that, exposed as it was to remolding influences, it remained so true to its own type and historic drift. The experience gained from the study of the English language is strengthened by all that we know of documented linguistic history. Nowhere do we find any but superficial morphological interinfluencings.

We may infer one of several things from this: — That a really serious morphological influence is not, perhaps, impossible, but that its operation is so slow that it has hardly ever had the chance to incorporate itself in the relatively small portion of linguistic history that lies open to inspection; or that there are certain favourable conditions that make for profound morphological disturbances from without, say a peculiar instability of linguistic type or an unusual degree of cultural contact, conditions that do not happen to be realized in our documentary material; or, finally, that we have not the right to assume that a language may easily exert a remolding morphological influence on another.

Meanwhile we are confronted by the baffling fact that important traits of morphology are frequently found distributed among widely differing languages within a large area, so widely differing, indeed, that it is customary to consider them genetically unrelated. Sometimes we may suspect that the resemblance is due to a mere convergence that a similar morphological feature has grown up independently in unrelated languages.

Yet certain morphological distributions are too specific in character to be so lightly dismissed. There must be some historical factor to account for them. Now it should be remembered that the concept of a "linguistic stock" is never definitive in an exclusive sense. We can only say, with reasonable certainty, that such and such languages are descended from a common source, but we cannot say that such and such other languages are not genetically related. All we can do is to say that the evidence for relationship is not cumulative enough to make the inference of common origin absolutely necessary.

May it not be, then, that many instances of morphological similarity between divergent languages of a restricted area are merely the last vestiges of a community of type and phonetic substance that the destructive work of diverging drifts has now made unrecognizable? There is probably still enough lexical and morphological resemblance between modern English and Irish to enable us to make out a fairly conclusive case for their genetic relationship on the basis of the present-day descriptive evidence alone.

It is true that the case would seem weak in comparison to the case that we can actually make with the help of the historical and the comparative data that we possess. It would not be a bad case nevertheless. In another two or three millennia, however, the points of resemblance are likely to have become so obliterated that English and Irish, in the absence of all but their own descriptive evidence, will have to be set down as "unrelated" languages.

They will still have in common certain fundamental morphological features, but it will be difficult to know how to evaluate them. Only in the light of the contrastive perspective afforded by still more divergent languages, such as Basque and Finnish, will these vestigial resemblances receive their true historic value. I cannot but suspect that many of the more significant distributions of morphological similarities are to be explained as just such vestiges.

The theory of "borrowing" seems totally inadequate to explain those fundamental features of structure, hidden away in the very core of the linguistic complex, that have been pointed out as common, say, to Semitic and Hamitic, to the various Soudanese languages, to Malayo-Polynesian and Mon-Khmer and Munda, to Athabaskan and Tlingit and Haida. We must not allow ourselves to be frightened away by the timidity of the specialists, who are often notably lacking in the sense of what I have called "contrastive perspective." Attempts have sometimes been made to explain the distribution of these fundamental structural features by the theory of diffusion. We know that myths, religious ideas, types of social organization, industrial devices, and other features of culture may spread from point to point, gradually making themselves at home in cultures to which they were at one time alien. We also know that words may be diffused no less freely than cultural elements, that sounds also may be "borrowed," and that even morphological elements may be taken over. We may go further and recognize that certain languages have, in all probability, taken on structural features owing to the suggestive influence of neighbouring languages.

2

Status of Language and Teaching

THE BACKDROP OF LANGUAGE

This is not a conventional history of English. Rather, it tries to show how the discipline of linguistic history may be pursued — a rather different matter. It does this by using selected phenomena in the history of English to exemplify the dynamic processes of change involved. In so doing it tries to address the question of linguistic change: why does change happen, and why does it happen at the time and in the way that it does? In answering these questions, this book, rather obviously, holds it as axiomatic that human language is both a cultural and a systematic phenomenon, and that both these characteristics need to be borne in mind when addressing the question of linguistic change. English, a West Germanic language originating in England, is the first language for most people in Australia, Canada, Ireland, New Zealand, the United Kingdom, and the United States.

It is used extensively as a second language and as an official language throughout the world, especially in the Commonwealth of Nations, in countries such as in India or South Africa, as well as in many international organizations. Modern English is sometimes described as the world lingua franca. English is the dominant international language in communications, science, business, aviation, entertainment, and diplomacy and also on the Internet. It has been one of the official languages of the United Nations since its founding in 1945 and is considered by many to be on its way to becoming the world's first universal language.

The influence of the British Empire is the primary reason for the language's initial spread far beyond the British Isles. Following World War II, the increased economic and cultural influence of the United States led to English permeating many other cultures, chiefly through development of telecommunications technology. Because a working knowledge of English is required in many fields, professions, and occupations, education ministries throughout the world mandate the teaching of English to at least a basic level in an effort to increase the competitiveness of their economies.

On the one hand, it is held here that the various changes at an intralinguistic level which are held to be the prime concern of writers of linguistic history-changes in writing systems, pronunciation, grammar or lexicon-cannot be meaningfully accounted for without reference to the extralinguistic contexts (historical, geographical, sociological) in which these phenomena are situated.

Language is plainly a social phenomenon-if societies did not exist, there would be no language-and it follows from this that an asocial approach to its study has a comparatively limited (because formal) interest. This conclusion applies most uncontroversially to diachronic linguistics (*i.e.,* time-situated linguistics). If we attempt to explain language change entirely intralinguistically, without ultimate reference to extralinguistic factors, then, it is argued here, the explanation will ultimately fail.

But it is also held here that linguistic change can operate intralinguistically, that is, without immediate reference to external, non-linguistic factors. The key argument in support of this axiom is that linguistic changes, once they have themselves been implemented, interact with each other to produce further change.

To clarify these points, it may be useful to model the structure of natural language diagrammatically. The deepest level of language, in this diagram, is semantics, that is, the level of meaning. (There are philosophical questions as to whether semantics can be deemed properly a part of the linguistic system, but, given that language is about the transmission of meaning (very broadly defined) it seems perverse to ignore it here.)

Meaning is expressed linguistically through the grammar and lexis of a language; in turn, the grammar and lexis of a language are transmitted to other language-users through speech or (a comparatively recent development in human history) through writing. The model of language has its uses, but it is important to be aware of its limitations. It is essentially a static model, a snapshot; it depicts what happens when a single linguistic 'event' (a word, a grammatical construction, a sound or a spelling) takes place.

It is hierarchical in orientation, placing semantics at the top of a tree in which transmission occupies a lowly position. Above all for the purposes of this book, it is limited because it does not indicate any point where change might take place. There are methodological advantages to treating each level of language (written and spoken transmission, grammar, semantics and lexicon) separately, for it is obvious that to attempt to cover every level at once brings with it a threat of incoherence. Nevertheless the approach has dangers.

What evidence we have indicates that the human brain uses each level of language in an integrated way, handling them all simultaneously and interactively, and in diachronic study it will frequently, if not generally, be found that change in one level of language relates intimately to change in others. If language is systematic-and it must be, for otherwise it would be impossible to use it to express meaning, however broadly we define that concept-then movement in one part of the system must have an effect or effects on other parts.

Languages, in short, are systems in which everything is connected to everything else. This structural notion is the major insight of linguistics since the modern discipline was founded in the nineteenth century, and it is at the heart of the subject's claim for non-trivial status. In sum, we must expect that any given linguistic event is the result of complex interaction between levels of language, and between language itself and the sociohistorical setting in which it is situated.

It is therefore necessary, in our modelling of language, to supplement the simple communicative model with a non-hierarchical one. This latter model allows for the process of change; disruption and subsequent reaction can happen at any point in the system, and thus any model of language reflecting these processes must be of necessity non-hierarchical.

The interactive nature of the phenomenon, of course, makes the investigation of linguistic change a matter of engaging with complexity; and this complexity might lead students of the history of English to despair of finding any generally acceptable truths on which to base their discipline. There is, in fact, a respected and respectable tradition in the linguistic sciences which holds that the only valid goal of diachronic linguistic enquiry is description, and that the discussion of causation is not a proper question for researchers to address.

The outcome of this distinction can be seen in the practice of diachronic linguistic enquiry. Some books are essentially lists of observations, and these may be termed chronicles-not necessarily a hostile criticism, for such collections of observations are the bedrock of deeper understanding. In a sense, the notion of 'chronicle' correlates with the synchronic (*i.e.,* time-independent) approach to linguistic study, in which the purpose of the discipline is to formalise the rules of a given state of language without relating these rules to their antecedents or successors; the true chronicle, with its annalistic approach, may be seen as a series of synchronic snapshots which happen to have been arrayed in chronological order, an ordering which makes no connective reference or causative link to what happens before or after.

Most of the readers of this book will have already encountered such annalistic approaches, and may have even formed the impression that such chronicles are what the historical study of English is about. But this conclusion, it is held here, is wrong; the practice of linguistic historiography is to do with the interpretation of these observations, and it is historiography, not chronicle-making. Since this book sets out to be an historical account, it is orientated in accordance with the practice of historiography as established by tradition: it seeks answers to the question 'why?' through the observation of correspondences. When historians seek to account for a particular event in the past-say, the French Revolution-then they will look for its causes in the state of society within which the event took place: the financial and political bankruptcy of the monarchy, the oppression of the Third Estate, the coexistence of advanced Enlightenment ideas in France with revolution in the United States, and so on. It is by seeking to answer such questions that the discipline of history progresses, although few historians nowadays would claim to have final solutions to the questions which history poses.

Similarly, the explanations put forward in this book for changes in the history of English have the validity of historiography; they are attempts to show why certain things happen when they do, argued (it is hoped) rationally from the observation of correspondences, and they are of course falsifiable, that is, open to being superseded by other explanations. Of course, it is widely accepted by scholars in many disciplines that neutral observation, the goal of the chronicle-maker, is something of a myth, for our position of observation (our point of view) conditions what is observed. Nevertheless, the disabling nature of this so-called 'observer's paradox' can be overstated.

Observers of language can strive for neutrality on the basis of shared terms of reference, even if they necessarily fail to achieve absolute objectivity because conditioned by their own intellectual horizons. The answer to the problem is not, it is held here, to cease making observations and hypotheses, but rather to continue to make observations and hypotheses from various points of view. The question has been addressed by philosophers since at least the eighteenth century. English is an Anglo-Frisian language brought to southeastern Great Britain in the 5th century AD by Germanic settlers from various parts of northwest Germany (Saxons, Angles) as well as Jutland (Jutes).

Prior to the invasion of Britain by these Germanic tribes, the native Britons spoke an early form of Brythonic (the ancestor of Modern Welsh). Unlike in Gaul and Hispania, the indigenous population did not adopt Latin as a native language during the Roman occupation, where it was mainly confined to the Roman cities and garrisons.

The degree to which the original Celtic-speaking inhabitants remained or were displaced by the Germanic invaders is a matter of some debate. Recent genetic studies together with a re-evaluation of archaeological evidence suggest that the native Celtic population were not substantially displaced in any part of Britain. If correct, this interpretation of events would imply that the native Celts in the south and east of Britain, gradually adopted the language and culture of a politically and socially dominant ruling class.

Celtic languages survived in parts of the island not colonised by the invaders: Scotland, Wales, Cornwall, and, to some extent, Cumbria. The dialects spoken by the invaders eventually coalesced to a degree and formed what is today called the Old English language, which resembled some coastal dialects in what are now northwest Germany and the Netherlands. Throughout the history of written Old English, it remained a highly synthetic language based on a single standard, while spoken Old English became increasingly analytic in nature, losing the more complex noun case system, with a heavier reliance on prepositions and fixed word-order.

This is evident in the Middle English period, when literature is first recorded in the various spoken dialects of English of the time, after written Old English lost its status as the literary language of the nobility. It has been postulated that the early development of the language may have also been influenced by a Celtic substratum.

Later, it was influenced by the related North Germanic language Old Norse, spoken by the Vikings who settled mainly in the north and the east coast down to London, the area known as the Danelaw. Then came the Norman Conquest of England in 1066. For about 300 years following, the Norman kings and the high nobility spoke only Anglo-Norman, which was very close to Old French.

A large number of Norman words found their way into Old English. Later, a large number of words were borrowed directly from Latin and Greek, especially for scientific and technical terms, leaving a parallel vocabulary that persists into modern times. The Norman influence strongly affected the evolution of the language over the following centuries, resulting in what is now referred to as Middle English.

During the 15th century, Middle English was transformed by the Great Vowel Shift, the spread of a standardised London-based dialect in government and administration, and the standardising effect of printing. Early Modern English can be traced back to around the time of William Shakespeare.

LANGUAGE CHANGE

So far, language change has been discussed without further definition or explanation. Yet the question 'what is language change?' has to be confronted at an early stage, for, as we shall see, its definition sets the goals for our enquiry. The distinction may be made between potential for change, implementation (itself including triggering or actuation) and diffusion.

The potential for change exists when a particular speaker or group of speakers makes a particular linguistic choice at a particular time; implementation takes place when that choice becomes selected as part of a linguistic system; and diffusion takes place when the change is imitated beyond its site of origin, whether in terms of geographical or of social distribution.

Strictly speaking, the first of these phenomena is not to be included as part of the typology of change. The continual flux of living languages means that new variant forms are constantly being created in a given linguistic state. However, these variants are not themselves linguistic changes; rather, they constitute the raw material which is a prerequisite for linguistic change.

A linguistic change happens only when a particular variable is selected and a systemic development follows. In that sense, language change begins with implementation; when implementation of potential for change is for some reason triggered in a linguistic system, then we can speak of a linguistic change. The diffusion of the phenomenon within a particular speech-community is, it is held here, a further process which can be counted as part of the particular change involved; it may, of course, itself have further effects.

It will be observed there that the potential for change, the set of 'variational spaces' within a given linguistic system, is always present. However, a particular interaction of processes-extralinguistic with intralinguistic, or intralinguistic with intralinguistic-at a particular time and in a particular place triggers the implementation of change, with subsequent diffusion of that change within and beyond a particular speech-community. Subsequently, other changes can be triggered in turn.

Form and Function

In pursuing the aims described, two key terms will be used on a number of occasions; it is therefore appropriate to offer some definitions at this initial stage. These are the terms *form* and *function*. These terms are used technically in many disciplines (*e.g.,* in architecture), so it is perhaps worth taking time to define the special ways in which they are used here.

By *function* is meant intralinguistically the role individual linguistic items play within an overall linguistic system, and-and this is an extension of traditional usage, although quite commonplace in sociolinguistic literature-also extra linguistically the role linguistic systems play in society. By *form* is meant the various linguistic items themselves.

Thus a pronoun (form) may act (function) as the subject or object of a clause; and a particular usage (form) may signal the role (function) of its user in relation to other users; or, to put matters less abstractly, a particular formal usage such as double negation *(I don't know nothing),* acting functionally in intralinguistic terms as an intensifying marker of negativity, typically functions extralinguistically in contemporary British society as a stigmatising item, signalling membership of a particular (and non-prestigious) social group.

Sociolinguistics and Pragmatics

The linguistic discipline which deals with the function of language in society may be subdivided into two related subdisciplines: sociolinguistics and pragmatics. Sociolinguistics is perhaps the better established of these two, in the sense that it has been practised for several decades by a number of major scholars of whom perhaps the most important are William Labov, Peter Trudgill, and James and Lesley Milroy. It deals with the ways in which membership of social groups is signalled through linguistic choices, and it will be observed that insights from sociolinguistics inform many aspects of this book.

The work of researchers like Labov, Trudgill and the Milroys has broken new ground in showing how linguistic usages of very delicate differentiation demonstrate membership of distinct social groups, and they have gone on from this insight to develop important perspectives on such matters as the linguistic difficulties suffered by underprivileged groups in society, and the causes and mechanisms of linguistic change.

The sociolinguistic approach is not, however, the only valid one in considering language in use. In recent years, another discipline has emerged which also deals with social interaction: pragmatics. Pragmatics, which has been defined as 'the study of how utterances have meanings in situations', emphasises how language functions as a means of communication, and various regulative principles have been identified which describe the pragmatic strategies of interpersonal communication which human language-users adopt. One of the most important of these is the philosopher H.P. Grice's Co-operative Principle, which sets out in maxim fashion the constraints which govern conversation.

The Principle may be summarised briefly as follows:

1. Quantity: Give the right amount of information, *i.e.,* (a) make your contribution as informative as required, (b) do not make your contribution more informative than is required.
2. *Quality:* Try to make your contribution one that is true, *i.e.,* (a) do not say what you believe to be false, (b) do not say that for which you lack adequate evidence.
3. *Relation:* Be relevant.
4. *Manner:* Be perspicuous, *i.e.,* (a) avoid obscurity of expression, (b) avoid ambiguity, (c) be brief (avoid unnecessary prolixity), (d) be orderly.

The Co-operative Principle, Grice held, governs all speaker-hearer/writer-reader communications. To communicate with someone else, it is necessary to co-operate with them linguistically; and, to co-operate with someone linguistically, it is necessary to use language they can understand. Thus extralinguistic pressures affect the linguistic usages of those subjected to those pressures.

It would perhaps be more correct to write of the re-emergence of pragmatics as a discipline. Students of the history of linguistic thought have shown that many modern notions of sociolinguistics and pragmatics have their origins in the work of nineteenth-century (and earlier) philologists and philosophers.

More recent work in the pragmatic and sociolinguistic analysis of speaker-interaction has distinguished between accommodation theory and identification theory, and these notions have significance for a more general theory of language change. Accommodation theory seeks to relate any given linguistic act to the relationship between particular interlocutors, and is a development of the cooperative notions set forth above. Identification is a broader notion which might be taken to comprehend accommodation theory. It tries to span the divide between pragmatics and sociolinguistics; it holds that any particular usage at any particular point in time is the result of an 'act of identity', in which speakers are seen as modifying their behaviour to accommodate to group norms.

Thus, 'the individual creates for himself the patterns of his linguistic behaviour so as to resemble those of the group or groups with which from time to time he wishes to be identified, or so as to be unlike those from whom he wishes to be distinguished'. It is an observed fact that speakers use language not just to communicate needs and to transmit information, but also to signal their and others' social standing. Identification theory is functional, in the broad sense used in this book, in that it situates any individual linguistic act in relation to its social setting.

Classification

The English language belongs to the western sub-branch of the Germanic branch, which is itself a branch of the Indo-European family of languages. The question as to which is the nearest living relative of English is a matter of some discussion. Apart from such English-lexified creole languages such as Tok Pisin, Scots (spoken primarily in Scotland and parts of Northern Ireland) is the Germanic variety most closely associated with English. Like English, Scots ultimately descends from Old English, also known as Anglo-Saxon.

The closest relative to English after Scots is Frisian, which is spoken in the Northern Netherlands and Northwest Germany. Other less closely related living West Germanic languages include German itself, Low German, Dutch, and Afrikaans. The North Germanic languages of Scandinavia are less closely related to English than the West Germanic languages. Many French words are also intelligible to an English speaker (though pronunciations are often quite different) because English absorbed a large vocabulary from Norman and French, via Anglo-Norman after the Norman Conquest and directly from French in further centuries.

As a result, a substantial share of English vocabulary is quite close to French, with some minor spelling differences (word endings, use of old French spellings, etc.), as well as occasional divergences in meaning, in so called "faux amis", or false-friends. Over 380 million people speak English as their first language. English today is variously estimated as the second, third, or fourth largest language by number of native speakers.

All estimates have it trailing Mandarin Chinese, and other estimates are mixed as to whether it outranks Hindi, Spanish, and a combination of the various Arabic dialects. However, when combining native and non-native speakers it is probably the most commonly spoken language in the world, though possibly second behind a combination of the Chinese languages. Estimates that include second language speakers vary greatly from 470 million to over a billion depending on how literacy or mastery is defined.

There are some who claim that non-native speakers now outnumber native speakers by a ratio of 3 to 1. The countries with the highest populations of native English speakers are, in descending order: United States (215 million), United Kingdom (58 million), Canada (17.6 million), Australia (17.5 million), Ireland (3.8 million), and New Zealand (3.4 million).

Of those nations where English is spoken as a second language, India has the most such speakers ('Indian English') and it has been claimed that, combining native and non-native speakers, India now has more people who speak or understand English than any other country in the world. Following India are the People's Republic of China, the Philippines, Nigeria, and Germany.

English is the primary language in Anguilla, Antigua and Barbuda, Australia (Australian English), the Bahamas, Barbados, Bermuda, Belize, the British Indian Ocean Territory, the British Virgin Islands, Canada (Canadian English), the Cayman Islands, Dominica, the Falkland Islands, Gibraltar, Grenada, Guernsey, Guyana, Isle of Man, Jamaica (Jamaican English), Jersey, Montserrat, Nauru, New Zealand (New Zealand English), Ireland (Hiberno-English), Pitcairn Islands, Saint Helena, Saint Lucia, Saint Kitts and Nevis, Saint Vincent and the Grenadines, Singapore, South Georgia and the South Sandwich Islands, Trinidad and Tobago, the Turks and Caicos Islands, the United Kingdom (various forms of British English), the U.S. Virgin Islands, the United States (various forms of American English), and Zimbabwe.

In many other countries, where English is not a first language, it is an official language; these countries include Cameroon, Fiji, the Federated States of Micronesia, Ghana, Gambia, India, Kiribati, Lesotho, Liberia, Kenya, Namibia, Nigeria, Malta, the Marshall Islands, Pakistan, Papua New Guinea, the Philippines, Puerto Rico, Rwanda, the Solomon Islands, Samoa, Sierra Leone, Singapore, Sri Lanka, Swaziland, Tanzania, Zambia, and Zimbabwe.

It is also one of the 11 official languages that are given equal status in South Africa ("South African English"). English is also an important language in several former colonies or current dependent territories of the United Kingdom and the United States, such as in Hong Kong and Mauritius. English is the language most often studied as a foreign language in the European Union (by 89per cent of schoolchildren), followed by French (32per cent), German (18per cent), and Spanish (8per cent).

It is also the most studied in the People's Republic of China, Japan, South Korea, and Taiwan. It is worth noting that English is not an official language in either the United States or the United Kingdom. Although the U.S. federal government has no official languages, English has been given official status by 25 of the 50 state governments.

Regional Varieties

The expansion of the British Empire and—especially since WWII—the primacy of the United States have spread English throughout the globe. Because of that global spread, English has developed a host of English dialects and English-based creole languages and pidgins.

The major varieties of English each include, in most cases, several sub varieties, such as Cockney slang within British English; Newfoundland English, and the English spoken by Anglo-Québecers within Canadian English; and African American Vernacular English ("Ebonics") and Southern American English within American English.

English is a pluricentric language, without a central language authority like France's Academic française; and although no variety is clearly considered the only standard, there are a number of accents considered as more formal, such as Received Pronunciation in Britain or, formerly, the upper-class Bostonian dialect in the U.S.

Scots developed — largely independently — from the same origins, but following the Acts of Union 1707 a process of language attrition began, whereby successive generations adopted more and more features from English causing dialectalisation. Whether it is now a separate language or a dialect of English better described as Scottish English is in dispute.

The pronunciation, grammar and lexis of the traditional forms differ, sometimes substantially, from other varieties of English. Because of English's wide use as a second language, English speakers have many different accents, which often signal the speaker's native dialect or language. For the more distinctive characteristics of regional accents, see Regional accents of English speakers, and for the more distinctive characteristics of regional dialects, see List of dialects of the English language.

Just as English itself has borrowed words from many different languages over its history, English loanwords now appear in a great many languages around the world, indicative of the technological and cultural influence of its speakers. Several pidgins and creole languages have formed using an English base, for example Tok Pisin began as one. There are many words in English coined to describe forms of particular non-English languages that contain a very high proportion of English words. Franglais, for example, is used to describe French with a very high English word content; it is found on the Channel Islands. Another variant, spoken in the border bilingual regions of Quebec in Canada, is called Frenglish. Norwenglish is a form of English containing many words or expressions directly copied from Norwegian.

STAGES OF SECOND LANGUAGE ACQUISITION

STAGE I: PRE-PRODUCTION

This is the silent period. English language learners may have up to 500 words in their receptive vocabulary but they are not yet speaking. Some students will, however, repeat every thing you say. They are not really producing language but are parroting.

These new learners of English will listen attentively and they may even be able to copy words from the board. They will be able to respond to pictures and other visuals.

They can understand and duplicate gestures and movements to show comprehension. Total Physical Response methods will work well with them. Teachers should focus attention on listening comprehension activities and on building a receptive vocabulary.

English language learners at this stage will need much repetition of English. They will benefit from a "buddy" who speaks their language. Remember that the school day is exhausting for these newcomers as they are overwhelmed with listening to English language all day long.

STAGE II: EARLY PRODUCTION

This stage may last up to six months and students will develop a receptive and active vocabulary of about 1000 words. During this stage, students can usually speak in one- or two-word phrases. They can use short language chunks that have been memorized although these chunks may not always be used correctly.

Here are some suggestions for working with students in this stage of English language learning:

- Ask yes/no and either/or questions.
- Accept one or two word responses.
- Give students the opportunity to participate in some of the whole class activities.
- Use pictures and realia to support questions.
- Modify content information to the language level of ELLs.
- Build vocabulary using pictures.
- Provide listening activities.
- Simplify the content materials to be used. Focus on key vocabulary and concepts.
- When teaching elementary age ELLs, use simple books with predictable text.
- Support learning with graphic organizers, charts and graphs. Begin to foster writing in English through labeling and short sentences. Use a frame to scaffold writing.

STAGE III: SPEECH EMERGENCE

Students have developed a vocabulary of about 3,000 words and can communicate with simple phrases and sentences. They will ask simple questions, that may or may not be grammatically correct, such as " May I go to bathroom? " ELLs will also initiate short conversations with classmates. They will understand easy stories read in class with the support of pictures.

They will also be able to do some content work with teacher support. Here are some simple tasks they can complete:

- Sound out stories phonetically.
- Read short, modified texts in content area subjects.
- Complete graphic organizers with word banks.
- Understand and answer questions about charts and graphs.
- Match vocabulary words to definitions.
- Study flashcards with content area vocabulary.
- Participate in duet, pair and choral reading activities.
- Write and illustrate riddles.
- Understand teacher explanations and two-step directions.
- Compose brief stories based on personal experience.
- Write in dialogue journals.

Dialogue journals are a conversation between the teacher and the student. They are especially helpful with English language learners. Students can write about topics that interest them and proceed at their own level and pace. They have a place to express their thoughts and ideas.

STAGE IV: INTERMEDIATE FLUENCY

English language learners at the intermediate fluency stage have a vocabulary of 6000 active words. They are beginning to use more complex sentences when speaking and writing and are willing to express opinions and share their thoughts. They will ask questions to clarify what they are learning in class. These English language learners will be able to work in grade level math and science classes with some teacher support. Comprehension of English literature and social studies content is increasing. At this stage, students will use strategies from their native language to learn content in English.

Student writing at this stage will have many errors as ELLs try to master the complexity of English grammar and sentence structure. Many students may be translating written assignments from native language. They should be expected to synthesize what they have learned and to make inferences from that learning. This is the time for teachers to focus on learning strategies. Students in this stage will also be able to understand more complex concepts.

STAGE V: ADVANCED FLUENCY

It takes students from 4-10 years to achieve cognitive academic language proficiency in a second language. Student at this stage will be near-native in their ability to perform in content area learning. Most ELLs at this stage have been exited from ESL and other support programmes. At the beginning of this stage, however, they will need continued support from classroom teachers especially in content areas such as history/social studies and in writing.

HISTORY OF ENGLISH LANGUAGE TEACHING

The English language teaching tradition has been subject to tremendous change, especially throughout the twentieth century. Perhaps more than any other discipline, this tradition has been practiced, in various adaptations, in language classrooms all around the world for centuries. While the teaching of Maths or Physics, that is, the methodology of teaching Maths or Physics, has, to a greater or lesser extent, remained the same, this is hardly the case with English or language teaching in general. As will become evident in this short paper, there are some milestones in the development of this tradition, which we will briefly touch upon, in an attempt to reveal the importance of research in the selection and implementation of the optimal methods and techniques for language teaching and learning.

THE CLASSICAL METHOD

In the Western world back in the 17th, 18th and 19th centuries, foreign languagc lcarning was associated with the learning of Latin and Greek, both supposed to promote their speakers' intellectuality.

At the time, it was of vital importance to focus on grammatical rules, syntactic structures, along with rote memorisation of vocabulary and translation of literary texts. There was no provision for the oral use of the languages under study; after all, both Latin and Greek were not being taught for oral communication but for the sake of their speakers' becoming "scholarly?" or creating an illusion of "erudition." Late in the nineteenth century, the Classical Method came to be known as the Grammar Translation Method, which offered very little beyond an insight into the grammatical rules attending the process of translating from the second to the native language.

It is widely recognised that the Grammar Translation Method is still one of the most popular and favourite models of language teaching, which has been rather stalwart and impervious to educational reforms, remaining a standard and sine qua non methodology.

With hindsight, we could say that its contribution to language learning has been lamentably limited, since it has shifted the focus from the real language to a "dissected body" of nouns, adjectives, and prepositions, doing nothing to enhance a student's communicative ability in the foreign language.

GOUIN AND BERLITZ - THE DIRECT METHOD

The last two decades of the nineteenth century ushered in a new age. In his The Art of Learning and Studying Foreign Languages, Francois Gouin described his "harrowing" experiences of learning German, which helped him gain insights into the intricacies of language teaching and learning. Living in Hamburg for one year, he attempted to master the German language by dint of memorising a German grammar book and a list of the 248 irregular German verbs, instead of conversing with the natives. Exulting in the security that the grounding in German grammar offered him, he hastened to go to the University to test his knowledge. To no avail. He could not understand a word! After his failure, he decided to memorise the German roots, but with no success. He went so far as to memorise books, translate Goethe and Schiller, and learn by heart 30,000 words in a dictionary, only to meet with failure. Upon returning to France, Gouin discovered that his three-year-old nephew had managed to become a chatterbox of French - a fact that made him think that the child held the secret to learning a language. Thus, he began observing his nephew and came to the conclusion (arrived at by another researcher a century before him!) that language learning is a matter of transforming perceptions into conceptions and then using language to represent these conceptions. Equipped with this knowledge, he devised a teaching method premised upon these insights.

It was against this background that the Series Method was created, which taught learners directly a "series" of connected sentences that are easy to understand. For instance, I stretch out my arm. I take hold of the handle. I turn the handle. I open the door. I pull the door.

Nevertheless, this approach to language learning was short-lived and, only a generation later, gave place to the Direct Method, posited by Charles Berlitz. The basic tenet of Berlitz's method was that second language learning is similar to first language learning. In this light, there should be lots of oral interaction, spontaneous use of the language, no translation, and little if any analysis of grammatical rules and syntactic structures. In short, the principles of the Direct Method were as follows:

- Classroom instruction was conducted in the target language
- There was an inductive approach to grammar
- Only everyday vocabulary was taught
- Concrete vocabulary was taught through pictures and objects, while abstract vocabulary was taught by association of ideas

The Direct Method enjoyed great popularity at the end of the nineteenth century and the beginning of the twentieth but it was difficult to use, mainly because of the constraints of budget, time, and classroom size. Yet, after a period of decline, this method has been revived, leading to the emergence of the Audiolingual Method.

THE AUDIOLINGUAL METHOD

The outbreak of World War II heightened the need for Americans to become orally proficient in the languages of their allies and enemies alike. To this end, bits and pieces of the Direct Method were appropriated in order to form and support this new method, the "Army Method," which came to be known in the 1950s as the Audiolingual Method.

The Audiolingual Method was based on linguistic and psychological theory and one of its main premises was the scientific descriptive analysis of a wide assortment of languages. On the other hand, conditioning and habit-formation models of learning put forward by behaviouristic phychologists were married with the pattern practices of the Audiolingual Method. The following points sum up the characteristics of the method:

- Dependence on mimicry and memorisation of set phrases
- Teaching structural patterns by means of repetitive drills
- No grammatical explanation
- Learning vocabulary in context
- Use of tapes and visual aids
- Focus on pronunciation
- Immediate reinforcement of correct responses

But its popularity waned after 1964, partly because of Wilga Rivers's exposure of its shortcomings. It fell short of promoting communicative ability as it paid undue attention to memorisation and drilling, while downgrading the role of context and world knowledge in language learning. After all, it was discovered that language was not acquired through a process of habit formation and errors were not necessarily bad or pernicious.

THE "DESIGNER" METHODS OF THE 1970S

The Chomskyan revolution in linguistics drew the attention of linguists and language teachers to the "deep structure" of language, while psychologists took account of the affective and interpersonal nature of learning. As a result, new methods were proposed, which attempted to capitalise on the importance of psychological factors in language learning. David Nunan referred to these methods as "designer" methods, on the grounds that they took a "one-size-fits-all" approach. Let us have a look at two of these "designer" methods.

SUGGESTOPEDIA

Suggestopedia promised great results if we use our brain power and inner capacities. Lozanov believed that we are capable of learning much more than we think. Drawing upon Soviet psychological research on yoga and extrasensory perception, he came up with a method for learning that used relaxation as a means of retaining new knowledge and material. It stands to reason that music played a pivotal role in his method. Lozanov and his followers tried to present vocabulary, readings, role-plays and drama with classical music in the background and students sitting in comfortable seats. In this way, students became "suggestible."

Of course, suggestopedia offered valuable insights into the "superlearning" powers of our brain but it was demolished on several fronts. For instance, what happens if our classrooms are bereft of such amenities as comfortable seats and Compact Disk players? Certainly, this method is insightful and constructive and can be practised from time to time, without necessarily having to adhere to all its premises. A relaxed mind is an open mind and it can help a student to feel more confident and, in a sense, pliable.

THE SILENT WAY

The Silent Way rested on cognitive rather than affective arguments, and was characterised by a problem-solving approach to learning. Gattegno held that it is in learners' best interests to develop independence and autonomy and cooperate with each other in solving language problems. The teacher is supposed to be silent - hence the name of the method - and must disabuse himself of the tendency to explain everything to them.

The Silent Way came in for an onslaught of criticism. More specifically, it was considered very harsh, as the teacher was distant and, in general lines, the classroom environment was not conducive to learning.

STRATEGIES-BASED INSTRUCTION

The work of O'Malley and Chamot (1990), and others before and after them, emphasised the importance of style awareness and strategy development in ensuring mastery of a foreign language. In this vein, many textbooks and entire syllabi offered guidelines on constructing strategy-building activities. Below there is an example of a list of the "Ten Commandments" for good language learning:

	Teacher's Version	Learner's Version
1	Lower inhibitions	Fear not!
2	Encourage risk-taking	Dive in
3	Build self-confidence	Believe in yourself
4	Develop intrinsic motivation	Seize the day
5	Engage in cooperative learning	Love thy neighbour
6	Use right-brain processes	Get the BIG picture
7	Promote ambiguity tolerance	Cope with the chaos
8	Practice intuition	Go with your hunches
9	Process error feedback	Make mistakes work FOR you
10	Set personal goals	Set your own goals

These suggestions cum injunctions are able to sensitise learners to the importance of attaining autonomy, that is, taking charge of their own learning, and not expecting the teacher to deliver everything to them.

COMMUNICATIVE LANGUAGE TEACHING

The need for communication has been relentless, leading to the emergence of the Communicative Language Teaching. Having defined and redefined the construct of communicative competence; having explored the vast array of functions of language that learners are supposed to be able to accomplish; and having probed the nature of styles and non-verbal communication, teachers and researchers are now better equipped to teach (about) communication through actual communication, not merely theorising about it.

At this juncture, we should say that Communicative Language Teaching is not a method; it is an approach, which transcends the boundaries of concrete methods and, concomitantly, techniques. It is a theoretical position about the nature of language and language learning and teaching.

FORMULATION OF SPEECH

Speech is so familiar a feature of daily life that we rarely pause to define it. It seems as natural to man as walking, and only less so than breathing. Yet it needs but a moment's reflection to convince us that this naturalness of speech is but an illusory feeling. The process of acquiring speech is, in sobre fact, an utterly different sort of thing from the process of learning to walk. In the case of the latter function, culture, in other words, the traditional body of social usage, is not seriously brought into play.

The child is individually equipped, by the complex set of factors that we term biological heredity, to make all the needed muscular and nervous adjustments that result in walking. Indeed, the very conformation of these muscles and of the appropriate parts of the nervous system may be said to be primarily adapted to the movements made in walking and in similar activities. In a very real sense the normal human being is predestined to walk, not because his elders will assist him to learn the art, but because his organism is prepared from birth, or even from the moment of conception, to take on all those expenditures of nervous energy and all those muscular adaptations that result in walking. To put it concisely, walking is an inherent, biological function of man.

Not so language. It is of course true that in a certain sense the individual is predestined to talk, but that is due entirely to the circumstance that he is born not merely in nature, but in the lap of a society that is certain, reasonably certain, to lead him to its traditions. Eliminate society and there is every reason to believe that he will learn to walk, if, indeed, he survives at all. But it is just as certain that he will never learn to talk, that is, to communicate ideas according to the traditional system of a particular society. Or, again, remove the new-born individual from the social environment into which he has come and transplant him to an utterly alien one. He will develop the art of walking in his new environment very much as he would have developed it in the old.

But his speech will be completely at variance with the speech of his native environment. Walking, then, is a general human activity that varies only within circumscribed limits as we pass from individual to individual. Its variability is involuntary and purposeless. Speech is a human activity that varies without assignable limit as we pass from social group to social group, because it is a purely historical heritage of the group, the product of long continued social usage. It varies as all creative effort varies — not as consciously, perhaps, but none the less as truly as do the religions, the beliefs, the customs, and the arts of different peoples.

Walking is an organic, an instinctive, function (not, of course, itself an instinct); speech is a non-instinctive, acquired, "cultural" function. There is one fact that has frequently tended to prevent the recognition of language as a merely conventional system of sound symbols, that has seduced the popular mind into attributing to it an instinctive basis that it does not really possess.

This is the well-known observation that under the stress of emotion, say of a sudden twinge of pain or of unbridled joy, we do involuntarily give utterance to sounds that the hearer interprets as indicative of the emotion itself. But there is all the difference in the world between such involuntary expression of feeling and the normal type of communication of ideas that is speech.

The former kind of utterance is indeed instinctive, but it is non-symbolic; in other words, the sound of pain or the sound of joy does not, as such, indicate the emotion, it does not stand aloof, as it were, and announce that such and such an emotion is being felt.

What it does is to serve a more or less automatic overflow of the emotional energy; in a sense, it is part and parcel of the emotion itself. Moreover, such instinctive cries hardly constitute communication in any strict sense. They are not addressed to any one, they are merely overheard, if heard at all, as the bark of a dog, the sound of approaching footsteps, or the rustling of the wind are heard.

If they convey certain ideas to the hearer, it is only in the very general sense in which any and every sound or even any phenomenon in our environment may be said to convey an idea to the perceiving mind. If the involuntary cry of pain which is conventionally represented by "Oh!" be looked upon as a true speech symbol equivalent to some such idea as "I am in great pain," it is just as allowable to interpret the appearance of clouds as an equivalent symbol that carries the definite message "It is likely to rain." A definition of language, however, that is so extended as to cover every type of inference becomes utterly meaningless. The mistake must not be made of identifying our conventional interjections (our oh! and ah! and sh!) with the instinctive cries themselves.

These interjections are merely conventional fixations of the natural sounds. They therefore differ widely in various languages in accordance with the specific phonetic genius of each of these. As such they may be considered an integral portion of speech, in the properly cultural sense of the term, being no more identical with the instinctive cries themselves than such words as "cuckoo" and "killdeer" are identical with the cries of the birds they denote or than Rossini's treatment of a storm in the overture to "William Tell" is in fact a storm. In other words, the interjections and sound-imitative words of normal speech are related to their natural prototypes as is art, a purely social or cultural thing, to nature.

It may be objected that, though the interjections differ somewhat as we pass from language to language, they do nevertheless offer striking family resemblances and may therefore be looked upon as having grown up out of a common instinctive base. But their case is nowise different from that, say, of the varying national modes of pictorial representation.

A Japanese picture of a hill both differs from and resembles a typical modern European painting of the same kind of hill. Both are suggested by and both "imitate" the same natural feature. Neither the one nor the other is the same thing as, or, in any intelligible sense, a direct outgrowth of, this natural feature. The two modes of representation are not identical because they proceed from differing historical traditions, are executed with differing pictorial techniques. The interjections of Japanese and English are, just so, suggested by a common natural prototype, the instinctive cries, and are thus unavoidably suggestive of each other.

They differ, now greatly, now but little, because they are builded out of historically diverse materials or techniques, the respective linguistic traditions, phonetic systems, speech habits of the two peoples. Yet the instinctive cries as such are practically identical for all humanity, just as the human skeleton or nervous system is to all intents and purposes a "fixed," that is, an only slightly and "accidentally" variable, feature of man's organism.

Interjections are among the least important of speech elements. Their discussion is valuable mainly because it can be shown that even they, avowedly the nearest of all language sounds to instinctive utterance, are only superficially of an instinctive nature. Were it therefore possible to demonstrate that the whole of language is traceable, in its ultimate historical and psychological foundations, to the interjections, it would still not follow that language is an instinctive activity. But, as a matter of fact, all attempts so to explain the origin of speech have been fruitless.

There is no tangible evidence, historical or otherwise, tending to show that the mass of speech elements and speech processes has evolved out of the interjections. These are a very small and functionally insignificant proportion of the vocabulary of language; at no time and in no linguistic province that we have record of do we see a noticeable tendency towards their elaboration into the primary warp and woof of language. They are never more, at best, than a decorative edging to the ample, complex fabric. What applies to the interjections applies with even greater force to the sound-imitative words. Such words as "whippoorwill," "to mew," "to caw" are in no sense natural sounds that man has instinctively or automatically reproduced. They are just as truly creations of the human mind, flights of the human fancy, as anything else in language. They do not directly grow out of nature, they are suggested by it and play with it.

Hence the onomatopoetic theory of the origin of speech, the theory that would explain all speech as a gradual evolution from sounds of an imitative character, really brings us no nearer to the instinctive level than is language as we know it to-day. As to the theory itself, it is scarcely more credible than its interjectional counterpart. It is true that a number of words which we do not: now feel to have a sound-imitative value can be shown to have once had a phonetic form that strongly suggests their origin as imitations of natural sounds. Such is the English word "to laugh."

For all that, it is quite impossible to show, nor does it seem intrinsically reasonable to suppose, that more than a negligible proportion of the elements of speech or anything at all of its formal apparatus is derivable from an onomatopoetic source. However much we may be disposed on general principles to assign a fundamental importance in the languages of primitive peoples to the imitation of natural sounds, the actual fact of the matter is that these languages show no particular preference for imitative words.

Among the most primitive peoples of aboriginal America, the Athabaskan tribes of the Mackenzie River speak languages in which such words seem to be nearly or entirely absent, while they are used freely enough in languages as sophisticated as English and German. Such an instance shows how little the essential nature of speech is concerned with the mere imitation of things.

The way is now cleared for a serviceable definition of language. Language is a purely human and non-instinctive method of communicating ideas, emotions, and desires by means of a system of voluntarily produced symbols. These symbols are, in the first instance, auditory and they are produced by the so-called "organs of speech."

There is no discernible instinctive basis in human speech as such, however much instinctive expressions and the natural environment may serve as a stimulus for the development of certain elements of speech, however much instinctive tendencies, motor and other, may give a predetermined range or mold to linguistic expression. Such human or animal communication, if "communication" it may be called, as is brought about by involuntary, instinctive cries is not, in our sense, language at all.

I have just referred to the "organs of speech," and it would seem at first blush that this is tantamount to an admission that speech itself is an instinctive, biologically predetermined activity. We must not be misled by the mere term.

There are, properly speaking, no organs of speech; there are only organs that are incidentally useful in the production of speech sounds. The lungs, the larynx, the palate, the nose, the tongue, the teeth, and the lips, are all so utilized, but they are no more to be thought of as primary organs of speech than are the fingers to be considered as essentially organs of piano-playing or the knees as organs of prayer.

Speech is not a simple activity that is carried on by one or more organs biologically adapted to the purpose. It is an extremely complex and ever-shifting network of adjustments — in the brain, in the nervous system, and in the articulating and auditory organs — tending towards the desired end of communication.

The lungs developed, roughly speaking, in connection with the necessary biological function known as breathing; the nose, as an organ of smell; the teeth, as organs useful in breaking up food before it was ready for digestion. If, then, these and other organs are being constantly utilized in speech, it is only because any organ, once existent and in so far as it is subject to voluntary control, can be utilized by man for secondary purposes.

Physiologically, speech is an overlaid function, or, to be more precise, a group of overlaid functions. It gets what service it can out of organs and functions, nervous and muscular, that have come into being and are maintained for very different ends than its own. It is true that physiological psychologists speak of the localization of speech in the brain.

This can only mean that the sounds of speech are localized in the auditory tract of the brain, or in some circumscribed portion of it, precisely as other classes of sounds are localized; and that the motor processes involved in speech (such as the movements of the glottal cords in the larynx, the movements of the tongue required to pronounce the vowels, lip movements required to articulate certain consonants, and numerous others) are localized in the motor tract precisely as are all other impulses to special motor activities.

In the same way control is lodged in the visual tract of the brain over all those processes of visual recognition involved in reading. Naturally the particular points or clusters of points of localization in the several tracts that refer to any element of language are connected in the brain by paths of association, so that the outward, or psycho-physical, aspect of language, is of a vast network of associated localizations in the brain and lower nervous tracts, the auditory localizations being without doubt the most fundamental of all for speech.

However, a speech- sound localized in the brain, even when associated with the particular movements of the "speech organs" that are required to produce it, is very far from being an element of language. It must be further associated with some element or group of elements of experience, say a visual image or a class of visual images or a feeling of relation, before it has even rudimentary linguistic significance. This "element" of experience is the content or "meaning" of the linguistic unit; the associated auditory, motor, and other cerebral processes that lie immediately back of the act of speaking and the act of hearing speech are merely a complicated symbol of or signal for these "meanings," of which more anon. We see therefore at once that language as such is not and cannot be definitely localized, for it consists of a peculiar symbolic relation — physiologically an arbitrary one — between all possible elements of consciousness on the one hand and certain selected elements localized in the auditory, motor, and other cerebral and nervous tracts on the other.

If language can be said to be definitely "localized" in the brain, it is only in that general and rather useless sense in which all aspects of consciousness, all human interest and activity, may be said to be "in the brain." Hence, we have no recourse but to accept language as a fully formed functional system within man's psychic or "spiritual" constitution. We cannot define it as an entity in psychophysical terms alone, however much the psycho-physical basis is essential to its functioning in the individual.

From the physiologist's or psychologist's point of view we may seem to be making an unwarrantable abstraction in desiring to handle the subject of speech without constant and explicit reference to that basis. However, such an abstraction is justifiable. We can profitably discuss the intention, the form, and the history of speech, precisely as we discuss the nature of any other phase of human culture — say art or religion — as an institutional or cultural entity, leaving the organic and psychological mechanisms back of it as something to be taken for granted.

Accordingly, it must be clearly understood that this introduction to the study of speech is not concerned with those aspects of physiology and of physiological psychology that underlie speech. Our study of language is not to be one of the genesis and operation of a concrete mechanism; it is, rather, to be an inquiry into the function and form of the arbitrary systems of symbolism that we term languages.

I have already pointed out that the essence of language consists in the assigning of conventional, voluntarily articulated, sounds, or of their equivalents, to the diverse elements of experience. The word "house" is not a linguistic fact if by it is meant merely the acoustic effect produced on the ear by its constituent consonants and vowels, pronounced in a certain order; nor the motor processes and tactile feelings which make up the articulation of the word; nor the visual perception on the part of the hearer of this articulation; nor the visual perception of the word "house" on the written or printed page; nor the motor processes and tactile feelings which enter into the writing of the word; nor the memory of any or all of these experiences.

It is only when these, and possibly still other, associated experiences are automatically associated with the image of a house that they begin to take on the nature of a symbol, a word, an element of language. But the mere fact of such an association is not enough. One might have heard a particular word spoken in an individual house under such impressive circumstances that neither the word nor the image of the house ever recurs in consciousness without the other becoming present at the same time.

This type of association does not constitute speech. The association must be a purely symbolic one; in other words, the world must denote, tag off, the image, must have no other significance than to serve as a counter to refer to it whenever it is necessary or convenient to do so. Such an association, voluntary and, in a sense, arbitrary as it is, demands a considerable exercise of selfconscious attention. At least to begin with, for habit soon makes the association nearly as automatic as any and more rapid than most.

But we have traveled a little too fast. Were the symbol "house " — whether an auditory, motor, or visual experience or image — attached but to the single image of a particular house once seen, it might perhaps, by an indulgent criticism, be termed an element of speech, yet it is obvious at the outset that speech so constituted would have little or no value for purposes of communication.

The world of our experiences must be enormously simplified and generalized before it is possible to make a symbolic inventory of all our experiences of things and relations; and this inventory is imperative before we can convey ideas. The elements of language, the symbols that ticket off experience, must therefore be associated with whole groups, delimited classes, of experience rather than with the single experiences themselves.

Only so is communication possible, for the single experience lodges in an individual consciousness and is, strictly speaking, incommunicable. To be communicated it needs to be referred to a class which is tacitly accepted by the community as an identity. Thus, the single impression which I have had of a particular house must be identified with all my other impressions of it.

Further, my generalized memory or my "notion" of this house must be merged with the notions that all other individuals who have seen the house have formed of it. The particular experience that we started with has now been widened so as to embrace all possible impressions or images that sentient beings have formed or may form of the house in question. This first simplification of experience is at the bottom of a large number of elements of speech, the so-called proper nouns or names of single individuals or objects. It is, essentially, the type of simplification which underlies, or forms the crude subject of, history and art. But we cannot be content with this measure of reduction of the infinity of experience. We must cut to the bone of things, we must more or less arbitrarily throw whole masses of experience together as similar enough to warrant their being looked upon — mistakenly, but conveniently — as identical. This house and that house and thousands of other phenomena of like character are thought of as having enough in common, in spite of great and obvious differences of detail, to be classed under the same heading.

In other words, the speech element "house" is the symbol, first and foremost, not of a single perception, nor even of the notion of a particular object, but of a "concept" in other words, of a convenient capsule of thought that embraces thousands of distinct experiences and that is ready to take in thousands more. If the single significant elements of speech are the symbols of concepts, the actual flow of speech may be interpreted as a record of the setting of these concepts into mutual relations.

The question has often been raised whether thought is possible without speech; further, if speech and thought be not but two facets of the same psychic process. The question is all the more difficult because it has been hedged about by misunderstandings.

In the first place, it is well to observe that whether or not thought necessitates symbolism, that is speech, the flow of language itself is not always indicative of thought. We have seen that the typical linguistic element labels a concept. It does not follow from this that the use to which language is put is always or even mainly conceptual. We are not in ordinary life so much concerned with concepts as such as with concrete particularities and specific relations.

When I say, for instance, "I had a good breakfast this morning," it is clear that I am not in the throes of laborious thought, that what I have to transmit is hardly more than a pleasurable memory symbolically rendered in the grooves of habitual expression. Each element in the sentence defines a separate concept or conceptual relation or both combined, but the sentence as a whole has no conceptual significance whatever. It is somewhat as though a dynamo capable of generating enough power to run an elevator were operated almost exclusively to feed an electric doorbell.

The parallel is more suggestive than at first sight appears. Language may be looked upon as an instrument capable of running a gamut of psychic uses. Its flow not only parallels that of the inner content of consciousness, but parallels it on different levels, ranging from the state of mind that is dominated by particular images to that in which abstract concepts and their relations are alone at the focus of attention and which is ordinarily termed reasoning. Thus the outward form only of language is constant; its inner meaning, its psychic value or intensity, varies freely with attention or the selective interest of the mind, also, needless to say, with the mind's general development.

From the point of view of language, thought may be defined as the highest latent or potential content of speech, the content that is obtained by interpreting each of the elements in the flow of language as possessed of its very fullest conceptual value. From this it follows at once that language and thought are not strictly coterminous. At best language can but be the outward facet of thought on the highest, most generalized, level of symbolic expression.

To put our viewpoint somewhat differently, language is primarily a pre-rational function. It humbly works up to the thought that is latent in, that may eventually be read into, its classifications and its forms; it is not, as is generally but naïvely assumed, the final label put upon the finished thought. Most people, asked if they can think without speech, would probably answer, "Yes, but it is not easy for me to do so. Still I know it can be done."

Language is but a garment! But what if language is not so much a garment as a prepared road or groove? It is, indeed, in the highest degree likely that language is an instrument originally put to uses lower than the conceptual plane and that thought arises as a refined interpretation of its content. The product grows, in other words, with the instrument, and thought may be no more conceivable, in its genesis and daily practice, without speech than is mathematical reasoning practicable without the lever of an appropriate mathematical symbolism.

No one believes that even the most difficult mathematical proposition is inherently dependent on an arbitrary set of symbols, but it is impossible to suppose that the human mind is capable of arriving at or holding such a proposition without the symbolism. The, writer, for one, is strongly of the opinion that the feeling entertained by so many that they can think, or even reason, without language is an illusion.

The illusion seems to be due to a number of factors. The simplest of these is the failure to distinguish between imagery and thought. As a matter of fact, no sooner do we try to put an image into conscious relation with another than we find ourselves slipping into a silent flow of words. Thought may be a natural domain apart from the artificial one of speech, but speech would seem to be the only road we know of that leads to it. A still more fruitful source of the illusive feeling that language may be dispensed with in thought is the common failure to realise that language is not identical with its auditory symbolism.

The auditory symbolism may be replaced, point for point, by a motor or by a visual symbolism (many people can read, for instance, in a purely visual sense, that is, without the intermediating link of an inner flow of the auditory images that correspond to the printed or written words) or by still other, more subtle and elusive, types of transfer that are not so easy to define.

Hence the contention that one thinks without language merely because he is not aware of a coexisting auditory imagery is very far indeed from being a valid one. One may go so far as to suspect that the symbolic expression of thought may in some cases run along outside the fringe of the conscious mind, so that the feeling of a free, non-linguistic stream of thought is for minds of a certain type a relatively, but only a relatively, justified one. Psycho-physically, this would mean that the auditory or equivalent visual or motor centres in the brain, together with the appropriate paths of association, that are the cerebral equivalent of speech, are touched off so lightly during the process of thought as not to rise into consciousness at all. This would be a limiting case-thought riding lightly on the submerged crests of speech, instead of jogging along with it, hand in hand.

The modern psychology has shown us how powerfully symbolism is at work in the unconscious mind. It is therefore easier to understand at the present time than it would have been twenty years ago that the most rarefied thought may be but the conscious counterpart of an unconscious linguistic symbolism.

One word more as to the relation between language and thought. The point of view that we have developed does not by any means preclude the possibility of the growth of speech being in a high degree dependent on the development of thought. We may assume that language arose pre-rationally — just how and on what precise level of mental activity we do not know — but we must not imagine that a highly developed system of speech symbols worked itself out before the genesis of distinct concepts and of thinking, the handling of concepts.

We must rather imagine that thought processes set in, as a kind of psychic overflow, almost at the beginning of linguistic expression; further, that the concept, once defined, necessarily reacted on the life of its linguistic symbol, encouraging further linguistic growth. We see this complex process of the interaction of language and thought actually taking place under our eyes.

The instrument makes possible the product, the product refines the instrument. The birth of a new concept is invariably foreshadowed by a more or less strained or extended use of old linguistic material; the concept does not attain to individual and independent life until it has found a distinctive linguistic embodiment. In most cases the new symbol is but a thing wrought from linguistic material already in existence in ways mapped out by crushingly despotic precedents. As soon as the word is at hand, we instinctively feel, with something of a sigh of relief, that the concept is ours for the handling. Not until we own the symbol do we feel that we hold a key to the immediate knowledge or understanding of the concept. Would we be so ready to die for "liberty," to struggle for "ideals," if the words themselves were not ringing within us? And the word, as we know, is not only a key; it may also be a fetter.

Language is primarily an auditory system of symbols. In so far as it is articulated it is also a motor system, but the motor aspect of speech is clearly secondary to the auditory. In normal individuals the impulse to speech first takes effect in the sphere of auditory imagery and is then transmitted to the motor nerves that control the organs of speech. The motor processes and the accompanying motor feelings are not, however, the end, the final resting point.

They are merely a means and a control leading to auditory perception in both speaker and hearer. Communication, which is the very object of speech, is successfully effected only when the hearer's auditory perceptions are translated into the appropriate and intended flow of imagery or thought or both combined. Hence the cycle of speech, in so far as we may look upon it as a purely external instrument, begins and ends in the realm of sounds. The concordance between the initial auditory imagery and the final auditory perceptions is the social seal or warrant of the successful issue of the process. As we have already seen, the typical course of this process may undergo endless modifications or transfers into equivalent systems without thereby losing its essential formal characteristics.

The most important of these modifications is the abbreviation of the speech process involved in thinking. This has doubtless many forms, according to the structural or functional peculiarities of the individual mind. The least modified form is that known as "talking to one's self" or "thinking aloud." Here the speaker and the hearer are identified in a single person, who may be said to communicate with himself.

More significant is the still further abbreviated form in which the sounds of speech are not articulated at all. To this belong all the varieties of silent speech and of normal thinking. The auditory centres alone may be excited; or the impulse to linguistic expression may be communicated as well to the motor nerves that communicate with the organs of speech but be inhibited either in the muscles of these organs or at some point in the motor nerves themselves; or, possibly, the auditory centres may be only slightly, if at all, affected, the speech process manifesting itself directly in the motor sphere.

There must be still other types of abbreviation. How common is the excitation of the motor nerves in silent speech, in which no audible or visible articulations result, is shown by the frequent experience of fatigue in the speech organs, particularly in the larynx, after unusually stimulating reading or intensive thinking.

All the modifications so far considered are directly patterned on the typical process of normal speech. Of very great interest and importance is the possibility of transferring the whole system of speech symbolism into other terms than those that are involved in the typical process. This process, as we have seen, is a matter of sounds and of movements intended to produce these sounds. The sense of vision is not brought into play. But let us suppose that one not only hears the articulated sounds but sees the articulations themselves as they are being executed by the speaker.

Clearly, if one can only gain a sufficiently high degree of adroitness in perceiving these movements of the speech organs,. the way is opened for a new type of speech symbolism — that in which the sound is replaced by the visual image of the articulations that correspond to the sound. This sort of system has no great value for most of us because we are already possessed of the auditory-motor system of which it is at best but an imperfect translation, not all the articulations being visible to the eye.

However, it is well known what excellent use deaf-mutes can make of "reading from the lips" as a subsidiary method of apprehending speech. The most important of all visual speech symbolisms is, of course, that of the written or printed word, to which, on the motor side, corresponds the system of delicately adjusted movements which result in the writing or typewriting or other graphic method of recording speech.

The significant feature for our recognition in these new types of symbolism, apart from the fact that they are no longer a by-product of normal speech itself, is that each element (letter or written word) in the system corresponds to a specific element (sound or sound-group or spoken word) in the primary system. Written language is thus a point-to-point equivalence, to borrow a mathematical phrase, to its spoken counterpart.

The written forms are secondary symbols of the spoken ones — symbols of symbols — yet so close is the correspondence that they may, not only in theory but in the actual practice of certain eye-readers and, possibly, in certain types of thinking, be entirely substituted for the spoken ones. Yet the auditory-motor associations are probably always latent at the least, that is, they are unconsciously brought into play. Even those who read and think without the slightest use of sound imagery are, at last analysis, dependent on it.

They are merely handling the circulating medium, the money, of visual symbols as a convenient substitute for the economic goods and services of the fundamental auditory symbols. The possibilities of linguistic transfer are practically unlimited. A familiar example is the Morse telegraph code, in which the letters of written speech are represented by a conventionally fixed sequence of longer or shorter ticks.

Here the transfer takes place from the written word rather than directly from the sounds of spoken speech. The letter of the telegraph code is thus a symbol of a symbol of a symbol. It does not, of course, in the least follow that the skilled operator, in order to arrive at an understanding of a telegraphic message, needs to transpose the individual sequence of ticks into a visual image of the word before he experiences its normal auditory image.

The precise method of reading off speech from the telegraphic communication undoubtedly varies widely with the individual. It is even conceivable, if not exactly likely, that certain operators may have learned to think directly, so far as the purely conscious part of the process of thought is concerned, in terms of the tick-auditory symbolism or, if they happen to have a strong natural bent towards motor symbolism, in terms of the correlated tactile-motor symbolism developed in the sending of telegraphic messages.

Still another interesting group of transfers are the different gesture languages, developed for the use of deaf-mutes, of Trappist monks vowed to perpetual silence, or of communicating parties that are within seeing distance of each other but are out of earshot. Some of these systems are one-to-one equivalences of the normal system of speech; others, like military gesture-symbolism or the gesture language of the Plains Indians of North America (understood by tribes of mutually unintelligible forms of speech) are imperfect transfers, limiting themselves to the rendering of such grosser speech elements as are an imperative minimum under difficult circumstances.

In these latter systems, as in such still more imperfect symbolisms as those used at sea or in the woods, it may be contended that language no longer properly plays a part but that the ideas are directly conveyed by an utterly unrelated symbolic process or by a quasiinstinctive imitativeness. Such an interpretation would be erroneous. The intelligibility of these vaguer symbolisms can hardly be due to anything but their automatic and silent translation into the terms of a fuller flow of speech. We shall no doubt conclude that all voluntary communication of ideas, aside from normal speech, is either a transfer, direct or indirect, from the typical symbolism of language as spoken and heard or, at the least, involves the intermediary of truly linguistic symbolism.

This is a fact of the highest importance. Auditory imagery and the correlated motor imagery leading to articulation are, by whatever devious ways we follow the process, the historic fountain-head of all speech and of all thinking. One other point is of still greater importance.

The ease with which speech symbolism can be transferred from one sense to another, from technique to technique, itself indicates that the mere sounds of speech are not the essential fact of language, which lies rather in the classification, in the formal patterning, and in the relating of concepts. Once more, language, as a structure, is on its inner face the mold of thought. It is this abstracted language, rather more than the physical facts of speech, that is to concern us in our inquiry. There is no more striking general fact about language than its universality.

One may argue as to whether a particular tribe engages in activities that are worthy of the name of religion or of art, but we know of no people that is not possessed of a fully developed language. The lowliest South African Bushman speaks in the forms of a rich symbolic system that is in essence perfectly comparable to the speech of the cultivated Frenchman.

It goes without saying that the more abstract concepts are not nearly so plentifully represented in the language of the savage, nor is there the rich terminology and the finer definition of nuances that reflect the higher culture. Yet the sort of linguistic development that parallels the historic growth of culture and which, in its later stages, we associate with literature is, at best, but a superficial thing.

The fundamental groundwork of language — the development of a clear-cut phonetic system, the specific association of speech elements with concepts, and the delicate provision for the formal expression of all manner of relations — all this meets us rigidly perfected and systematized in every language known to us.

Many primitive languages have a formal richness, a latent luxuriance of expression that eclipses anything known to the languages of modern civilization. Even in the mere matter of the inventory of speech the layman must be prepared for strange surprises. Popular statements as to the extreme poverty of expression to which primitive languages are doomed are simply myths.

Scarcely less impressive than the universality of speech is its almost incredible diversity. Those of us that have studied French or German, or, better yet, Latin or Greek, know in what varied forms a thought may run. The formal divergences between the English plan and the Latin plan, however, are comparatively slight in the perspective of what we know of more exotic linguistic patterns. The universality and the diversity of speech lead to a significant inference.

We are forced to believe that language is an immensely ancient heritage of the human race, whether or not all forms of speech are the historical outgrowth of a single pristine form. It is doubtful if any other cultural asset of man, be it the art of drilling for fire or of chipping stone, may lay claim to a greater age. I am inclined to believe that it antedated even the lowliest developments of material culture, that these developments, in fact, were not strictly possible until language, the tool of significant expression, had itself taken shape.

LANGUAGE TESTING

In language assessment, particular language tests are designed for particular purposes (*i.e.,* proficiency, diagnosis, placement, and progress), and if applied to other purposes, may result in inappropriate evaluations of students' language ability. Tests have specific uses, and classroom tests can be used to evaluate specific curricula. Gronlund says that validity is "the extent to which inferences made from assessment results are appropriate, meaningful, and useful in terms of the purpose of the assessment".

Language proficiency tests and diagnostic tests are not specific to any one curriculum, but on the other hand, progress assessments should evaluate students' ability to implement the language knowledge and skills that they have learned through their studies in a particular course, and placement assessment seeks to determine the level of students' knowledge/skill with reference to placement within a particular curriculum.

With respect to assessment to place students into a specific curriculum, test content needs to be based on the material presented in the curriculum, which in turn should be based upon real-world tasks of English language use. Bailey says, "Since the purpose of a placement test is to assign students to particular levels of a programme, then it makes sense that the content of the test should be related to the curricula of those levels". Thus, the purposes of programme level placement tests in non-Western developing countries differ from those of high-stakes international tests (such as the Test of English for International Communication - TOEIC or International English Language Testing System — IELTS), which evaluate general English language proficiency. But often such general proficiency tests are used for placement purposes in developing countries simply because they are readily available and have high face validity. This practice can be a problem because these standardized tests are not meant to evaluate specific curricular content.

In fact, they are designed to lessen cultural bias by removing explicit cultural references - references that are the regional uses of English that the language learners in particular regions do in fact need to know. Educational Testing Service and University of Cambridge ESOL Examinations, the developers of two widely used, high stakes tests (the TOEIC and IELTS), have taken considerable measures to exclude content that could be offensive or highly inappropriate for test takers world-wide who are from extremely diverse cultural backgrounds.

Green and Jay (2005), in discussing quality control for IELTS content, explain efforts "to ensure that all material is culturally appropriate and accessible world-wide".

The *TOEIC Technical Manual* states "every effort is made to ensure that the test is unbiased and culturally relevant to our many candidates worldwide". Also, the Association of Language Testers in Europe (2005) recommends avoiding cultural bias in choosing texts for assessment, citing problematic materials such as local newspapers, or texts referring to war, death, politics, or religion.

Despite increased awareness of issues of culturally inappropriate content in English materials, culturally inappropriate content is still a problem. While it can be argued that inappropriate use of tests is the responsibility of the users, that is, ministries of education and/or school administrators, test users in developing countries may have few options when the only tests available are designed for other contexts.

Yet by eliminating problematic culturally explicit content (a practice appropriate for large-scale international tests), the ability to evaluate accurately real-world English language use in specific regions is lessened. Invalid testing due to cultural differences between test maker and test taker is a form of test bias, known as cultural bias. In language assessment, Bachman and Palmer consider the effect of cultural bias in second/foreign language testing, including assessing cultural bias as part of evaluation of the test's usefulness.

They note the possibility of decreased reliability in the sense that test takers would not be able to perform to the best of their ability as would be possible for them in their own cultural setting, and the consequently different test results would be a manifestation of the testing procedure instead of the students' ability. Palomba and Banta point out that test "data are unreliable to the extent that score variance is due to measurement error". If measurement error were to result from cultural bias, it would decrease test reliability.

In addition to affecting reliability in assessment, cultural bias impacts construct validity. In other words, a test does not actually measure the construct that it was designed to evaluate if it is distorted by cultural bias. Culturally biased test content is a threat to validity through construct under-representation or construct-irrelevant variance, meaning that the attribute in question is not being fully evaluated and that factors unrelated to that attribute may affect the outcome of the evaluation.

If a developing nation's department of education desires its citizens to learn English as a lingua franca within the national sociocultural context, yet language assessment is based on Western sociocultural norms, then questions of construct under representation and construct-irrelevant variance in the assessment may legitimately be raised.

English Language Use in Non-Western Regions

If we are to measure real-world uses of English in non-Western regions, we need to know how English is used in such communities. Bachman and Palmer (1996) say, "In order for a particular language test to be useful for its intended purposes, test performance must correspond in demonstrable ways to language use in non-test situations", in this case, non-Western English use in developing nations, that is, in Asia, the Middle East, and Africa. Research into non-Western English language use reveals diverse needs among different regions of the world.

Kharma (1998) mentions social and educational needs of English learners in the Arabian Gulf countries in international communication (business, diplomacy, and travel; air traffic control; science and technology; and books and entertainment). In Asia, Indonesian uses of English are identified by Winter, Inkiriwang, and Senduk as including university studies and tests, employment, entertainment, interaction with English-speaking people, and overseas travel.

Not only is English used in international business with native-English speakers, but it is also used in many non-Western countries as a lingua franca for local communication needs, as in India and the Philippines. Other non-Western uses of English are seen in countries with large expatriate populations that use English as the language of communication, such as in the Arabian Gulf, or when people from nations with several regional languages may use English as an intranational language to communicate with others from their own country, as in India and the Philippines. Often the English used in these non-Western settings, by necessity, is different from the English of the USA, UK, or Canada.

Language Instruction, and Language Assessment

Recognizing the importance of correspondence between target language use, instruction, and assessment is an important step in finding a solution to the problem of inappropriate language instruction and testing, particularly when it stems from sociocultural bias from the use of Western tests in non-Western regions.

Bachman and Palmer state that testers want to "make inferences about test takers' ability to use language in a target language use domain... a set of specific use tasks that the test taker is likely to encounter outside of the test itself". Brown and Bailey, among other assessment experts, suggest that placement test content be based upon the instructional content of the curriculum into which students are to be placed.

Thus we see in task-based assessment a three-fold relationship between tasks of real-world English language use, tasks for English instruction, and tasks for English language placement. The Connecting Point between Teachers, Testers, and Learners, illustrates the centrality of real-world English language use tasks to language instruction and assessment.

In developing countries, there is a need for culturally appropriate tests of real world non-Western English language use to place students into language programmes which are seeking to instruct them in the English that they need in their specific region.

If the purpose of language assessment is to measure the practical language ability of students in real-life settings, then language assessment must correspond to tasks of target language use in authentic contexts. Assessment based on such real-world use of English language use has the advantage of being culturally specific, thus removing culturally inappropriate content. Brown, Hudson, Norris and Bonk suggest that, although there are challenges yet to be overcome, task-based language performance assessment offers a considerable advantage in evaluating test takers' ability to use the target language (*i.e.*, English) in real-world communication.

Such task-based language performance assessment would be based on needs analysis of daily tasks in real-world settings that require the use of English in actual communication. Once tasks of real-world English language use are identified, test items can be developed for placement testing. But first it is necessary to identify how the target language is used in daily life. Various writers have defined task differently, and in this report, "task" focuses on authentic language use tasks accomplishing a real-world goal.

In developing placement tests, language teachers and school administrators ultimately want to know if their students are able to use the target language in real-life communication (which ideally are addressed by the curriculum). Referring to tasks to be used in language assessment, Bachman says, "Task specifications constitute the definition of the content domain to which our assessment-based inferences about ability extrapolate or the domain of real-life tasks which we want to predict".

Such tasks can be identified through sociolinguistic research investigating how language is used in social interaction. Specifically, this research investigates task descriptions of non-Western English language use, utilizing Bachman and Palmer's (1996) definition: "an activity that involves individuals in using language for the purpose of achieving a particular goal or objective in a particular situation".

In particular, this project identifies three tasks of non-Western English language use that are culturally appropriate in some regions but inappropriate in others. The resulting task descriptions are the informants' accounts of regionally specific uses of English explained in their own words.

Analysis Instrument for Developing Countries

Baine, in the field of special education, observed the same problem of Western-designed tests being culturally inappropriate and irrelevant for use in developing countries. He describes his ecological inventory as a needs analysis instrument that he specifically designed for use in developing countries. This ecological inventory surveys activities of daily life in home, work, school, and community domains. Baine proposed using this inventory to identify tasks for instruction and assessment to address special education needs in developing regions.

Tasks identified using the inventory are then to be used to develop criterion-referenced tests appropriate for specific regions to evaluate students' ability to carry out the targeted daily life activities. Although Baine's inventory is designed for special education purposes, it provides an excellent instrument for sociolinguistic research into tasks of non-Western English language use.

Research Question 1 seeks to discover three tasks that are considered inappropriate by the majority of informants yet which are deemed appropriate by some of the informants, specifically:

1. What are three tasks of non-Western English language use (in home, work, and community domains) that were rated as culturally appropriate/somewhat appropriate for assessment in by informants from some non-Western regions but were rated as inappropriate by the majority of the informants?

The wording of a test task makes a difference in its effectiveness in assessment for many reasons, but pertinent to this research is that wording reflecting cultural bias can decrease the task's validity. Thus it is helpful to know why a test task is inappropriate in specific regions, so that appropriate changes can be made if or when that task is to be used in other regions, changes that are often required to adapt content for use in testing English as a foreign language in non-Western regions. Therefore, Research Question #2 addresses the issue of why these three tasks were rated as culturally inappropriate by the majority of the informants, specifically:

2. What are factors that could cause these three tasks to be culturally inappropriate in some non-Western regions?

This research project utilized a reiterative process that gathered data in two phases: (1) semi-structured interviews with the 29 informants, resulting in a data base of task descriptions of non-Western English language use; and (2) a confirmation survey, based on the collective task descriptions, which gave the informants the opportunity to evaluate each other's task descriptions for appropriateness in their home regions.

But in other regions language identity was an issue. Edwards mentions "the power association between language and nationalism," and says that because nationalism "is, among other things, a pronounced and often mobilizing sense of groupness, it follows that any language component will be carefully delineated". For some of these multilingual informants, particularly in intranational political communication, group identification was crucial, and choice of language was an indication of group identification.

India 5, who rated Task 3 as inappropriate, said that government forms would use English in southern India, but she emphasized the importance of the Tamil language in her state in India, viewing it as a way to assert Tamil identity in opposition to the dominance of Hindi. Uganda/Kenya 1, who also rated Task 3 as inappropriate, said that in Kenya "even those who speak Swahili, they will do their paperwork in English." But in terms of public speaking, she said, "you go by your audience.

If most of them are Swahili-speaking, then you speak Swahili, because those who speak English, they know Swahili." Lebanon 1 said that even though her country is multilingual (Arabic, English, French, and Armenian), it is an Arabic country, and she emphasized the importance of Arabic identity. For these informants, language identity was more important than official government language policy, and for India 5 and Uganda/Kenya 1 the official language did not automatically determine the choice of language in political campaign speeches.

One way to make this task of political speeches appropriate in more regions is to change the setting from speaking to local people to addressing a multinational audience where English would be the common language, either internationally or internationally. Such a focus could make the use of English in speeches a real-world use of English appropriate in many non-Western regions.

Adjusting this task to be appropriate in other regions could result in wording such as "make speeches to an international audience" or "make speeches for the international news media."

LANGUAGE TEACHING

What have all these problems got to do with those of us who are foreign-language educators? Isn't our job just to teach grammar, vocabulary, and communication skills?

There are several good reasons why we should care about world problems. One is ethical and personal. Many language teachers find it morally wrong to just stick their heads into their textbooks and pretend these problems don't exist. Another reason concerns our aspirations to be a language-teaching "profession." The idea that the professions have a moral responsibility to society in the practice of their specialized skills goes back to the Hippocratic Oath in ancient Greece where doctors swore to use their professional skills for the good of society. The past 20 years have seen a rapid increase in the number of professional groups working to solve world problems through research in their field, education of the public, and political action. Physicians for Social Responsibility and the 1985 Nobel Peace Prize winner, International Physicians for the Prevention of Nuclear War, are two such groups. Similar groups exist for scientists, lawyers, psychologists, and other fields. If language teachers truly aspire to be a "profession" in the real sense of the word, then they must consider this aspect of social responsibility.

Another reason for dealing with global issues in language teaching concerns our status within the field of education. The education profession has always recognized its unique responsibility in promoting peace, justice, and an active concern for the world's problems. The World Confederation of Organizations of the Teaching Profession, for example, clearly states that its aims include the promotion of equality, peace, justice, freedom, and human rights among all peoples. The US organization, Educators for Social Responsibility, confirms the importance of the three ₹ of traditional education—reading, 'riting and 'rithmetic—but argues that we need to extend these to make "responsibility" the fourth R of education.

The 1974 United Nations Educational, Scientific, and Cultural Organization *Recommendation Concerning Education for International Understanding, Cooperation and Peace and Education Relating to Human Rights and Fundamental Freedoms* calls for a global perspective at all levels of education, understanding, and respect for other cultures; an awareness of the rights of individuals and groups; and a readiness on the part of the individual to participate in solving the problems of his or her community, nation, and the world.

For language teachers, the most significant attempt to deal with language teaching and world problems is UNESCO's Linguapax project. The name comes from the Latin words *lingua* (language) and *pax* (peace) and refers to a series of seminars dealing with language teaching for international understanding. The first Linguapax conference, held in 1987 in Kiev, USSR, brought together such groups as the International Association of Applied Linguistics, International

Association for the Development of Cross-cultural Communication, and World Federation of Modern Language Associations to discuss "Content and Methods of Teaching Foreign Languages and Literature for Peace and International Understanding." The resulting Linguapax Kiev Declaration made four recommendations to foreign-language teachers:

- Be aware of their responsibility to further international understanding through their teaching.
- Increase language teaching effectiveness so as to enhance mutual respect, peaceful coexistence, and cooperation among nations.
- Exploit extracurricular activities such as pen-pal programmes, videoexchanges, and overseas excursions to develop international understanding.
- Lay the basis for international cooperation through classroom cooperation using language-teaching approaches responsive to students' interests and needs.

Fur ther recommendations called for UNESCO and its member nations

- to take steps to inform students and their families of the potential of foreign languages to promote better knowledge of world issues and concerns; and
- to organize workshops for foreign-language teachers and students on contemporary world issues of direct relevance and interest to young people, such as environmental protection and the struggle against poverty and hunger.

VIEWS OF LANGUAGE EDUCATORS

Over the past decade, a number of leaders within the worldwide English-language teaching (ELT) profession have addressed the importance of global education for teachers of English as a second language (ESL) and English as a foreign language (EFL). Some stress how global issues can provide meaningful content for language classes. Others stress the mission language teachers have to teach for a better world. The following quotes from two well-known educators highlight the rationale for a global education approach to English-language teaching:

Global issues are real: the spoliation of the rainforests, the thinning of the ozone layer, acid rain, nuclear waste, population growth, the spread of AIDS, state violence and genocide in Kurdistan, Tibet and Bosnia, ecological disaster and war in Ethiopia and Somalia... the list is depressingly long. What has this to do with the teaching of EFL? English language teaching has been bedevilled with three perennial problems: the gulf between classroom activities and real life; the separation of ELT from mainstream educational ideas; the lack of a content as its subject matter. By making Global Issues a central core of EFL, these problems would be to some extent resolved. —Alan Maley (1992: 73)

Global, peace and environmental issues intrinsically affect every human being on earth. These issues provide content for your content- based humanized ESL teaching of the 90's. We teachers have a mission, a mission of helping everyone in this world communicate with each other to prevent the global disaster ahead. The 90's are in your hands. —H. D. Brown (1990)

The idea that foreign-language teaching can contribute to creating a better world is not new, of course. Indeed, much traditional language teaching makes vague references to global education ideals. However, as one noted language educator points out, this has mostly remained wishful thinking:

It may be well to ask ourselves whether international understanding, let alone world peace, can be said to have been promoted by the considerable amount of foreign language teaching in the world. Diligent learning of foreign words and phrases, laborious copying and recitation of irregular verb paradigms, and the earnest deciphering of texts in the foreign language can hardly be considered powerful devices for the development of international understanding and good will.

If our language students are truly to become socially responsible world citizens, then global issues and the four goals of global education (knowledge, skills, attitudes, and action) must appear explicitly in our language-teaching curriculum.

GLOBAL ISSUES IN THE LANGUAGE CLASSROOM

EFL instructors around the world integrate global issues and global education into their teaching in a variety of ways that involve language-teaching content, methods, materials, course design, teacher training, and extracurricular activities.

Global Education Content

Language has a certain degree of flexibility of topic that other subjects do not. It is not surprising, then, that content is one area of teaching where many instructors are integrating a global education perspective. This approach is described by one Japan-based language educator as follows:

"Global issues" and "global education" are hot new buzzwords in the language teaching world. Global education is the process of introducing students to world issues, providing them with relevant information and developing the skills they will need to help work towards solutions. Those who support global education usually defend it in this way: we all need to use reading passages, dialogues and discussions in our teaching, so why not design these with content that informs students of important world issues and challenges them to consider solutions?

Global issues can be included in teaching content even when students are just starting to learn the sounds of the foreign language. One example is the

Japanese junior high school EFL text *Cosmos English Course*,which teaches the sounds of English by using the example word "peace" to teach the English sound /p/. Grammar, usually felt by students to be one of the dullest areas of language study, can also be taught with a global perspective through a change of content. Starkey, for example, describes how teaching past, present, and future tenses becomesmore meaningful when students study the past, present, and future of global issues. This could involve students studying the historical background of an issue such as environmental pollution, looking at pollution today in their community or country, and then doing future-oriented activities to solve this problem. Comparatives can similarly be practiced by comparing human rights in different countries or by contrasting global inequalities of First World wealth and Third World poverty. Some innovative teachers have designed exercises to teach students the conditional "if...then" while promoting environmental awareness. These efforts revolve around pattern practice based on model sentences such as "If we all recycled paper, we'd save more trees" or "If we all picked up the litter at our university, we'd have a clean and beautiful campus."

Reading, writing, listening, and speaking can also be integrated with global issues content. One British English instructor, for example, has based a complete English four-skills lesson on the international human rights organization Amnesty International. This begins with students *listening* to information about Amnesty International,*speaking* their opinions concerning human rights, *reading* about the work of Amnesty International in its English newsletter, and then *writing* English letters calling for the release of prisoners of conscience around the world.

TEACHING METHODS

Global education is as much a matter of how we teach as of what we teach. For many teachers, this involves a shift from passive to active learning, from teacher- to student-centered classes, from language as structure to language for communication about the world. This shift in teaching method often stimulates instructors to experiment with new approaches such as experiential learning.

This can lead to trying out class simulations and role-plays that get students out of their seats and actively involved in exploring global issues in the foreign language. This can result in language-teaching lessons in which students practice their foreignlanguage skills while role-playing blacks and whites in apartheid South Africa, taking the parts of logging companies and tribal peoples in a tropical rainforest simulation, or acting as UN ambassadors in a model UN simulation. Other teachers try to bring the world into the classroom by inviting guest speakers such as visitors from Africa or representatives from groups such as Greenpeace to promote communicative English skills as well as interest in world cultures and global issues. Yet other teachers attempt to develop global awareness and language skills through student projects such as social issue interview surveys or oral class presentations on global organizations such as United Nations Children's Fund (UNICEF) and Oxfam.

GLOBAL EDUCATION MATERIALS

A global education approach to language teaching requires that teaching materials impart the knowledge, skills, and attitudes required to help language students become socially responsible world citizens. In many textbooks, however, world problems are conspicuous by their absence. Even when textbooks do touch upon global issues, they often tend to treat them trivially as an overlay on the linguistic syllabus. Starkey, among others, criticizes the "tourist-consumer" flavour of many language texts, with their focus on shopping, travel, and fashion, and concludes that "foreign language textbooks provide fertile grounds for discovering bias, racism and stereotype".

Happily, more foreign-language textbooks now include lessons dealing with global themes. A look at Asian textbooks of English as a foreign language will turn up language lessons ranging from topics such as Martin Luther King and tropical rainforests to Mother Teresa and world hunger. A growing number of commercially published English language textbooks are also appearing which deal specifically with global issue themes, including*Making Peace*,*Global Views*,*The Global Classroom*,*Environmental Issues*,*Earthwatch*,*Impact Issues*,and *The World Around Us*.

Language teachers unable to find the global teaching materials they want often write their own language lessons on topics as diverse as refugees, recycling, and world religions. Yet others design their teaching materials around the many exciting global education textbooks, teaching packs, CD-ROMS, and videos used in the US and United Kingdom.

GLOBAL EDUCATION COURSE DESIGN

Many language teachers in Asia and abroad are experimenting with global education course design. One English language course I have developed for my Japanese university students is Global Issues. In this course, students focus each week on a different world problem—the environment, human rights, apartheid, world hunger—and explore in English the issue, its causes, and solutions through video, games, quizzes, discussions, role-plays, and simulations.

A number of teachers have devised similar courses on cultures of the world, in which students practice English skills while deepening their interest in foreign countries. Others have built English courses around audio-visual resources such as films. Fukunaga, for example, teaches English through Global Issue Movies where students practice language skills while studying films such as *Mississippi Burning* (civil rights), *The Killing Fields*(war and peace), and *Dances with Wolves* (intercultural understanding). One Tokyo-based EFL teacher has even built an entire college English course around the movie *Gandhi* to improve students' English skills while time allowing them to explore themes such as apartheid, racism, colonialism, and non-violence.

Some teachers around the world are attempting to bring a global perspective into the teaching of English for special purposes through the design of courses such as English for Doctors or Business English. One teacher designed a 20-hour intensive English for Engineering course aimed at producing socially responsible, environmentally aware engineers. The course concerned the building of an imaginary dam and involved students in reading proand anti-dam arguments, role-playing loggers and environmentalists, then presenting oral and written environmental assessments of the project.

Extracurricular Activities

Extracurricular activities also allow language teachers to combine global issues with the study of foreign languages. Some language colleges in Japan, for example, hold annual international awareness seminars as part of their fall school festivals, featuring English speech contests on global themes or English-speaking guest lecturers from groups such as UNESCO or Friends of the Earth.

Out-of-class volunteer activities comprise another area where language teachers can help to internationalize their students. As one Japan-based teacher puts it,

Volunteer work with global issues can be a perfect context for teacher-student contact outside class. Personally, because I'm committed to a just world free of war, hunger and poverty, and because I'm committed to my students learning English, I find there's no better combination than working on global issues with students outside the classroom. While students get the language practice that I need them to get to complement my classes, we are working together for the future world of our choice.

One out-of-class activity carried out by Bamford was a charity walkathon in Tokyo where students and teachers practice English while walking 35 kilometers to raise money to help end world hunger.

Overseas school tours are another way to promote international understanding among language learners. Many schools in Japan, for example, send groups of students abroad for summer language practice and overseas homestay programmes. Although these undoubtedly promote students' language ability and intercultural awareness, such visits center on countries like the US, tend to focus on Disneyland and other tourist sights, and sometimes involve more shopping than intercultural understanding. A number of language educators in Japan, in contrast, are increasingly trying to awaken the interest of Japanese students to other areas of the world. One college English teacher in Tokyo, for example, regularly leads English school trips to India, where her Japanese students stay with Indian families and learn about life, culture, and social issues. Another Japanbased teacher has taken Japanese students to the Philippines to help them improve their English as they learn about problems and issues facing developing nations. Another English teacher takes her Japanese high-school girls to South Korea to visit their sister school. Since English is the only common language between the Korean and Japanese girls, her students come home with improved English skills as well as a greater understanding of South Korea, its people, its sad history of Japanese colonial occupation, and the need to work for better relations between the two countries.

Global Education Teacher Training

Teacher training is another area of language education where interesting global education initiatives are taking place, such as the intensive summer workshop run by the Language Institute of Japan for high-school English teachers. This brings together classroom English teachers from Japan and from countries throughout Asia who study together to improve their teaching methodology and language skills while using English to explore topics involving world cultures and social issues.

Another initiative is a graduate-level English teacher-training course, Global Issues and Cooperative Learning, offered by Teachers College, Columbia University of New York at its Tokyo campus as part of its international Master of Arts in the Teaching English as a Second Language programme. This course, which I've taught for the past 10 years, gives graduate students in the field of Englishlanguage teaching the chance to explore teaching ideas, resources, and activities from fields such as global education, peace education, human rights education, and environmental education. These teachers then go on to practice designing and teaching model Englishlanguage lessons on global education themes for use in their own schools.

Beyond the classroom

Being a global teacher, of course, doesn't have to stop at the schoolyard gate. Language teachers can help to stimulate and inspire students through their daily lives by becoming active "world citizen" role models for students to emulate. One of the easiest things for language teachers is to support, with our money or time, global organizations working to solve world problems. Changing our lifestyles is another way to work for a better world. This might mean travelling to school by bicycle, using more public transportation, or photocopying less.

When shopping, this could include buying from "fair trade" organizations, looking for environmentally friendly products, and using the new consumer handbooks that identify which companies have military contracts, destroy rainforests, or exploit Third World workers.

Language teachers can have an even greater impact by persuading their schools, companies, or language-teaching organizations to similarly consider global issues and social responsibility. This might include discussing with your colleagues, school administrator, university dean, or office staff how your institution could contribute to a better world by reducing waste, by raising funds for worthwhile causes, and by working to change unjust or environmentally harmful school practices.

LANGUAGE TEACHING IN INDIA

Soft Skills are part of Communication Skills. Soft skills comprises of the skills which an individual uses to inform, to persuade, to explain, to present, to understand, elicit information. One may hate soft skills as he/she does n't posess the essential skills of persuading, explaining, understanding a spoken word. But today one cannot ignore the roll of soft skills in any learning process, more so in learning and teaching a language.

As English has turned into a universal language, its presence and value in the world has expanded enormously in the past decades. Many money-earning activities such as BPO, Medical Transcription and IT add to the importance and relevance of English in every walk of life. Prof. Jacob Tharu says, "English is no longer some remote but a powerful mystery, lying hidden in the world of textbooks and examination."

CONVENTIONAL ENGLISII LANGUAGE TEACHING

In the past, students were introduced to English only in their sixth standard. Students learned English just as another subject like Physics and Mathematics and got very little opportunity to using it within the school as well as outside the school.

The above context was appropriate for the use of methods that did not focus much on communicative competence. Language teachers adopted and followed some or all of the different methodologies listed below to teach the language.

Grammar Translation Method

Grammar translation method was used by the teacher to teach young children, where teacher explained every word to students in the native language to make him understand and learn English. But in this method there was at least one disadvantage. Both the teacher and the student concentrated more on L1 rather than L2. In this method English language class seemed to be L1 class rather than L2 class. Students got only limited benefit through this method.

Unfortunately, this method is still in use in many rural schools throughout India. This method is also supported by the methods used to teach mother tongue in our schools.

Bilingual Method

May be we should declare this as the method, our own favourite method in our schools. Most teachers follow the bilingual method to teach the students in Indian schools, where the teacher first of all explains the entire English sentence in L1 and then asks the students to perform activities in English. Here, it used to be a main assumption that only the teachers have the freedom to take the help of L1 and students are not supposed to use it, However, this constraint is found mostly on paper, not in the classroom. When a student is in the process of composing his or her English sentences, abundant help through the use of mother tongue sentences is provided. This method does not help fluency and naturalness in language expression. Thus, this method became beneficial to, students in learning the second language only up to some extent.

Direct Method

Earlier, teachers used to follow the direct method to teach Indian students mostly in private schools, which usually charge a higher tuition fee, etc. These teachers will stick to the practice of using only English, without depending on L1. Here, teacher is not supposed or authorized to use any single word from L1. This forced seclusion made students from many families with no past history of learning or using English face great difficulty in understanding certain words and their meanings. But this method turned to be more useful for the students to learn language than any other method as this method creates more encouraging language environment for students in the class room.

IN THE CONTEXT OF ENGLISH AS A SUBJECT

All the above methods have their own advantages and disadvantages, where the students learned English only as a subject rather than as language. They were also unable to put their learning into practice due to lack of a favourable environment.

In addition to the above constraints, the teachers used to have very limited teaching hours, mostly from three to six hours per week which are not enough to teach the language elaborately giving emphasis for the basic elements of language.

Another limitation seen in Indian teachers is that some of the English teachers are not familiar with the latest developments in ELT pedagogy. The situation is no better even at the college level as Robert Bellarmine observes, "The most serious problem in the teaching of English in our country is the appallingly small quantity and atrociously poor quality of English to which our learners are exposed." Teaching of English in India is examination-oriented only.

A CHALLENGE IN TEACHING ENGLISH TODAY

Challenges before the English Language teachers in India are enormous and apparent. They should be able to cater to the practical needs of learners, to make them competent enough to interact with one another and also to retrieve information all over the world.

English has a base in several countries and is considered as the most suitable and convenient tool for International Communication. The people who have proficiency in this language could access large number of jobs and also were seen holding high positions in many National and International Organizations.

In the earlier days English was just like a Library language, but now that notion has changed totally. At present the challenges visible before the English language teachers in India are diverse and it is necessary for them to shape up accordingly to meet the demands of the day.

METHODS ADAPTED TO IMPROVE SPOKEN SKILLS

Group Discussions

Now due to the world wide growing trends in English, teachers give more emphasis to communicative approach rather than the lecture mode. Their main goal is to make the students effective communicators in English both inside and outside the class room. To achieve this, they involve the students to participate more in classroom activities so that they will acquire adequate command over speaking skills. To create this environment, teachers can conduct group discussions, where students are supposed to speak only in English. Here, they can give their views, ideas and thoughts in English due to which they develop the habit of speaking fluently in English like they do in their mother tongue.

Various types of discussions also help students to improve their general awareness and understanding about current affairs. It gives a lot of scope for good imagination and deep thoughts. This type of discussions helps the students to listen to the views of fellow students which in turn helps them to gain knowledge and enrich the vocabulary also.

Debates

Debates too play an important role to improve the speaking ability of the students both at school and at higher level. Debates not only make the students to speak boldly and fluently but also help them to take one stand and be firm and consistent on that. Along with this advantage of reasoning, it gives students some experience to control their emotions without losing their temper. This also helps them to organize their thoughts and ideas in a specific way while speaking.

Role Plays

Role-plays are another important task that can improve the basic colloquial English of the learners. In role plays, the students assume themselves as one of the characters and behave and speak accordingly involving in the given character completely. In these types of activities teachers have to play a vital role as instructors and guide the students properly so that they can act appropriately to meet the situation. They should help the students now and then to understand and take up the role given to get a grip on the tone of voice.

Computer Assisted Language Learning (CALL)

Now-a-days computer has become a part and parcel of our day to day life. It plays a vital role in the process of teaching and learning. It can be used to learn a foreign language like English. Computers have made language learning easy and also made the language learning process interesting and enjoyable for both teacher and student throughout the world.

CALL has reduced the burden of the teacher whose teaching methods will be out dated to teach language to present day generation of the world. It is described as one of the interactive methods that can help a learner according to their own ability to learn, which enriches their language skills. CALL enables the learner to look beyond the conventional mode of learning and encourages self learning.

ENGLISH FOR SPECIFIC PURPOSES

As English has emerged as a global language, it also plays a vital part in every profession with respect its importance and demand. Every profession has its own professional terminology which is used frequently in that particular profession. For example, certain terms used by the doctors, lawyers, et al. are quite different from those of other professionals. So, to benefit these professionals, English for specific purposes is introduced so that specific English words related to that particular profession can be taught by those professionals. Jargon related to one profession is different from the other. Hence every professional is taught in a particular manner that fits in well with his professional demands.

TEACHING LANGUAGE THROUGH VISUAL AIDS

One of the innovative methods used by the teacher to teach language in class room is visual aids. The teacher distributes visual aids to students by dividing them into various groups. The students are then given stipulated time to extract relevant information on the given aids.

After that, those learners are supposed to speak about the visual aids given to them. This method expands the analyzing capacity of the students. By looking at the picture, the learner should think and come out with innovative thoughts which also help in learning language by creating fun-filled environment around them.

The teacher acts as facilitator who motivates the students to talk freely. As each person gets their own unique thinking it helps to sharpen their thinking process.

LANGUAGE GAMES

In addition to the above mentioned methods teachers also use various language games to teach English language apart from the conventional ways of language teaching, which helps in developing vocabulary from the language that is being learned.

1. Crossword puzzles
2. Games to teach basics of grammar to the students through various structures.

3

General Linguistic in English

Learning a second or a foreign language is more than learning a description of it. It is developing the ability to use the language on habit level. This is true of not only second language learning but also of first language learning. Fundamentally, all language learning involves the processes of listening, speaking, reading and writing. These processes involve both linguistic and psychological aspects. This leads us to understand that all language learning is based on certain well-defined principles derived from linguistic science as well as psychological science.

LINGUISTIC

One potent implication of linguistic theory is that language teaching should recognize the fact that experiences in L_1 should be related to the teaching of the target language. The first language acquired has a tremendous impact in the learning of the second language. Therefore, care must be taken to ensure that a conducive environment is created for language acquisition of a growing infant. This will facilitate his development of Language Acquisition Device; the innate potentiality which pre-conditions the ultimate acquisition and learning of languages. Language tests should be designed in such a way that the areas of disparities between L_1 and the target language are identified through contrastive language testing. This would provide an excellent frontier where error analysis model assists in diagnosing the inhibitions to learning, thereby providing clues for facilitation of language learning.

More so, the teaching of rules should be seen as a pre-requisite before a teacher proceeds to the functional use of the language in the classroom situation. The linguistic performance of every learner should be seen as a necessity which must be accomplished. Hence, the methodology should allow for active participation of students in the teaching process. The testing procedures should utilize the receptive skills of the learners in perfecting their productive skills. For instance, the use of descriptive language testing stands out as a prominent tool of measurement which enhances the learners' communicative competence in a given language.

PSYCHOLOGICAL

Herman (1961) cited in Finocchiaro (1969) identifies five steps through which the speakers of other languages proceed in learning a new language. These steps include anticipation, initial conformity, discouragement, crisis and adjustment and integration. The teacher needs to be extremely skillful in tackling problems of psychology. The students learning potential will also play a leading role in determining the content of each lesson. If a pupil finds himself in a group where all the pupils need help in building the basic experiential concepts, the problem is generally not one of great magnitude. If on the other hand, he finds himself in a group where other pupils possess experiential concepts in the language, the problem assumes a tremendous proportion.

So, by implication, the language teacher is expected to vary his methodology in order to cater for the psychological disparities (individual differences) in the learners. Since the theory emphasizes learning by association, the teaching of language should entail both the diachronic and synchronic study of the L_2 from the standpoint of the L_1. The theory posits that the more a stimulus is presented, the better perception a learner has. This appropriates the audio-lingual strategies of language teaching by memorization, rote learning, practice and repetition. However, the problem with the approach is that the points of language deficiency in individual learner might be difficult to identify and analyze. Simultaneous practice facilitates learning when L_1 and L_2 are studied together. The testing in language skill should be objective in order to sustain students' interest in learning. Motivation is a basic necessity in language teaching and testing situations. Therefore, adequate reinforcements (*e.g.*, applauding correct responses) and enough impetus (*e.g.*, availability of instructional resources) must be put in place to enhance performance.

Another vital implication of the psychological theory is that it advocates for a clearly suitable strategy which imposes on the learning; experiences which are in line with their innate potentialities. The learners' language ego feel reinforced when they are confronted with learning experiences at the crucial points of 'needs' in target language. This means that giving a test which has no functional essence in relation to learners' use of the target language could be annoying and frustrating.

SOCIOLOGICAL

The cultural context in which the language is being taught and tested is of fundamental importance for full understanding and evaluation. The cultural and social situation should be clarified and taught concomitantly with the features of language. This is done by simulating real life situations in the classroom. Learners should be allowed to practice language use in its cultural context. The community in which the school is located should not be ignored as well. The implication here is that cultural norms should be taken into consideration in the development of language curriculum, evaluation, administration and testing. Language teachers and students should see language as a social instrument of communication which is relative to role play and context. What this theory advocates is that pragmatics should be given more attention in the teaching and testing of any language. If truly the essence of language is communication, then, the 'communicative competence' or 'linguistic performance' should be the striking goal of any language teaching curriculum. Learners should be made to understand the variant complexity into which functional use of a language may be put.

By inference, for a judicious manipulation of the variables of language teaching methodology, the idea of 'natural situation' or immersion method should be put to play here; most especially in the areas of phonology and pragmatics. The implication that this has for testing is that the assessment (or mode of assessment) should neither be rigid or mono-directional. Tests should be designed in such away that the actual use of language (performance) in certain contexts by learners is measured rather than the knowledge (competence) of a language which may not necessarily guarantee the use (communicative competence). It is also important to know that when students err; the faulty responses should be corrected almost immediately within the framework of the context.

The notion of communicative competence is vital in sociolinguistic purviews. The idea stemmed from the premise that language is a functional instrument of socio-cultural expression. So, if the use of a language is hinged on the sociological realities, then, the use of pragmatic, true-to-life modules of imparting linguistic knowledge should be intensified. Consequently, this approach requires a testing module which can adequately appraise not only the linguistic knowledge but the appropriate use of codes that fit different circumstances. This is why communicative language testing which, in addition, examines the extent to which the learners are able to demonstrate their linguistic knowledge in meaningful communicative situation seems imperative. This view is also shared by Morrow (1979) and Canale (1984). To Weir (1988:9),

The performance tasks candidates are faced with in communicative tests should be representative of the type of task they might encounter in their own real-life situation and should correspond to normal language use where an integration of communicative skills is required with little time to perfect on, or monitor language input and output.

Sociological theory has a far-reaching implication for language teaching and testing. This is because it emphasizes ESP teaching and testing considering their provisions which seek to meet the diverging needs of learners in different situation.

PEDAGOGICAL

This indicates that the teaching of language should be practical if truly the rationale behind competence is performance. Learners should be put at the centre of the learning experience. Also in the centre are the teacher and the school. It has often been said "there are no good or bad methods, there are only good or bad teachers". According to Finocchiaro (1969), the personality of the teacher coupled with his attitude towards the pupils and his works will determine the extent to which a programme will be carried out. The general teaching skills of a teacher coupled with his linguistic ability facilitate or inhibit learning depending on his quality. A teacher who is proficient in language usage finds it easy to emphasize similar or contrasting elements in the target language, prepare appropriate approaches and materials and appreciate the difficulties faced by learners.

The objective, the curriculum and the evaluative procedure should be a joint thinking and planning of the school supervisor and the teacher. This co-operation will be reflected in the classroom instructional programme. The teacher who feels secured in the co-operation and understanding of the supervisor will experiment with new practices, modify the curriculum and develop the facets of a topic more thoroughly. The teacher may find it necessary to determine or change the size of his class in order to prepare materials for varying ability levels and modify the teaching activities to suit him and the class.

Immersion method, didactic strategy and situational dialogues which are student-centred enhance learning. The language learning experience must be organized in such away that it easily coheres with learners experiences in the assimilation of rules. Also, direct use of referencing should be adopted in the teaching of literary aspects of language.

In the area of testing, the pedagogical theory assumes that an ideal language test must not be fuzzy or abstract. Learners should be able to identify the relevance of test items in their communicative use into which a language is put. This underscores the use of communicative language testing over other descriptive ones which are largely grammar-governed but context-insensitive. Tinuoye (1991) identifies four phases of language testing. These are the traditional approach, the psychometric-structuralist model, integrative testing and communicative language testing. Of all these, communicative language testing seems to be the best because it is applicable to all the theories of language teaching discussed in this chapter.

LINGUISTIC IMPERIALISM

English includes some words that can be written with accent marks. These words have mostly been imported from other languages, usually French. But it is increasingly rare for writers of English to actually use the accent marks for common words, even in very formal writing. The strongest tendency to retain the accent is in words that are atypical of English morphology and therefore still perceived as slightly foreign. For example, *café* and *paté* both have a pronounced final *e*, which would be "silent" by the normal English pronunciation rules. Some examples: appliqué, attaché, blasé, bric-à-brac, brötchen, café, cliché, crème, crêpe, façade, fiancé(e), flambé, naïve, naïveté, né(e), papier-mâché, passé, piñata, protégé, raison d'être, résumé, risqué, über-, vis-à-vis, voilà.

For a more complete list, see List of English words with diacritics.Some words such as *rôle* and *hôtel* were first seen with accents when they were borrowed into English, but now the accent is almost never used. The words were considered very French borrowings when first used in English, even accused by some of being foreign phrases used where English alternatives would suffice, but today their French origin is largely forgotten. The accent on "élite" has disappeared from most publications today, though *Time* magazine still uses it. For some words such as "soupçon" however, the only spelling found in English dictionaries (the OED and others) uses the diacritic.

Italics, with appropriate accents, are generally applied to foreign terms that are uncommonly used in or have not been assimilated into English: for example, *adiós, coup d'état, crème brûlée, pièce de résistance, raison d'être, über (übermensch), vis-à-vis.* It was formerly common in English to use a diaeresis to indicate a syllable break: for example, coöperate, daïs, reëlect. One publication that still uses a diaeresis for this function is the *New Yorker* magazine. However, this is increasingly rare in modern English. Nowadays the diaeresis is normally left out (cooperate), or a hyphen is used (co-operate). It is, however, still common in loanwords such as naïve and noël.

Written accents are also used occasionally in poetry and scripts for dramatic performances to indicate that a certain normally unstressed syllable in a word should be stressed for dramatic effect, or to keep with the metre of the poetry. This use is frequently seen in archaic and pseudoarchaic writings with the "-ed" suffix, to indicate that the "e" should be fully pronounced, as with *cursèd*.

In certain older texts (typically British), the use of ligatures is common in words such as archæology, diarrhœa, and encyclopædia. Such words have Latin or Greek origin. Nowadays, the ligatures have been generally replaced in British English by the separated letters "ae" and "oe" ("encyclopaedia", "diarrhoea") and in American English by "e" ("encyclopaedia", "diarrhea"); however, the spellings "oeconomy" and "oecology" are now generally replaced by "economy" and "ecology" outside the U.S. as well.

For further information on how one can type diacritics and ligatures, see British and American keyboards, keyboard layouts.

In the nineteenth century, though, such norms were still seen as something to be established, and once established, spread. As Tony Crowley emphasizes, the "forces of centripetalisation... were not confined to a united language internal to the British state". Many British scholars believed that English, by right of the accomplishments of its speakers, was on its way towards being, and deserved to become, the universal language.

As one apologist for imperialism proclaimed, "English is emphatically the exponent of commerce, of civilization, of social and religious freedom, of progressive intelligence, and of an active catholic philanthropy; and beyond any tongue ever used by man, it is of right the cosmopolite speech".

One might observe in this argument for linguistic imperialism more going on than Locke's requirements for recording and communicating ideas. By now, another notion had become imported into British linguistic discourse, one justifying the belief that language reflected, indeed created character.

This notion encouraged British linguist G. F. Graham, for example, to describe language as follows: Language is the outward expression of the tendencies, turn of mind, and habits of thought of some one nation, and the best criterion of their intellect and feelings. If this explanation be admitted, it will naturally follow that the connexion between a people and their language is so close, that the one may be judged of it by the other; and that the language is a lasting monument of the nature and character of the people.

The belief that the character and intelligence of a people was determined by their language descended not from Bacon or Locke, but from Condillac, who in his Essay on the Origin of Human Knowledge had declared not only that "every language expresses the character of the people that speak it" and that a nation's great works begin only "when the language begins to have fixed principles and a settled standard", but also, more importantly, that "the language of rude and ignorant people obstructs the progress of the mind," an obstruction that cannot "diminish, but in proportion to the degrees of perfection added to that language".

Such pronouncements lent authority to the ideologues' plan to impose a standardized French throughout the country. In the late eighteenth century, they sought to replace not only foreign languages but also French dialects. According to Hans Aarsleff,

The chief support for these efforts came in fact from the non-French speakers who wished to be part of the events they did not understand. Since the republic was one and indivisible under a single law and the equality of patriots, it must also have one language and do away with the distinction between the French-speaking elite and the rest of the population. The aim was liberation, not repression.

However noble the intent of the ideologues may have been, their project to standardize the language within French borders soon combined with the idea that some languages were better, because more "rational," than other languages, and therefore it was equally noble to impose a more rational language upon the speakers of those less so. An important linguist whose work sometimes was used to support such linguistic imperialism — although he himself did not support it — was Wilhelm von Humboldt.

His influential text, The Diversity of Human Language-Structure and Its Influence on the Mental Development of Mankind (1836), claimed, as its title suggests, that the language and mental capability of a people were identical, "For," as he explains, "intellectuality and language allow and further only forms that are mutually congenial to one another".

According to Humboldt's theory, some language types more closely reflect the principles of universal grammar than others because they have had, from their very origin, a better intuitive grasp of the goals of speech. A language's "primordial form" determines from the start its ultimate development, just as the initial configuration of a crystal determines its ultimate structure.

Humboldt concluded that certain linguistic properties such as regular inflection were more conducive to creativity and intellectual rigour. Accordingly (to continue my analogy), just as it is legitimate to value a diamond more than a quartz crystal, it is legitimate to value some languages (as it turns out, unsurprisingly, "Sanskrit" or Indo-European languages) more than others. Humboldt does not want to eliminate the inferior languages anymore than he would want to eliminate "inferior" crystals and gems. As he put it,

I can never avoid a clear and open adoption of the decisive contrast between languages of purely regular form, and those of a form that deviates from this. It is my sincere conviction that what is expressed thereby is just an undeniable fact. The excellence of even these deviant languages, with the particular advantages it confers, the artistry of their technical construction, is neither misapprehended nor despised; we simply deny them the capacity to act, of themselves, in so ordered, so versatile and so harmonious a fashion upon the mind.

Later British efforts to standardize English, as Crowley has noted, "did not exclude differences but hierarchished them: posited as the central form, it [standard English] then ranged around it dialectal, class, gender and race-related differences in an inferior relation to its own powerful status".

Humboldt clearly provides a rationale for such a hierarchalization. Deriving his standard from the values held by his own society and then imposing it upon others, thus "proving" that otherness leads to inferiority, Humboldt set the pattern for later attempts to purify languages and cultures of foreign elements.

Humboldt's main argument for such purification, however, came from his habit of describing the differences among languages as being analogous to differences among works of art.

Previously, Condillac had described languages as developments of an initial, formative analogy, one that continues to govern the language's structure and give it its unity. A language's beginning, Condillac had said, may be arbitrary, but afterwards linguistic relationships are not: "Signs are arbitrary the first time they are employed, which is the reason perhaps that some imagine they can have no character. But I would fain know whether it be not natural for every nation to combine their ideas according to their own peculiar genius". Humboldt took this idea further to claim that the totality of a language was, like an artistic genius' initial inspiration, inherent in the sparking analogy that initiates the development of a language:

"Language, as is evident from its very nature, is present to the soul in its totality. Every detail in it, that is, behaves in such a way as to correspond to another that has yet to become clear, and to a whole given, or rather capable of creation, by the sum of the phenomena and the laws of the mind. The actual development goes on gradually, however, and the new increment is formed by analogy with what is already present."

For Humboldt, then, a language is like organic art. And, like art, when conceived organically, a language suffers when it is not kept pure. As Hans Aarsleff explains:

"For Condillac the genius of each language is controlled by the analogy that determines its individuality and organization. It is by virtue of its analogy that a language can be said to be an organism, and for Condillac as well as Humboldt this analogy and thus also the organism are impaired when a language becomes mixed with elements taken from a language that obeys another analogy."

Humboldt understands language as the working out of an intrinsic relationship between an initial "form" or "analogy" that cannot be artificially created and a totality that has yet to be realized but whose intimated nature as an integral whole determines what does and does not belong to it. Despite major differences between Humboldt's romanticism and the rationalisms of Locke, Leibniz, and Condillac — including the obvious difference of Humboldt's insistence upon the "genius" of the initial formation — Humboldt presumes as the rationalists did that nature itself is an integrated system and that ideally language mirrors that integrative totality.

Even so, a very important difference exists between Humboldt's theory and those of the universal grammarians on the one side and the Lockian conventionalists on the other. The difference lies in Humboldt's treating language as a process rather than a product.

We usually think of language as being the lexicon and the grammatical laws that determine the correctness of speech. Humboldt says, on the contrary, that "the break-up into words and rules is only the dead makeshift of scientific analysis". Such structures are descriptions of moments of stasis that in fact do not occur: "Language, regarded in its real nature, is an enduring thing, and at every moment a transitory one.... In itself it is no product, but an activity".

This language activity, or speech, Humboldt sometimes describes as a "labour," or a "work of the spirit", and sometimes as an "inner striving" of the individual to, on the one hand, express the requirements of a particular situation and, on the other, to be understood, which requires submitting to the way in which a listener "under similar circumstances, would have spoken to [the speaker]".

Such "labour," which "produces the expression of thought, is always directed at once upon something already given; it is not purely creative, but a reshaping activity". Humboldt claims that the "labour operates in a constant and uniform way", according to a certain form — or what he sometimes, following Condillac, calls the central "analogy."

This form, not grammatical form, constitutes the very essence of language, and language, therefore, cannot be regarded as a totality of signs and a set of rules for their combination. We can regard "only the totality of this speaking as the language". Only particular utterances are "present."

V. N. Volosnov, in his germinal text Marxism and the Philosophy of Language, has described Humboldt as "the most important representative" and founder of one of the two most important trends in language theory prior to his own work in the 1930s. That trend, individualistic subjectivism, adhered to four basic principles:

1. Language is activity, an unceasing process of creation (energeia) realized in individual speech acts;
2. The laws of language creativity are the laws of individual psychology;
3. Creativity of language is meaningful creativity, analogous to creative art;
4. Language as a ready-made product (ergon), as a stable system (lexicon, grammar, phonetics), is, so to speak, the inert crust, the hardened lava of language creativity, of which linguistics makes an abstract construct in the interests of the practical teaching of language as a ready-made instrument.

The opposing major trend, established by Ferdinand de Saussure, Volosinov called abstract objectivism, and he gives these as its basic principles:

1. Language is a stable, immutable system of normatively identical' linguistic forms which the individual consciousness finds ready-made and which is incontestable for that consciousness.
2. The laws of language are the specifically linguistic laws of connection between linguistic signs within a given, closed linguistic system. These laws are objective with respect to any subjective consciousness.
3. Specifically linguistic connections have nothing in common with ideological values (artistic, cognitive, or other). Language phenomena are not grounded in ideological motives. No connection of a kind natural and comprehensible to the consciousness or of an artistic kind obtains between the word and its meaning.

4. *Individual* acts of speaking are, from the viewpoint of language, merely fortuitous refractions and variations or plain and simple distortions of normatively identical forms; but precisely these acts of individual discourse explain the historical changeability of linguistic forms, a changeability that in itself, from the standpoint of the language system, is irrational and senseless. There is no connection, no sharing of motives, between the system of language and its history. They are alien to one another.

I borrow Volosinov's antithetical contrast here because it highlights nicely the difference between the Romantic and Modernist conceptions of the grounds of meaning, the nature of discursive force, and the individual's relationship to a language.

Whereas the Romantics believed that discursive force originated from the individual's grasp of a core analogy that generates an organic linguistic whole, the Modernists, like the eighteenth-century Rationalists, saw the whole itself as the ground.

The chief differences between the Modernists and their Rationalist predecessors, of course, were that while the Rationalists thought the whole in question was Nature, the Modernists thought it was language; and while the Rationalists thought language could be fixed and altered to correspond to the logic governing the universe, the Modernists thought that language was not subject to the individual's control.

Just as Darwin argued that the success or failure of the individual act or life had no effect upon the evolution of its species, except insofar as that act or life is the consequence of an accidental mutation affecting the individual's inheritable capacities correlated with accidental alterations in the species' environment, Saussure argued that the system of language that mediates speech, that determines or limits what an individual thinks, and that "in great part... makes the nation" that speaks it, is completely "unassailable by the human will" and changes only by chance.

Saussure's founding methodological premises are well known. He defines language (la langue) and speech (la parole) in terms of a difference between "the product passively registered by the individual" and "an individual act of the will and the intelligence". This distinction allows him to establish language as an isolated, homogeneous object for a science distinct from those appropriate to studying speech.

Language as the object of linguistics is a closed system of arbitrary signs, and signs are "real objects", unities of signifiers and signifieds whose identities are determined by their differences from one another within the closed system. His very definition of language therefore compels him to distinguish between synchronic linguistics (the study of a language at a particular moment in time) and diachronic linguistics (the study of historical changes in states of the system).

Apparently, Saussure intended for these constitutional definitions to establish only a particular point of view, one that would not delegitimate the study of individual speech or motivated discourse but would assign to such studies entirely different methodologies.

However, his claims that signs are real and not merely analytical abstractions and, more importantly, that the history of a language is conceptually and causally independent of the state of a language, led inevitably to "structuralism" and the belief in the abyss between desire and knowledge, motive and effect, that structuralistic thinking supposedly reveals.

This "abyss," however, is less a revelation than a presupposition.

That this is so can best be observed by revisiting Saussure's explanation of the difference between "static linguistics" and "evolutionary linguistics." In this section of his Course, as in several other places, Saussure draws an analogy between a language and a game of chess.

The recurrence of this analogy leads me to believe that Saussure consciously modeled his theory on the game. Whether he did so or not, the analogy provides considerable insight to the limitations of the theory.

Saussure offers three points of comparison between chess and language in order to illuminate his distinction between synchrony and diachrony. First, he says, "a state of a chessboard corresponds exactly to a state of the language.

The value of the chess pieces depends on their position upon the chess board, just as in the language each term has its value through its contrast with all the other terms". This correspondence tells us a number of things. For one, it reminds us that the capacity of a sign to substitute for an idea is conditioned by the sign's comparative relationship to other signs in the system.

Saussure, when explaining the difference between value and meaning, said that "the content of a word is determined in the final analysis not by what it contains [*i.e.*, by "the concept or meaning for which it is a token"] but by what exists outside it. As an element in a system, the word has not only a meaning but also — above all — a value."

And that value is "assessed against comparable values, by contrast with other words". In the analogy with chess, then, the "meaning" of a knight is "can move up two spaces and over one," while its value is the product of that capacity and its position on the board in relation to the other pieces, each with its own meaning and value. This correspondence also suggests that the board itself, its configuration and size, is not determined by the play even if the board's order determines the potential value of every piece on it.

What in language corresponds to the board? "It is true," Saussure notes, "that the values also depend ultimately upon one invariable set of conventions, the rules of the game, which exist before the beginning of the game and remain in force after each move". These rules, he says, correspond to "the unchanging principles of semiology." So the rules, no doubt, establish the board. Still, we have no idea what in language might correspond to it.

But the only thing the board could correspond to in Saussure's system is reality, which, for his system to work, would have to be a fixed scheme, like the scheme of squares on the board. As Saussure says, though, "If words had the job of representing concepts fixed in advance, one would be able to find exact equivalents for them as between one language and another.

But this is not the case". Instead of "predetermined categories" or "ideas given in advance" are "values emanating from a linguistic system." Furthermore, "If we say these values correspond to certain concepts, it must be understood that the concepts in question are purely differential.... What characterizes each most exactly is being whatever the others are not". In other words, Saussure presupposes a reality that is formally fixed but blank; in itself it is meaningless, like the squares of a chess board, except when a linguistic game is being played upon it. What the squares "mean" is nothing; their value is determined by the pieces upon them, just as are the values of the pieces themselves.

The board, then, is Saussure's metaphor as the chora, the ground of discourse. It may be helpful to compare Saussure's notion of the ground as a fixed structure, a notion typical of philosophies of being, with a more historicized notion of ground typical of philosophies of becoming. Julia Kristeva, for instance, has argued that chora's "organization is subject to... an objective ordering [ordonnancement], which is dictated by natural or sociohistorical constraints such as the biological difference between the sexes or family structure". In contrast, Saussure's theory clearly implies that changes in linguistic order have no effect upon social order as such, even if various "moves" may effectively re-value elements within the social order. Individuals remain in the grip of a system with no rational means of altering it.

We may draw similar conclusions from Saussure's second and third points of comparison between chess and language. The second is that "the system is only ever a temporary one. It varies from one position to the next.

" The third is that "in order to pass from one stable position to another or, in our terminology, from one synchronic state to another, moving one piece is all that is needed". The consequence of these characteristics is that changes in the linguistic order are necessarily irrational, senseless. Any one move "has a repercussion upon the whole system," but "it is impossible for the player to foresee exactly where its consequences will end".

Prediction is impossible because there is an absolute break between diachrony and synchrony. "In a game of chess," as in linguistics, any given state of the board is totally independent of any previous state of the board. It does not matter at all whether the state in question has been reached by one sequence of moves or another sequence. Anyone who has followed the whole game has not the least advantage over a passerby who happens to look at the game at that particular moment.

In order to describe the position on the board, it is quite useless to refer to what happened ten seconds ago. All this applies equally to a language. Although alterations in linguistic systems usually take place through "blind forces of change," even deliberate changes are necessarily irrational.

As Saussure says, "If the game of chess were to be like the operations of a language in every respect, we would have to imagine a player who was either unaware of what he was doing or unintelligent". Just as to Darwin the evolution of life is not going anywhere in particular; to Saussure the evolution of language is not going anywhere.

Both the physical environment and the social order are beyond the individual's control; just as the survival value of an individual's genetic characteristics and the value of a sign's meaning are products of previous changes in the system, changes that will have taken place through "blind force" and that no one could have predicted. The net result is a view of discourse that implies that anyone who is surviving or making sense now has every reason to try to maintain the system exactly as it is and has no reason at all to try to change it.

THE CONSEQUENCES OF LINGUISTIFICATION

Discourse about discourse has tended towards what I will call "linguistification" — towards more and more emphasis upon language as a medium of force between "mind" and "reality," one of greater or lesser transparency, but always towards more formality, abstraction, and disconnection from historical process and individuals' situations and their desires. Linguistic discourse has been hardly value-free, "objective," or descriptive; instead, the ideal of formal coherence has almost always been its goal.

Once this goal has been articulated, the desire for linguistic standardization or purification has been the usual unfortunate consequence. Only in a few historic instances has the "substantiality" of the others' discourse been recognized at all. Even in these, however, recognition of the other has depended upon first subordinating the other's discourse to some authoritative standard: Erasmus's copia, although acknowledging a multiplicity of finite perspectives, relied not only upon a community of Latinity, but ultimately upon Papal authority to achieve final consensus; Vico, although fighting the substitution of Cartesianism for common sense, saw Cartesian logic not as being itself imbued with the temporality that prudence accounts for, but as being actually universal, although in need of being supplemented by common sense; and Humboldt, as pathbreaking as his view was of discourse as a struggle or labour of the individual desire and the particular instant against the petrified or crystallized remains of prior linguistic activity, he still saw true discourse as a struggle towards a new form of coherence and unity that required a cleansing of alien elements to achieve its destined perfection.

The remaining theories of discourse, from Augustine through Saussure, tend to suppress completely the effects of individual speech acts, particular discursive situations, and others' opinions about speech. Therefore, linguistification tends to suppress, if not bury completely from view, the effects of power at work in discourse.

Instead of a flow of discursive process, it presents a sequence of linguistic states; and instead of the effective word, it presents the arbitrary sign. As "language," discourse is set apart from reality, thus obscuring the way things are. Language is said to have a different ontological status from reality and to operate according to different sets of laws; accordingly, language is understood differently from the way we understand "reality as such."

Moreover, linguistification implies that because languages are unified wholes, we have numerous, incommensurable languages. And it is not just that Swahili differs from French, but that poetic languages differ from scientific languages, and that both differ from "ordinary" languages. Such languages are said to be "translatable" into the others only insofar as they "refer" to the same thing in a world that is presumed to be unaffected by mere discourse.

By the same logic, or rather by the same need to grasp "meaning" as sets of relations within integrated totalities, language itself is said to be split into incommensurable "levels," so that what can be said to be true at the level of phonetics cannot be said to be true at the level of syntax, and so on. Of course, such beliefs about language led to spectacular attempts to impose the syntax of the sentence upon wholes greater than the sentence (structuralism), attempts to reconcile the event of speech, which can be "deviant" and new, with the grammar of the language, and attempts to locate and distinguish the levels of discourse that function according to different sets of rules than those of the sentence.

All this breaking up of discourse, this cognitive shattering of the world, underwrites "alienation," the central "problem" of discourse. Ironically, alienation is a problem only to the processes of linguistification, a fact that is obscured by understanding discourse in terms of language. Because they defined the phenomena of discourse as "language" problems, whole generations of intellectuals ignored the rhetorical tradition with its emphasis upon concrete discursive situations, social constraints, choice, responsibility, and persuasive force.

As late modernist and postmodernist writers began to tackle the problems that had been caused by linguistification, they did so within linguistic terminology, usually completely in ignorance of the rhetorical alternatives available to them.

This forgetting of the tradition is especially evident in European scholarship. Chaim Perelman, for instance, could, upon visiting The Pennsylvania State University in the late 1960s, be genuinely surprised to find out that what he thought he had discovered had been the subject of debate for centuries. He could then go on in The New Rhetoric to reclaim this "lost" tradition.

Other Europeans, however, seem to have never acknowledged rhetoric or seem to have had a very limited view of its issues. Mikail Bakhtin, J. L. Austin, Michel Foucault, Jacques Derrida, Stephen Toulmin, and many others who have battled against alienating dichotomies of modernism and who have sought to reclaim an understanding of discourse as situated events, apparently have done so completely without the benefit of knowing the work of their predecessors who had fought to prevent the splits from occurring in the first place.

Of course, this neglect of the tradition is understandable since what was left to the discipline of rhetoric after Plato split it from philosophy, and after Ramus and then Bacon eliminated invention from its canon, was distributed after the Enlightenment into logic, literary criticism, anthropology, psychology, linguistics, etc. But removing a particular subject from the rhetorical field could not remove rhetoricity from the subject. Eventually, the twentieth century had to account for the discursive processes of all these disciplines. Sooner or later, they have all had to confront the fact that the saying is never innocent of what is being said, that appearance is a mode of reality.

Regrettably, attempts to account for the effects of saying were made so not by resubordinating the disciplines to the study of what the Sophists had called logos but by importing linguistics into the various disciplines, on the assumption that linguistics explained scientifically how discourse worked. Richard Rorty book The Linguistic Turn explains marvelously how this occurred in philosophy. Similar "turns" took place in the other "human sciences."

Rorty has suggested that the "three hundred years' worth of attempts to bridge the gap which the Cartesian, representationalist picture of knowledge and inquiry led us to imagine existed" is coming to an end. Would that it were so simple! Rorty's hopeful comment reveals just how deeply the picture he deplores still dominates even the best of us, for it suggests that that picture is just an illusion, an appearance, with no real effects, and so it can be simply dismissed and forgotten.

But, as I have said several times in this book, even if belief in such a picture cannot produce the effects the belief would lead us to expect, it produces effects nevertheless. However unnecessarily or inappropriately, people *do* interpret and persuade through linguistic and cultural conceptual schemes.

Given this, our interpretive and rhetorical strategies must take these beliefs and effects into account. We may say there are situations where it would be better if there were no linguistic effects in discourse. We may say linguistification and culturalization have produced situations we find undesirable, situations we would prefer to alter.

If so, we may want to develop a study of discourse that has as its purpose de-linguistification and de-culturalization, one that produces alternative ways of interpreting and persuading to those who do rely upon ideas of "culture" or "language," when these are understood as "structured [media] of representation, capable of standing in determinate relations to a distinct entity called 'the world' ".

LINGUISTIC CHOICES

The challenge for all language users is to create texts that realize the expected social context; cohesive texts that are coherent with respect to register. Texts that fail to effectively signal the context in which and for which they are created are often seen as lacking coherence. Children who do not present their sharing time contributions with the expected register variables, for example, are often judged negatively by their teachers, even when their contribution is comprehensible. Informal definitions likewise fail to signal the academic context that the formal definition signals participation in.

Texts that do not signal understanding of the school context present the language user as a person who is not responding adequately to the situation in realizing the language task. The following sections show how the situational variables of field, tenor, and mode are realized in ideational, interpersonal, and textual choices in the grammar, and how these choices are different in interactional and school-based contexts. Each of the situational variables is analyzed in terms of the grammatical choices that are relevant for understanding how that aspect of the situation is realized through particular register choices.

For example, the presentation of ideas, the field variable, typically draws on broadly different kinds of lexical and grammatical choices in informal conversation and the language of schooling. Similarly for tenor and mode, the different role relationships and different kinds of texts that are typical of these two broadly defined different situational contexts are realized in different register choices.

The spoken texts that illustrate the points in this chapter come from group interviews with children who explored questions about students and teachers interacting in the classroom. Although these interviews took place at school, they were structured to encourage discussion among the students, and so the patterns of language that the students draw on to jointly construct texts in this context contrast strongly with the kind of language that they encounter in their reading and have to produce in their writing.

Informal conversation in other contexts is even more distinct from the kind of language students need to engage in for success at school. The written texts used as examples in this chapter come from textbooks as well as from students' writing. Although all contexts and texts have their own relationships and features that can be specified at greater levels of detail, the differences between the spoken interaction and written texts analyzed in this chapter enable us to identify some register features that are particularly important for participation in interaction, on the one hand, and in the texts typical of schooling, on the other.

Lexical explicitness is one way that the ability to use language successfully in school tasks is often characterized. This "explicitness" should be seen not in cognitive terms, but in linguistic terms, as an ability to draw on lexical resources that are effective in particular contexts. Such ability requires knowledge of the social expectations of the task as well as control of the range of vocabulary needed to construe meanings precisely. Explicitness, then, in these terms, is manifested through selections from the grammatical elements related to the construction of the field of discourse.

The field of discourse, what the language is about, is closest to ordinary notions of what it means to use language effectively. Students know that they need to use the "right words" if they are going to demonstrate what they have learned. The field variable is realized primarily in nouns, verbs, and other content words. What a text is about emerges to a great extent from vocabulary choices. At school, much vocabulary is subject-specific, contributing to text creation in particular content areas.

Texts (1) and (2) illustrate some differences in realization of the field variable in academic registers and interactional registers. Text (1) is an example of the kinds of text students read at school, a paragraph on sedimentary rock from a seventh-grade science textbook. The paragraph describes two ways, both involving water, that sedimentary rocks are formed.

1. The formation of sedimentary rocks is closely associated with water. One type forms when water carries soil, pebbles, and other particles to the ocean floor where these sediments become rock. The second method involves chemicals dissolved in water. By evaporation and precipitation of substances like calcium carbonate, sedimentary rocks can form.

Text (2), an excerpt from a group discussion of third-grade students, shows some typical features of an interactional register. The children are talking about what makes a student a "good responder" in the classroom. They discuss how teachers decide whom to call on. Matthew makes the point that sometimes teachers call on students who have not raised their hands in order to catch people who aren't paying attention. This means that sometimes students raise their hands even when they don't know the answer, hoping the teacher will call on people who are not raising their hands.

But he adds that a student takes a risk if he assumes that the teacher will not call on him. If the teacher calls on him anyway, and he doesn't know the answer, he needs some excuse such as "I wasn't raising my hand, I was just stretching. " Here's how the discussion went:

2. *Matthew:* And um, like um sometimes if, um, like you think that the teacher? um, if you raise your hand and she says "No" so she'll pick on the peoples that don't know it? so you raise your hand she picks you and you go "Well, I think, I didn't, um, well. "
   Boyd: I was just stretching
   Cara: Gosh.
   Matthew: Yeah
   A little later:
   Boyd: The other thing is, the teachers usually try to call on people that aren't paying attention=
   Cara: I know
   Boyd: =which happens to me a lot.
   Justin: And they surprise us.
   Matthew: That's what I said like the people raise their hand? and- and she because they think they're going to pick the person who don't know it? and when she picks on you she says, ... "Oh. "
   Cara: I know, I used to do that.

Lexical Choices

Learning to use language in specialized ways is one of the challenges of schooling, and vocabulary choices that realize field are typically different in interactional and school-based texts. The lexis of school based texts is often technical and abstract, as seen in (1), where the lexical choices identify it as a science text. Science texts depend on technical terms to make precise meanings. Text (1) draws on a technical lexis (formation, chemicals, calcium carbonate, sedimentary rock) to describe a geological process.

Text (2), on the other hand, shows typical lexical choices for interactional texts, where lexis tends to be more ordinary and generic. Even the lexical terms that relate to schooling are non-technical and concrete (teacher, raise hand, pick you, etc.). This difference between the "everyday" and the "specialist" lexis is a major way that the language of academic texts differs from the ordinary interactional language of daily life.

Another way that field is construed is in the types of processes that different text types draw on. From a functional perspective, an English clause can include a process, typically realized in a verb or verbal group; participants, typically realized in nouns or nominal groups; and circumstances, typically realized in prepositional phrases or adverbs. An example of this analysis is provided at (3):

3. Halliday describes six types of processes: material, behavioural, mental, verbal, relational, and existential. He shows how each type of process assumes a constellation of participants in the process and grammatical relationships between process and participants that are realized in different ways. A complete explanation of this way of analyzing clauses is beyond the scope of this book, but examples of the six types of processes.

Different registers draw on different constellations of processes as they realize different situational contexts. Research and pedagogical approaches that use the identification of different process types and show how they are functional for constructing different types of texts include.

Comparing the processes in (1) with those in (2) shows how this kind of analysis illuminates differences between the situational contexts that these texts realize. The differences are indicative of the kinds of processes that are typical of these two types of text, (1) and (2). In (2), the interactional discussion about events, material processes (raise, pick) construe the events, behavioural processes (stretching, paying attention) construe human behaviours, and verbal and mental processes (says, know) construe the saying and thinking of the participants involved, enabling Matthew to talk about the actions of the student and teacher and his feelings about them. An existential process (the other thing is) enables the introduction of a new topic.

In (1), on the other hand, the author chooses material processes to describe the way sedimentary rock forms, and relational processes such as is associated with and involves constructing the scientific theory that explains this natural occurrence. These differences in the kinds of processes are typical of differences between the two registers, as interactional language more frequently focuses on individual actions and personal viewpoints, while the textbook presents information and constructs new understandings about the physical world.

The more frequent use of relational processes, in particular, characterizes school-based registers, describe more fully. Experientially, then, texts realize the contextual variable of field through their lexical choices, whether technical or ordinary, including the choice of process type and associated participants and circumstances.

Logical Relationships

Another important field variable is the realization of logical relationships within texts. The kinds of logical meanings that contribute to the realization of field include relationships of time, consequence, comparison, and addition.

Differences between everyday, interactional registers and the registers that construe school-based texts can be illustrated in the way conjunctions are typically used.

Use of conjunctions is one of the options in the system of logical connection within and between clauses. In spoken interaction, conjunctions are a pervasive feature, and a few commonly used conjunctions can construe a wide range of meanings in this register. Occurring more frequently in speech than in writing, conjunctions construe generalized meanings in interactional discourse that require more specific choices in academic texts. This means that spoken discourse frequently employs a few commonly occurring conjunctions to realize a variety of logical links.

This can be seen clearly in (2), repeated at (4) to highlight how Matthew uses conjunctions to make logical connections in his explanation. Conjunctions introduce all but three of the nine non-embedded clauses in the first part of the explanation about raising his hand:

4. a. <u>And</u> um, <u>like</u> um sometimes <u>if</u>, um, <u>like</u> you think that the teacher?
   b. um, <u>if</u> you raise your hand
   c. <u>and</u> she says "No"
   d. <u>so</u> she'll pick on the peoples that don't know it?
   e. <u>so</u> you raise your hand
   f. she picks you
   g. <u>and</u> you go
   h. "Well, I think,
   i. I didn't, um, well. "

Matthew begins his explanation at (a) with the clause "And um, like um sometimes if, um, like you think." He uses several conjunctions as he makes his point. The if marks the clause as introducing a hypothetical case, but the other conjunctions he uses suggest that what he is about to say is linked to previous discourse (and) and that it will introduce an example (like). The next segment (b)–(d), introduces a further hypothetical (if) clause describing what a student might do, followed by the next event in the evolving scenario, the teacher's possible response, introduced with and and elaborated with so.

At (e)–(g) Matthew then describes an instance in which a student does what has been described in (b)–(d), introduced with a causal marker (so) at (e), followed by the next event in the sequence (f), with the consequence of that event described at (g)–(i), again introduced with and. This frequent use of conjunctions to introduce clauses, typical of spoken discourse, illustrates two major functions of conjunctions in speech: to display generalized semantic meanings and to mark text structure with discourse markers.

In (2), only a few different conjunctions are used with generalized meanings. Matthew's use of coordinating conjunctions, especially and, to link his clauses in this oral discourse is a major strategy for maintaining coherence in speech.

A study by Lazaraton (1992), for example, found five times more clauses connected by and in speech than writing. She reports that clauses connected by and in the narrative and comparison/contrast spoken texts she analyzes exhibit a wider range of meanings compared with the same genres of written texts. For example, sequence and addition are common meanings displayed by clauses connected by and in her spoken corpus, but not in writing, where other ways of marking these logical relationships are used.

In (4), a variety of logical relationships exists between clauses connected with and; for example, the and at (c) links clauses that could also have been linked with but to highlight the adversative aspect of the teacher's refusing to call on a student who "knows it." In informal spoken explanations, the same conjunctions can construe different logical meanings, and the clauses they link do not necessarily display the explicit semantic relationship that is associated with the conjunction in a more decontextualized reflection on its meaning.

These variable meanings can also be illustrated by looking at one aspect of the linking relationships signaled by conjunctions; that is, whether the links are internal or external. Internal conjunctions signal logical relationships that construct the text as text, while external conjunctions signal logical relationships that are present in the world outside the text. Internal conjunctions can indicate speaker or text-based links.

For example, Martin describes two environments for internal relations; in interactional exchanges, to mark challenges to moves or links between exchanges, while across a variety of text types, internal relationships help to mark the structure of the text. Internal conjunction reflects the rhetorical organization of text, or the speaker's knowledge base or attitude, rather than relating events in the world.

In (4), for example, Matthew's like at (a) is an internal link that indicates he is presenting an example. The rest of Matthew's explanation uses external conjunction to link a series of clauses that depict the scenario Matthew is presenting, a scenario that illustrates how a student might think the teacher would act in response to a student raising his hand. The conjunctions if, and, and so [(b)–(g)] are external links that introduce the conditional/causal logic that motivates the sequence of events. Internal conjunctive links construct the logical relationships between one part of a text and another, while external conjunctive links construe the logical relationships in the situation being discussed. Conjunction and logical linking is an area of English grammar that varies considerably according to register. Both interactional and academic texts use internal and external conjunction, but they draw on internal conjunctive resources for different purposes.

In speech, the same frequently occurring conjunctions can be used to make both internal and external links. In (5), for example, from the same children's discussion, Matthew uses because both internally and externally:

5. Well like I have a partner that hardly anybody likes because they make fun of her name because it's Halley like Halley's comet.

Matthew's first because introduces the evidence he uses to justify his statement that the other children don't like his partner. This because makes an internal link that introduces the reason Matthew can make the judgement he has made. His second because, on the other hand, makes an external link by explaining why the children make fun of Halley's name. Use of conjunctions to signal internal links, like the basis for Matthew's judgement, are typical of interactional registers.

In informal conversation, conjunctions can carry less semantic weight, as intonation and interactional context contribute to the meanings that are made. This use of conjunctions does not transfer well to academic registers, however, where different grammatical strategies are expected when evidence is presented. This is one aspect of the challenge of reasoning in the ways expected at school. In academic registers, a more varied set of conjunctions is used in more restricted ways. Conjunctions like however, furthermore, and nevertheless, for example, not typical of informal conversation, can link and mark the logical relationships between the parts of a text in academic registers. When conjunctions like because and but are used, they are generally expected to construe their core semantic meanings and not the range of meanings that they are able to make in informal talk.

This means that students need to learn alternative strategies in school-based texts for realizing the logical relationships that they use common conjunctions for in informal speech. This is typically done through entirely different ways of casting sentences, involving different forms of clauses and clause combinations.

Logical relationships that are typically signaled by conjunctions in speech are typically realized in other ways in academic texts. Example (1) from the science textbook, reproduced here as (6), illustrates this, with the text separated into its finite, non-embedded clauses:

6. a. The formation of sedimentary rocks is closely associated with water.
   b. One type forms
   c. When water carries soil, pebbles, and other particles to the ocean floor
   d. Where these sediments become rock.
   e. He second method involves chemicals dissolved in water.
   f. Yevaporation and precipitation of substances like calcium carbonate,
   e. Entary rocks can form.

While in informal spoken discourse, logical connections are most often made with conjunctions, in academic registers, logical connections are more typically made through nouns and verbs. Here the causal links are made with nominal and verbal expressions (is closely associated with, forms, involves, by evaporation ...). The conjunctive relationships are integrated into the clause, rather than being expressed between clauses. Causal conjunctions such as because or so are not needed to make the logical connections.

These issues of discourse organization and clause structuring are taken up in greater detail below in the presentation of the textual resources of the grammar, where the implications of such conjunctive choices for the overall structuring of academic texts are illustrated. In analyzing how field is construed in informal conversation and school-based texts, then, the focus is on the experiential resources of nominal and verbal elements and on how resources that make logical connections are deployed. This focus illuminates how the language of schooling challenges students to draw on more specialized lexical and grammatical resources that enable them to reason in particular, valued ways.

Taking a Stance

Tenor is the contextual variable that is realized in the interpersonal elements of the grammar. It is through choices from the interpersonal component that speakers and writers demonstrate their understanding of the role relationships inherent in each context and express their stance towards the texts they are creating. Academic language has different expectations from interactional language regarding presentation of self. In academic contexts, students are typically expected to project a non-interacting and distanced relationship with the listener/reader in their writing and formal speaking. Ways of presenting judgements and evaluation also differ in informal interaction and school-based texts.

Certain grammatical and lexical features can be identified that construe different tenors as they make a text more or less distanced and authoritative in the way information is presented and evaluation is realized. This section contrasts the interpersonal features that are typical of the tenor of informal spoken interaction with those typical of the tenor of the texts students work with at school.

Mood is a major resource for establishing tenor. Mood is the grammatical resource that helps realize interactivity and negotiation. English has three mood options, declarative, interrogative, or imperative, as illustrated in (7):

7. Declarative mood: You are learning about functional grammar.
   Interrogative mood: Are you learning about functional grammar?
   Imperative mood: Learn about functional grammar!

Selection of mood is a choice that presents the language user as someone who states, questions, or commands, and each choice suggests a different relationship between speaker/listener or writer/reader. Dialogic conversation typically has varied mood structure, as speakers share information and question and urge each other to act. The typical mood choice in academic texts, on the other hand, is declarative, as the speakers/writers present themselves as knowledgeable providers of information. School-based registers typically do not emerge through the active interaction of interlocutors. While they also have elements that construe the speaker/ writer's awareness of audience, these are different from the give and take of conversational interaction, where interrogative and imperative forms are common.

This can be illustrated by a text that draws on the mood structure of an interactional register in an academic context, revealing the infelicity of the grammatical choices for presenting a reasoned position. Texts (8) and (9) are examples from a text written by a high school student who is responding to an essay by Wendell Berry:

8. Wendell Berry thinks that escaping nature is what we seek for satisfaction, but how can that be so? Today, more than ever, there is a great demand for environmental engineers because there has been a tremendous increase of interest for the environment. Wendell Berry also believes that we dislike confronting with the sun, the air and the temperatures but if that were the case, then why do so many people insist in migrating to California? He also mentions, "Life will become a permanent holiday." That is impossible! Even if high-tech machinery were invented, human beings would be needed to operate them.
9. Let us not part from nature nor from technology, instead let us carry them both with us into the future!

In (8), the student expresses her disagreement with Berry through rhetorical questions which she answers briefly, with little development. In (9), she uses an imperative structure to appeal to her audience in a hortatory way.

This essay construes a context of high involvement and emotional appeal, a dialogic stance that is not typically highly valued in the expository essay, where instead an assertive author is expected to present information in measured ways, and to use more subtle resources than interrogative and imperative structures to persuade others to adopt a point of view. Example (10) demonstrates how another student writer draws on academic register resources in expressing disagreement with Berry's thesis:

10. Although technology has caused many people to lose sight of their own capabilities and talents, we cannot overlook the medical advances and research possibilities that it has allowed us and still allows us.

This writer takes a similar stance towards Berry's thesis that the writer of (8) and (9) has, disagreeing with Berry's view of technology, but the writer of (10) begins with a concession to Berry (the Although clause) and then brings out the points on which she will disagree. Instead of interrogative or imperative mood, she draws on the resources of modality in arguing that we cannot overlook what technology offers. Modality is a resource for presenting propositions non-categorically, enabling the expression of degrees of probability, certainty, necessity, and other meanings. Modal verbs and adjuncts enable the expression of interpersonal meanings that construe the stance of the speaker/writer. Rather than expressing opinions starkly as the writer of (8) does (That is impossible!), the writer of (10) uses the modal choice cannot that makes this position a matter of inability and necessity, enabling her to state her position in a way that does not depend on a hortatory style that construes a context of argumentative interaction. The grammatical choices in (10) enable the writer both to concede a point and to challenge Berry's ideas.

It is also possible to end an essay with an injunction about what should be done, as the writer of (9) has, but in a style that construes a less hortatory perspective. Text (11) illustrates this:

11. My point is that satisfaction should not come from only working with nature, as Berry believed. People should get satisfaction from helping others, getting good grades, building new inventions, making people happy, etc. The list is endless. Satisfaction should come from accomplishing something useful.

Without making a direct appeal to the reader, as the writer of (9) does, the writer of (11) still presents a clear point of view and recommendation. Instead of the grammatical choice Let us, this writer uses the modal verb should to accomplish the purpose of suggesting what should be done. It is the lexical and grammatical choices that make a presentation appear more "reasoned."

This is not to say that a rhetorical question or hortatory injunction is never appropriate in an academic text. But that will show that a hortatory text has a different purpose from an analytical text, and adopting a hortatory stance when analysis is called for can result in a less effective text that can more easily be discounted. Although the well-placed rhetorical question can enhance an academic text, students who rely too heavily on dialogic features in their writing enact an interpersonal stance that may detract from the points they are making. In (12), for example, the student's use of varied mood structure in rhetorical questions and exclamations, along with first person pronouns, gives the essay a tone of personal involvement:

12. How come he also believe that unsatisfaction is achieved by people not doing the things we hate or don't want to do? Is he telling me that I should work in a cold or hot environment? Expose myself under the sun all day? or even expose myself to wind and rain. All these conditions inflict pain on the human body. The pain can be endured, but why would anyone chose too? For satisfaction? I believe not!

This writer's disagreement with Berry's thesis is construed as emotional and reactive. Eschewing the varied mood structures of conversational interaction and adopting the impersonality of third person declarative sentences requires that students understand how to use the features of academic registers to convey their feelings and attitudes at the same time that they present themselves as objective experts with information to communicate to others.

The expectation for "reasoned" presentation reflects a value that is placed on arguments that are supported by evidence and presented objectively. Without controlling the grammatical resources that enable an argument to be challenged in the detached, rather than involved, style that is more highly valued in academic contexts, writers risk having their views dismissed as merely emotional reactions.

Developing writers are challenged to construe interpersonal meaning without being able to draw on intonation for this purpose. In spoken texts, intonation can construe interpersonal meanings that are not otherwise lexicalized. In (2), for example, Matthew's intonation as he says "Well, I think, I didn't, um, well" conveys all the embarrassment and chagrin that he felt during this episode. In academic texts, meanings are typically construed without drawing on this resource, so lexical and grammatical choices, along with some punctuation and formatting conventions, realize meanings that would be realized in intonation in spoken interaction.

Text (13), for example, taken from the same textbook as (1), shows how a text in an academic register can convey the attitudes and personal judgements of the author towards what is said in the absence of intonational cues:

13. Many astronomers now believe that the radio sources inside quasars are objects known as black holes. The existence of black holes is more or less taken for granted by many astronomers, although no one has ever seen one. Black holes, if they exist, are in fact invisible!

A black hole, according to the theory, is the result of matter that has been super-compressed. For example, if the sun were compressed from its present diameter of 1,390,000 km down to a diameter of just 6 km, it would become a black hole. The gravitational attraction of such a heavy object would be so great that nothing, not even light, could escape from it.

The author takes advantage of orthographic resources such as bolding, italics, and exclamation points to highlight terms and emphasize key points. This mimics the role of intonation in spoken language. However, this text has other features that realize interpersonal meaning in ways that are quite different from what is typical of informal speech.

One aspect of this text's meaning is the expression of tentativeness about the existence of black holes that pervades this selection without being explicitly stated. Although this text is about black holes, the author is not fully committed to black holes as a theoretical construct. In order to grasp the full meaning of the passage, the reader needs to link the expression of doubt in the although clause (although no one has ever seen one) and the if clause (if they exist) with other signals of possible skepticism about the existence of black holes, realized in expressions including Many astronomers now believe, more or less taken for granted, and according to the theory.

The cumulative effect of all of these is to raise questions about the existence of black holes. The point that black holes are in fact invisible is marked with an exclamation point, and students need to draw on the meanings of all of the linguistic resources used by the author in order to understand that astronomers might have doubts about the existence of black holes.

The understanding that this is a theoretical construct and may not actually exist has to be gleaned through linguistic features that never make this point directly.

It is typical of written school-based texts that the writer often suggests interpersonal or attitudinal stances towards what is being presented without explicitly marking them as such. As in (13), interpersonal meanings important for comprehension of a text are often stated inexplicitly and draw on many areas of the grammar. An approach in the systemic functional linguistics framework that focuses on ways of construing evaluation is appraisal analysis.

This approach identifies grammatical resources for making three kinds of interpersonal meaning: resources for passing judgements, resources for positioning the writer with respect to the meanings in the text, and resources for modifying the interpersonal force or focus of the message. From the perspective of appraisal analysis, any element of the grammar can contribute to making these kinds of attitudinal meanings.

In (13), for example, the writer uses a variety of structural elements to construe an attitude towards black holes and indicate a position with respect to them (*e.g.,* taken for granted, if they exist, in fact, according to the theory), as well as modifying the force of the assertions (*e.g.,* many astronomers now believe, more or less).

The fact that attitudinal meanings pervade a text, realized in nouns, verbs, adjectives, and clause constructions, means that interpersonal meaning, like intonational patterns in spoken language, is construed throughout the grammar, as the attitude of the speaker/writer towards what is being said or written is incorporated throughout the text.

Although valuable resources for interpersonal meaning in speech, such as varied mood structure and intonation, are typically not central to academic registers, attitudinal meanings are still always present. In school-based texts, attitudinal meanings emerge in modality and other resources for attitudinal meaning that are often implicit in the overall stance and judgements they construe.

Mode: Structuring a Text

The third contextual variable that is always realized through grammatical choices is mode. The choices for mode reflect the different ways that a text is presented and organized, related to the role that language plays in realization of the context of situation. Here there are major differences between the registers of informal spoken interaction and the registers of schooling, as texts participate in very different ways in these contexts. In informal conversation, the interlocutors are engaged in mutually constructing meaning, and the way the text is structured helps realize this co-construction.

In academic texts, on the other hand, the meanings are built up as the text progresses without co-construction by an interlocutor. This requires different grammatical strategies. In either case, elements from the textual component of the grammar enable the speaker or writer to control the flow of information, repeating and emphasizing where necessary and introducing details and asides where appropriate.

But different modes use different kinds of linguistic resources, or use the resources in different ways, to accomplish this. The resources for realizing mode that are considered here include cohesive devices, especially conjunctions, and their role in clause structuring, as well as thematic development and other resources for structuring information.

Cohesion, Conjunctions, and Clause-Combining Strategies

Cohesive elements are one set of resources for forming texts. Cohesion refers to the way that linkages are made in texts across clause boundaries. Reference is one resource for cohesion by which pronouns and deictic expressions.

In interactional contexts, they are often used exophorically, pointing to participants in the immediate context, where the situation disambiguates the referent. In academic texts, on the other hand, this and that are more often used endophorically to make links between segments of text. For example, in (14), (again from a response to the Berry essay) after a discussion about what satisfaction means, the student uses that to connect her next sentence to the previous text:

14. That is what society must learn, satisfaction is not having success or money or things handed to you but suffering to attain them and learning from the experience.

This is different from the that that points to something in the external context; instead, it points to the previous text. Students need to learn to use reference in different ways as they work with school-based texts.

Conjunction is another resource for cohesion in texts. The discussion of field showed that the way logical relationships are indicated differs between interactional and school-based registers, as school-based texts less often use explicit conjunctive links and more often incorporate the logical relation in nominal or verbal elements. Here the focus is on conjunction more abstractly, as a strategy for realizing mode through the way the discourse is organized, where conjunctions themselves are only one means of creating links from one part of the text to another.

Some examples of the variety of ways that logical connections can be made in English text are shown at (15):

15. a. Rain ruined the picnic.
    b. The picnic was ruined by the rain.
    c. The picnic was ruined because it rained.
    d. It rained. The picnic was ruined.

The connection between picnic and the rain can be expressed through predication (with a verb, ruined), through a minor predication (with a preposition, by), with a conjunction (because), or as two separate sentences with no structural relationship. The real-world connection is the same in each case, but the grammatical options represent different degrees of integration of the logical relationship into the clausal structure. With the two elements, rain and the ruining of the picnic as the central ideas, (a) is the most integrated expression of this proposition, with the participants and processes represented as the main elements of the clause.

In (b), on the other hand, the actor (rain) is presented in a prepositional phrase. In (c), the rain is presented as a verbal element in a separate clause, introduced by a causal conjunction (because). And in (d), the events are represented in two separate sentences, with no overt conjunctive link. The grammar of English provides different ways of expressing the same real-world relationships, with some ways of expression integrated into clause structure and other ways relying on conjunctions or other means of clause combining.

Differences in ways of reasoning, whether through conjunctions, prepositions, verbs, or nouns, are a key aspect of register differences. In academic texts, reasoning with nouns, verbs, and prepositions is typical. This is because the function of much school-based language is expository, presenting ideas that can be analyzed and interpreted. In academic texts the dense presentation of information means that more integrated logical relations are typically more highly valued. The emergent and co-constructed nature of informal spoken interaction, on the other hand, means that explicit conjunctions linking finite clauses are more common. Text (16) shows a typical conjunctive structure of academic registers.

16. At one time, socializing and visiting with family and friends was a very common event. Our "advances" in communication have, in a way, set us back. The invention of the telephone has made it more convenient for people to talk with those that they cannot usually see and spend time with, but the telephone has also become a substitute for spending time with loved ones. Instead of getting everyone together and having a picnic or day together at someone's house, the telephone has seemed to replace this.

Many spend more time inside away from other people, talking on the telephone or watching television, rather than spending time outside enjoying nature and others' company.

In (16), conjunctions are used primarily for noun phrase coordination, as in socializing and visiting with family and friends. Only one case of clause-linking uses conjunction, the but in the third sentence. On the other hand, a variety of logical relationships is still signaled throughout the text. The primary logical relation in this paragraph is contrast. Rather than joining clauses with but to signal this contrast, however, the writer uses at one time, instead of, and rather than to make the contrastive links.

For example, in the sentence Instead of getting everyone together and having a picnic or day together at someone's house, the telephone has seemed to replace this, the prepositional phrase instead of signals the relationship of contrast. In conversational interaction, the speaker might alternatively have said something like "We used to get everyone together and have a picnic, but the telephone has replaced this."

Other logical relationships are also expressed through verbs. For example, in the sentence The invention of the telephone has made it more convenient for people to talk with those that they cannot usually see and spend time with, the conjunctive relationship of cause is expressed by the verbal has made instead of, for example, the conjunction so (The telephone was invented, so it is more convenient ...). These different choices result in texts whose overall structure and density of information vary considerably. A key challenge for students is to learn to condense meanings in denser clause structures that incorporate logical relationships rather than stringing together one clause after another with conjunctions as they do in spoken interaction. This means learning the more restricted meanings for conjunctions as they are used in academic registers and alternative strategies for introducing the logical relationships that conjunctions offer.

Clauses can be linked with each other in different ways, and different clause combining strategies are functional for creating different kinds of texts. Creating interactional texts requires that speakers continually monitor information, often adding background or motivating circumstances as they proceed. An emergent organizational structure is achieved as speakers develop ideas and co-construct discourse with clauses chained by conjunctions.

In academic texts, on the other hand, organization is more often hierarchical, with embedded clauses and nominal structures used to pack more information into each sentence. This variation in ways of combining clauses is part of the resources available to the speaker/ writer for structuring information in a text.

Taking a functional approach to the different ways clauses can be combined means considering the way the clauses participate in the broader textual context.

The categories "dependent" or "subordinate" and "independent" are insufficient in analyzing the different kinds of relationships between clauses and how clauses link with each other to form cohesive texts in speaking and writing.

This is because the category subordinate clause includes two functionally very different types of clauses. Some subordinate clauses participate in discourse structuring; these are referred to as hypotactic clauses. Others function as a nominal group or part of a nominal group and do not make an independent contribution to discourse structure; these are called embedded clauses. Hypotactic clauses are dependent on but not constituents of another clause.

They may be introduced by subordinating conjunctions such as if, when, or because as they are linked with a prior or subsequent clause. Embedded clauses, on the other hand, function within another clause; for example, as a postmodifier in a nominal group. We see this in a sentence from the explanation of black holes, reproduced at (17):

17. A black hole ... is the result of matter that has been super-compressed.

The restrictive relative clause that has been super-compressed is embedded in the nominal group that has matter as its head. This clause does not make an independent contribution to discourse structure, but instead functions as part of the nominal group. Other examples of embedded clauses are comparative clauses and nominalized clauses that function as subject or complement.

In addition to these two types of subordinate clause, clauses can also be linked in a coordination relationship of parataxis. Paratactic clauses are linked to a prior clause with a coordinating conjunction or merely juxtaposed, and include direct quotations. Spoken interaction relies heavily on parataxis to link from clause to clause. This three-way distinction of clause linkages as paratactic, hypotactic, or embedded, distinguishes between clauses that independently contribute to discourse structure (hypotactic and paratactic) and those that function as part of another clause (embeddings).

Different choices in clause structuring are characteristic of different registers, and result in differences in lexical density in informal and academic texts. Lexical density is a measure of the number of content words per non-embedded clause in a text. According to Halliday, "the average lexical density for spontaneous spoken English barely exceeds two lexical words per clause".

The lexical densities of (1) and (2) differ considerably, with (1) more than three times as lexically dense as (2). Such a difference is typical of these two types of discourse. The more highly structured nature of school-based texts contributes to their lexical density. Through lexical density, academic registers pack more information into each clause, making it possible to build up the information in a text efficiently.

Conjunctions, as a cohesive resource, contribute in different ways to interactional and academic texts, with a lesser reliance on conjunctions for clause linking and realization of logical connections and a greater use of embedded clauses in school-based texts that are more densely structured.

Theme and Information Structuring

Thematic development is another textual resource that contributes to organizational differences in texts. Theme is a construct of functional grammar that reveals how a clause in English is organized as a message. The theme of an English clause is the linguistic element that occurs first in the clause. It serves as the "point of departure", or starting point, for the clause as a whole. The remainder of the clause is called the rheme; "the part in which the Theme is developed".

Different kinds of linguistic elements can serve as clause themes, as shown at (18), with themes underlined:

18. Themes are often the subject of the clause. But conjunctions can also be part of the theme. Naturally, elements that contribute interpersonal meaning also occur first in the clause and contribute to the expression of theme. In some clauses, prepositional phrases or other experiential elements occur in initial position and serve as themes.

In (18), themes are realized in experiential (Themes, conjunctions, elements that contribute interpersonal meaning, In some clauses), interpersonal (Naturally), and textual (But) elements. A full explication of the analysis of theme requires more space than is available here, but for the purposes of this book, theme can be identified as the elements up to and including the first experiential element at the beginning of a clause. In a clause beginning with a verb, the verb is the theme. When a clause participant is the theme, the whole nominal group is analyzed as the theme. Where conjunctions occur, they are also part of theme, as are interpersonal elements such as the adjunct naturally.

Analysis of the thematic structure of a text reveals the method of development in the text, as choice of the starting point of the clause indicates the perspective the speaker/writer is taking. Different kinds of themes indicate different approaches to the organization of the text and are also related to differences in register. The clause themes differ in the two texts. In (2), the themes of Matthew's clauses are conjunctions and pronominal subjects, along with the Well that introduces his reported response to the teacher's calling on him.

These themes are functional for realizing the scenario that Matthew is developing, as the conjunctions scaffold the sequence of actions by the teacher and Matthew's response. In (1), on the other hand, the author uses the theme position to progressively build an understanding of how sedimentary rocks are formed. The first theme, the formation of sedimentary rocks, presents the notion that sedimentary rocks form, and the further themes explicate the types of formations (one type; the second method).

The theme of the where clause picks up the elements that were presented in the rheme of the when clause (soil, pebbles, and other particles), calling them these sediments. Finally, the theme of the last clause, by evaporation and precipitation of substances like calcium carbonate, enables the author to elaborate the details of the secondmethod introduced in the prior sentence as the point of departure for the next clause, and end the paragraph with a restatement of the point of the paragraph as a whole, how sedimentary rocks can form.

Academic registers often thematize noun phrases that condense prior information and present what has already been said so that further comment can be made about it, as shown above, where these sediments was picked up as clause theme. The creator of an academic text can exploit the functionality of theme for controlling the method of development of the text. An example of this is seen in the first two sentences in (13), presented at (19):

19. Many astronomers now believe that the radio sources inside quasars are objects known as black holes. The existence of black holes is more or less taken for granted by many astronomers, although no one has ever seen one.

The second sentence begins with the thematic element The existence of black holes. This theme takes the information that was new in the rheme of the previous sentence, that there are objects known as black holes, and re-presents it as a nominalized element in the second sentence, as the point of departure for further discussion about black holes.

The theme of a clause is often also the subject of the clause, but the functions of subject and theme are not the same. In functional grammar, subject is the "element ... on which the validity of the information is made to rest"; a nominal group "by reference to which the proposition can be affirmed or denied". Subject is a useful construct for identifying the pivotal participants in a clause, but since not all clauses begin with subjects, incorporating the notion of theme in the grammatical analysis is a means of better understanding how information is structured in academic texts.

Looking at clause subjects alone also reveals information about differences in the two registers, but not about the method of development. The subjects alone reveal the key participants, but it is the themes that show how the text is developing, as conjunctions and initiating phrases help scaffold the organization. The interactional text, (2), relies heavily on pronominal subjects, while the academic text, (1), draws on lexical subjects. The subjects of (2) are pronouns, with the most frequent subjects you (a generalized third person singular pronoun meaning a person), she (the teacher), and I.

Such choices, typical of interactional discourse, are described by Chafe (1986) as "light subjects." They reflect the fact that participants in conversation typically engage in exchanges in which their clauses begin with a shared pronominal referent and add new information about that referent in clause complements. Such pronominal subjects are often deictic elements (you and I) that point to conversational participants and create involvement.

Various studies have confirmed that in conversation, pronominal subjects are typical. The subjects of the textbook passage, on the other hand, are lexicalized and include expanded nominal groups. The you and I that characterize interactional speech do not appear here, and lexicalized subjects appear instead. This text is not about propositions that hinge on you and me, but instead on the formations, types, and methods that are discussed in the textbook.

It is useful to distinguish between theme and subject in order to analyze the organizational structure and development of information in a text. In informal interactional texts, pronominal subjects often occur in theme position, and new information is increasingly built up in the clause rhemes. In academic texts, the author is challenged to progressively build an argument, summarizing and recapitulating prior discourse as each clause expands the discussion.

For this purpose, the academic texts use noun phrases that condense given information as the point of departure so that further comment can be made. Information from the rheme of one clause occurs again as the theme in the following clause, contributing to the density of academic texts and to the kind of organization which is often described as more complex.

LINGUISTICS PHILOLOGY

Before doing so, however, it must be noted that such a linking of textual analysis to more general linguistic concerns is not a feature of scholarly practice which has been invariably accepted by all linguistic historians.

Since the end of the Second World War, two traditions of enquiry into the history of English can be distinguished: the 'philological' and the 'linguistic'. These traditions have from time to time been seen as mutually antagonistic, although there are signs that a scholarly rapprochement between them is beginning to emerge.

The term 'philology' has a number of meanings; on the continent of Europe, for instance, it is often used to refer to literary rather than to linguistic studies. Perhaps its most common use, however, is to refer to the close study of the language of individual texts from the past, as opposed to 'linguistics', which may be crudely defined as the scientific study of language, whereby observed facts are placed within a larger conceptual framework.

Many scholars have come to see philology as old-fashioned, not concerned with the larger theoretical picture which is considered by some the true domain of historical linguistics, and therefore trivial; traditional philology certainly suffered, at least in British universities, from such atomism, and it is probably for this reason that it has come, at least for the time being, to lose its centrality within the larger domain of English studies.

Philology seemed to be-or perhaps more correctly seemed to have become-not so much 'theory-free' as 'theory-innocent', and thus ultimately intellectually unsatisfying.

Yet it could be argued that a tendency has developed amongst some modern linguists to allow theory to overwhelm data; and the data-centred discipline of philology can be regarded therefore as useful corrective to a tendency to overgeneralise.

The necessity of bringing together these two approaches to the historical study of language is emphasised when we judge the evidence for the history of English. In the Old and Middle English periods, the main sources of information are literary and documentary manuscripts, supplemented to a limited extent by inscriptions on stone, wood, metal or bone, and by place-names, and complex questions of context and transmission surround all these texts.

In the Early Modern English period, things seem at first sight more hopeful; the evidence of the manuscript is supplemented not only by that of the printed book but also by that offered by the first serious writers on the English language: the spelling-reformers, the early phoneticians and grammarians and the early lexicographers.

Many of these scholars were excellent observers of the language of their time; however, their evidence always needs to be judged in the light of contemporary prescriptive attitudes to speech and writing. Only in the nineteenth and twentieth centuries, with the rise of the scientific study of contemporary language, does the evidence become in any sense complete; but, even then, there are problems to do with the sheer quantity and range of the material collected, and with the theoretical assumptions which governed its collection.

Hie direct evidence for past states of the language, therefore, survives in patchy and fragmentary ways; and, although this direct evidence can be supplemented by the indirect evidence to be derived from processes of linguistic reconstruction, these latter methods not only present problems of their own but also themselves depend on the historical record.

Unlike the modern sociolinguist or diaiectologist, historical linguists cannot choose their informants for their social class or geographical setting; we have to make do with what the vagaries of time have left us, and, very frequently, we depend on the merest hints to help us construct our hypotheses about past states of the language.

It is therefore important not to draw linguistic conclusions from textual data without first subjecting the texts to careful examination. 'Every text has its own history' could be taken as the key axiom which underlies-or should underlie-philological practice. To refer simply to diatopic ('through-space', *i.e.*, geographical) and diachronic ('through-time', *i.e.*, historical) variation in texts is not enough; texts need to be contextualised, so that the true status of the information they contain may be ascertained.

WRITTEN ENGLISH

A version of the language almost universally agreed upon by educated English speakers around the world is called formal written English. It takes virtually the same form no matter where in the English-speaking world it is written. In spoken English, by contrast, there are a vast number of differences between dialects, accents, and varieties of slang, colloquial and regional expressions. In spite of this, local variations in the formal written version of the language are quite limited, being restricted largely to the spelling differences between British and American English.

Languages are more to us than systems of thought transference. They are invisible garments that drape themselves about our spirit and give a predetermined form to all its symbolic expression. When the expression is of unusual significance, we call it literature. Art is so personal an expression that we do not like to feel that it is bound to predetermined form of any sort.

The possibilities of individual expression are infinite, language in particular is the most fluid of mediums. Yet some limitation there must be to this freedom, some resistance of the medium. In great art there is the illusion of absolute freedom. The formal restraints imposed by the material — paint, black and white, marble, piano tones, or whatever it may be — are not perceived; it is as though there were a limitless margin of elbow-room between the artist's fullest utilization of form and the most that the material is innately capable of. The artist has intuitively surrendered to the inescapable tyranny of the material, made its brute nature fuse easily with his conception.

The material "disappears" precisely because there is nothing in the artist's conception to indicate that any other material exists. For the time being, he, and we with him, move in the artistic medium as a fish moves in the water, oblivious of the existence of an alien atmosphere. No sooner, however, does the artist transgress the law of his medium than we realise with a start that there is a medium to obey.

Language is the medium of literature as marble or bronze or clay are the materials of the sculptor. Since every language has its distinctive peculiarities, the innate formal limitations — and possibilities — of one literature are never quite the same as those of another. The literature fashioned out of the form and substance of a language has the colour and the texture of its matrix.

The literary artist may never be conscious of just how he is hindered or helped or otherwise guided by the matrix, but when it is a question of translating his work into another language, the nature of the original matrix manifests itself at once. All his effects have been calculated, or intuitively felt, with reference to the formal "genius" of his own language; they cannot be carried over without loss or modification. Croce is therefore perfectly right in saying that a work of literary art can never be translated.

Nevertheless literature does get itself translated, sometimes with astonishing adequacy. This brings up the question whether in the art of literature there are not intertwined two distinct kinds or levels of art — a generalized, non-linguistic art, which can be transferred without loss into an alien linguistic medium, and a specifically linguistic art that is not transferable. I believe the distinction is entirely valid, though we never get the two levels pure in practice.

Literature moves in language as a medium, but that medium comprises two layers, the latent content of language — our intuitive record of experience — and the particular conformation of a given language — the specific how of our record of experience. Literature that draws its sustenance mainly — never entirely — from the lower level, say a play of Shakespeare's, is translatable without too great a loss of character. If it moves in the upper rather than in the lower level — a fair example is a lyric of Swinburne's — it is as good as untranslatable. Both types of literary expression may be great or mediocre.

There is really no mystery in the distinction. It can be clarified a little by comparing literature with science. A scientific truth is impersonal, in its essence it is untinctured by the particular linguistic medium in which it finds expression. It can as readily deliver its message in Chinese as in English.

Nevertheless it must have some expression, and that expression must needs be a linguistic one. Indeed the apprehension of the scientific truth is itself a linguistic process, for thought is nothing but language denuded of its outward garb. The proper medium of scientific expression is therefore a generalized language that may be defined as a symbolic algebra of which all known languages are translations.

One can adequately translate scientific literature because the original scientific expression is itself a translation. Literary expression is personal and concrete, but this does not mean that its significance is altogether bound up with the accidental qualities of the medium.

A truly deep symbolism, for instance, does not depend on the verbal associations of a particular language but rests securely on an intuitive basis that underlies all linguistic expression. The artist's "intuition," to use Croce's term, is immediately fashioned out of a generalized human experience — thought and feeling — of which his own individual experience is a highly personalized selection.

The thought relations in this deeper level have no specific linguistic vesture; the rhythms are free, not bound, in the first instance, to the traditional rhythms of the artist's language. Certain artists whose spirit moves largely in the non-linguistic (better, in the generalized linguistic) layer even find a certain difficulty in getting themselves expressed in the rigidly set terms of their accepted idiom. One feels that they are unconsciously striving for a generalized art language, a literary algebra, that is related to the sum of all known languages as a perfect mathematical symbolism is related to all the roundabout reports of mathematical relations that normal speech is capable of conveying.

Their art expression is frequently strained, it sounds at times like a translation from an unknown original — which, indeed, is precisely what it is. These artists — Whitmans and Brownings — impress us rather by the greatness of their spirit than the felicity of their art.

Their relative failure is of the greatest diagnostic value as an index of the pervasive presence in literature of a larger, more intuitive linguistic medium than any particular language. Nevertheless, human expression being what it is, the greatest — or shall we say the most satisfying — literary artists, the Shakespeares and Heines, are those who have known subconsciously to fit or trim the deeper intuition to the provincial accents of their daily speech. In them there is no effect of strain.

Their personal "intuition" appears as a completed synthesis of the absolute art of intuition and the innate, specialized art of the linguistic medium. With Heine, for instance, one is under the illusion that the universe speaks German. The material "disappears."

Every language is itself a collective art of expression. There is concealed in it a particular set of esthetic factors — phonetic, rhythmic, symbolic, morphological-which it does not completely share with any other language. These factors may either merge their potencies with those of that unknown, absolute language to which I have referred — this is the method of Shakespeare and Heine — or they may weave a private, technical art fabric of their own, the innate art of the language intensified or sublimated.

The latter type, the more technically "literary" art of Swinburne and of hosts of delicate "minor" poets, is too fragile for endurance. It is built out of spiritualized material, not out of spirit. The successes of the Swinburnes are as valuable for diagnostic purposes as the semi-failures of the Brownings. They show to what extent literary art may lean on the collective art of the language itself.

The more extreme technical practitioners may so over-individualize this collective art as to make it almost unendurable, One is not always thankful to have one's flesh and blood frozen to ivory. An artist must utilize the native esthetic resources of his speech.

He may be thankful if the given palette of colours is rich, if the springboard is light. But he deserves no special credit for felicities that are the language's own. We must take for granted this language with all its qualities of flexibility or rigidity and see the artist's work in relation to it. A cathedral on the lowlands is higher than a stick on Mont Blanc.

In other words, we must not commit the folly of admiring a French sonnet because the vowels are more sonorous than our own or of condemning Nietzsche's prose because it harbours in its texture combinations of consonants that would affright on English soil. To so judge literature would be tantamount to loving "Tristan und Isolde" because one is fond of the timbre of horns. There are certain things that one language can do supremely well which it would be almost vain for another to attempt. Generally there are compensations.

The vocalism of English is an inherently drabber thing than the vowel scale of French, yet English compensates for this drawback by its greater rhythmical alertness. It is even doubtful if the innate sonority of a phonetic system counts for as much, as esthetic determinant, as the relations between the sounds, the total gamut of their similarities and contrasts. As long as the artist has the wherewithal to lay out his sequences and rhythms, it matters little what are the sensuous qualities of the elements of his material.

The phonetic groundwork of a language, however, is only one of the features that give its literature a certain direction. Far more important are its morphological peculiarities. It makes a great deal of difference for the development of style if the language can or cannot create compound words, if its structure is synthetic or analytic, if the words of its sentences have considerable freedom of position or are compelled to fall into a rigidly determined sequence. The major characteristics of style, in so far as style is a technical matter of the building and placing of words, are given by the language itself, quite as inescapably, indeed, as the general acoustic effect of verse is given by the sounds and natural accents of the language.

These necessary fundamentals of style are hardly felt by the artist to constrain his individuality of expression. They rather point the way to those stylistic developments that most suit the natural bent of the language. It is not in the least likely that a truly great style can seriously oppose itself to the basic form patterns of the language. It not only incorporates them, it builds on them.

The merit of such a style as W. H. Hudson's or George Moore's is that it does with ease and economy what the language is always trying to do. Carlylese, though individual and vigorous, is yet not style; it is a Teutonic mannerism. Nor is the prose of Milton and his contemporaries strictly English; it is semi-Latin done into magnificent English words.

It is strange how long it has taken the European literatures to learn that style is not an absolute, a something that is to be imposed on the language from Greek or Latin models, but merely the language itself, running in its natural grooves, and with enough of an individual accent to allow the artist's personality to be felt as a presence, not as an acrobat. We understand more clearly now that what is effective and beautiful in one language is a vice in another.

Latin and Eskimo, with their highly inflected forms, lend themselves to an elaborately periodic structure that would be boring in English. English allows, even demands, a looseness that would be insipid in Chinese. And Chinese, with its unmodified words and rigid sequences, has a compactness of phrase, a terse parallelism, and a silent suggestiveness that would be too tart, too mathematical, for the English genius.

While we cannot assimilate the luxurious periods of Latin nor the pointilliste style of the Chinese classics, we can enter sympathetically into the spirit of these alien techniques. I believe that any English poet of to-day would be thankful for the concision that a Chinese poetaster attains without effort. Here is an example: Wu-river stream mouth evening sun sink, North look Liao-Tung, not see home. Steam whistle several noise, sky-earth boundless, Float float one reed out Middle-Kingdom.

These twenty-eight syllables may be clumsily interpreted: "At the mouth of the Yangtsze River, as the sun is about to sink, I look north towards Liao-Tung but do not see my home. The steam-whistle shrills several times on the boundless expanse where meet sky and earth. The steamer, floating gently like a hollow reed, sails out of the Middle Kingdom." But we must not envy Chinese its terseness unduly.

Our more sprawling mode of expression is capable of its own beauties, and the more compact luxuriance of Latin style has its loveliness too. There are almost as many natural ideals of literary style as there are languages. Most of these are merely potential, awaiting the hand of artists who will never come. And yet in the recorded texts of primitive tradition and song there are many passages of unique vigour and beauty. The structure of the language often forces an assemblage of concepts that impresses us as a stylistic discovery. Single Algonkin words are like tiny imagist poems.

We must be careful not to exaggerate a freshness of content that is at least half due to our freshness of approach, but the possibility is indicated none the less of utterly alien literary styles, each distinctive with its disclosure of the search of the human spirit for beautiful form.

Probably nothing better illustrates the formal dependence of literature on language than the prosodic aspect of poetry. Quantitative verse was entirely natural to the Greeks, not merely because poetry grew up in connection with the chant and the dance, but because alternations of long and short syllables were keenly live facts in the daily economy of the language.

The tonal accents, which were only secondarily stress phenomena, helped to give the syllable its quantitative individuality. When the Greek metres were carried over into Latin verse, there was comparativly little strain, for Latin too was characterized by an acute awareness of quantitative distinctions. However, the Latin accent was more markedly stressed than that of Greek. Probably, therefore, the purely quantitative metres modeled after the Greek were felt as a shade more artificial than in the language of their origin. The attempt to cast English verse into Latin and Greek molds has never been successful. The dynamic basis of English is not quantity, but stress, the alternation of accented and unaccented syllables.

This fact gives English verse an entirely different slant and has determined the development of its poetic forms, is still responsible for the evolution of new forms. Neither stress nor syllabic weight is a very keen psychologic factor in the dynamics of French.

The syllable has great inherent sonority and does not fluctuate significantly as to quantity and stress. Quantitative or accentual metrics would be as artificial in French as stress metrics in classical Greek or quantitative or purely syllabic metrics in English. French prosody was compelled to develop on the basis of unit syllable-groups. Assonance, later rhyme, could not but prove a welcome, an all but necessary, means of articulating or sectioning the somewhat spineless flow of sonorous syllables.

English was hospitable to the French suggestion of rhyme, but did not seriously need it in its rhythmic economy. Hence rhyme has always been strictly subordinated to stress as a somewhat decorative feature and has been frequently dispensed with. It is no psychologic accident that rhyme came later into English than in French and is leaving it sooner. Chinese verse has developed along very much the same lines as French verse.

The syllable is an even more integral and sonorous unit than in French, while quantity and stress are too uncertain to form the basis of a metric system. Syllable-groups — so and so many syllables per rhythmic unit — and rhyme are therefore two of the controlling factors in Chinese prosody. The third factor, the alternation of syllables with level tone and syllables with inflected (rising or falling) tone, is peculiar to Chinese. To summarize, Latin and Greek verse depends on the principle of contrasting weights; English verse, on the principle of contrasting stresses; French verse, on the principles of number and echo; Chinese verse, on the principles of number, echo, and contrasting pitches.

Each of these rhythmic systems proceeds from the unconscious dynamic habit of the language, falling from the lips of the folk. Study carefully the phonetic system of a language, above all its dynamic features, and you can tell what kind of a verse it has developed — or, if history has played pranks with its phychology, what kind of verse it should have developed and some day will.

Whatever be the sounds, accents, and forms of a language, however these lay hands on the shape of its literature, there is a subtle law of compensations that gives the artist space. If he is squeezed a bit here, he can swing a free arm there. And generally he has rope enough to hang himself with, if he must. It is not strange that this should be so. Language is itself the collective art of expression, a summary of thousands upon thousands of individual intuitions.

The individual goes lost in the collective creation, but his personal expression has left some trace in a certain give and flexibility that are inherent in all collective works of the human spirit. The language is ready, or can be quickly made ready, to define the artist's individuality. If no literary artist appears, it is not essentially because the language is too weak an instrument, it is because the culture of the people is not favourable to the growth of such personality as seeks a truly individual verbal expression.

WRITING AND SPEECH

Perhaps the most important point to make about the evidence for past states of the language is that, until the very end of the nineteenth century, direct (as opposed to reconstructed) evidence is to be found solely in the written record. Thus the most important act of evidential contextuali-sation needed in an historical study of English is a clarification of the relationship between the written and spoken modes of language.

For most of the language's history, the written mode is all that survives; and this fact raises problems of how far writing maps onto speech. It is, of course, obvious that the writing-systems of the world used today do not have any clear relationship to the sounds which, often at some removes, they represent: the relationship between symbol and sound is arbitrary, not necessary.

Thus, in alphabetic scripts, Cyrillic 'means', whereas Roman 'means' [w] in English and so on. This complexity is compounded by the appearance of conventional uses based upon distributional distinctions (*e.g.*, has two different phonic significances in Present-Day English yacht, many), and by diachronic variation. As an example of the latter, the representation of might be examined, for this sound has been represented very variously in spelling during the history of English.

An examination of the Linguistic Atlas of Late Mediaeval English yields a broad range of forms for Present-Day English sh- in 'shall' as recorded in manuscripts, for instance chal, scal, schal, shal, ssal, sal, xal; with the possible exception of the initial x- in xal, none of these spelling-variants seems to signify any sound other than.

At a more general level, the written mode is traditionally taken to represent a more formal register than the spoken mode: thus the distinction between language appropriate for, say, a conversation and, for example, a learned article. On the other hand, and despite the existence of conventional usages (*e.g.*, 'silent ' or 'silent ' in forms such as life, knight), it is plain that English alphabetic script has evolved so that the symbols generally and typically represent vowels of some kind, whereas etc. are used generally and typically to represent consonants.

And there are obviously areas of discourse where the distinction between formal written language and less formal speech becomes hard to draw, such as in the academic lecture. There are two important points to make here. One is that the modes of speech and writing should be treated by historians of a language as distinct manifestations of that language, with important implications for the methodology of linguistic historiography.

The second point, however, is equally valid: there is an obvious connection between the written and spoken modes, because both are manifestations of (*i.e.,* transmission-mechanisms for) the 'same' language.

EVIDENCE FOR ENGLISH

The problem of evidence for the history of English is at its most acute for the period up to c. 1250, that is, the Old English and post-Old English periods.

It is usual to classify the extant Old English texts as belonging to four dialect-groupings: Old Northumbrian and Old Mercian, West Saxon and Old Kentish. We will be returning to the meaning of these labels shortly; ut, before we do so, we might note that the evidence for each of these dialect-groupings varies in extent very considerably, both diachronically and diatopically.

It includes the major inscriptions in runes, the ancient Germanic alphabetic system. The virtue of the table given below is that it shows up the massive gaps in the written record, and that the pattern of gaps and entries does seem to correlate with historical events.

Thus the seventh and eighth centuries, the period of Northumbrian hegemony in England, are unsurprisingly also the time when most texts traditionally called 'Old Northumbrian' survive; in the eighth and ninth centuries Mercia held primacy amongst the Anglo-Saxon kingdoms, and 'Old Mercian' texts predominate; and, in the tenth and eleventh centuries, the period of the supremacy of Wessex, by far the largest number of texts are 'West Saxon'.

The table has obvious flaws, however, and these need to be spelt out rather carefully. First of all there is the question of what we mean by the labels 'Northumbrian', 'Mercian', 'Kentish' and 'West Saxon'.

Northumbrian	*Mercian*	*Kentish*	*West Saxon*	*Date (century)*
Ruthwell Cross; early texts of Cædmon's Hymn; Bede's Death Song; Auzon Casket	Corpus glossary	-	-	seventh/eighth
Liber Vitae	Epinal/ Erfurt glossaries; Vespasian Psalter Gloss	*Codex Aureus; Charters*	Early WS texts names (e.g. Parker Chronicle)	ninth
Lindisfarne Gospels Gloss; Ru2	Ru1; Chad; (ancestor of AB-language)	*Psalms; Hymns; Glosses*	Late WS texts (e.g. certain MSS of Ælfric)	tenth/eleventh

It is obvious, from their descendants in the much better attested Middle English period, that these various Old English dialects can be given a roughly geographical ordering, even if the placings can scarcely be as accurate as that achieved in detailed surveys of present-day varieties of English. It is perhaps best to see these terms as typological expressions, useful ways of expressing broad diatopic relationships between bodies of texts.

Just how rough these expressions are, however, is indicated when we move to a second caveat about the table: the way in which it places each text in a clear-cut relationship of descent and difference. The trouble is that many-if not most-of these texts are situated in quite complex linguistic and textual networks. Thus the Erfurt glossary was almost certainly copied by a scribe whose first language was not English, with all the implications that has for the status of the text as linguistic evidence.

The Vespasian Psalter Gloss, although the major ninth-century Mercian text, was copied in Canterbury, possibly by a non-Mercian scribe working from a Mercian original. The ninth-century Kentish Charters differ from the tenth-century Kentish Psalms in that many of the former show (so it is often, if controversially, claimed) the impact of Mercian orthographic tradition while the latter are influenced by West Saxon remarks, 'West Saxon is fighting against the strong tradition of Mercian spelling'.

The whole question of the relationship between the corpora of Early and Late West Saxon texts is a complex one; it has been traditional to refer to the writings of King Alfred's day (the late ninth century) as exemplifying 'Early West Saxon' whereas those of Abbot Ælfric's time (the early eleventh century) are often termed 'Late West Saxon', yet the relationship between Early West Saxon and Late West Saxon is distorted if the material remains which make up the latter are taken as descended straightforwardly from the former.

The relationship between the Lindisfarne Gospels Gloss and the Mercian portion of the Rushworth Glosses ('Ru1') is an intricate one; but this did not stop Farman, the Mercian glossator of this part of the Rushworth Gospels, feeling and reflecting the impact of what must have been an incipient West Saxon standardised written language. This list of special cases could be greatly expanded.

Finally, some broad coverage across the country. Such an impression is quite fallacious. Apart from West Saxon, the dialect materials from Anglo-Saxon England are slight and fragmentary, and major parts of the country are almost entirely unrepresented (*e.g.*, East Anglia).

It seems that what the written evidence of Anglo-Saxon England supplies us with is a set of snapshots of individual usages, of varying evidential value, giving us an idea of the kinds of language found in a few regional centres of the period. This picture corresponds with what we know of Anglo-Saxon writing abilities in the vernacular: something restricted to the monastic scriptorium.

It is in this sense that some distinguished scholars have spoken of the impossibility of Old English dialectology, if our aim is to produce something comparable to the modern Survey of English Dialects; and it seems certain, despite some researchers' gallant attempts, that quantitative surveys comparable to those carried out by modern sociolinguists are not an appropriate methodology for the study of the language of this period-the material remains to allow for statistical analysis of the kind favoured by such investigations are simply not to be had. However, it is possible to make some interesting typological statements, and the investigation of scriptorial practices remains a valid goal of enquiry.

A similar situation may be found when we turn to the manuscript-evidence for the post-Old English/transitional Middle English period, that is, from the Norman Conquest up to c. 1250. Until the middle of the thirteenth century, manuscripts in the vernacular continued to be produced in England; a remarkable fact is that more manuscripts in what is conventionally called 'Old English' survive dating from after the Norman Conquest than from before it.

But these texts were generally produced under a conservative scriptorial system which survived in only a few regional centres, for instance Worcester, and which could enforce a normative spelling-system; in less geographically and politically peripheral scriptoria, such as Canterbury, the vernacular was replaced much earlier by Latin as the language of written record.

Even in the West Midlands, this scriptorial system had broken down by the middle of the thirteenth century as a result of wider vernacular literacy and demand for books; it has usually been argued that, sustained by the close supervision associated with monastic discipline, the system could not survive in the looser institutional structures needed to produce books rapidly. And in some parts of the country, such as the North or the extreme South-West, conditions were such that vernacular literacy to all intents and purposes seems to have disappeared for much of the Middle English period. The evidence for post-Old English remains patchy.

Moreover, the manuscripts which do survive raise textual problems in many ways similar to those raised by the Old English evidence; for instance, the texts associated with and derived from the much-copied early-thirteenth-century handbook for solitary religious women, Ancrene Wisse, make up a very high proportion of the texts located on this map. Without them, a large portion of the evidence for transitional Middle English would disappear.

And yet there is evidence that these texts were in some sense and at some point in their transmission standardised, that is, focused on a conventionalised usage, traditionally localised at the North Herefordshire religious house of Wigmore Abbey. The evidence for the central period of Middle English is much fuller. The most important source of information for much of this period, as for Old English, continues to be the corpus of surviving manuscripts.

But whereas the manuscript-remains from the period up to 1250 are comparatively scanty, the manuscript-evidence for Middle English after that date is very considerable indeed. Moreover, its evidential value is qualitatively distinct. Middle English is 'dialectal' rather than 'standardised'; a debased vernacular for much of the period, English did not achieve the status of availability for all possible registers until well after the end of the Middle Ages-arguably, not until the nineteenth century, when French was replaced by English as the language of acts of parliament.

The reason for this debasement of English is historical. Although there is good evidence that the Norman aristocracy learnt English fairly quickly after the Conquest-a trend encouraged by the events of 1204, when the rulers of England lost control of Normandy and those barons who owned land in both countries (as many did) had to choose between their English and Norman estates-nevertheless French remained the language of prestige and sophistication during the Middle Ages. Since no general norm of written English was taught until at least the fifteenth century, the written mode of Middle English reflects the diatopic variation of the spoken medium more clearly than ever since.

Despite this plethora of evidence for contemporary linguistic variation, however, it was until comparatively recently (and, in some circles, remains) scholarly practice to confine the discussion of the dialectal manifestations of Middle English to a rather small set of texts considered to be of first-class evidential value: thus the primacy in this scholarly tradition of authorial holographs, which are supposed to give precise information about the language of a (comparatively) fully contextualised individual.

During the Middle English period, such texts are unhappily few: Dan Michel's Ayenbite of Inwyt is one such, as are the holograph writings of the poet and scribe Thomas Hoccleve (early fifteenth century), or much of the fascinating late-medieval collection of papers and letters collected by and for the Paston family of Norfolk.

To these might be added-albeit somewhat controversially-the English poetry of John Gower, William Langland and possibly even Geoffrey Chaucer himself, all of whose usages may be reconstructed from the evidence of manuscripts copied around or just after the time of the poets' deaths. Any discussion of the language of these authors, especially in the field of phonological reconstruction, has in the past been usually restricted to the analysis of poetic rhyming or metrical practice. Such an emphasis on authors derives from the traditional primary philological goal of textual criticism: the construction of the 'critical edition', whereby the authorial text could be presented to a modern audience free from an assumed overlay of scribal accretion and corruption.

However, the completion of the Linguistic Atlas of Late Mediaeval English (LALME) in 1986 has meant a massive addition to the body of localised and localisable texts for the period 1350-1450, and hence a liberation from the restricted corpus hitherto studied.

The focus of LALME is on individual scribal usage rather than on that of the author-thus scribes are granted equal importance to authors in terms of their status as linguistic informants-and on the written language as an object of interest in its own right rather than as indirect evidence for the spoken mode. LALME covers the period 1350-1450, and the reasons why it ends at the later date are obvious: it is from that time that standardisation of the written mode obscures the earlier pattern of richly recorded dialectal variation.

By the sixteenth century, in England at least, the public written mode of the vernacular had become standardised-focused-in a way which points forward to the fixed and educationally enforced standard of present-day written English. The use of printing for reproducing English texts from the end of the fifteenth century provided prescriptive norms for contemporary manuscript-usage, a development which correlates with the contemporary growth in vernacular literacy.

Printing was introduced into England, it seems, as the result of popular demand for the rapid production of books. Its invention correlates with the growth of a larger distinct reading public, that is, notably in London and the rest of the prosperous South and East, a literate, upwardly mobile, urban middle class.

It is worth recording that upper-class readers still demanded lavishly decorated manuscripts for presentation to them; printed books were essentially aimed at the emerging middle classes, for whom the traditional workaday manuscripts were a poor second-best. During this period, the origins of Present-Day English society, with its modern class-gradations, may be detected; and these class differences are marked by linguistic standardisation in both written and spoken modes.

For information about the spoken mode during the Early Modern English period we depend not so much, as in the Old and Middle English periods, on the evidence supplied by variant spellings and grammatical forms in written texts (although informal writings from the period do sporadically reflect contemporary speech-habits in ways which are disguised in contemporary printed books, and deserve more attention than they are often given).

Rather, students of Early Modern English speech depend on the interpretation of contemporary statements about the language: the works of the orthoepistical writers and the early English grammarians and lexicographers. Even here, it is important to note that the evidence of these early commentators cannot itself be taken at face value. A number of writers claim usages as authentic which are at obvious variance with the facts, misled by their own conception of what is more or less prestigious practice. Helpful extra information about pronunciation is given by rhyming practices and, even, puns; and there is also the evidence provided by, for instance, writers of the time attempting to represent, frequently for the purposes of parody, the variousness of contemporary spoken language; good examples of the latter are to be found in Shakespeare's representation of non-standard speech, such as in Edgar's 'countryman's' language in King Lear.

However, these practices, too, can be affected by the growth of prescriptive norms, and a degree of formalisation cannot be ruled out even (perhaps especially) in parodic writing-just as present-day stage Glaswegian is not to be too closely identified with the actor's target for imitation, 'real' Glaswegian. Rhymes and puns, archaistic grammar or vocabulary, can be conventional, and not a true reflection of the spoken mode of the time. It is therefore important, in studying the language of this period, for a third source of evidence to be brought into consideration: the evidence of Present-Day English itself. Present-Day English is made up of many varieties; and many of these varieties themselves contain residualisms which illuminate the earlier history of the language.

RECONSTRUCTION

So far in this chapter, we have been concerned with the analysis of direct, that is extant, evidence for the historical study of English. There is, of course, another, indirect source of evidence for states of the language in the past, which has proved particularly useful when engaging with pre-historic matters (*i.e.*, discussion of linguistic events which take place before the period of written records). This source lies in the well-established methodologies associated with comparison of recorded language-states and subsequent reconstruction of common unrecorded ancestor-forms.

A simple example of comparative reconstruction (as it is called), that is, reconstruction based on the data of more than one related language or variety, is given by Lehmann, who cites the contrast between British, Australian and North American pronunciations of the words atom, bitter and little. In some varieties of American English (AE), the medial -t- is voiced, so that atom and Adam, bitter and bidder are pronounced alike (*i.e.,* they are homophones); this usage contrasts with that of British English, where atom, bitter have medial/t/ beside medial/d/in Adam, bidder.

Pronunciations like those of British English (BE) are also found in other varieties of English, for example in Australia (AusE). Such comparisons enable the linguist to reconstruct a *proto-form* or *etymon*. The implication of this diagram is that American English had undergone an innovation not experienced by the other varieties in question.

This simple reconstruction is supported by an examination of words made from the same base in American English, such as hitter American English/'h d r/beside hit American English/h t/. The voiceless/t/in the verb suggests that the American English pronunciation of hitter with/d/, the derived noun, not shared by British English and Australian English, is an innovation.

Beside comparative reconstruction, historical linguists also have had recourse to *internal reconstruction*. Internal reconstruction, as its name suggests, uses data from within one variety-which itself might be reconstructed-for reconstructing its ancestor. Again, Lehmann gives a simple example of this procedure. He notes that an earlier American English/t/became/d/in certain environments.

Both methods are well established in scholarship, and have proved themselves to be a valuable resource of indirect evidence for historical study. However, there are problems about these methods which, when the disciplines of reconstruction were first established during the nineteenth century, were perhaps not addressed as fully as they might have been.

Table. Internal Reconstruction

tick	sin	bid	hit
ticker	sinner	bidder	hitter
ticking	sinning	bidding	hitting
ticks	sins	bids	hits
red	black	fast	fat
redder	blacker	faster	fatter

In essence, these problems centre on the question of uniformity that the proto-language represents a uniform state from which subsequent varieties have diverged. The evidence of present-day and historically recorded languages is that such uniformity is a fiction; any single language is a congeries of varieties which have emerged through processes of complex interaction with each other.

Furthermore, the techniques of reconstruction can be taken only so far back. It has been a presumption of most linguists that all human languages have an ultimate common ancestor, but the reconstruction of this ultimate proto-language has not proved possible. Languages borrow material from other languages as well as inherit it from their ancestors, and the further back the reconstruction is taken, and the more languages there are for comparison, the smaller the amount of inherited material there is.

In such circumstances, it is worth reminding ourselves that any set of reconstructed proto-forms is an abstract representation of an underlying system, not reflecting the surface variation of which natural languages consist; a useful formalisation, but limited if our aim is to use such formalisations as evidence for the processes involved in linguistic change.

It is for this reason that this book, although it deals with a few problems where reconstruction of some kind is necessary, has avoided dealing with language-states such as Proto-Germanic, where only reconstructed forms can be adduced as evidence. It is worth noting, moreover, that reconstructions of proto-languages depend on the earliest historical data available; and the earliest data for English from the Anglo-Saxon period themselves need textual analysis before they in turn can be used for reconstruction.

PROBLEMS OF TEXTUAL ANALYSIS

At the beginning of this chapter, reference was made to the necessity for textual analysis before linguistic deductions can be legitimately made. In what remains, some textual problems characteristic of the various periods of English conventionally distinguished will be discussed, exemplifying the kinds of difficulty which the diachronic linguist needs to confront.

An Old English Problem

The first example will be taken from the Old English period that is the period roughly from the arrival of the Anglo-Saxons in England up to the Norman Conquest of 1066. A typical linguistic innovation, observable in Present-Day English and referred to from time to time elsewhere in this book, is that which scholars refer to as 'misadaptation' or 'hyperadaptation' or, sometimes, 'hypercorrection'. Hyperada-ptation is characteristic of socially mobile, upwardly aspiring people; such folk are weakly tied to the social network they are attempting to leave, and similarly weakly tied to the target-class at which they are aiming.

A good example in Present-Day English is the spread of initial by habitual 'h-droppers' to environments where it is not used in 'standard' speech and where it has no etymological justification, for instance for 'I'. Such innovations can become objects of mirth and parody. But they are of interest to linguists because they display the classic features of an innovation, being produced by a group of upwardly aspiring people with weak ties in the community both to their social origins and to their social target.

Such hyperadaptations can be found early in the history of English. An eighth/ninth-century copy of the Gospels in Latin, was given an Old English interlinear gloss in the tenth century by two scribes whose names are recorded in the manuscript: Farman and Owun. The book belonged in 1650 to John Rushworth, deputy clerk to the House of Commons, and he donated it to the Bodleian; it is therefore known as the Rushworth Gospels. Farman's portion consisted of the gloss to Matthew, Mark 1-2, and a small portion of John; Owun wrote the rest.

The colophon indicates that Farman wrote 'æt harawuda', usually identified as Harewood near Leeds in Yorkshire. Owun seems to have been a Northumbrian. The two scribal contributions are traditionally known as Ru1 and Ru2 respectively. It has long been recognised that Farman's glossing differs linguistically from the Old Northumbrian of Owun, but accounting for the difference was controversial before R. Menner's study of 1934. Until that date, it was a persistent belief that Ru1 was 'a kind of mixture of Mercian and West

Saxon'; and some scholars had concluded that this mixed variety existed because Farman was copying a West Saxon gloss and interlarding it with his own (Old Mercian) forms. Menner showed convincingly that Farman was a translator of the exemplar before him. The basis of his proof was that, in his glossing of Mark, Farman used as his exemplar the Old Northumbrian gloss to the Lindisfarne Gospels, which still survives: 'this is obvious...from his frequently copying the variant glosses and even a marginal expansion from Lindisfarne'; the gloss to Matthew, however, was derived independently. Careful comparison of the two sets of glosses in Ru1 shows few linguistic differences between them. What differences there are can be explained in terms of what has been called 'constrained usage':

One may...risk the deduction that in copying another gloss Farman would avoid a word that did not belong to his own dialect, but might on the contrary follow his original in the use of words that would not be his choice in an independent translation.

Although Menner vindicated Farman's usage as his own, his work left a number of questions unanswered. In terms of the traditional Old English dialect typology, Farman's language remained mixed in appearance, and his writing included a number of forms which seemed not to be etymologically justified.

The key work on Farman's usage remains Kuhn's study of e and œ in Ru1. Kuhn demonstrated that Farman's peculiarities could be accounted for in terms of hyperadaptation (although Kuhn did not use the term) in the direction of West Saxon, a dialect which, in the generations after Farman, became prestigious and was therefore imitated in the written mode outside its area of origin.

Probably the clearest instance of this behaviour, fully documented by Kuhn, is Farman's use of œ for the isolative development of both West Germanic a and West Germanic e. As a Mercian, Farman might have been expected to share the development of these sounds found in the chief Old English 'Mercian' text, the ninth-century gloss to the Vespasian Psalter; but there are some interesting differences.

Because of a prehistoric Old English sound-change known as 'second fronting', the gloss to the Vespasian Psalter has e for West Germanic a where West Saxon has œ. Farman, however, generally has œ; beside dœg, other common forms are œfter, fæder, hrœgl etc. He uses e only rarely, for instance hweþre. Kuhn shows that Farman uses œ to e as the reflex of West Germanic a in the proportion 25:2.

Farman's usage here may seem unexceptionable; we know little enough about the true geographical extent of second fronting in the Old English period, and it could be argued that the sound-change simply did not reach 'æt harawuda'. However, this position cannot be sustained when we examine the reflexes of West Germanic e in Farman's glosses.

Unless affected by neighbouring sounds, the reflex of West Germanic e has been astonishingly stable in the history of English, and e is the usual form in all Old English dialects. Yet Farman uses œ for e in West Germanic e-words in the proportion of 5 *œ* to 9 *e*-a remarkable statistic. Thus forms such as *œfne, cwœþende, stœfn, þœc, þægn, wœr* appear. A. Campbell objected to a 'general identification of œ and e' in Farman's idiolect, and drew attention to the restricted set of words in which œ for e occurred.

Campbell did not, however, make as clear a distinction as he might have done between writing and speech; and this held him back from accepting Kuhn's explanation of these forms, even though he felt that the 'cause of these abnormal spellings requires investigation'. Kuhn, having found similar behaviour in the eleventh-century *Worcester Chronicle,* explained Farman's usage as follows: Farman was a Mercian whose native speech must have been essentially the same as that of the scribe who glossed the Vespasian Psalter, but whereas the latter was writing with a minimum of outside influence, Farman was trying to imitate the language of his temporal and ecclesiastical superiors.

As a consequence of this imitation, he introduced numerous Saxonisms into his glosses, among them œ instead of e for [West Germanic] a. He, like the Worcester scribe, carried the imitation too far, and wrote œ frequently for [West Germanic].

In other words, Farman hyperadapted in the written mode. His hypercorrection, moreover, can be accounted for in terms of what may be termed weak cultural ties; Farman was not a West Saxon, but aspired to West Saxonism. This makcs him a typical innovator; but it also makes his evidence for Old Mercian problematic.

A Middle English Problem

Until quite recently, Middle English scholars generally held to the dictum, perhaps most clearly enunciated by J.R.R. Tolkien, that the language of a Middle English text was a reflection of its textual transmission.

Since Middle English was the age when dialectal variation was reflected in the written mode, and therefore scribal idiolects varied very considerably, and since most Middle English texts other than authorial holographs were the result of scribes copying the work of other scribes whose idiolects almost necessarily differed to a greater or lesser extent from their own, it was assumed that any given scribal copy was written in what became called a Mischsprache, a 'mixed language', to which each scribe involved in transmitting the text had contributed some element.

It was therefore assumed that texts other than holographs-which were felt to be in some sense 'pure'-were of very limited linguistic value. The publication of LALME has, however, revised scholarly opinion on this matter. It is now held that the problems of interpretation raised by scribe-author interaction in the copying of Middle English texts can be overcome. The means by which this has been done have been set out in a series of ground-breaking articles, which established a typology of scribal practice. This typology, which is clinal, divides the habits of copyists of Middle English manuscripts into three categories:

1. *Literatim*-copying, whereby a scribe reproduced, letter-by-letter, the forms of an exemplar;
2. Translation, whereby scribes converted the language of their exemplars into their own language;
3. Something between these two poles.

Examples of all three kinds of behaviour are not hard to find in Middle English texts:

- The Cotton text of The Owl and the Nightingale, although copied by one hand throughout, is written in two distinct spelling-systems which fall into two distinct sets of stints.
- A comparison of William Caxton's text of Malory with Caxton's own prose shows that, in this instance, the printer had imposed his own spellings on whatever exemplar was being presented to him. This was not Caxton's usual practice, as is demonstrated by his retention of particular spelling-usages characteristic of especially prestigious text-descent, *e.g.,* his prints (in verse) of John Gower's Confessio Amantis or (in prose) of Nicholas Love's translation of the Mirror of the Blessed Life of Jesus Christ.
- The Titus manuscript of Ancrene Riwle seems to be written in a mixture of 'AB-language' and North-West Midland Middle English; even if the manuscript were still written by a literatim-copyist, it suggests very strongly that a mixed language lies somewhere in the ancestry of the text.

M. Benskin and M. Laing, as well as engaging with the mechanisms involved here, distinguish subcategories, for example progressive translators, who begin as literatim-scribes but become translators as copying proceeds, or constrained scribes, whose repertoire of forms is partially but not wholly activated by their exemplars.

They conclude that, during the period covered by LALME, 2-type scribes, or scribes who tended towards 2-type behaviour, were by far the most common kind. This insight makes scribes as well as authors legitimate objects of investigation. The processes involved in scribal translation may be illustrated by an examination of four texts of a major Middle English poem, the Cursor Mundi.

This lengthy (about 30,000 lines) spiritual history of humanity from the Creation to the Day of Judgement survives in nine fourteenth-century manuscripts or manuscript-fragments in a number of Middle English dialects.

Short parallel passages derived from four manuscripts. All contractions have been silently expanded, but the texts are otherwise as they appear in the manuscripts. MS C has a number of features which characterise it as Northern. Late Old English a is reflected as in strang 'strong' 5, bald 'bold' 7; the weak adjective ending -e, which was lost early in Northern England, has disappeared in the strang strijf 'the furious strife' 5, even though the stress-pattern of the verse indicates that it probably appeared in the authorial original, and the present plural ending is -is in lesis 'lose' 6; Norse-derived pronominal forms, þer, þam 'their', 'them' appear in 6, 26, and sere 'various' 12, 23 is also of Scandinavian derivation.

MS F is similarly marked by Northern forms. Late Old English â appears as in nane 'none' 10; *-e* seems no longer to reflect any phonetic fact, and thus appears unhistorically, for example þousande 'thousand'; the present plural ending in -s appears in dos 'do' (rubricated heading); a Norse-derived form, þaire 'their' 6 appears beside native ham 'them' 26; sere 'various' is replaced by native mony 12, but retained as sere 23. Probable Norse-derived forms in MS F but not in MS C include til 'to' 14.

MS G is something of a mixture. Late Old English â appears as in strong 5, bolde 7, non 'none' 10. The weak adjective is no longer inflectionally marked: þe strong strijf 5, but this practice is more widespread in late-fourteenth-century Middle English than it was earlier in the century. However, men cals 'men call' in the rubric at the head of the passage shows the characteristic Northern present plural ending, þaim 'them' 26 appears, and sere 'various' 23 is retained.

MS T is in a markedly distinct dialect from the other three manuscripts. Old English â appears as, in longe 5, bolde 7, noon 'none' 10 etc. There is some evidence for the retention of the weak adjective as a living feature of the language: þe longe strif 5; and the present plural is the Midland -en in callen (rubric), ernen 'desire' 1, duden 'did' 12. hem 'them' 26 appears for MS C's þam, and mony appears instead of sere.

It is from the evidence of such texts, both localised by internal reference and localisable by subsequent deduction, that LALME was created. The coverage it achieved is illustrated in the map already referred to, which indicates the locations of every localised and localisable text used in the published atlas.

The distinction between 'localised' and 'localisable' is methodologically important; localised texts form a group of materials, largely documentary and thus usually brief, which are firmly identified with a particular locality. They supply the anchors to which other longer texts, generally literary, may be 'tied' or 'fitted' typologically (both terms frequently used in the literature).

The following hypothetical and simplified example may illustrate the process. A short document, which we shall call Text Z, contains a for 'he', meche for 'much', scholle(n) for 'shall'. Another, much larger literary text, Text Y, contains the same features, and thus may be associated with Text Z; but the larger text by its very nature yields a good deal more information about other items and their forms as well as a, meche, scholle(n). Thus the information gained from the exercise is greatly increased.

The fit-technique, as it is known, is typologically governed; thus a further text, Text X, may have a, meche but not scholle(n), and is therefore to be placed at some remove from Texts Y and Z in the direction of other texts which do not have scholle(n). Once fitted, the literary texts localised in this way may themselves be used for further localisations; a typological matrix has been established within which other texts as yet unstudied may be placed.

As with the Old English example of Farman, however, it is sometimes dangerous to take Middle English texts at face value. MS Manchester, Chetham's Library, A.6.11 (6696) is an early-sixteenth-century copy of John Gower's late-fourteenth-century poem, the Confessio Amantis. At the end of the manuscript appears the name 'Notehurste'.

This word also appears in another manuscript, MS Glasgow, University Library, Hunterian V.2.8, a copy of the alliterative Gest Hystoriale of the Destruction of Troy, and it refers to Nuthurst in South Lancashire, where the Chetham family lived. Both manuscripts were copied by the same scribe, Thomas Chetham (c. 1490-1546), probably for his own use. The Glasgow Gest Hystoriale is localised entirely plausibly by LALME to the South-East Lancashire/Cheshire border; but the linguistic evidence presented by the manuscript needs to be judged with some care.

It seems probable that Chetham's behaviour here is of the kind called 'constrained'. In such an interpretation, mony etc. would represent Chetham's core repertoire of forms-forms which he will always use, because others are outside his linguistic 'horizon'-while his variation between, for example, she when copying Gower and ho in the Glasgow Gest shows the activation of one of two possible variables in his repertoire when one of them appears in his exemplar.

If this hypothesis is correct, it reminds us of the vagaries of textual survival; if the Chetham Gower had not survived, then we would not be aware that Chetham's repertoire of possible variation covered such a comparatively wide spectrum of forms.

PROBLEMS OF TEACHING ENGLISH

English is the *'Lingua Fraznca'* of the world. With the IT Revolution and most of software and operating system being in English Language, a new utility for written and oral communication in English Language has emerged. English is said to be the world's most important language having communicative and educative value. English is used all over the world not out of any imposition but because of the realization that it has certain advantages. A very important reason for regarding English as a world language is that the world's knowledge is enshrined in English. It is a progressive language. It is dynamic and flexible. Over and above English is universally renowned for its power of expression and its rich literature.

We are going to have children in other parts of the world besides England, speaking English as their first language. But the gap still remains like those of the haves and have-nots, developed and developing, urban and the rural. Much is required to be done by the linguists, the polyglots, the scholars and the teachers to bridge the gap between the English literate and the English illiterate population of the world. We have to go into the intricacies of the English language and simplify the methodology.

Whatever English now represents or has represented over centuries of colonization, it belongs to every one. It is a global language, the first of its kind. The Australian poet Peter Porter emphasized the point in a World Conference *Welcome Poem*, published in the *Times Literary Supplement* (28th February 1992) to the effect that:

'Everything will be exposed in English
So delegates and lovers understand'

Education has been the primary factor in the more formal transmission of English around the world. There developed an indigenous, modernizing, reform movement in Bengal during the early decades of the nineteenth century. It was led by Ram Mohan Roy. When Macaulay in his famous 1835 'Minutes' set out the case for the intellectual improvement of the country; arguing that, while he himself had not knowledge of the indigenous languages, he had never found an Orientalist 'who could deny that a single shelf of a good European library was worth the whole native literature of India and Arabia; and that henceforth available funds should be employed in imparting knowledge of English literature and science through the medium of English language.' Not only were schools and colleges set up as a result of Macaulay's initiative, but English replaced Persian as the official state language, and more gradually, English procedures and assumptions replaced Indian in law and administration.

English symbolizes in Indian minds, better education, better culture and higher intellect. In present times, English is the most preferred language. The Indians and the Indian English language press uses many words derived from Indian language. Indian accent is sometimes difficult for non-Indians to understand. Actually English has co-existed in the Indian sub-continent alongside thousands of local languages. It has remained at the heart of the Indian society. According to recent surveys, approximately 4 per cent of the Indian population use English. That figure might seem insignificant, but out of the total population it represents 35 million speakers. It means India is the largest English speaking community outside USA and the UK. As India celebrates its 60th year of independence from British rule, English continues to expand its empire. English is virtually the mother-tongue for many educated South Asian, but for the vast majority, it remains second language. So English, spoken by such speakers is heavily influenced by speech patterns of their ethnic language.

Language learning is a natural process for the natives. The approach to this learning process is called the 'behavioristic approach'. But for the students of other languages, deliberate efforts are required to learn a foreign language which requires a 'mentalistic approach'. The students of rural and semi-urban areas in India face such problems because English is not their mother-tongue. It is neither instinctive nor intuitive. Language acquisition seems to be a process of both of analogy and application, nature and nurture. Teachers of language have adopted and invented a variety of methods to teach English. Edward M. Anthony says in 'Approach, method and Technique-Teaching English as a Second language', "Method is an overall plan for the orderly presentation of language material no part of which contradicts and all of which is based upon, the selected approach. Approach is axiomatic and a method is procedural. ' The orderly presentation of language to students is influenced by several factors. The teacher has to keep in mind the age of the student, his native language, his cultural background and his previous experience with English. The experience of the teacher and his level of English mastery are equally important. To achieve the desired effects, the goal of a course much be kept in mind-whether it is aimed at reading, fluency in speech, inculcating translation skill. All these objects shape methodology.

Students of the rural colleges face a number of problems. English is their second language. Learning a second language means acquiring a system of rules, but just as a very little is known about these rules, even less is known about how such rule systems are acquired. Students find themselves unable to express in English. They have no idea of proper sentence structure. They do not know proper pronunciation, spellings and grammatical rules. The sole objective of the teacher and the learner remain to clear the exams. The students never realize the importance of learning English as a language. In the past, in rural areas, English was introduced to students in the fifth class. But now there is no dearth of English medium schools in such area yet the standards of English are falling rapidly. If we compare a graduate of present time with a graduate of the past, the result is shockingly amazing. The emphasis on passing the exams lies so heavy on the students that they opt for the cramming method. Such an approach helps unscrupulous elements to flourish. They help the students in achieving their goals of passing the exams. The inter-disciplinary relation of teaching and learning process brings home the fact that the problems of the teachers can be solved if we concentrate on the causes of the problem of the students.

The changing times have witnessed the growing importance of English language in all walks of life. It does not seem that we are using English language as non-native speakers or as a second language. Conscious and unconscious use of the words in our everyday conversation from the English language bears evidence to this fact. Even the English illiterates in the rural areas use such words effortlessly. May be that is the flexibility of English language to let foreign, cultural influences mould, and shape and enrich it. The result is that we have about 40,000 words from the Hindustani incorporated in the world famous dictionaries like Oxford English Language Dictionary, COD, Collins Cobuild English Dictionary. To cite a few examples of such words we may say;

'Kachha, pucca, Thug, Thuggee, Jungle, Stations, School-bags, Computers, Television, Programme, Malls, College Convert, Dinner, Lunch, Breakfast, Airport' and even in our own people settled in European and America Countries:

Pump, Agriculture, Medicine, Medical college, Construction Building, Readymade Garments, cupboards, Jewellery, Tailor, Master, Library, Pictures, CD, Cell phones,.............' We may continue to add to the common usages from the English Language as a part of our daily conversation in the rural, semi-urban areas. Even the designations of officers are political authorities are frequently used. It is quite ironical that in spite of such a good store of English Language words our students and in some cases even teachers cannot either write or speak English language properly.

Because of the rapidly increasing web of Educational facilities, the rural areas have been enjoying the facilities of the convents. But it has neither helped in raising the level of the students, nor made them learn English as a language. The infrastructure of such schools is weak. Some teachers have good accent, but they do not posses a good command over the language. Now In the rural and semi-Urban areas, study of English language begins at an early age, at the KG level, it continues up to Senior Secondary or first Degree level.

Even in the Professional Courses, the teaching of English as a communication skill is an integral part of the curriculum or the course obligations. It is quite unfortunate that whatever our English language teachers gain in the completion of their course or education as eligibility for seeking a job or an employment, it stays there and the teaching learning stagnates. The process of teaching is not updated even after the passage of years. So much so as the experience shows in many cases, they have no idea of good dictionaries meant for the students or for themselves or even for the office managers or Administrators. It may be pertinently mentioned here that to cater to the tremendously growing demand for English Language teachers and learners, there exists 'the bank of English" with an envious corpus of about 400 million words of written and spoken English. For this purpose, they are using a wide range of different types of writing and speech from hundreds different sources: Newspapers, Magazines fiction and Non-Fiction, Books, Brochures, Leaflets, Reports Letter Radio, T.V. Airports. Informal spoken language is represented by recording of everyday casual conversations, meetings, interview and discussions.

Students of the rural areas do not realize the importance of English as a language of communication whereas this is the most important aspect of this global language. They lack the confidence to speak in English; expression in the language is weak. First reason is that they have been taught English through Grammar-Translation Method. This method makes them dependent on their mother tongue. Whatever they read, they translate it into their own vernacular. During the time of exams, they cram the expected questions because they cannot write one original sentence of their own. Because of GT Method, they have no vocabulary of English words. While writing, they depend on the cheap material from the help books.

The hackneyed, stereotyped and traditional pattern of exams aims at clearing English not as a language but as a subject. The students, therefore, are guided to practice pick and chose method from the sub-standard material available in the market. So that students merely pass the subject far from learning any level of the Language. It is more shocking to learn that even the questions that students are supposed to answer are told to learn through translation from English to their own vernacular. Poor performance in translation, lack of proper vocabulary, no knowledge proverbs all are results of a casual approach. Even after reading English for 14 or 15 years the level of the students remains poor.

To solve all the problems, a systematic approach should be followed. The teachers should aim at teaching primarily, not knowledge but skill, the different skills required for good Listening-Speaking-Reading-Writing. Teachers should find some way of helping pupils to enjoy their language activities, and of building their confidence. A teacher who tries to help his pupils in this way has rightly rejected the image of the teacher who acts as the arbitrary dispenser of all knowledge. As children learn by way of imitation, similarly, the students tend to follow the example set by their teacher. The English teacher should have the wide-ranging enthusiasm and Imagination, It can make English course 'a sort of clearing house for ideas and interests which branch out into all the other subjects that the pupils are studying in school, and beyond them.'

To tackle with the problem of lack of vocabulary in the students, Productive and receptive Use of words should be kept in mind. The students should be made to learn simple words. This will help in inculcating a habit of learning new words in them. Their newly learnt words will become a part of their own vocabulary and they will be in a position to use those words. This is the natural process of movement at need from receptive to productive use of the words. This enhancement of vocabulary will result into better expression. The common errors made by the students in the different usages of the same word can be cured by this technique. Normally, the students can not differentiate between Noun and Verb, adjective or adverb. They should be clearly guided about the difference between the parts of speech by practice. They can be made aware of the different parts of a word; root, suffix, prefix and how can they change the total meaning of the word by adding suffix or prefix with the root *i.e.,*

(i) Nouns related to verbs and marked by suffix:

a. Deny (verb) Noun: Denial
b. Close (verb) Noun: Closure
c. Mock (verb) Noun: Mockery
d. Collide (verb) Noun: Collision
e. Use (verb) Noun: Usage
f. Flatter (verb) Noun: Flattery
g. Apply (verb) Noun: Application
h. Achieve (verb) Noun: Achievement

(ii) Nouns related to adjectives and marked by suffix:

a. Frail (adjective) Noun: Frailty
b. Close (adjective) Noun: Closeness
c. Capable (adjective) Noun: Capability
d. Intense (adjective) Noun: Intensity

Such practices will help them enjoying their play with words. They can understand the importance of suffixes and prefixes. They can be given exercise of making words negatives from positives by prefixes for example: dis as a prefix changes the meaning of the word: (all the following words are negative in meaning) 'dislike, disobey, displeasure, disorder, disloyal, disprove, dishonorable',

They can enjoy these exercise and they can also strengthen their vocabulary. It will help in breaking the monotonous routine of the class. Regular tests can be held to evaluate the progress of the students. After laying stress on their vocabulary building, students should be given exercises of Reading. Books provide most pupils with the situations in which learning take place. Reading is the core of Language learning. Students can acquire the speed and skills for practical purposes. In our literate society, professional competence depends on reading skills. Practice in exact reading should occur frequently, at least once a week and preferably twice. The vocabulary drills can help them understand the usages of words in the books. They should be made to underline the Noun, Verb, adjective, and Adverb, in the given passage of reading. Similarly, they can be taught the proper usage of Articles, Determiners, Proposition and Conjunctions. They should be guided to mark the idioms and how the use of idioms makes the expression better. They should notice the difference between.

Put up, Put of, Put on, and Put with'
Laugh at, Laugh with, Laugh away'

By noticing all such components of the language they can enjoy the richness and flexibility of language. Once their interest is aroused, they will show tremendous improvement. Reading can also help them in making aware of spellings. When the students have practiced different uses of words and have developed habit of reading, they can avoid the common errors of Translations. In rural areas, the students tend to choose the literal way of translating the sentences from Hindi or Punjabi into English. Some examples need consideration here. Students make errors while translation of the following sentences:

1. He is my underwear friend.
2. Oh mother Ganga, send me telegram!
3. He killed my ten rupees.

Such problems arise because of translating each word of English into Hindi or Punjabi and vice versa. Whereas the students should be made aware of the fact that it is impossible to find an exact equivalent for every English word.

After the usages of all such practices in the classrooms, the students should be given exposure. There can be no learning without exposure. Group discussions can be arranged. Texts should be read loudly by the students. Simple usage of words will become a part of their speech only when they are exposed to deliver a speech and express their own ideas. The zeal for learning will help them in their own advancement. The problems of the students and the teachers are inter-related. It is necessary to assure that the learner makes a tremendous contribution in the process.

English has been successfully taught through literature for many years. But now when the students are taking their exams of other subjects of post graduation *i.e.,* History, Political Science, Economics etc. in Hindi or Punjabi, their interest and efficiency in English is decreasing. Even those students, who have passed their post graduation in English, are not able to write and speak it accurately. Whereas the fluency in the spoken language should be stressed. Teachers should aim at teaching of pragmatics. Pragmatic competence is central to Communication 'the ability to use language effectively to fulfill intentions and goals'. Different languages use differ strategies.

It is important that the learners of English are given such information as possible the ways in which to use their language. English should be taught as a language, not as a subject. The course material should be designed in such a manner that emphasis on language should be there. For example while teaching a simple poem like Daffodils by Wordsworth to the students, the teacher can ask the student to underline the different words used by the poet for the expression of happiness.

'Sprightly, glee, jocund, pleasure'. Similarly cryptic, pithy, terse and valuable lines of Pope can be taught to them. Students will make those lines a part of their memory. Teaching can be enjoyed by both the teacher and the students in this manner. Students do enjoy poetry and drama provided the feed back is given in the same spirit. The enthusiasm, the zeal and interest of the teacher can kindle the spark of learning in the students. Presentations by the students can help them enhancing their level of confidence.

Teacher can change subject matter from prose to poetry, from essay writing to letter writing to prevent the class from monotonous routine. Audio-Visual aids can add to the presentation of the topic. Students can be encouraged to listen to English news and English commentaries broad cast on Radio and telecast on TV. Motivation in the initial phase, proper methodology in the next phase should be followed. Teacher's own personality and command over language counts a lot. Faculty improvement programmes should be held. Teachers should be made aware of the latest techniques and methods. An English language teacher should be capable of arising the interest and imagination of the students. As a seasoned teacher of English once warned a callow colleague: 'Never forget, my, boy that the English teacher's business is with the imagination'. If the students enjoy literature, only then they can quote from it. Literature taught in such a way will be enjoyed and remembered for a long time.

If we take into consideration the role of teacher and learner in acquiring the knowledge of a language; the problems can be solved effectively. Only then the students will realize the practical use of English language. English will be used by them as a medium of expression.

They will be able to use English as a language of communication. Fluency in the speech, proper knowledge of sentence structure, confidence of speaking in the public will make them able to keep their pace with the developing world. It will also help in raising the standards of English as a language at the college level.

On the basis of suggestions given above, the critical situations in the teaching of English can be checked from further deteriorations. Decidedly one or two persons can't do anything solid. Let everyone concerned with it take the responsibility. Only then we can create a congenial environmental and we can be able to achieve better results in the teaching and learning of English.

GENERAL PRINCIPLES OF TEACHING ENGLISH

The modern approach to all language learning and teaching is the scientific one and is based on sound linguistic principles. They are subject to change in the light of new facts exposed by linguists and language users. These principles are general principles and are applicable to English language.

- Principle 1. Give Priority to Sounds: The sounds of English should receive priority. Sounds should be given their due place in the scheme of teaching. Sounds should not be presented in isolation. They should appear in proper expressions and sentences spoken with the intonation and rhythm which would be used by a native speaker.
- Principle 2. Present Language in Basic Sentence Patterns: Present, and have the students memorise, basic sentence patterns used in day to day conversation. From small utterances the students can easily

pass on to longer sentences. In case of learning mother-tongue, the student's memory span can retain much longer sentences than those of a foreign language. The facility thus gained in a foreign language enables the learners expand the grasp of the language material in respect of sounds and vocabulary items.

- Principle 3. Language Patterns as Habits. Real language ability is at the habit level. It does not just mean knowing about the language. Make language patterns as habit through intensive pattern practice in variety of situations. The students must be taught to use language patterns and sentence constructions with appropriate vocabulary at normal speed for communication. In fact the habitual use of the most frequently used patterns and items of language, should take precedence over the mere accumulation of words.
- Principle 4. Imitation. Imitation is an important principle of language learning. No leaner by himself ever invented language. Good speech is the result of imitating good models. The model should be intelligible. Imitation followed by intensive practice helps in the mastery of the language system.
- Principle 5. Controlled Vocabulary. Vocabulary should be kept under control. Vocabulary should be taught and practised only in the context of real situations. This way, meaning will be clarified and reinforced.
- Principle 6. Graded Patterns: "To teach a language is to impart a new system of complex habits, and habits are acquired slowly." (R.Lado) So, language patterns should be taught gradually, in cumulative graded steps. This means, the teacher should go on adding each new element or pattern to previous ones. New patterns of language should be introduced and practised with vocabulary that students already know.
- Principle 7. Selection and Gradation: Selection of the language material to be taught is the first requisite of good teaching. Selection should be done in respect of grammatical items and vocabulary and structures.

Selection of language items should involve:

frequency	(how often a certain item or word is used)
range	(in what different contexts a word or an item can be used)
coverage	(how many different meanings a word or an item can convey)
availability	(how far an item is convenient to teach)
learnability	(how far an item is easy to learn)
teachability	(how far and item is easy to teach - in the social context)

Gradation of the language material means placing the language items in an order. Grading involves grouping and sequence. Grouping concerns (i) the system of language, and (ii) its structures. Grouping the system of language means what sounds, words, phrases and meanings are to be taught.

Thus we have:

(i) Phonetic grouping, *i.e.* grouping according to sounds. For example, words having the same sound are placed in the one group as, cat, bat, mat, pat, fat, sat; it, bit, fit, hit, kit, it, etc.

(ii) Lexical grouping, *i.e.*, grouping according to lexical situations. Example:school, teacher, headmaster, peon, class-room, library. All these words are grouped around "school."

(iii) Grammatical grouping, *i.e.*, grouping according to similar patterns as, my book/ his book, (pattern grouping): in the room, in the corner/ in the class/in the garden, etc. (phrase grouping)

(iv) Semantic grouping, *i.e.*, grouping according to meaning. Example: school, college, university; bicycle, rickshaw, car, tonga, train, aeroplane, etc,.

(v) Structure grouping, *i.e.*, grouping in the structures means how the selected items fit one into the other-the sounds into the words, the words into phrases, the phrases into the clauses and sentences, and the sentences into the context.

Sequence meants what comes after what. Sequence should be there in the arrangement of sounds (phonetic sequence), phrases (grammatical sequence) words (lexical sequence) and in meaning (semantic sequence). Sequence of structures implies direction, expansion, variation and length of the structures.

- Principle 8. The Oral Way. Experts believe that the oral way is the surest way to language learning. Prof. Kittson rightly observes,. "Learning to speak a language is always the shortest road to learning to read and write it." Prof Palmer also writes,. "We should refrain from reading and writing any given material until we have learnt to use its spoken form."
- Principle 9. Priorities of Language Skills: Listening (with understanding), speaking, reading and writing are the four fundamental skills. Listening and speaking areprimary skills, while reading and writing are secondary skills. Reading and writing are reinforcement skills. They reinforce what has been learnt through understanding and speaking. In fact, understanding and speaking speed up the reading process. Writing should be introduced after reading.
- Principle 10. Multiple Line of Approach: "The term multiple line implies that one is to proceed simultaneously from many different points towards the one and the same end. We should reject nothing except the useless material and should selected judiciously and without prejudice all that is likely to help in our work". In teaching a language, it implies attacking the problem from all fronts. Say, for example, there is a lesson on 'Holidays' in the text book. The teacher can have a number of language activities connected with the topic

such as oral drill, reading, sentence writing, composition, grammar, translation, language exercises etc.

- Principle 11. Language Habit through Language Using: A language is best learnt through use in different contexts and situations. Prof. Eugene A. Nida rightly observes, "Language learning means plunging headlong into a series of completely different experiences. It means exposing oneself to situations where the use of language is required." Another expert expresses a similar opinion by saying: "Learning alanguage means forming new habits through intensive practice in tearing and speaking. The emphasis should always be on language in actual use".
- Principle 12 Spiral Approach. The "spiral" approach to language learning should be followed. Previously taught vocabulary and structures should be reintroduced in subsequent units whenever logical or possible. This is "spiral approach.
- Principle 13. Use Mother-tongue Sparingly. The mother-tongue should be sparingly and judiciously used during teaching English. Of course, at the early stage, some explanations will have to be given in pupil's mother tongue. It is important that students do not use their mother-tongue in the classroom.

4

Forms and Structure of Language Development

LANGUAGE DEVELOPMENT

For the majority of children, starting school means confronting new ways of using language. These include using language to accomplish new types of tasks and new expectations for how they will structure what they say. Schooling brings new kinds of interaction, where students are often required to state information that in an everyday context could be taken for granted, and to specify relationships between concepts in some detail. Language is a beautiful gift. With it we can share our wants, our needs, our thoughts, our feelings, and everything that makes us human. If you spend time with a child, you have the power to give and nurture this gift of communication.

Many factors affect the rate at which a child develops language. *Sometimes language development slows down while a child is learning other skills*, such as standing or walking. In other words, the bulk of the child's concentration and energy may be going to gross motor development at this point with little reserve for the development of language.

The amount and kind of language the child hears may also affect the rate of language development. For example, if the child is hearing two languages at home, his or her brain is trying to learn two sets of vocabulary, process two sets of speech sounds, and understand two sets of grammatical rules. That is a lot of work! It may take longer to begin talking, and still the child may at first feel comfortable speaking in only one of the languages. Some children who are immersed in a new language at school may be silent for a long period of time.

In addition, students are expected to begin using language in a new mode, writing, which brings with it new ways of grammatical organization. These new ways of meaning-making enable participation in a wider range of tasks and contexts, so it is important that all students have opportunities to develop their language potential as they progress in schooling. Some children's ways of making meaning with language enable them to readily respond to the school's expectations, but the ways of using language of other students do not. The language students bring from their communities to school is the means through which they engage new "schooled" knowledge.

For this reason, it is important to value a wide range of ways of using language at school, giving different languages, dialects, and ways of meaning more social value by having them shared in the schooling context. But it is also important to provide all students with access to academic ways of using English so they can participate in new kinds of learning at school. All children enter school with language resources that have served them well in learning at home and that have enabled them to be interactive and successful members of their families and local communities.

But many children lack experience in making the kinds of meanings that are expected at school, or with the kinds of written texts and spoken interaction that prepare some children for school-based language tasks. This lack of experience makes it difficult for these students to learn and to demonstrate their learning. Schooling is a context in which the kinds of meanings that are made are quite different from the meanings made in more informal contexts of everyday life.

Language is used in school contexts in ways that are integral to construing the academic and social knowledge that schools aim to develop. As students move into middle school and secondary school, the tasks they are asked to do become more and more dependent on control of a wide range of linguistic resources.

While these ways of making meaning may appear to set up barriers for children from backgrounds that have not prepared them for participation in this context, the ways of meaning are integral to accomplishing the goals of schooling.

Learning and language are closely related, and for success at school, students need to come to understand the context of schooling and the linguistic choices that realize that context. Under the influence of the work of Vygotsky, among others, there has been increased recognition of the role that language plays in the development of social and cognitive processes. Vygotsky argues that language and thinking develop simultaneously in social interaction.

The development of particular ways of thinking occurs through the linguistic tools that the society uses and that become part of the socio cultural experiences of the child. This means that the kinds of conceptual knowledge that children develop depend on their social experiences and ways of interacting with others, with language the primary semiotic system through which this interaction takes place.

Much of the knowledge that schooling aims to develop in the child is not available just through everyday experience in the world; it needs to be articulated in ways that abstract from everyday life as children engage in structured experiences that provide new perspectives on the world and enable them to generalize their experience. Vygotsky describes such knowledge as "scientific" concepts, different from the "everyday" concepts that emerge through the less structured experiences of everyday life.

Vygotsky believes that both scientific and everyday concepts develop through scaffolded interaction with more experts others who work with learners to help them perform at levels that they would be unable to achieve independently; what Vygotsky calls the "zone of proximal development." Through social interaction of this kind, children are challenged to do more than they can on their own. This suggests that a clear understanding of the role language plays in this socialization would require analysis of the structure and uses of language itself.

But in fact, language is the element of learning that is most unanalyzed and least often explicitly addressed. A Vygotskyan perspective illuminates how differences in socialization practices mean that students from different backgrounds come to school with divergent preparation for using language in the ways expected at school, but does not offer concrete solutions that are specifically bound to the nature of language. A linguistic approach, on the other hand, can show how the structuring of new kinds of knowledge depends on new ways of using language and can identify the features of the language that enable schooled ways of learning.

Describing learning from a linguistic perspective, Halliday focuses on developments in the grammar that are needed to accommodate the construal of more complex kinds of meanings as children learn. Using a complementarily similar to that of Vygotsky's "everyday" and "scientific" concepts, Halliday describes how children learn to reconstrue "common sense" knowledge in a more abstract mode as they reproduce it as "educational" knowledge, and finally to construe knowledge in specialized and technical language.

This perspective offers a framework for understanding how language evolves over time in the child in ways that enable learning, as learning and learning new language occur simultaneously. Adopting this view of the relationship between language and social context and language and thinking has major implications for how the challenges of schooling are understood.

The activities that students are asked to engage in result in the development of knowledge and language related to the goals of those activities. Language is the primary means through which school activities are conducted and students' development is realized and evaluated. Both Halliday and Vygotsky view language learning as integral to, not separate from or prior to, cognitive development.

In learning language in interaction with others, children "appropriate the knowledge and practices of their culture" as they develop scientific, non-everyday concepts that draw on ways of using language that are not part of everyday experience. A better understanding of the ways language construes academic knowledge is important for students and teachers, linguists and language researchers, textbook writers and administrators. This research that demonstrates the ways language socialization practices prepare some children for the contexts of schooling. It also reviews descriptions of school language use that highlight the linguistic choices that are highly valued in school tasks.

It is these choices that can be characterized as the language of schooling. The functional linguistic analysis that follows in later chapters links the language features with the social contexts they realize to show the close relationship between language and context, and to illustrate the challenges for students whose socialization has not prepared them to participate fully in the school context.

Life Experience

Language use in the classroom differs from language use in other social situations in many ways. It involves the sharing of ideas and knowledge rather than the sharing of personal relationships and accomplishment of activities together in familiar contexts. Power relationships, expectations for participation, and the forms that discourse takes also differ at home and school. When they go to school, children engage in new kinds of tasks and need to use language for new purposes.

Sociolinguistic research has shown that many children come from homes and communities that do not use language in the ways associated with typical school contexts. The study of classroom language and its relationship to the social and cultural contexts of home language has demonstrated that there are major discontinuities for many children between language use in school and community. Children from non-mainstream backgrounds have had different experiences and developed different linguistic resources from those that are typically assumed in the school setting.

The ability to draw on the linguistic features that construe academic contexts depends on experience with those contexts that may not be available in the home or community for many students, especially those who speak English as a second language, who speak non-standard dialects of English, or whose home and community experience has not socialized them into the ways of making meanings that are expected at school. Children's different out-of-school experiences with language affect their knowledge about expectations for language use at school, as the language and discourse forms expected at school are foreign to many children's experiences.

Knowledge about "schooled" ways of using language is differentially distributed in society; resulting in differences among students in the ways they realize in language use what is apparently the same context. How we learn and what we learn about language depends on the context of learning. Students cannot just transfer the spoken language they have developed in their homes and communities to the school context. Their experiences in school need to help them develop facility with the ways of using language that are valued there.

Although it has often been noted that the language tasks that are required of children at school are different from those that many of them engage in at home, what is not always recognized is that these new situational contexts and tasks also require new uses of the linguistic resources of the grammar. Some children come to school with prior experience drawing on linguistic features that reflect school-like tasks, having had practice with such tasks in their homes and communities.

Other children have not, and so has had little experience hearing or using linguistic resources in the ways expected at school. Scollon and Scollon, for example, identify practices that help young children develop resources that will serve them well later in school. One of these practices is what they call "vertical constructions," a means by which caregivers interact with children to assist them in adding new information to their utterances. For example, in (1), the adult helps the child construct a statement about the tape recorder:

1. *Child:* tape recorder use it use it
   Adult: Use it for what?
   Child: talk recorder talk Brenda talk

The child is able to progressively elaborate what she says with the help of the adult interlocutor, developing, in such interaction, use of new language structures. The authors suggest that this and other types of interaction, such as the construction of narratives, are facilitative for the development of academic language because they promote the creation of a grammatically and lexically marked information structure which is high in new information and which fictionalizes the roles of author and audience.

Parents and children in the middle-class families studied by Snow also engage in activities that model the language of schooling as they tell or read stories in which the author is impersonal, the setting is distanced, and contextual references have to be understood from the writer's or speaker's point of view. These forms of interaction are not universal, however. Scollon and Scollon also document the language development of Athabaskan children who do not gain experience with these language functions; instead, they develop expertise in alternative ways of using language.

Competence with school language involves knowing how to act in a particular context, being willing to assume the expected role relationships and having knowledge about linguistic expectations for performance of school-based tasks. As Mehan pointed out, "to be successful in the classroom, students not only must know the content of academic subjects, they must learn the appropriate form in which to cast their academic knowledge". Even from the earliest school tasks, teachers have certain expectations of students for how they should use language. These expectations are typically not articulated in terms of grammatical or discourse structure, but instead in terms of admonitions to "be explicit," "use the right words," "be more detached," or "be better organized." But these values are expressed and realized through particular grammatical choices that are common to school-based language tasks.

Some children are able, even in kindergarten, to draw on the grammatical structures that approximate the styles expected by their teachers, but others are not. In producing the highly valued styles, children evoke the context of schooling that matches the teacher's expectations. These children are then considered "successful." Some students' social experience in early childhood prepares them for effective participation in the language-based tasks of schooling, and others' do not.

Because the school draws predominantly on middle-class ways of making meaning, children with those linguistic experiences are at an advantage. Wells, for example, found that fluency and facility with spontaneous oral language, while fairly evenly distributed among the preschool children in his longitudinal study, did not necessarily lead to success with reading and writing tasks at school. In fact, as soon as the children were assessed at school, a strong relationship emerged between social class and linguistic skills.

He suggests that this is because the school assesses written language and preparation for literacy rather than competence with spoken language. The majority of students are able to cope with the speaking and listening demands of the classroom. What differentiates them and predicts subsequent achievement is their preparation to display the literacy skills that are valued by the school. Wells suggests, then, that what has been called linguistic disadvantage should be understood as relative unfamiliarity with the purposes and forms that language takes in literacy tasks.

Orientation to Meaning

Understanding the role of social experience is especially important in light of the fact that unfamiliarity with the language of schooling is closely related to social class membership. Bernstein's theory provides an explanation for this, suggesting that people develop different coding orientations, or ways of using language, related to their social class and culture.

These different coding orientations are manifested in the ways we participate in interaction. We have different senses of what is significant and relevant and have different ways of engaging in and responding to what might on the surface seem like the same contexts, based on the social relations that are characteristic of our experiences in a particular social class and culture. These different social relations and experiences are related to the power and control that people in different social groups are able to exercise in their material lives.

Orientation to interactional practices emerges from social class membership. Socialization experiences result in different senses of what is expected or valued in different interactional contexts. So even when participating in the same contexts, such as schooling, students from different class and cultural backgrounds will use language in different ways. Bernstein, for example, found that middle-class and working-class children responded very differently to interview situations; not in the amount of speech they produced, but in the extent to which their speech used verbal strategies that are expected in such formal contexts as schooling.

Bernstein found that middle-class children understood that when asked an open-ended question by an adult in an interview context, they were expected to construct particular kinds of texts using particular verbal strategies. They understood, for example, that in certain contexts questions which seemed open were actually testing questions, requiring a particular kind of response.

Bernstein emphasizes the importance of distinguishing between "recognising when a verbal strategy is contextually relevant, possessing the strategy and using it". Hawkins' analysis of the speech of 5-year-old middle-class and working-class children also demonstrates these differences.

Middle-class and working class children employed linguistic features such as explicit noun phrases and deictic reference in different ways in language elicited by structured interviews. Middle-class children used more specific referents, while "working class children oriented towards a type of reference which is less specific and takes for granted a greater degree of common knowledge shared by speaker and addressee".

When asked to describe a detailed picture, working-class children used exophoric reference (that; this), whereas middle-class children used nouns. When they were unsure, middle-class children used verbs of tentativeness and first person pronouns (it seems to me), whereas working-class children used you see, or interactive tags like isn't it and don't they. The children's grammatical choices reflected the social strategies they adopted in different tasks.

The frequency of adjectives produced was different by social class in one task because middle-class children were using a form of social control that involved saying someone was naughty, bad, and cross, whereas working-class children used imperative forms of the verb to accomplish the social control, saying Stop that or Don't do that rather than You're being naughty. Hawkins suggests that these differences reflect the children's social experiences with different ways of using language to accomplish similar tasks.

More recent research using Bernstein's framework is reported in Hasan's study of mother—child dyads in Australia. Using a more nuanced definition of social class to avoid the use of such ambiguous terms as middle class and working class, Hasan divides the mothers in her study into two categories,

Low Autonomous Professions (LAP) and High Autonomous Professions (HAP). This conceptualizes social class in terms of how possible it is for the breadwinner to make work-related policy decisions which affect any aspect of the work-life of others in the place of work; and whether the breadwinner has the possibility of passing such decisions on to others who could then act as instruments for the execution of these decisions.

Such a view of social class focuses on the degree of autonomy and control experienced by the parents in their workplaces. Hasan shows how differences by social class are relevant to socialization practices that prepare children for their different positioning in society.

For example, in the language used by mothers to control children, mothers from LAP families are overtly controlling in their use of language and allow conflict. Mothers from HAP families are more manipulative and avoid conflict. For example, in (2), a LAP mother wants Karen to get out of the bathtub:

2. *Karen:* I'm not getting out
   Mother: you'll get out.
   Karen: no, I won't
   Mother: yes
   Karen: no
   Mother: yes
   Karen: I'm not standing up
   Mother: I'll drag you out if I have to

In (3), a HAP mother urges Donna to get out of the bath:

3. *Mother:* you tell me when you're ready to get out
   Donna: OK now
   Mother: you're not ready until the plug's out
   Donna: well, I lost my hands and foots
   Mother: then you'd better find them
   Donna: ooh, they're in the front so I'm getting out
   Mother: no you're not please pull the plug out, Donna
   Donna: can't feel it's not anywhere ... I feel it now
   Mother: good I thought you'd see it my way

The mother in (2) exercises control directly, using threats (I'll drag you out)to make her authority clear. The mother in (3), on the other hand, uses more indirect means of control (you'd better; please). Children, then, learn these different linguistic strategies.

The linguistic choices construe social contexts in particular ways and lead children to have different linguistic responses to what seem to be similar circumstances. Different ways of "doing" with language focus children on different aspects of the interaction. In other words, the role of social experience is key in shaping and understanding the options for language use that children experience and learn. Early childhood experiences prepare some children to have an orientation to learning through definitions, or to attending to principles underlying categories.

Painter demonstrates, for example, how the development of use of hypothetical if clauses enables a young child to construe contexts beyond personal experience. Children first hear such clauses from their parents (If you see [a snake], don't touch it because they're dangerous) and then later try them out themselves (3year-old Stephen: If you fell down bump really, really hard [you might cry, too]). In the same way, certain kinds of interaction and the development of certain kinds of grammatical resources also enable the child to use particular ways of reasoning; with syllogisms, for example. Children who live in contexts where these kinds of interaction take place develop resources that prepare them for the ways language will be used in schooling.

An individual child's ability to use language for particular purposes varies according to the specific demands and expectations of the context. Hasan demonstrates, for example, that some 7-year-olds are able to tell someone who is not present how to make something, but the same children may not be able to tell about an event they have participated in. In her study, those who could fluently describe what they had done had difficulty doing the other task, and used halting and ungrammatical structures in their attempts.

She concludes that "the growth of language in an individual is the function of that individual's engagement in a varied set of activities, calling for the use of language". In other words, language abilities develop through participation in contexts where those abilities meet needs and accomplish meaningful purposes. This means that children come to school with different strategies for language use.

As students move on in school, advanced literacy tasks require that they read and write texts that analyze unfamiliar topics in dense and abstract language that draws on linguistic resources that are unfamiliar to the everyday experience of many children. Rose, for example, has shown how textbooks in technical and scientific subjects often do not make explicit the causal nature of the relationship between events in an explanation.

Instead, students are expected to recognize implicit expression of causality in order to understand the logic of the text. Social experience with language prepares some children, but not others, to recognize the meanings in this way of presenting causal relationships. "Children of middle-class families, in which prohibitions and prescriptions are more frequently explained, sequences of why questions and answers encouraged, and obligation expressed more implicitly, may be advantaged in learning to recognize implication sequences and interpret the implicit causal relations which organize them logically".

He argues that the ability to interpret logical relations, typically interpreted as a cognitive skill, depends on understanding the logic of cause that particular institutions' or disciplines' texts typically express. Both grammatical and lexical issues are relevant to understanding the challenges of school-based language. Corson, for example, focuses on the Graeco-Latin vocabulary of English and the difficulty it poses for students from different class, cultural, or linguistic backgrounds.

He suggests that "exposure to the culture of literacy gives us the necessary foundations for vocabulary development within meaning systems that derive from it". Corson cites research that concludes that the difference between the word knowledge performances of high and low achieving students "comes from events outside school, not from school itself". Not everyone has the same exposure, as many students rarely encounter Graeco-Latin words in print outside of school.

Corson points out that "... knowing the meaning of an academic word is knowing how to use it within an appropriate meaning system.... The necessary raw materials for this word learning lie in frequent encounters with words in the many contexts that display the rules for their application, and in regular opportunities to play these 'language games' at a high standard of performance".

The Language of Schooling

One approach to addressing differences between home and school language use has been to suggest that all parents adopt the practices of the middle-class parents as a way of preparing children for school. In particular, joint book reading is often recommended, based on research that finds that children who come from homes where books are frequently read do better in school. Cox et al., for example, compared children at two preschools and found that higher income children are more likely to control "literate register options," but that regardless of income, children who controlled the written-like register came from homes that provided strong, child-centreed book experiences.

These children were able to successfully reconstruct a written-like monologue from a familiar storybook and were able to modify their own spoken stories based on personal experience to realize a "literate" register.

On the basis of studies like these, parents have been urged to prepare children for school by reading to them. The underlying idea is that by engaging in practices that mimic the middle class ways of interacting, all parents can prepare their children for success in school tasks. But Williams questions whether such strategies can be successful. He demonstrates that joint book reading is not the same situational context for all families that engage in it.

Social class differences still manifest themselves in joint book reading, and the supposed benefits for developing the "literate register options" do not automatically result from the activity itself. In reading books aloud to children, caretakers from different social class backgrounds use language in different ways and thereby co-construct different kinds of meanings with the child.

Williams' study of joint book reading provides evidence that it is not the activity itself, but the way language is used and the semantic meanings that are realized that provide the preparation for schooling that comes for some children through this activity. Following Hasan's model in investigating the joint book reading behaviour of mothers and children from different social classes, Williams found that mothers in the LAP and HAP groups read similar amounts but that the total number of interactive messages exchanged between mother and child during the reading activity was three times greater for the HAP group.

Although the mothers and children in both groups initiated interaction through demands for information at similar rates, there were differences in the kind of interaction that ensued. HAP mothers more frequently asked children to elaborate comments about something in the book or some aspect of their own experience and then expanded children's responses to extend beyond a first specific comment.

HAP mothers' questions were prefaced significantly more often than LAP mothers' with options that elicited the child's perspective, such as "do you think ...?" In general, the HAP mothers engaged their children much more in interactive discourse that pushed the child to talk about himself or herself in relation to the story and to evaluate the book as a text. Such interactions are mirrored in school-based literacy tasks in which stories are discussed and evaluated. Heath also describes differences in joint book reading behaviour of mothers and children from different social groups.

It is important to stress that Williams found many similarities between the book reading of mothers and children in the two social groups. All mothers read fluently and dramatically, all addressed questions to the children and prompted the children for adequate responses, and all responded to their children's initiations. In both groups, children spontaneously initiated conversation during the reading and predicted what was to come next in the narrative.

It was only in a careful analysis of the deeper differences between the groups that the semantic variation and its significance became apparent. These differences manifested themselves in the extent of linguistic interaction that mothers and children had around the text itself as object, in the kinds of questions asked by the mothers, and in the kinds of interpretive work that the children engaged in to answer those questions.

Although all mothers asked questions that demanded information, many demands for information were focused on ensuring that the child noticed key features of the illustrations, or clustered around one particular moment in the narrative they were reading. Only the HAP mothers asked the children for explanations, and this type of question occurred frequently in that interaction.

It is such questions that engage the mother and child in joint co-construction of the type described by Scollon and Scollon, where the mother guides the child's interpretations in response to the child's initiatives and responses, helping the child attend to particular kinds of meanings that prepare a child for the kinds of interaction and language use that schooling also develops.

It is this kind of interaction, associated with dominant social groups, that is also privileged in schooling contexts. Williams asks what the major social prerequisites would be for LAP families to adopt such practices. He points out that the social institutional status of families and their location in social formations through that status varies by social class, and that this status is reflected in and in turn construed by the kinds of interaction caregivers and children engage in during activities such as joint book reading.

He argues that parents cannot be advised to ask certain kinds of questions and have it be expected that thereby the same kinds of meanings will be construed as those construed by parents whose whole relationship to the social world is of a different sort; where their status gives them power and control in ways that the status of other families does not. Williams argues that it is contexts that seem similar that lead to misrecognition of deeper differences related to social status.

He calls this "sameness but difference" as he demonstrates how the HAP interaction extends meaning relations beyond a specific instance, and so has the potential to develop children's "individuated literate consciousness." His statistical analysis of a large corpus of joint book reading shows significant differences in the semantic features of the activity according to social class. It is through the careful analysis of the linguistic choices and the meanings they construe that differences in underlying contexts are revealed.

Even when interaction is ostensibly "doing the same thing," the meanings that are construed can be different. So it is not just engaging in an activity such as joint book reading that is important, but how meanings are made in interaction that prepares some children to easily engage in similar kinds of activities at school. A child's orientation to particular ways of using language has both social and psychological dimensions, as it develops in social interaction, but manifests itself as the particular skills of the individual child.

In Bernstein's formulation, social class membership shapes and positions children in terms of what they perceive as significant and relevant in their interactions with others. Each context activates certain kinds of meanings that prompt children to draw on particular lexical and grammatical resources that in turn realize the context in particular ways. This makes for a dialectical relationship between language and context as the meanings language makes always shape and are shaped by the social context.

While language use provides evidence for the differences in children's backgrounds, more importantly, from a functional linguistics perspective, the language provides evidence about how the context is being understood by the children. With different life experiences with language, children inevitably come to school with different orientations to meaning, prepared to attend to different kinds of meanings and to construe meanings in different ways.

Differences in ways of construing meaning are functional for the kinds of lives that people in different social circumstances live in our society. Cultural differences are part of this, but as there are many similarities between the same social classes in different cultures, a focus on social class is important for understanding the different kinds of social and interactional experiences children have outside of school and for providing the social experiences at school that enable students to participate in the contexts of society that schooling aims to prepare students for.

As Painter points out, "variation in ways of meaning according to social class membership is interpretable not in terms of richer or poorer linguistic experience, but in terms of a linguistic experience which enables the learners, within the family, to construe the social system in a way adjusted to their social positioning".

But if one of the goals of schooling is to extend students' ability to participate in a range of social and academic contexts, then one of the tasks of schooling should be to enable students to make new kinds of meaning. The next sections explore what this implies for students' performance in school language tasks.

STRUCTURE IN LANGUAGE

English grammar displays minimal inflection compared with most other Indo-European languages. This is caused by deflexion. For example, Modern English, unlike Modern German or Dutch and the Romance languages, lacks grammatical gender and adjectival agreement. Case marking has almost disappeared from the language and mainly survives in pronouns. The patterning of strong (*e.g., speak/spoke/spoken*) versus weak verbs inherited from Germanic has declined in importance and the remnants of inflection (such as plural marking) have become more regular. At the same time as inflection has declined in importance in English, the language has become more analytic, and developed a greater reliance on features such as modal verbs and word order to convey grammatical information.

Auxiliary verbs are used to mark constructions such as questions, negatives, the passive voice and progressive tenses. The question of form in language presents itself under two aspects. We may either consider the formal methods employed by a language, its "grammatical processes," or we may ascertain the distribution of concepts with reference to formal expression. What are the formal patterns of the language? And what types of concepts make up the content of these formal patterns? The two points of view are quite distinct.

The English word unthinkingly is, broadly speaking, formally parallel to the word reformers, each being built up on a radical element which may occur as an independent verb (think, form), this radical element being preceded by an element (un-, re-) that conveys a definite and fairly concrete significance but that cannot be used independently, and followed by two elements (-ing, -ly; -er, -s) that limit the application of the radical concept in a relational sense. This formal pattern — (b) + A + (c) + (d) -is a characteristic feature of the language. A countless number of functions may be expressed by it; in other words, all the possible ideas conveyed by such prefixed and suffixed elements, while tending to fall into minor groups, do not necessarily form natural, functional systems.

There is no logical reason, for instance, why the numeral function of -s should be formally expressed in a manner that is analogous to the expression of the idea conveyed by -ly. It is perfectly conceivable that in another language the concept of manner (-ly) may be treated according to an entirely different pattern from that of plurality.

The former might have to be expressed by an independent word (say, thus unthinking), the latter by a prefixed element (say, plural -reform -er). There are, of course, an unlimited number of other possibilities. Even within the confines of English alone the relative independence of form and function can be made obvious. Thus, the negative idea conveyed by uncan be just as adequately expressed by a suffixed element (-less) in such a word as thoughtlessly.

Such a twofold formal expression of the negative function would be inconceivable in certain languages, say Eskimo, where a suffixed element would alone be possible. Again, the plural notion conveyed by the -s of reformers is just as definitely expressed in the word geese, where an utterly distinct method is employed.

Furthermore, the principle of vocalic change (goose — geese) is by no means confined to the expression of the idea of plurality; it may also function as an indicator of difference of time (*e.g.,* sing — sang, throw — threw). But the expression in English of past time is not by any means always bound up with a change of vowel.

In the great majority of cases the same idea is expressed by means of a distinct suffix (die-d, work-ed). Functionally, died and sang are analogous; so are reformers and geese. Formally, we must arrange these words quite otherwise.

Both die-d and re-form-er-s employ the method of suffixing grammatical elements; both sang and geese have grammatical form by virtue of the fact that their vowels differ from the vowels of other words with which they are closely related in form and meaning (goose; sing, sung). Every language possesses one or more formal methods for indicating the relation of a secondary concept to the main concept of the radical element. Some of these grammatical processes, like suffixing, are exceedingly wide-spread; others, like vocalic change, are less common but far from rare; still others, like accent and consonantal change, are somewhat exceptional as functional processes. Not all languages are as irregular as English in the assignment of functions to its stock of grammatical processes. As a rule, such basic concepts as those of plurality and time are rendered by means of one or other method alone, but the rule has so many exceptions that we cannot safely lay it down as a principle.

Wherever we go we are impressed by the fact that pattern is one thing, the utilization of pattern quite another. A few further examples of the multiple expressions of identical functions in other languages than English may help to make still more vivid this idea of the relative independence of form and function.

In Hebrew, as in other Semitic languages, the verbal idea as such is expressed by three, less often by two or four, characteristic consonants. Thus, the group sh-m-r expresses the idea of "guarding," the group g-n-b that of "stealing," n-t-n that of "giving." Naturally these consonantal sequences are merely abstracted from the actual forms. The consonants are held together in different forms by characteristic vowels that vary according to the idea that it is desired to express. Prefixed and suffixed elements are also frequently used. The method of internal vocalic change is exemplified in shamar "he has guarded," shomer "guarding," shamur "being guarded," shmor "(to) guard." Analogously, ganab "he has stolen" goneb "stealing," ganub "being stolen," gnob "(to) steal." But not all infinitives are formed according to the type of shmor and gnob or of other types of internal vowel change.

Certain verbs suffix a t-element for the infinitive, *e.g.,* ten-eth "to give," heyo-th "to be." Again, the pronominal ideas may be expressed by independent words (*e.g.,* anoki "I"), by prefixed elements (*e.g.,* e-shmor "I shall guard"), or by suffixed elements (*e.g.,* shamar-ti "I have guarded"). In Nass, an Indian language of British. Columbia, plurals are formed by four distinct methods.

Most nouns (and verbs) are reduplicated in the plural, that is, part of the radical element is repeated, *e.g.,* gyat "person," gyigyat "people." A second method is the use of certain characteristic prefixes, *e.g.,* an'on "hand," ka-an'on "hands"; wai "one paddles," lu-wai "several paddle." Still other plurals are formed by means of internal vowel change, *e.g.*, gwula "cloak," gwila "cloaks." Finally, a fourth class of plurals is constituted by such nouns as suffix a grammatical element, *e.g.,*, waky "brother," wakykw "brothers."

From such groups of examples as these — and they might be multiplied ad nauseam — we cannot but conclude that linguistic form may and should be studied as types of patterning, apart from the associated functions. We are the more justified in this procedure as all languages evince a curious instinct for the development of one or more particular grammatical processes at the expense of others, tending always to lose sight of any explicit functional value that the process may have had in the first instance, delighting, it would seem, in the sheer play of its means of expression.

It does not matter that in such a case as the English goose — geese, foul — defile, sing — sang — sung we can prove that we are dealing with historically distinct processes, that the vocalic alternation of sing and sang, for instance, is centuries older as a specific type of grammatical process than the outwardly parallel one of goose and geese.

It remains true that there is (or was) an inherent tendency in English, at the time such forms as geese came into being, for the utilization of vocalic change as a significant linguistic method. Failing the precedent set by such already existing types of vocalic alternation as sing — sang — sung, it is highly doubtful if the detailed conditions that brought about the evolution of forms like teeth and geese from tooth and goose would have been potent enough to allow the native linguistic feeling to win through to an acceptance of these new types of plural formation as psychologically possible.

This feeling for form as such, freely expanding along predetermined lines and greatly inhibited in certain directions by the lack of controlling types of patterning, should be more clearly understood than it seems to be. A general survey of many diverse types of languages is needed to give us the proper perspective on this point. We saw that every language has an inner phonetic system of definite pattern. We now learn that it has also a definite feeling for patterning on the level of grammatical formation.

Both of these submerged and powerfully controlling impulses to definite form operate as such, regardless of the need for expressing particular concepts or of giving consistent external shape to particular groups of concepts. It goes without saying that these impulses can find realization only in concrete functional expression. We must say something to be able to say it in a certain manner.

Let us now take up a little more systematically, however briefly, the various grammatical processes that linguistic research has established. They may be grouped into six main types: word order; composition; affixation, including the use of prefixes, suffixes, and infixes; internal modification of the radical or grammatical element, whether this affects a vowel or a consonant; reduplication; and accentual differences, whether dynamic (stress) or tonal (pitch). There are also special quantitative processes, like vocalic lengthening or shortening and consonantal doubling, but these may be looked upon as particular sub-types of the process of internal modification.

Possibly still other formal types exist, but they are not likely to be of importance in a general survey. It is important to bear in mind that a linguistic phenomenon cannot be looked upon as illustrating a definite "process" unless it has an inherent functional value. The consonantal change in English, for instance, of book-s and bag-s (s in the former, z in the latter) is of no functional significance. It is a purely external, mechanical change induced by the presence of a preceding voiceless consonant, k, in the former case, of a voiced consonant, g, in the latter. This mechanical alternation is objectively the same as that between the noun house and the verb to house. In the latter case, however, it has an important grammatical function, that of transforming a noun into a verb. The two alternations belong, then, to entirely different psychological categories. Only the latter is a true illustration of consonantal modification as a grammatical process.

The simplest, at least the most economical, method of conveying some sort of grammatical notion is to juxtapose two or more words in a definite sequence without making any attempt by inherent modification of these words to establish a connection between them. Let us put down two simple English words at random, say sing praise. This conveys no finished thought in English, nor does it clearly establish a relation between the idea of singing and that of praising.

Nevertheless, it is psychologically impossible to hear or see the two words juxtaposed without straining to give them some measure of coherent significance. The attempt is not likely to yield an entirely satisfactory result, but what is significant is that as soon as two or more radical concepts are put before the human mind in immediate sequence it strives to bind them together with connecting values of some sort. In the case of sing praise different individuals are likely to arrive at different provisional results.

Some of the latent possibilities of the juxtaposition, expressed in currently satisfying form, are: sing praise (to him)! or singing praise, praise expressed in a song or to sing and praise or one who sings a song of praise (compare such English compounds as killjoy, *i.e.,* one who kills joy) or he sings a song of praise (to him). The theoretical possibilities in the way of rounding out these two concepts into a significant group of concepts or even into a finished thought are indefinitely numerous. None of them will quite work in English, but there are numerous languages where one or other of these amplifying processes is habitual. It depends entirely on the genius of the particular language what function is inherently involved in a given sequence of words.

Some languages, like Latin, express practically all relations by means of modifications within the body of the word itself. In these, sequence is apt to be a rhetorical rather than a strictly grammatical principle. Whether I say in Latin hominem femina or femina hominem videt or hominem videt femina or videt femina hominem makes little or no difference beyond, possibly, a rhetorical or stylistic one. The woman sees the man is the identical significance of each of these sentences.

In Chinook, an Indian language of the Columbia River, one can be equally free, for the relation between the verb and the two nouns is as inherently fixed as in Latin. The difference between the two languages is that, while Latin allows the nouns to establish their relation to each other and to the verb, Chinook lays the formal burden entirely on the verb, the full content of which is more or less adequately rendered by she-him-sees. Eliminate the Latin case suffixes (-a and -em) and the Chinook pronominal prefixes (she-him-) and we cannot afford to be so indifferent to our word order. We need to husband our resources.

In other words, word order takes on a real functional value. Latin and Chinook are at one extreme. Such languages as Chinese, Siamese, and Annamite, in which each and every word, if it is to function properly, falls into its assigned place, are at the other extreme. But the majority of languages fall between these two extremes.

In English, for instance, it may make little grammatical difference whether I say yesterday the man saw the dog or the man saw the dog yesterday, but it is not a matter of indifference whether I say yesterday the man saw the dog or yesterday the dog saw the man or whether I say he is here or is he here? In the one case, of the latter group of examples, the vital distinction of subject and object depends entirely on the placing of certain words of the sentence, in the latter a slight difference of sequence makes all the difference between statement and question.

It goes without saying that in these cases the English principle of word order is as potent a means of expression as is the Latin use of case suffixes or of an interrogative particle. There is here no question of functional poverty, but of formal economy. We have already seen something of the process of composition, the uniting into a single word of two or more radical elements. Psychologically this process is closely allied to that of word order in so far as the relation between the elements is implied, not explicitly stated. It differs from the mere juxtaposition of words in the sentence in that the compounded elements are felt as constituting but parts of a single word-organism.

Such languages as Chinese and English, in which the principle of rigid sequence is well developed, tend not infrequently also to the development of compound words. It is but a step from such a Chinese word sequence as jin tak "man virtue," *i.e.,* "the virtue of men," to such more conventionalized and psychologically unified juxtapositions as t'ien tsz "heaven son," *i.e.,* "emperor," or shui fu "water man," *i.e.,* "water carrier."

In the latter case we may as well frankly write shui-fu as a single word, the meaning of the compound as a whole being as divergent from the precise etymological values of its component elements as is that of our English word typewriter from the merely combined values of type and writer. In English the unity of the word typewriter is further safeguarded by a predominant accent on the first syllable and by the possibility of adding such a suffixed element as the plural -s to the whole word. Chinese also unifies its compounds by means of stress. However, then, in its ultimate origins the process of composition may go back to typical sequences of words in the sentence, it is now, for the most part, a specialized method of expressing relations. French has as rigid a word order as English but does not possess anything like its power of compounding words into more complex units. On the other hand, classical Greek, in spite of its relative freedom in the placing of words, has a very considerable bent for the formation of compound terms.

It is curious to observe how greatly languages differ in their ability to make use of the process of composition. One would have thought on general principles that so simple a device as gives us our typewriter and blackbird and hosts of other words would be an all but universal grammatical process. Such is not the case. There are a great many languages, like Eskimo and Nootka and, aside from paltry exceptions, the Semitic languages, that cannot compound radical elements.

What is even stranger is the fact that many of these languages are not in the least averse to complex word formations, but may on the contrary effect a synthesis that far surpasses the utmost that Greek and Sanskrit are capable of. Such a Nootka word, for instance, as "when, as they say, he had been absent for four days" might be expected to embody at least three radical elements corresponding to the concepts of "absent," "four," and "day."

As a matter of fact the Nootka word is utterly incapable of composition in our sense. It is invariably built up out of a single radical element and a greater or less number of suffixed elements, some of which may have as concrete significance as the radical element itself. In the particular case we have cited the radical element conveys the idea of "four," the notions of "day" and "absent" being expressed by suffixes that are as inseparable from the radical nucleus of the word as is an English element like -er from the sing or hunt of such words as singer and hunter.

The tendency to word synthesis is, then, by no means the same thing as the tendency to compounding radical elements, though the latter is not infrequently a ready means for the synthetic tendency to work with. There is a bewildering variety of types of composition. These types vary according to function, the nature of the compounded elements, and order.

In a great many languages composition is confined to what we may call the delimiting function, that is, of the two or more compounded elements one is given a more precisely qualified significance by the others, which contribute nothing to the formal build of the sentence. In English, for instance, such compounded elements as red in redcoat or over in overlook merely modify the significance of the dominant coat or look without in any way sharing, as such, in the predication that is expressed by the sentence.

Some languages, however, such as Iroquois and Nahuatl, employ the method of composition for much heavier work than this. In Iroquois, for instance, the composition of a noun, in its radical form, with a following verb is a typical method of expressing case relations, particularly of the subject or object. Imeateat, for instance, is the regular Iroquois method of expressing the sentence I am eating meat. In other languages similar forms may express local or instrumental or still other relations.

Such English forms as killjoy and marplot also illustrate the compounding of a verb and a noun, but the resulting word has a strictly nominal, not a verbal, function. We cannot say he marplots. Some languages allow the composition of all or nearly all types of elements. Paiute, for instance, may compound noun with noun, adjective with noun, verb with noun to make a noun, noun with verb to make a verb, adverb with verb, verb with verb. Yana, an Indian language of California, can freely compound noun with noun and verb with noun, but not verb with verb.

On the other hand, Iroquois can compound only noun with verb, never noun and noun as in English or verb and verb as in so many other languages. Finally, each language has its characteristic types of order of composition. In English the qualifying element regularly precedes; in certain other languages it follows. Sometimes both types are used in the same language, as in Yana, where "beef" is "bitter-venison" but "deerliver" is expressed by "liver-deer." The compounded object of a verb precedes the verbal element in Paiute, Nahuatl, and Iroquois, follows it in Yana, Tsimshian, and the Algonkin languages.

Of all grammatical processes affixing is incomparably the most frequently employed. There are languages, like Chinese and Siamese, that make no grammatical use of elements that do not at the same time possess an independent value as radical elements, but such languages are uncommon. Of the three types of affixing-the use of prefixes, suffixes, and infixes — suffixing is much the commonest.

Indeed, it is a fair guess that suffixes do more of the formative work of language than all other methods combined. It is worth noting that there are not a few affixing languages that make absolutely no use of prefixed elements but possess a complex apparatus of suffixes. Such are Turkish, Hottentot, Eskimo, Nootka, and Yana. Some of these, like the three last mentioned, have hundreds of suffixed elements, many of them of a concreteness of significance that would demand expression in the vast majority of languages by means of radical elements.

The reverse case, the use of prefixed elements to the complete exclusion of suffixes, is far less common. A good example is Khmer (or Cambodgian), spoken in French CochinChina, though even here there are obscure traces of old suffixes that have ceased to function as such and are now felt to form part of the radical element.

A considerable majority of known languages are prefixing and suffixing at one and the same time, but the relative importance of the two groups of affixed elements naturally varies enormously. In some languages, such as Latin and Russian, the suffixes alone relate the word to the rest of the sentence, the prefixes being confined to the expression of such ideas as delimit the concrete significance of the radical element without influencing its bearing in the proposition.

A Latin form like remittebantur "they were being sent back" may serve as an illustration of this type of distribution of elements. The prefixed element re- "back" merely qualifies to a certain extent the inherent significance of the radical element mitt- "send," while the suffixes -eba-, -nt-, and -ur convey the less concrete, more strictly formal, notions of time, person, plurality, and passivity. On the other hand, there are languages, like the Bantu group of Africa or the Athabaskan languages of North America, in which the grammatically significant elements precede, those that follow the radical element forming a relatively dispensable class. The Hupa word te-s-e-ya-te "I will go," for example, consists of a radical element -ya- "to go," three essential prefixes and a formally subsidiary suffix.

The element te- indicates that the act takes place here and there in space or continuously over space; practically, it has no clear-cut significance apart from such verb stems as it is customary to connect it with. The second prefixed element, -s-, is even less easy to define. All we can say is that it is used in verb forms of "definite" time and that it marks action as in progress rather than as beginning or coming to an end.

The third prefix, -e-, is a pronominal element, "I," which can be used only in "definite" tenses. It is highly important to understand that the use of -eis conditional on that of -s- or of certain alternative prefixes and that te- also is in practice linked with -s-. The group te-s-e-ya is a firmly knit grammatical unit. The suffix -te, which indicates the future, is no more necessary to its formal balance than is the prefixed re- of the Latin word; it is not an element that is capable of standing alone but its function is materially delimiting rather than strictly formal.

It is not always, however, that we can clearly set off the suffixes of a language as a group against its prefixes. In probably the majority of languages that use both types of affixes each group has both delimiting and formal or relational functions. The most that we can say is that a language tends to express similar functions in either the one or the other manner. If a certain verb expresses a certain tense by suffixing, the probability is strong that it expresses its other tenses in an analogous fashion and that, indeed, all verbs have suffixed tense elements.

Similarly, we normally expect to find the pronominal elements, so far as they are included in the verb at all, either consistently prefixed or suffixed. But these rules are far from absolute. We have already seen that Hebrew prefixes its pronominal elements in certain cases, suffixes them in others. In Chimariko, an Indian language of California, the position of the pronominal affixes depends on the verb; they are prefixed for certain verbs, suffixed for others. It will not be necessary to give many further examples of prefixing and suffixing. One of each category will suffice to illustrate their formative possibilities. The idea expressed in English by the sentence I came to give it to her is rendered in Chinook by i-n-i-a-l-u-d-am. This word — and it is a thoroughly unified word with a clear-cut accent on the first a — consists of a radical element, -d- "to give," six functionally distinct, if phonetically frail, prefixed elements, and a suffix. Of the prefixes, i- indicates recently past time; n-, the pronominal subject "I"; -i-, the pronominal object "it"; -a-, the second pronominal object "her"; -l-, a prepositional element indicating that the preceding pronominal prefix is to be understood as an indirect object (-her-to-, *i.e.,* "to her"); and -u-, an element that it is not easy to define satisfactorily but which, on the whole, indicates movement away from the speaker. The suffixed -am modifies the verbal content in a local sense; it adds to the notion conveyed by the radical element that of "arriving" or "going (or coming) for that particular purpose."

It is obvious that in Chinook, as in Hupa, the greater part of the grammatical machinery resides in the prefixes rather than in the suffixes. A reverse case, one in which the grammatically significant elements cluster, as in Latin, at the end of the word is yielded by Fox, one of the better known Algonkin languages of the Mississippi Valley.

We may take the form eh-kiwi-n-a-m-oht-ati-wa-ch(i) "then they together kept (him) in flight from them." The radical element here is kiwi-, a verb stem indicating the general notion of "indefinite movement round about, here and there." The prefixed element *eh-* is hardly more than an adverbial particle indicating temporal subordination; it may be conveniently rendered as "then."

Of the seven suffixes included in this highly-wrought word, -n- seems to be merely a phonetic element serving to connect the verb stem with the following -a-; -a- is a "secondary stem" denoting the idea of " flight, to flee"; -m- denotes causality with reference to an animate object; -o(ht)- indicates activity done for the subject (the socalled "middle" or "medio-passive" voice of Greek); -(a)ti- is a reciprocal element, "one another"; -wa-ch(i) is the third person animate plural (-wa-, plural; -chi, more properly personal) of so-called "conjunctive" forms.

The word may be translated more literally (and yet only approximately as to grammatical feeling) as "then they (animate) caused some animate being to wander about in flight from one another of themselves." Eskimo, Nootka, Yana, and other languages have similarly complex arrays of suffixed elements, though the functions performed by them and their principles of combination differ widely.

We have reserved the very curious type of affixation known as "infixing" for separate illustration. It is utterly unknown in English, unless we consider the -n- of stand (contrast stood) as an infixed element. The earlier Indo-

European languages, such as Latin, Greek and Sanskrit, made a fairly considerable use of infixed nasals to differentiate the present tense of a certain class of verbs from other forms (contrast Latin vinc-o "I conquer" with vic-i "I conquered"; Greek lamb-an-o "I take" with e-lab-on "I took").

There are, however, more striking examples of the process, examples in which it has assumed a more clearly defined function than in these Latin and Greek cases. It is particularly prevalent in many languages of southeastern Asia and of the Malay archipelago. Good examples from Khmer (Cambodgian) are tmeu "one who walks" and daneu "walking" (verbal noun), both derived from deu "to walk." Further examples may be quoted from Bontoc Igorot, a Filipino language.

Thus, an infixed -in- conveys the idea of the product of an accomplished action, *e.g.*,, kayu "wood," kinayu "gathered wood." Infixes are also freely used in the Bontoc Igorot verb. Thus, an infixed -um- is characteristic of many intransitive verbs with personal pronominal suffixes, *e.g.*,, sad- "to wait," sumid-ak "I wait"; kineg "silent," kuminek-ak "I am silent." In other verbs it indicates futurity, *e.g.*,, tengao- "to celebrate a holiday," tumengao-ak "I shall have a holiday." The past tense is frequently indicated by an infixed -in-; if there is already an infixed -um-, the two elements combine to -in-m-, *e.g.*,, kinminek-ak "I am silent."

Obviously the infixing process has in this (and related) languages the same vitality that is possessed by the commoner prefixes and suffixes of other languages. The process is also found in a number of aboriginal American languages. The Yana plural is sometimes formed by an infixed element, *e.g.*,, k'uruwi "medicine-men," k'uwi "medicineman"; in Chinook an infixed -l- is used in certain verbs to indicate repeated activity, *e.g.*,, ksik'ludelk "she keeps looking at him," iksik'lutk "she looked at him" (radical element -tk).

A peculiarly interesting type of infixation is found in the Siouan languages, in which certain verbs insert the pronominal elements into the very body of the radical element, *e.g.*,, Sioux *cheti* "to build a fire," *chewati* "I build a fire"; *shuta* "to miss," *shuunta-pi* "we miss." A subsidiary but by no means unimportant grammatical process is that of internal vocalic or consonantal change.

In some languages, as in English (sing, sang, sung, song; goose, geese), the former of these has become one of the major methods of indicating fundamental changes of grammatical function. At any rate, the process is alive enough to lead our children into untrodden ways. We all know of the growing youngster who speaks of having brung something, on the analogy of such forms as sung and flung. In Hebrew, as we have seen, vocalic change is of even greater significance than in English. What is true of Hebrew is of course true of all other Semitic languages. A few examples of so-called "broken" plurals from Arabic will supplement the Hebrew verb forms that I have given in another connection. The noun balad "place" has the plural form bilad; gild "hide" forms the plural gulud; ragril "man," the plural rigal; shibbak "window," the plural shababik. Very similar phenomena are illustrated by the Hamitic languages of Northern Africa, *e.g.*,, Shilh izbil "hair," plural izbel; a-slem "fish," plural i-slimen; sn "to know," sen "to be knowing"; rmi "to become tired," rumni "to be tired"; ttss "to fall asleep," ttoss "to sleep."

Strikingly similar to English and Greek alternations of the type sing — sang and leip-o "I leave," leloip-a "I have left," are such Somali cases as al "I am," il "I was"; i-dah-a "I say," i-di "I said," deh "say!" Vocalic change is of great significance also in a number of American Indian languages. In the Athabaskan group many verbs change the quality or quantity of the vowel of the radical element as it changes its tense or mode. The Navaho verb for "I put (grain) into a receptacle" is bi-hi-sh-ja, in which -ja is the radical element; the past tense, bi-hi-ja', has a long a-vowel, followed by the "glottal stop"; the future is bi-h-de-sh-ji with complete change of vowel.

In other types of Navaho verbs the vocalic changes follow different lines, *e.g.*,, yah-a-ni-ye "you carry (a pack) into (a stable)"; past, yah-i-ni-yin (with long i in -yin; -n is here used to indicate nasalization); future, yah-a-di-yehl (with long e). In another Indian language, Yokuts, vocalic modifications affect both noun and verb forms.

Thus, buchong "son" forms the plural bochang-i (contrast the objective buchong-a); enash "grandfather," the plural inash-a; the verb engtyim "to sleep" forms the continuative ingetym-ad "to be sleeping" and the past ingetymash. Consonantal change as a functional process is probably far less common than vocalic modifications, but it is not exactly rare. There is an interesting group of cases in English, certain nouns and corresponding verbs differing solely in that the final consonant is voiceless or voiced.

Examples are wreath (with th as in think), but to wreathe (with th as in then); house, but to house (with s pronounced like z). That we have a distinct feeling for the interchange as a means of distinguishing the noun from the verb is indicated by the extension of the principle by many Americans to such a noun as rise (*e.g.*,, the rise of democracy) — pronounced like rice — in contrast to the verb to rise (s like *z*).

In the Celtic languages the initial consonants undergo several types of change according to the grammatical relation that subsists between the word itself and the preceding word. Thus, in modern Irish, a word like bo "ox" may under the appropriate circumstances, take the forms bho (pronounce wo) or mo (*e.g.*,, an bo "the ox" as a subject, but tir na mo "land of the oxen," as a possessive plural).

In the verb the principle has as one of its most striking consequences the "aspiration" of initial consonants in the past tense. If a verb begins with t, say, it changes the t to th (now pronounced h) in forms of the past; if it begins with g, the consonant changes, in analogous forms, to gh (pronounced like a voiced spirant g or like y, according to the nature of the following vowel). In modern Irish the principle of consonantal change, which began in the oldest period of the language as a secondary consequence of certain phonetic conditions, has become one of the primary grammatical processes of the language.

Perhaps as remarkable as these Irish phenomena are the consonantal interchanges of Ful, an African language of the Soudan. Here we find that all nouns belonging to the personal class form the plural by changing their initial g, j, d, b, k, ch, and p to y (or w), y, r, w, h, s and f respectively; *e.g.*,, jim-o "companion," yim-'be "companions"; pio-o "beater," fio-'be "beaters." Curiously enough, nouns that belong to the class of things form their singular and plural in exactly reverse fashion, *e.g.*, yola-re "grass-grown place," jola-je "grass-grown places"; fitan-du "soul," pital-i "souls."

In Nootka, to refer to but one other language in which the process is found, the t or tl of many verbal suffixes becomes hl in forms denoting repetition, *e.g.*, hita-'ato "to fall out," hita-'ahl "to keep falling out"; mat-achisht-utl "to fly on to the water," mat-achisht-ohl "to keep flying on to the water." Further, the hl of certain elements changes to a peculiar h-sound in plural forms, *e.g.*, yak-ohl "sore-faced," yak-oh "sore-faced (people)."

Nothing is more natural than the prevalence of reduplication, in other words, the repetition of all or part of the radical element. The process is generally employed, with self-evident symbolism, to indicate such concepts as distribution, plurality, repetition, customary activity, increase of size, added intensity, continuance. Even in English it is not unknown, though it is not generally accounted one of the typical formative devices of our language.

Such words as goody-goody and to poohpooh have become accepted as part of our normal vocabulary, but the method of duplication may on occasion be used more freely than is indicated by such stereotyped examples. Such locutions as a big big man or Let it cool till it's thick thick are far more common, especially in the speech of women and children, than our linguistic text-books would lead one to suppose. In a class by themselves are the really enormous number of words, many of them sound-imitative or contemptuous in psychological tone, that consist of duplications with either change of the vowel or change of the initial consonant-words of the type sing-song, riff-raff, wishy-washy, harum-skarum, roly-poly. Words of this type are all but universal.

Such examples as the Russian ChudoYudo (a dragon), the Chinese ping-pang "rattling of rain on the roof," the Tibetan kyang-kyong "lazy," and the Manchu porpon parpan "blear-eyed" are curiously reminiscent, both in form and in psychology, of words nearer home. But it can hardly be said that the duplicative process is of a distinctively grammatical significance in English. We must turn to other languages for illustration. Such cases as Hottentot go-go "to look at carefully" (from go "to see"), Somali fenfen "to gnaw at on all sides" (from fen "to gnaw at"), Chinook iwi iwi "to look about carefully, to examine" (from iwi "to appear"), or Tsimshian am'am "several (are) good" (from am "good") do not depart from the natural and fundamental range of significance of the process. A more abstract function is illustrated in Ewe, in which both infinitives and verbal adjectives are formed from verbs by duplication; *e.g.*, yi "to go," yiyi "to go, act of going"; wo "to do," wowo "done"; mawomawo "not to do" (with both duplicated verb stem and duplicated negative particle).

Causative duplications are characteristic of Hottentot, *e.g.*, gamgam "to cause to tell" (from gam "to tell"). Or the process may be used to derive verbs from nouns, as in Hottentot khoe-khoe "to talk Hottentot" (from khoe-b "man, Hottentot"), or as in Kwakiutl metmat "to eat clams" (radical element *met-* "clam").

The most characteristic examples of reduplication are such as repeat only part of the radical element. It would be possible to demonstrate the existence of a vast number of formal types of such partial duplication, according to whether the process makes use of one or more of the radical consonants, preserves or weakens or alters the radical vowel, or affects the beginning, the middle, or the end of the radical element. The functions are even more exuberantly developed than with simple duplication, though the basic notion, at least in origin, is nearly always one of repetition or continuance.

Examples illustrating this fundamental function can be quoted from all parts of the globe. Initially reduplicating are, for instance, Shilh ggen "to be sleeping" (from gen "to sleep"); Ful pepeu-'do "liar" (*i.e.*, "one who always lies"), plural fefeu-'be (from fewa "to lie"); Bontoc Igorot anak "child," ananak "children"; kamu-ek "I hasten," kakamu-ek "I hasten more"; Tsimshian gyad "person," gyigyad "people"; Nass gyibayuk "to fly," gyigyibayuk "one who is flying." Psychologically comparable, but with the reduplication at the end, are Somali ur "body," plural urar; Hausa suna "name," plural sunana-ki; Washo gusu "buffalo," gususu "buffaloes"; Takelma himi-d- "to talk to," himim-d- "to be accustomed to talk to." Even more commonly than simple duplication, this partial duplication of the radical element has taken on in many languages functions that seem in no way related to the idea of increase.

The best known examples are probably the initial reduplication of our older IndoEuropean languages, which helps to form the perfect tense of many verbs (*e.g.*, Sanskrit dadarsha "I have seen," Greek leloipa "I have left," Latin tetigi "I have touched," Gothic lelot "I have let"). In Nootka reduplication of the radical element is often employed in association with certain suffixes; *e.g.*, hluch- "woman" forms hluhluch-'ituht "to dream of a woman," hluhluchk'ok "resembling a woman." Psychologically similar to the Greek and Latin examples are many Takelma cases of verbs that exhibit two forms of the stem, one employed in the present or past, the other in the future and in certain modes and verbal derivatives. The former has final reduplication, which is absent in the latter; *e.g.*, *al-yebeb-i'n* "I show (or showed) to him," al*yeb-in* "I shall show him." We come now to the subtlest of all grammatical processes, variations in accent, whether of stress or pitch. The chief difficulty in isolating accent as a functional process is that it is so often combined with alternations in vocalic quantity or quality or complicated by the presence of affixed elements that its grammatical value appears as a secondary rather than as a primary feature.

In Greek, for instance, it is characteristic of true verbal forms that they throw the accent back as far as the general accentual rules will permit, while nouns may be more freely accented. There is thus a striking accentual difference between a verbal form like eluthemen "we were released," accented on the second syllable of the word, and its participial derivative lutheis "released," accented on the last.

The presence of the characteristic verbal elements e- and -men in the first case and of the nominal -s in the second tends to obscure the inherent value of the accentual alternation. This value comes out very neatly in such English doublets as to refund and a refund, to extract and an extract, to come down and a come down, to lack luster and lack-luster eyes, in which the difference between the verb and the noun is entirely a matter of changing stress. In the Athabaskan languages there are not infrequently significant alternations of accent, as in Navaho ta-di-gis "you wash yourself" (accented on the second syllable), ta-di-gis "he washes himself" (accented on the first). Pitch accent may be as functional as stress and is perhaps more often so.

The mere fact, however, that pitch variations are phonetically essential to the language, as in Chinese (*e.g.*, feng "wind" with a level tone, feng "to serve" with a falling tone) or as in classical Greek (*e.g.*, lab-on "having taken" with a simple or high tone on the suffixed participial -on, gunaik-on "of women" with a compound or falling tone on the case suffix -on) does not necessarily constitute a functional, or perhaps we had better say grammatical, use of pitch.

In such cases the pitch is merely inherent in the radical element or affix, as any vowel or consonant might be. It is different with such Chinese alternations as chung (level) "middle" and chung (falling) "to hit the middle"; mai (rising) "to buy" and mai (falling) "to sell"; pei (falling) "back" and pei (level) "to carry on the back." Examples of this type are not exactly common in Chinese and the language cannot be said to possess at present a definite feeling for tonal differences as symbolic of the distinction between noun and verb. There are languages, however, in which such differences are of the most fundamental grammatical importance.

They are particularly common in the Soudan. In Ewe, for instance, there are formed from subo "to serve" two reduplicated forms, an infinitive subosubo "to serve," with a low tone on the first two syllables and a high one on the last two, and an abjectival subosubo "serving," in which all the syllables have a high tone. Even more striking are cases furnished by Shilluk, one of the languages of the headwaters of the Nile. The plural of the noun often differs in tone from the singular, *e.g.*, yit (high) "ear" but yit (low) "ears." In the pronoun three forms may be distinguished by tone alone; e "he" has a high tone and is subjective, -e "him" (*e.g.*, a chwol-e "he called him") has a low tone and is objective, -e "his" (*e.g.*, wod-e "his house") has a middle tone and is possessive.

From the verbal element gwed- "to write" are formed gwed-o "(he) writes" with a low tone, the passive gwet "(it was) written" with a falling tone, the imperative gwet "write!" with a rising tone, and the verbal noun gwet "writing" with a middle tone.

In aboriginal America also pitch accent is known to occur as a grammatical process. A good example of such a pitch language is Tlingit, spoken by the Indians of the southern coast of Alaska. In this language many verbs vary the tone of the radical element according to tense; hun "to sell," sin "to hide," tin "to see," and numerous other radical elements, if low-toned, refer to past time, if hightoned, to the future.

Another type of function is illustrated by the Takelma forms hel "song," with falling pitch, but hel "sing!" with a rising inflection; parallel to these forms are sel (falling) "black paint," sel (rising) "paint it!" All in all it is clear that pitch accent, like stress and vocalic or consonantal modifications, is far less infrequently employed as a grammatical process than our own habits of speech would prepare us to believe probable.

Because English is so widely spoken, it has often been referred to as a "global language", the *lingua franca* of the modern era. While English is not an official language in many countries, it is currently the language most often taught as a second language around the world. Some linguists believe that it is no longer the exclusive cultural sign of "native English speakers", but is rather a language that is absorbing aspects of cultures worldwide as it continues to grow.

It is, by international treaty, the official language for aerial and maritime communications, as well as one of the official languages of the European Union, the United Nations, and most international athletic organisations, including the International Olympic Committee. Books, magazines, and newspapers written in English are available in many countries around the world.

English is also the most commonly used language in the sciences. In 1997, the Science Citation Index reported that 95per cent of its articles were written in English, even though only half of them came from authors in English-speaking countries.

THE CHALLENGES OF "LITERATE" LANGUAGE

In today's complex world, literacy means far more than learning to read and write in order to accomplish particular discrete tasks. Instead, literacy is a form of social action where language and context co-participate in making meaning. Although much research has focused on the features of early reading and writing in school contexts, less work has been done related to the kinds of tasks that challenge students in middle school, high school, and postsecondary education. These advanced literacy contexts call for a kind of meaning-making that is also required for participation in many of the institutions of today's world.

An individual's growth and development and ability to participate in society require ever-expanding knowledge and control over meaning-making in new contexts and through new linguistic resources. Students need to use language in particular ways in order to be successful in science, history, and other subjects; to develop interpretations, construct arguments, and critique theories.

Learning to use language in ways that meet the school's expectations for advanced literacy tasks is a challenge for all students, but it is especially difficult for those who have little opportunity for exposure to and use of such language outside of school. Our schools serve students who speak different languages and dialects, who have been socialized in different ways, and who face different kinds of challenges in their daily lives.

Students whose cultural practices are similar to those of the school may be able to transfer those practices to the school setting, but students from other backgrounds may need to focus on the ways that language contributes to meaning-making as they engage in new social and cultural practices in order to succeed in achieving advanced literacy.

The functional linguistics approach that this book takes focuses on the ways that social contexts are always realized in the linguistic choices speakers and writers make in constructing texts of different types. It is the social contexts that need to remain at the forefront of our thinking about the linguistic challenges of schooling so that our approach to research and pedagogy can reveal the true expectations that the tasks of advanced schooling present to the diverse students in today's schools.

Much research on students' language development and much analysis of school-based language focus on the differences between speech and writing, describing the challenges that come with the need to deal in a written mode at school. From this perspective, "literate" texts have been described as decontextualized, explicit, and complex. These features, in this view, make this language more cognitively demanding than the language of spoken interaction.

Decontextualization, explicitness, and complexity are inadequate characterizations of the real challenges of the language through which schooling is realized, however. Such characterizations of "literate" language are motivated by the linguistic features of this language, but these terms carry values that can distract us from attending to the social contexts of language use and the ways those contexts are realized in particular grammatical and lexical choices.

School-based texts accomplish particular purposes in schooling by construing the kinds of experience and interpersonal relationships that are expected in the schooling context, which itself has particular cultural purposes.

By recognizing how different linguistic choices are functional for construing experience, presenting one's perspective, and constructing particular kinds of texts, we keep the focus on the role of language as a social force.

This perspective expands the teaching arena, enabling the teacher to be proactive in new ways in helping students learn the ways language is used to construe knowledge in different subject areas. Because all language use contributes to the construal of the social contexts in which it occurs, a functional theory of language enables us to identify the linguistic choices that realize particular kinds of contexts.

The notion of linguistic "choice" is a key feature of the analysis presented here. Rather than seeing language as a set of rules, the functional linguistic perspective sees the language system as a set of options available for construing different kinds of meanings.

Although the language as a whole offers a broad set of options, each speaker may be aware of only some part of the total set, based on that speaker's experiences. Unfamiliarity and lack of social experience with the way language is used in school, rather than the intrinsic cognitive challenges of the content or subject matter, may underlie the difficulties many students experience in schooling.

Recognizing the socially constructed nature of the language of schooling also enables us to see that it can be taught and learned. The next sections of this chapter discuss the inadequacy of thinking about the linguistic challenges of schooling in terms of the decontextualization, explicitness, and complexity of the language itself. An alternative functional linguistic perspective is then introduced to highlight the social and cultural dimensions of the linguistic challenges.

DECONTEXTUALIZATION

The view of school language as "decontextualized" has its origins in work such as Olson's (1977) distinction between text and utterance. In that influential and frequently cited article, Olson (1977) argues that "... language development is not simply a matter of progressively elaborating the oral mother tongue ...". Instead, he suggests, a whole new way of using language emerged in the western essayist tradition, leading to the development of what he calls "text"; more conventionalized and explicit than the "utterance" of oral language.

As this essayist tradition developed historically, according to Olson, the focus of the author has been to try to put the total meaning into the text; that is, to fully conventionalize meaning, minimizing dependence on the situated knowledge that we use in understanding ordinary conversation by drawing on linguistic conventions that are designed to make texts more explicit.

This enables written texts to be understood, according to Olson (1977), on their own terms, without recourse to context and speaker presuppositions.

In writing, as different from in speaking, "the meaning is in the text". Spoken language, on the other hand, appeals to shared experiences and knowledge for interpretation. Olson suggests that formal schooling is a process of teaching children to "speak a written language, " and that the transition from oral language to written text is "one of increasing explicitness, with language increasingly able to stand as an unambiguous or autonomous representation of meaning".

Olson's arguments have been extensively critiqued. Although Olson himself has somewhat modified the strong position he put forth in 1977, the views expressed in that article are still influential. The notion of "autonomous text" has influenced others to consider some uses of language "decontextualized, " with implications for school success. Catherine Snow and her colleagues, who have also been influential in shaping a view of the relationship between language, learning, and home and school experience, provide particularly clear statements of these issues in relation to pedagogical concerns.

For Snow (1983), decontextualized language is language used "without the support of conversational context". Examples of such language use include presenting monologues, doing abstract verbal reasoning, and giving metalinguistic judgements such as judging sentences as grammatical or ungrammatical, identifying ambiguity, and giving definitions.

These tasks require skills in providing a "coherent, comprehensible, informationally adequate account without signals from an interlocutor". She focuses particularly on the distanced relationship between reader and writer. Snow characterizes "decontextualized" language as explicit, distanced, and complex and highly structured. By explicit, she means that the vocabulary choices are precise and elaborated.

Distanced refers to the relationship between speaker/writer and listener/ reader. In decontextualized language, the student has to make the message clear without the help of an interlocutor, and the speaker/writer's view of the listener/ reader's perspective and participation in the text is reflected in the way reference is made to what is being talked about. The deictic this or that, for example, that refer to something that can be pointed to in a shared context, cannot be used as a resource for making meanings clear in decontextualized texts. Such texts are also complex and highly structured, with lexical and syntactic means used to show how one part of a text relates to what has been said before.

The features of decontextualized language that Snow points to are stated in linguistic terms, especially in terms of linguistic choices that need to be made for reference and linking.

In her study of how children in middle-class homes are prepared for the literacy demands of schooling, Snow (1983) shows that some caregivers use these "literate" features even in their oral discourse with children. Snow suggests that such language does not draw on the shared physical context and is not molded in response to a present interlocutor, as ordinary spoken interaction typically does and is.

The functional view taken in this book also recognizes that written language has developed over time in ways that are quite different from the ways that oral language has developed. However, the interpretation of these differences focuses on how the written ways of meaning are functional for doing the kinds of things with language that are typical of contexts like schooling. Rather than talk about such language as decontextualized and explicit, the functional focus reveals the kinds of contexts that written, school-based texts realize.

It is important to make this distinction because of the judgements that follow from characterizing the task and challenges in different ways. Characterizing texts as "autonomous" suggests that students who are able to effectively read and write school-based texts have the ability to distance themselves from the present context and deal with decontextualized knowledge.

This seems like a very advanced skill, indeed, and it is not surprising that this ability would be valued. But if, on the other hand, it is recognized that contexts are in fact evoked in the language choices made in constructing every text, then the role of social experience in preparing a student to use language in ways expected in school tasks can be explicitly acknowledged and incorporated into language development theory and pedagogy.

To call the kind of texts that students need to work with at school decontextualized suggests that these texts are somehow outside of any particular context. But school-based texts are difficult for many students precisely because they emerge from discourse contexts that require different ways of using language than students experience outside of school. Reading, writing, and speaking the kinds of texts that are valued in school calls for drawing on a different constellation of linguistic resources from what is typical or expected in everyday conversation.

Informal spoken interaction has key features such as deictic pronouns and demonstratives that reflect the context of situation in which the speakers find themselves. But written texts also reflect the contexts from which writers proceed, requiring different kinds of contextualizing features for understanding. The point is not that written language is decontextualized, but that it typically draws on different lexical and grammatical resources and genre conventions than informal spoken interaction because it generally realizes different situational contexts.

It is familiarity with the expectations of the situation and with the kinds of grammatical choices that construe particular contexts that enables a speaker/writer to produce a text that has the "written" features. Olson and Snow both suggest that decontextualized language creates autonomous texts that can be understood out of the contexts of their creation.

The research and pedagogical implications of this way of thinking about language would seem to be that students need to learn to be more explicit, distanced, and complex in their language use as their writing develops. But examination of constructs like "explicitness" and "complexity" suggests that they can be misleading in the way they lead us to think about the cognitive demands of schooling.

And characterizing any language use as decontextualized distracts us from a focus on the actual linguistic features that construe different contexts. The alternative view developed in this book is that a more appropriate and effective way to focus on language development is to help students understand the contexts that the texts of advanced literacy emerge from and how the linguistic choices of writers construe particular kinds of meanings.

Explicitness

Studies that characterize academic language as explicit typically focus on linguistic features such as the use of full noun phrases instead of pronouns, avoidance of deictic expressions that require situational context for understanding, and use of markers of organizational structure as evidence for greater explicitness. Teachers promote this type of explicitness when they push students to lexicalize referents that might otherwise be expressed as deictics, pronouns, or gestures, and to expand ellipsis, as seen in (1):

1. *K:* They were hunting for—
   T: Ok, they were hunting for—
   Ss: Wari [type of animal in the story]
   T: Hold on. Who was hunting?
   K: Three brothers.
   T: Ok, three brothers were ... hunting.

This fifth-grade teacher is unwilling to accept a summary of a story which specifies referents pronominally instead of lexically, even when all students share knowledge of this story and the characters.

Studies of child language have shown that children follow a developmental path in their ability to be explicit in these terms, and that their social and cultural experiences prepare them to do this in particular contexts and not others. Through social experiences they learn when and how to provide a context for their interlocutor that does not rely on a shared situation. Romaine's study of children's language development, for example, focusing on devices for topic specification and elaboration such as modifiers, prepositional phrases, and relative clauses, finds great variability in the extent to which children provide elaborated referents, depending on the situation.

The same children who have trouble specifying and elaborating a topic in some contexts are able to do so when they understand that the speech situation calls for such specification and elaboration. Romaine points out that all children are familiar with the syntactic constructions needed to make a text lexically explicit. How children differ is in knowing what is assumed and what must be made explicit in a particular situation. Because this is a function of the purpose and role of the text that is being created and of the degree of shared knowledge that can be assumed at a given moment, a child's tendency to be "explicit" reflects that child's familiarity with the expectations of a particular discourse situation.

Explicitness is always relative, since presuppositions and background knowledge are called on in the interpretation of all texts. Lexicalization in itself does not necessarily make a text more unambiguous. Informal spoken texts typically use exospheric referents, pronouns, and generalized conjunctions, but the meanings constructed in such interaction are usually clear to the interlocutors, even with disfluencies, false starts, and elliptical structures. The broader illocutionary force of an utterance, combined with the shared context, even make it possible for interlocutors to comprehend and move forward in a conversation when someone mis-speaks.

In any case, lexicalization is not the same thing as the clarity of meaning that is suggested by the term explicit. Nystrand and Wiemelt point out that explicit is typically used to mean that there is no doubt about possible meaning. They suggest that explicitness in these terms is valued because it is said to reflect the full and careful articulation of thought. Learning to be explicit, from this perspective, means learning to think carefully. But as they point out, formal explicitness, in the sense of lexicalization, may not imply clarity of meaning.

Whether a referent is explicit or not in academic texts depends on the presuppositions of the writer/speaker and the background knowledge of the reader/listener, just as in conversational texts, the explicitness of referents depends on shared situational context and background knowledge. Explicitness emerges from a match between the context in which a text is used and the reader's purposes, situations, and cultures.

In fact, inferencing on the basis of background assumptions plays a central role in the interpretation of all texts. Highly complex and abstract background assumptions which are not spelled out are often necessary for the interpretation of written language, especially in school contexts. Sinclair argues that it is not possible to make written language fully explicit, because contextual assumptions are always important to interpretation. If students lack the necessary background assumptions, they will fail to comprehend even the most lexically explicit texts.

As is demonstrated in later chapters, the technicality and abstraction that are functional and necessary for engaging in advanced literacy tasks in school subjects often obscure agency (who is responsible), making the texts inexplicit in order to give priority to the processes rather than participants. Explicitness, then, is achieved in context-appropriate text. It does not necessarily mean the text is unambiguous. This is why explicit may be a misleading characterization of written texts and school-based language.

No language that participates in social processes is decontextualized. To say that school-based language is decontextualized ignores the fact that the classroom is its own context with its own expectations for language use, and that this context is more familiar to children of some backgrounds than to others. The background knowledge and expectations of participants in school-based genres are situated in particular socio cultural contexts which are defined by larger class relations and other power structures of society.

There is no doubt that much of what is taught in school is different from how things are typically learned in ordinary life. For example, learning vocabulary words and their meanings before reading a passage, or in a spelling list, is quite different from learning new words incidentally in contexts where they are functional. But using the term decontextualized in reference to texts of language itself misleadingly presents some texts as being fully comprehensible in and of themselves.

Notions of explicitness and decontextualization ignore the cultural knowledge and knowledge about language use needed to make the link between text and context. All texts reflect the contexts of their creation, but not all students are familiar with the contexts that are evoked. To call language decontextualized when referents are lexicalized fails to recognize that to lexicalize known referents is also a convention that evokes a particular context. Making the linguistic choices that realize academic contexts requires experience and willingness to participate in such contexts along with knowledge of the grammatical and lexical choices that are highly valued.

Language is always used in particular cultural ways that are learned through experience. From a functional point of view, then, the language of schooling is not decontextualized, just unfamiliar to many students. It is the knowledge and experience of the listener or reader, and not the language itself that determines whether or not a particular text is contextualized. Arguing that texts are autonomous underestimates the challenges for those who do not have an insider's understanding of the conventions for the creation of academic texts.

So instead of characterizing the language of schooling as explicit and decontextualized, we need to recognize what the linguistic features are that lead to such characterizations and understand how these features are functional for making school-based texts effective in and for their contexts.

Snow and Olson both recognize the role of context and experience, although they do not highlight these aspects. Olson, for example, recognizes that student' difficulties in interpreting sentence meaning in "decontextualized" ways may indicate lack of experience in suspending prior knowledge and expectancies. Snow also recognizes that context includes historical context— that is, that previous experience contextualizes tasks for students familiar with such tasks.

The functional linguistics approach foregrounds the relationship between context and language by focusing on the ways this relationship is realized in different kinds of spoken and written texts. Students' learning and language development can be analyzed in terms of the kinds of contexts their linguistic choices realize as they engage with the spoken and written tasks of schooling.

Complexity

The written language typical of schooling is also described as more "complex" than the language of ordinary spoken interaction. Here again, however, a functional linguistic perspective can enrich and nuance our understanding of a construct like complexity. Halliday argues that speech and writing have different kinds of complexity, manifested in different but functional ways in each case in the creation of different kinds of texts.

Spoken language is complex in its introduction and elaboration of background as it is needed, in its linking of various structures into a coherent text by use of conjunctions and discourse markers, and in its use of intonation to mark information structure. In academic texts we find a different kind of complexity, with elabouration through nominal elements expanded with pre- and post modification by adjectives, prepositional phrases, and embedded clauses.

Participles, adverbial phrases, and other devices allow for expansion of clause-internal structure at the same time that infinitive clauses, those clauses, restrictive relative clauses, and other such structures allow for the embedding and integration of ideas in complex clauses. Written, school-based texts tend to be complex in their internal clause structure, while spoken interaction tends to be complex in the way clauses are chained and linkages are indicated from one part of a larger discourse to another. To call only the organization of written text "complex" privileges one kind of complexity.

Assessing students' language by calling only certain grammatical choices complex gives them value that is often interpreted cognitively in ways that are inappropriate. Some forms of complexity are part of conversational competence, too, and grammatical analysis needs to take account of these different kinds of complexity, recognizing that spoken and written modes typically call for different kinds of linguistic structuring without a bias or privileging of one mode by calling it more complex. A functional linguistic analysis shows, for example, that a construct like subordination, frequently used as a measure of language complexity in educational and linguistic research, can actually serve different functional roles and introduce different kinds of complexity into texts.

Relative clauses, complement clauses, and adverbial clauses introduced by subordinators such as because, although, if, before, since, and others are typically considered subordinate clauses, but some "subordinate" clauses play non-subordinating roles as broader discourse links. It has also been shown that subordinate clauses do not necessarily co-occur with other linguistic elements associated with formal, literate style.

Not all subordinate clauses are equally "complex," and a functional approach can analyze how the different types of clauses called "subordinate" contribute to text structure and complexity in different ways. Analysis of subordination is often used in studies of spoken and written discourse to draw conclusions about the linguistic skills of a speaker, or about the complexity of the discourse which is analyzed.

Beaman, for example, uses subordination as an index of complexity in speech and writing, and Kalmar uses the development of subordination as an indication of a higher evolutionary level of a language. In several studies during the 1960s and later, researchers showed a correlation of use of subordinate structures with school success.

Loban states the underlying assumption of this approach when he says "both logical analysis and previous studies of language designate subordination as a more mature and difficult form of language expression than simple parallel statements connected by and or but".

The equation of subordination with complexity in measurement of language performance, and the further equation of linguistic complexity and cognitive skill, suggests that an accurate definition and analysis of complexity is an important issue for both educational and linguistic research. Subordination is considered a complex use of language because it represents the embedding of one clause within another in a hierarchical relationship.

Romaine points out that "children's language development has often been assessed in terms of measures which rely on the assumption that having strategies for subordinating and embedding sentences within each other is indicative of greater cognitive skill and verbal ability".

She questions this assumption, as her research shows that certain constructions may be acquired and used only in certain contexts, such as school, and suggests that studies of syntactic structure must focus on the pragmatic and semantic, as well as the syntactic, aspects of these constructions. Her view is that all children have competence in using complex syntax, but that situationally such use may be differentially displayed, due to different experiences in use of language and expectations about the context in which the language is elicited.

Studies that measure language complexity have an impact not only on research but also on the practice of education. Loban, for example, makes curricular recommendations, stressing the importance of oral language as a basis for literacy, and arguing that students need to develop "syntactic complexity" in speech before writing.

Such recommendations are of course crucially dependent on clear definitions of syntactic complexity, and on definition of what counts as complex in speech and writing. Both spoken and written language can be shown to be complex, depending on the variables that are in focus for the analyst. This suggests that the demands of school-based texts are better framed in linguistic terms rather than in the cognitive terms that a word like complexity suggests.

Cognitive Demand

When terms such as decontextualized, explicit, and complex are used to characterize language, these terms are often interpreted cognitively. The characterization of academic language as more cognitively demanding than ordinary conversational interaction is articulated by Cummins (1984), who posits two dimensions on which language tasks can be evaluated: according to the amount of contextual information available to make the language comprehensible, and according to the amount of cognitive involvement needed to do the task.

Cummins defines cognitive demand as the degree to which "linguistic tools have become largely automatized (mastered) and thus require little active cognitive involvement for appropriate performance". He suggests that "cognitive involvement can be conceptualized in terms of the amount of information that must be processed simultaneously or in close succession by the individual in order to carry out the activity".

Others have used the notion of cognitive demand to categorize the level of difficulty presented by teachers' questions, suggesting that "thinking skills" can be taught by asking students questions that elicit "higher order" thinking. But it is important to keep in mind that the degree to which a task is cognitively demanding depends on the particular context and on students' prior familiarity and experience with the topic and task. Categorizing teachers' questions as being more or less cognitively demanding in terms of the responses they would seem to elicit from students, for example, obscures important differences in how questions are asked and answered that can be determined only by looking at the way the question/answer sequence unfolds during classroom discourse.

The level of cognitive demand of a particular question depends on what the teacher's goals are, what the students have already learned, and the point in the lesson at which the question is asked. A determination of the cognitive level of teacher questions needs to be made by analyzing the interaction which results, not just the form of the elicitation.

Text (2) is an example of this from a sixth-grade science lesson on mealworms. The teacher is asking students questions about what they have learned:

2. *Teacher:* Do they have ears?
   Student: No.
   Teacher: How do you know? How do you know whether they have (any of those) or whether they do not. Karen?

Karen: Well, I know that they have eyes 'cause it was on the chart. And I knew that they didn't have noses 'cause I looked it up, but I don't know if they have ears or not.

While the teacher's question, How do you know? would seem to call for some reasoning on the part of the student, in this case the response only reports where the student found the factual information. So rather than presenting "higher cognitive demand, " this question, when analyzed retrospectively to account for the student's response, is seen to actually involve little cognitive demand at all.

The level of cognitive difficulty is negotiated at the level of the interactive task in which the teacher and student(s) are engaged, rather than being determined by the linguistic form of the question itself. As Mehan said, "the meaning of an act initiated by the teacher ... is prospective. Its actual meaning is realized retrospectively, when the act performed by the student is evaluated by the teacher".

Just as with the other notions discussed in this chapter, the notion of language as inherently cognitively demanding is problematic. The cognitive demand of any particular activity or text is a product of the students' prior experience (including experience with language). Therefore, out of context, no particular task can be called cognitively demanding.

Language is more cognitively demanding when it is less familiar and automatic, so school-based language use may typically be more cognitively demanding than conversational interaction for the learner who has used English primarily in informal situations. Context-dependence and cognitive demand may be useful constructs for language teachers to consider in setting appropriate tasks for learners, since providing context for understanding and monitoring the level of information processing required of students should enhance their learning opportunities. But cognitive demand must be seen as residing in the relationship between task and learner rather than in the task or text itself.

5

Concept of Grammar Method

BASIC GRAMMAR

The children have usually acquired a measure of English from their caregivers and have consequently generated grammar though they don't know the names for the grammar rules. The adult beginners will already have grammar from their native language and will need to translate that knowledge to English. However, no matter where the beginner starts, the body of knowledge remains the same.

PARTS OF SPEECH

- Beginners should learn that every word they are using has a purpose and is labeled appropriately as a part of speech. Children should learn about nouns, pronouns, verbs, adjectives, adverbs, prepositions, conjunctions and interjections. These will give each part of the sentence a role to play and, as more is learned, it will fit into this schema.

  Once the beginners have mastered parts of speech, they should learn concepts such as syntax and that every language fits together in a certain way. From the lessons on vocabulary students can be introduced to the parts of a sentence and should be shown how words go together in phrases and clauses. Students can learn how to create simple sentences with just one verb and, once mastering this, they can progress onto complex and compound sentences with more clauses and phrases. This should be followed by exercises in which these are practiced and learned so that the concepts become part of the students' mental schema.

VERB TENSES

- People who are new to a language often mix up their tense agreements, and it is no different with English beginners. Students should be taught that the verbs they learn to recognize have many aspects that make up good grammar. For instance, all verbs have four principal parts: a base form, a present participle, a simple past form and a past participle. There are regular and irregular verbs, and each type forms tenses in different ways.

Students can then be taught about verb tenses explicitly with present, past and future tenses. After the students have mastered grammar, they can be taught about the perfect tenses, but beginners do not need this yet.

VOICE AND MOOD

- In English grammar the verbs are the most difficult to learn, as they are the moving or active force behind the language. It is important, therefore, that learners be taught about active (performing the action) and passive (action performed) voice. Verbs are also used to express mood and are found in three moods: indicative (making a statement), imperative (giving an order) and subjunctive (state of being). The subject of English grammar is huge, and learners can proceed as far as they want. Once they have mastered the use of verbs and sentence formation, vocabulary can be added as they encounter it, which will always add to their knowledge of grammar.

GRAMMAR PLANS

- Step 1:
  Set goals for your lesson. Decide what element of grammar the lesson will cover and set several objectives for your students to accomplish during the lesson. Consider what your students already know about grammar when writing your goals and objectives.
- Step 2:
  Write an introduction for the grammar lesson. Your introduction must show your ESL students why the grammar skills you are teaching are important for them to master. Include examples of the specific grammar element being used correctly.
- Step 3:
  Begin your lesson plan by including a few minutes when you will model the correct use of the grammar skill you will be teaching. Give several written and spoken examples for your students.
- Step 4:
  Create activities your students can complete to learn the grammar skill you are teaching. Try to use activities that will work with a variety of learning styles.
- Step 5:
  Include time for your students to practice the grammar skill you will

be teaching. Divide them into pairs to practice using the skill verbally. Let them practice the skill in writing, too.

- Step 6:
  Conclude your lesson plan with a way to measure your students' success. Whether you choose to give them a written or oral test or to have them demonstrate correct use of the grammar skill, you must be able to decide if they have learned the desired skill.

GRAMMAR QUESTIONS

Circle the best answer.

1. Many grammatical errors can be avoided – and flow improved – by reading your written work aloud and listening for the sound. This is called
   a. busy work;
   b. writing by ear;
   c. writing by feel;
   d. peer editing.
2. Shorter sentences are a good idea for beginning writers because they are
   a. in shorter paragraphs;
   b. fragments;
   c. what Hemingway wrote;
   d. easier to control.
3. Words at the beginning of sentences in a piece of writing should be
   a. varied;
   b. the same;
   c. nouns;
   d. verbs.
4. A phrase is a group of related words that
   a. function as a single part of speech;
   b. are nouns;
   c. has both a subject and predicate;
   d. has both an adjective and adverb.
5. A clause is a group of related words that
   a. function as a single part of speech;
   b. are verbs;
   c. has both a subject and predicate;
   d. has both a preposition and interjection.
6. Commas are used in all of these instances EXCEPT
   a. to separate items in a series;
   b. to separate clauses joined by a conjunction;
   c. to separate prepositional phrases;

d. to separate parenthetical phrases in a sentence.

7. The flow of writing can be improved by
   a. combining sentences;
   b. writing run-on sentences;
   c. eliminating unnecessary words;
   d. both a and c.
8. Paragraphs are connected by ________________
   a. declarative sentences;
   b. transitions;
   c. conjunctions;
   d. antecedents.
9. Strong writing will include all of these EXCEPT
   a. vivid verbs;
   b. precise descriptions;
   c. many adjectives in each sentence;
   d. a narrative that flows smoothly.
10. Pronouns must have ________________, which are the nouns they refer to.
    a. antecedents;
    b. clauses;
    c. adjectives;
    d. pre-nouns.
11. Attribution is necessary to show
    a. possession or ownership;
    b. who is speaking in dialogue;
    c. who is the subject of the sentence;
    d. the setting of the story.
12. The kinds of sentences include all of these EXCEPT
    a. declarative;
    b. interrogative;
    c. imperative;
    d. mandatory.
13. The subject is the part of a sentence
    a. that shows action;
    b. about which something is said;
    c. shows a relationship between words;
    d. is a group of related words that have a theme.
14. The predicate is the part of the sentence
    a. about which something is said;
    b. which ends it;
    c. that shows action or says something about the subject;
    d. that modifies a verb.

15. (1) *"I will always remember my first visit to Portland."*
    (2) *"My first visit to Portland will always be memorable to me."*
    a. 2 is better because you should avoid starting sentences with "I";
    b. 1 is better because it uses the active voice and is therefore more vigorous;
    c. 2 is better because the passive voice is more creative;
    d. either sentence is fine.
16. The topic sentence
    a. tells readers what the paragraph is about;
    b. provides supporting details;
    c. connects one paragraph to another;
    d. presents a picture of a person, place or thing.
17. Types of paragraphs include all of these EXCEPT
    a. expository;
    b. descriptive;
    c. persuasive;
    d. classified.
18. Writing should be
    a. ambiguous;
    b. clear;
    c. heavily modified;
    d. clichéd.
19. A closing sentence in a paragraph
    a. always ends the essay;
    b. can link to the next paragraph;
    c. can review the subject of the sentence;
    d. both b & c.
20. A sentence with one independent clause and no dependent clauses is
    a. simple;
    b. compound;
    c. complex;
    d. compound-complex.
21. Dialogue is
    a. characters talking in a story;
    b. the same as narrative;
    c. sentence fragments;
    d. complex attribution.
22. An apostrophe is used for all these reasons EXCEPT
    a. to form some plurals;
    b. to show possession;
    c. to form contractions;
    d. to indicate dialogue.

23. A complex sentence will have
    a. one independent clause only;
    b. two independent clauses.
    c. two simple phrases;
    d. one independent clause and one or more dependent clauses.
24. An expository paragraph will primarily
    a. persuade;
    b. tell a story;
    c. inform;
    d. describe.

Part II. Matching.

Match the term at left with its definition.

1.	Noun	a.	Often follows an interjection; shows strong feelings
2.	Question mark	b.	Indicates an explanation follows; introduces lists, etc.
3.	Verb	c.	Used to emphasize a point – can also set off explanations
4.	Comma	d.	Connects related ideas in a sentence; very useful
5.	Preposition	e.	Part of speech that shows surprise or strong feeling
6.	Semicolon	f.	Used in place of a noun
7.	Conjunction	g.	Indicates dialogue; word-for-word; emphasis
8.	Adverb	h.	Modifies a noun or pronoun
9.	Exclamation Point	i.	A word that shows action or being
10.	Adjective	j.	A person, place, thing or idea
11.	Pronoun	k.	Shows a relationship between words in a sentence
12.	Period	m.	Used following an inquiry
13.	Ellipsis	n.	Used to show possession or missing letters in contractions
14.	Interjection	o.	Indicates a pause or missing words
15.	Colon	p.	Separates clauses, items in a series – a pause
16.	Quotation Marks	r.	Placed at the end of a sentence
17.	Apostrophes.	s.	Modifies a verb, adjective or an adverb
18.	Dash	t.	Part of speech that connects words, sentences, phrases, etc.

Part III. Comma usage.

Indicate the reason commas are used:

A. To separate the elements in a series.
B. To connect two independent clauses joined by a conjunction.
C. To set off introductory elements.
D. To set off parenthetical elements.

1. Once the rain washed the air clean, we could smell the piney woods.

2. She threw the rocks hard, fast, accurately and with delight.
3. He walked the transit centre, and decided to board the next bus and see where he ended up.
4. Rossellini Bridge, which spans Lake Washington, is the longest floating bridge in the world.
5. After jumping out of the plane, Alex spread his arms and tried to enjoy the free fall.
6. The cat was grumpy, lazy, demanding, gluttonous and hairy.
7. Paul Newman, the late actor, was also a race car driver and philanthropist.
8. On the way to Mount St. Helen's, they stopped and purchased some binoculars.
9. She road her bicycle to work, but swimming was her favourite form of exercise.
10. The Redwoods, majestically soaring into the clouds, were the highlight of the vacation.

Part IV. Punctuation.

Punctuate the following passage. You will use periods, commas, question marks, semicolons, exclamation points, quotation marks, dashes and apostrophes.

Note: "*Expotition*" is intentionally misspelled by author A.A. Milne; he was having fun, showing how youngsters might mistakenly spell *Expedition* — a journey of discovery.

Hint: Many lines are dialogue and thus include quotation marks.

Each line is worth 1 point; you will get 0 points, ½ point or 1 point per line.

Oh Piglet said Pooh excitedly we re going on an Expotition all of us with things to eat To discover something

To discover what asked Piglet anxiously

Oh just something

Nothing fierce

Christopher Robin didn t say anything about fierce He just said it had an x

It isn t their necks I mind said Piglet earnestly It s their teeth But if Christopher Robin is coming I don t mind anything

I didn t ask them explained Rabbit carelessly They just came They always do They can march at the end after Eeyore

What I say said Eeyore is that it s unsettling I didn t want to come on this what Pooh said I only came to oblige But here I am and if I am the end of the Expo what we re talking about then let me be the end But if every time I want to sit down for a little rest I have to brush away half a dozen of Rabbit s smaller friends and relations first then this isn t an Expo whatever it is at all it s simply a Confused Noise That s what I say

TEACHING ADVANCE GRAMMAR

Your advanced ESL class can hone their skills on conversation, popular media, literature, and a host of other activities. There will still be weak areas of grammar to address and watch for. With the proper guidance from you, the instructor, a higher confidence level and greater command of the English language can be achieved by every student in the class.

Test the students. At this level there will be a wide range of ability, and weak areas will show up in different places for individual students. You will need to test both their oral and written communication levels to see where you need to focus your efforts at the advanced level of grammar instruction.

Base grammar lessons around weak areas. Pronouns, possessives, verb forms, problem words, idiomatic expressions and a host of other issues can all be addressed in the context of listening and responding to excerpts from current news and popular culture.

Have the students keep a notebook. They should be writing down the unfamiliar words they come across in their reading, and the words they have to look up in order to express a thought. Make sure they are studying and memorizing these.

Make notes while they're speaking. You don't want to interrupt the students, but jot down the areas that they're getting right, along with what they're missing. Praise and correct them when they are done speaking. Have them write down the corrected sentences and practice them. Give additional practice on the concepts if necessary.

Be friendly and encouraging. Students won't learn if they're afraid to make mistakes. Keep reminding them that the more mistakes they make, the faster they'll master the English language. Always remind them of what great progress they're making, especially when they get something right that they've missed in the past.

GOOD EXPLANATION

be correct

It is surprising how many incorrect explanations you find in TEFL books. A good example is the distinction usually made between some and any, which goes something like:

- Use some+plural countable/uncountable noun in affirmative sentences.
- Use any+plural countable/uncountable noun in negative sentences and questions.
- Higher level books may go on to add that you use some in questions if you expect an affirmative answer, or in invitations, or various other situations. Not only does this 'rule' score low on generality, it still fails to explain:

Take any one you want.
Any of the assistants at the desk will be able to help you.
I didn't like some of his books.

Compounds (somebody, somewhere etc) also create problems for this explanation, as many of them have to be explained separately.

An explanation based on the difference in meaning between some and any might eliminate many of these problems. Such an explanation might be along the lines of:

- any+noun refers to an indeterminate subset of the collection of nouns referred to.
- some+noun refers to a particular subset of the collection of nouns referred to.

This explanation is not particularly clear here, but can be made so by being presented in an adequate context. It does have the advantage of being a reasonable approximation to what the difference between some and any actually is.

The advantage of the traditional explanation is that it is easy to teach, which can be important for lower level classes, multi-lingual classes, and classes given by inexperienced teachers. However, ease of teaching should not be a prime concern - it is the teachers job to get their head around such problems. Ease of learning is more of an issue, but I don't think this is promoted by giving explanations which students will soon see being contradicted. At lower levels, if you must give an incorrect explanation, a lot of problems will be saved if you make the limitations of your explanation clear. In the above example, you might give the first explanation as a 'rule of thumb', emphasizing that, although it provides a guide for most situations, it is not to be considered a hard and fast rule.

be consistent

Fairly obvious this. An explanation shouldn't contradict itself, or any other explanations the student might have been given. Of course, if the student has previously been given an inadequate explanation (such as some/any referred to above) then you are going to have to contradict what they have learnt.

be simple

The explanation should be as simple as possible, but no simpler. Never over-simplify - again, some/any is a good example of this. The problem is that students soon come across examples that contradict what you have taught them. Obviously, the explanation also has to be comprehensible, which may provide problems for lower levels or younger learners. If you can't come up with a suitably comprehensible explanation, maybe the structure in question is not suitable for the level you are teaching.

have no exceptions

An explanation with exceptions is going to create problems as soon as a student comes across one of them, and then says 'but you told us...', which leaves you looking pretty silly. You should explain how apparent exceptions fit in with the rule you are teaching, or, if there are dealing exceptions to the rule you are teaching, you should point them out to students. For example, you might explain that the present perfect is *never* used with adverbs of finished time, but you should also point out that 'just' is *not* an adverb of finished time (something that has never seemed immediately obvious to me!)

be complete

Each of the following explanations for the present perfect is more 'complete' than the one preceding it:

The present perfect is used to describe experiences.

The present perfect is used with adverbs of unfinished time.

The present perfect is used for actions which can still happen, or can happen again.

How well do they explain:

I've been to Paris.

I had cornflakes for breakfast today.

The teacher hasn't arrived yet.

I've done my homework.

The first three examples can be explained by the third explanation given above; the first two explantions fall down at the second an third examples.

The third explanation can cover all three examples and so can be considered complete in the sense that it explains all similar situations without any need for 'speacial pleading'.

The fourth example, however, cannot be explained by any of the above explanations, and requires treatment as a separate situation or 'use' of the present perfect. See my page on the present perfect for a full analysis of situations where the present perfect is used.

be exhaustive

At lower levels it's fairly normal to leave out some of the more subtle details; at advanced levels this is not really an option as if you don't give the students the information you can't assume anyone else will. For example:

It's years since I went to Scotland.

It's years since I've been to Scotland.

The first form would be included in most explanations (since + point in time), the second requires a bit more effort. If you compare the following examples, however:

It's years since I left school.

INCORRECT *It's years since I've left school.*

it becomes clear that the present perfect can be used *after* since only if the action can still happen - I can go to Scotland again, but I can't leave school again. This is the kind of explanation which, despite being simple, is omitted by most TEFL books.

Another example:

INCORRECT? The car was too fast for me to follow it.

The car went too fast for me to follow it.

Why can't 'it' be included in the first? Because here *fast* is an adjective and complement of the subject. In the second sentence *fast* is an adverb, and as it doesn't describe the subject we need to include an object for 'follow'. This is another explanation which is conspicuous by its absence from most TEFL books.

A slightly differentproblem is that with some structures, such as inversions, there are a *lot* of different cases to cover - it's difficult to be completely exhaustive.

be general

The explanation should be at the most general level possible. For example, we often teach that 'will' is not used in if-clauses.

However, this is just a consequence of the fact that we don't use 'will' (for future reference) in *subordinate* clauses. By teaching the latter, possibly in the context of a lesson on conditionals, you are giving the student information which is much more widely applicable. The end result is that the student has a lot less to learn. You also avoid giving the (false) impression that English is a language that is full of exceptions and ad hoc rules.

be productive

No matter how good an explanation is, it's not much use if it leaves the student asking 'why would I want to say that?' The passive is a good example; it's fairly easy to explain the syntax, but unless you give examples of where it is usually used, students aren't likely to use it very much.

In general, explanations along the lines of 'this structure emphasises...' are not very useful for helping students to decide when to use a structure.

'The present perfect continuous emphasises the activity...' is a typical example. How does this help us to choose between:

I've chopped the onions.

I've been chopping onions.

Not very much. When to use one form or the other becomes much clearer if you explain that each sentence refers to a differnet *type* of result, so:

I've chopped the onions. (They're ready to fry.)

I've been chopping onions. (That's why I'm crying.)

With this information, students can choose the form to use depending on the message thay actually want to get across.

enable discrimination

This is similar to (the same as?) the previous point. The explanation should enable students to discriminate between when to use one structure and when to use another.

For example, you should teach students the *difference* between If only and I wish. If you don't, how can they choose which to use in a given situation? The obvious problem here is that it can be very difficult to explain subtle differences between forms - assuming you can work out the difference.
Examples:

I wish you hadn't done that.
If only you hadn't done that.

The first sentence regrets the effect your action had on the speaker, the second expresses regret for the effect it had in general.

The second, unlike the first, can be used to express sympathy.

I wish I had studied harder.
If only I had studied harder.

In the second sentence here the negative effects of my not studying are being felt now or 'immediately'. The first sentence might be referring to a negative effect at some time in the past.

I wish he didn't go on so much.
I wish he wouldn't go on so much.

The first sentence expresses regret about a fact that the speaker doesn't like. In the second the speaker also shows that he would like the situation to change. A full understanding of how we use will and would are required to analyse the second sentence, although it usually include in sections on wish/If only.

be 'memorizable'

A good explanation should be easy for students to remember. This is not likely to be the case for long and rambling explanations, or for those that require students remember lots of arbitrary information, such as the explanation for adjective order found in most books - can you remember the order?

TRANSLATION METHOD OF GRAMMAR

The (Grammar Translation Method) is a cross lingual technique. It is used in language learning. Grammar is given more importance in this method. Learners understand the grammar rules better. The exercises in this method put the learner into an active problem-solving situation. In the schools, the teachers often follow the traditional method of translation technique. It is an easy way to explain things. Great Indian leaders is the past had attained remarkable progress in this method. Reading and writing are the major focus.

Vocabulary selection is based solely on the text used. The words are introduced through bilingual word lists dictionary and memorization. The grammar rules are presented. A list of vocabulary items is presented with their translation meanings. Translation exercises are prescribed. Grammar is taught inductively. Mother tongue is the medium of instruction.

STEPS INVOLVED IN GRAMMAR TRANSLATION METHOD

1. The teacher asks the students to read few lines from the text. He asks them to translate into L1 and he helps them with new words.
2. The teacher answers all their questions in L1
3. The students write the answers for the questions
4. The answers are checked by them. Mistakes are corrected by the teacher. He speaks in L1
5. The students are asked to translate the words listed into their L1. The teacher helps them in synonyms, Antonyms and Meanings for these words.
6. The teacher works the grammar exercises and he presents grammar rules. The students do the exercises and translate the sentences into L1.
7. The students translate the lines from the text into L1. They memorize the read out listed words and frame sentences for the vocabulary items.
8. Students write a composition based on the passage.

DEMERITS

This GTM was in use for 100 years from 1840 to 1940. It had its own drawnbacks.

1. It failed to produce oral fluency in English.
2. Students found the method boring as they had to memorize words and rules.
3. It does not develop confidence among the learners.
4. The use of L1 is more predominantin the class.
5. No link between the text words and real life situations.
6. The learner was unable to use English in day to day Communication
7. This method focused only in reading and writing. Little attention is paid to speaking.

THE DIRECT METHOD

The salient features of the Direct Method are

1. The use of everyday vocabulary and structures is the object of language teaching.
2. The learner is expected to use the language to the outside situations.
3. Oral skills are developed in this method. (Question-answer session, Interaction exercises and intensive drills). Speech habits are developed by initiation drill.
4. Grammar is taught inductively
5. It focuses on the second language learning in a natural way.

6. Concrete meanings are taught through situational approach. The meaning of a word is not given in L1 and L2.
7. Abstract meanings are taught through association of ideas.
8. Both oral and listening skills are taught.
9. Translation method is avoided.
10. Good pronunciation is aimed at.
11. Writing skill is secondary.

The Direct Method was introduced in France and Germany. In the U.S., it is known as Berlitz Method. The main aim of this method is to help the students to speak the target language (L2) fluently and correctly.

In this method, a short text is presented and difficult words are explained in L2 to the learners. The understanding is tested by questioning and the students learn grammar rules on their own. Question-answer sessions, interaction exercises, intensive classroom drills, dictation, free composition, pronunciation are done in the classroom to develop and strengthen L2.

DEMERITS

- Its procedures and techniques were difficult.
- Teachers had difficulty in explaining the difficult words.
- Fluency in L2 is necessary.
- No selection and grading of vocabulary and structures.
- It was a success in private language schools but not in public secondary schools.
- There was less time and less opportunity available in the classroom.

THE BILINGUAL METHOD

Dr.C.J.Dadson developed the Bilingual method. This method needs L1 and L2. The approach begins from Bilingual and becomes monolingual at the end. The teacher uses both mother tongue (L1) and the target language (L2) in the classroom. This may be considered as a combination of the Direct Method and the Grammar Translation Method.

The principles followed in this method are:

- Any Foreign Language or Second language can be learned with the help of L1.
- Mother tongue is not used as Translation.
- Teacher only uses L1 in the class room
- Students are not allowed to use their mother tongue.
- Sentence is the unit of teaching
- L1 is used by the teacher to achieve his communication or explanation.
- Teacher gives meanings in L1 for meaningful parts or sentences.
- When the students achieve sufficient communicative proficiency, L1 is withdrawn by the teacher.

PROCEDURE/STEPS IN TEACHING

1. First the teacher reads out a dialogue to the class. The students listen to the teacher with their books closed.
2. The students repeat the lines with the teacher with their books opened in the second reading.
3. The teacher gives sentence wise or meaningful parts wise L1 equivalents (meanings)
4. The teacher says each sentence of the dialogue twice with L1 version (meanings)

DEMERITS

- The focus is on the grammatical structures not on the day-to-day conversation
- The teacher must be proficient (fluent) in L1 and L2.
- It does not follow any set theory
- Students become dependent on their mother tongue
- The methods and procedures are not different

S.O.S (The Structural-Oral-Situational Approach)

The SOS approach was officially accepted by the Madras Presidency in 1950. Till 1990, the SOS has been practiced in schools in South India. It is a communication of certain aspect of the Direct Method, oral and Audio Lingualism.

The basic importance features of this approach are:

1. Learning a language is not only learning its words but also the syntax
2. Vocabulary is presented through grades.
3. The four skills of (LSRW) Listening, Speaking, Reading and Writing are presented in order.
4. Sentence patterns exist and can form the basis of a language course.
5. Class room teaching and learning are made enjoyable.
6. Concrete linguistic items are taught through Demonstration
7. Abstract ideas are taught through association.
8. It helps to develop learners competence in the use of structure in L2.

TEACHING OF ADJECTIVES

Example: Practical Application: Use of small + so + such + Noun/s

Teacher:

1. The books are small and thin.
2. The books are so small that I can put three of them in my pocket.
3. These are such small books that I can put three of them in my pocket.

Similar sentences are presented by the teacher.

DEMERITS

1. The situations are not real-life situation.
2. The teacher had to carry a lot of TLM's
3. Explanation of abstract ideas is very difficult
4. It is viable only in the elementary level
5. The approach has been found inadequate and ineffective.

LATER TRENDS

Communicative Language Teaching (CLT)

CLT is a functional approach to language learning. In 1972, this language course was proposed in Europe. The main aim is to develop the communicative competency of the learner. His need of understanding and expressing in the L2 is the main focus of this method.

OBJECTIVES OF CLT:

1. To produce effective communicative competency in learners.
2. The focus is on meanings and functions of the language.
3. More importance on the learner and his learning.
4. Language is acquired in CLT.
5. The teacher is a facilitator in language acquisitions.
6. Involve the learner in the learning process thro' problem solving, tasks, participation and interaction.
7. All the four LSRW skills are equally treated.

It is an eclectic approach. CLT involves many classroom activities like group work, pair work, language games, role play, question-answer sessions. It is not confined to any set of text books. The learners are mostly introduced task based and problem solving situations.

GRAMMAR-TRANSLATION APPROACH

This approach was historically used in teaching Greek and Latin. The approach was generalized to teaching modern languages.

Classes are taught in the students' mother tongue, with little active use of the target language. Vocabulary is taught in the form of isolated word lists. Elaborate explanations of grammar are always provided. Grammar instruction provides the rules for putting words together; instruction often focuses on the form and inflection of words. Reading of difficult texts is begun early in the course of study. Little attention is paid to the content of texts, which are treated as exercises in grammatical analysis. Often the only drills are exercises in translating disconnected sentences from the target language into the mother tongue, and vice versa. Little or no attention is given to pronunciation.

COMPONENTS OF GRAMMAR AND SYNTAX

- The principle elements of the sentence
  - Subject
  - Verbs and verb phrases
  - Direct and indirect object(s)
  - Complements with verbs that express feeling, appearing, being and seeming
  - Modifiers
  - Clauses
  - Phrases
- Parts of speech and their functions within sentences
  - Nouns and nominals (infinitives, gerunds, etc.)
  - Articles
  - Verbs
  - Pronouns
  - Adjectives
  - Adverbs
  - Prepositions
  - Conjunctions
  - Interjections
- Types of sentences and their syntax
  - Simple
  - Compound
  - Complex
  - Basic and variations on basic sentence patterns
  - Sentence structure: Complete, incomplete, run-on, coordination of verb tenses
- Verb Usage
  - Agreement
  - Tense
  - Mood
  - Active or passive voice
  - Sequence and consistency of tenses
  - Modals
  - Phrasal verbs
- Word usage or lexicon
  - Idiomatic constructions
  - Formulaic expressions
  - Use of phrases within sentences

Steps

- Motivate the teaching of structures by showing how they are needed in real-life communication.

- State the objective of the lesson.
- Review the familiar items, *e.g.* calendar, time, name of objects, auxiliary verbs in the target language that will be needed to introduce, explain, or practice the new item.
- Use the new structure (adjective of colour, for example) in a brief utterance in which all the other words are known to the students.
- Model the utterance several times.
- Engage in full class, half-class, group and individual repetition of the utterance.
- Give several additional sentences in which the structure is used. Class and groups will repeat with you.
- Write two of the sentences on the board. Underline the new structure and (where relevant) use curved arrows or diagrams to illustrate the relationship of the structure to other words and/or parts of the sentence.
- Point to the underlined structure as you ask questions that will guide students to discover the sounds, the written form, the position in the sentence and the grammatical function of the new structure. ("What does it tell us?")
- Help students (age 11 or older) to verbalize the important features of the structure. Use charts and other aids to relate to other familiar structures such as verb tenses.
- Engage the students in varied guided oral practice.
- Require students to consciously select the new grammatical item from contrasting one learned in the past.
- Have the students use the structure with communi-cative expressions and familiar or new notions.
- Where feasible, do a translation exercise (provided this will not promote interference from L1).

SENTENCE TRANSFORMATION: FROM BASIC TO COMPLEX SENTENCES

- Take a basic sentence:
  Juan lost his book.
- Expand on it:
  Juan lost his science book.
- Expand again with additional information:
  Juan lost his science book at the playground.
- Combine two sentences:
  Juan lost his science book. He was playing on the swings.
  Juan lost his science book while playing on the swings.
  Juan lost his science book while playing on the swings at the playground.

- Make substitutions:
  Juan lost his science homework...
  Juan lost his math book...etc.
- Transform a sentence to elaborate or link ideas:
  Juan lost his math book. Did Juan lose his science book, too?
- Add information and construct a short narrative around the sentences students have created:
  Juan was playing on the swings at the playground when he lost his math book. Juan also lost his science homework because it was in his math book.

Sentence Transformation

Focusing on Specific Points of Grammar
Subject pronouns
I, you, he, she, we, they
Forms of verb to be
_____ are running down the hill.
_____ is going to school.
_____ was at the school play.
_____ were not at the school play.
Changes in verb tense
Bill is sitting down. Bill will sit down.
Mary walks too fast. Mary walked too fast.
"When" clauses
Mr. Black will sit down. Mr. Black will take off his coat.
When Mr. Black sits down, he will take off his coat.
The girls will arrive at school. The bell will be ringing.
When the girls arrive at school, the bell will be ringing.
Relative Clauses
The book is on the desk. The book is red.
The book that is on the desk is red.
The girl is in the kitchen. The girl is my sister.
The girl who is in the kitchen is my sister.
Negatives
He likes to go for a walk after dinner.
He doesn't like to go for a walk after dinner.
Mary likes to go for a walk after dinner.
She isn't thinking about her homework.
Interrogatives ((Is/Are)
John is running away from the wolf.
Is John running away from the wolf?
Interrogatives (Do/Does)

We walk to the market every afternoon.
Do we walk to the market every afternoon?
Do you walk to the market every afternoon?
Interrogatives (Modals-Can)
(Can) My brother can ride his bike to school.
Can my brother ride his bike to school?
What can your brother do on his bike?

SENTENCE RECOMBINATION

Sentence recombination is an effective activity for teaching sentence structure, paragraph structure, punctuation, transition and coherence, and parts of speech. Students must also use critical thinking skills to cluster and organize ideas and concepts.

Sentence recombination exercises are thematic and can be easily constructed in advance by the teacher or as a group activity with the students. Here is an example.

Combine these sentences into a passage by using compound subjects, compound predicates and other compound sentence elements. In rewriting, be sure to include introduction and transition sentences so the passage flows smoothly.

- People all over the world build houses.
- People all over the world like their homes.
- Houses are built in many shapes.
- Houses are built in many sizes.
- Houses are built of grass.
- Houses are built of palm leaves.
- Houses are built of wood.
- Houses are built of steel.
- Houses are built of stone.
- Houses are built of adobe.
- Houses are built of plaster.
- Houses are built of concrete.
- Houses are built of other materials.
- The construction may be simple.
- The construction may be complex.
- Construction must be adapted to the climate.
- Construction must be adapted to the materials available.
- Construction must be adapted to the skills of the workers.

There are many variations on the paragraph or composition that students can create in this exercise.

Evaluate the product based on linguistic and conceptual complexity and coherence.

DIRECT APPROACH OF GRAMMAR

This approach was developed initially as a reaction to the grammar-translation approach in an attempt to integrate more use of the target language in instruction.

Lessons begin with a dialogue using a modern conversational style in the target language. Material is first presented orally with actions or pictures. The mother tongue is NEVER, NEVER used. There is no translation. The preferred type of exercise is a series of questions in the target language based on the dialogue or an anecdotal narrative. Questions are answered in the target language. Grammar is taught inductively—rules are generalized from the practice and experience with the target language. Verbs are used first and systematically conjugated only much later after some oral mastery of the target language. Advanced students read literature for comprehension and pleasure. Literary texts are not analyzed grammatically. The culture associated with the target language is also taught inductively. Culture is considered an important aspect of learning the language.

READING APPROACH OF GRAMMAR

This approach is selected for practical and academic reasons. For specific uses of the language in graduate or scientific studies. The approach is for people who do not travel abroad for whom reading is the one usable skill in a foreign language.

The priority in studying the target language is first, reading ability and second, current and/or historical knowledge of the country where the target language is spoken. Only the grammar necessary for reading comprehension and fluency is taught. Minimal attention is paid to pronunciation or gaining conversational skills in the target language.From the beginning, a great amount of reading, both in and out of class. The vocabulary of the early reading passages and texts is strictly controlled for difficulty. Vocabulary is expanded as quickly as possible, since the acquisition of vocabulary is considered more important that grammatical skill. Translation reappears in this approach as a respectable classroom procedure related to comprehension of the written text.

COMMUNITY LANGUAGE LEARNING

This methodology is not based on the usual methods by which languages are taught. Rather the approach is patterned upon counseling techniques and adapted to the peculiar anxiety and threat as well as the personal and language problems a person encounters in the learning of foreign languages. Consequently, the learner is not thought of as a student but as a client. The native instructors of the language are not considered teachers but, rather are trained in counseling skills adapted to their roles as language counselors.

The language-counseling relationship begins with the client's linguistic confusion and conflict. The aim of the language counselor's skill is first to communicate an empathy for the client's threatened inadequate state and to aid him linguistically. Then slowly the teacher-counselor strives to enable him to arrive at his own increasingly independent language adequacy. This process is furthered by the language counselor's ability to establish a warm, understanding, and accepting relationship, thus becoming an "other-language self" for the client. The process involves five stages of adaptation:

STAGE 1

The client is completely dependent on the language counselor.

1. First, he expresses only to the counselor and in English what he wishes to say to the group. Each group member overhears this English exchange but no other members of the group are involved in the interaction.
2. The counselor then reflects these ideas back to the client in the foreign language in a warm, accepting tone, in simple language in phrases of five or six words.
3. The client turns to the group and presents his ideas in the foreign language. He has the counselor's aid if he mispronounces or hesitates on a word or phrase. This is the client's maximum security stage.

STAGE 2

1. Same as above.
2. The client turns and begins to speak the foreign language directly to the group.
3. The counselor aids only as the client hesitates or turns for help. These small independent steps are signs of positive confidence and hope.

STAGE 3

1. The client speaks directly to the group in the foreign language. This presumes that the group has now acquired the ability to understand his simple phrases.
2. Same as 3 above. This presumes the client's greater confidence, independence, and proportionate insight into the relationship of phrases, grammar, and ideas. Translation is given only when a group member desires it.

STAGE 4

1. The client is now speaking freely and complexly in the foreign language. Presumes group's understanding.
2. The counselor directly intervenes in grammatical error, mispronunciation, or where aid in complex expression is needed. The client is sufficiently secure to take correction.

STAGE 5

1. Same as stage 4.
2. The counselor intervenes not only to offer correction but to add idioms and more elegant constructions.
3. At this stage the client can become counselor to the group in stages 1, 2, and 3.

SILENT WAY

This method begins by using a set of coloured rods and verbal commands in order to achieve the following:

To avoid the use of the vernacular. To create simple linguistic situations that remain under the complete control of the teacher To pass on to the learners the responsibility for the utterances of the descriptions of the objects shown or the actions performed. To let the teacher concentrate on what the students say and how they are saying it, drawing their attention to the differences in pronunciation and the flow of words. To generate a serious game-like situation in which the rules are implicitly agreed upon by giving meaning to the gestures of the teacher and his mime. To permit almost from the start a switch from the lone voice of the teacher using the foreign language to a number of voices using it. This introduces components of pitch, timbre and intensity that will constantly reduce the impact of one voice and hence reduce imitation and encourage personal production of one's own brand of the sounds.

To provide the support of perception and action to the intellectual guess of what the noises mean, thus bring in the arsenal of the usual criteria of experience already developed and automatic in one's use of the mother tongue.To provide a duration of spontaneous speech upon which the teacher and the students can work to obtain a similarity of melody to the one heard, thus providing melodic integrative schemata from the start.

MATERIALS

The complete set of materials utilized as the language learning progresses include:

A set of coloured wooden rods A set of wall charts containing words of a "functional" vocabulary and some additional ones; a pointer for use with the charts in Visual Dictation A colour coded phonic chart(s) Tapes or discs, as required; films Drawings and pictures, and a set of accompanying worksheets Transparencies, three texts, a Book of Stories, worksheets

AUDIOLINGUAL METHOD

This method is based on the principles of behaviour psychology. It adapted many of the principles and procedures of the Direct Method, in part as a reaction to the lack of speaking skills of the Reading Approach.

New material is presented in the form of a dialogue. Based on the principle that language learning is habit formation, the method fosters dependence on mimicry, memorization of set phrases and over-learning. Structures are sequenced and taught one at a time. Structural patterns are taught using repetitive drills. Little or no grammatical explanations are provided; grammar is taught inductively. Skills are sequenced: Listening, speaking, reading and writing are developed in order. Vocabulary is strictly limited and learned in context. Teaching points are determined by contrastive analysis between L1 and L2. There is abundant use of language laboratories, tapes and visual aids. There is an extended pre-reading period at the beginning of the course. Great importance is given to precise native-like pronunciation. Use of the mother tongue by the teacher is permitted, but discouraged among and by the students. Successful responses are reinforced; great care is taken to prevent learner errors. There is a tendency to focus on manipulation of the target language and to disregard content and meaning.

HINTS FOR USING AUDIO-LINGUAL DRILLS IN TEACHING

- The teacher must be careful to insure that all of the utterances which students will make are actually within the practiced pattern. For example, the use of the AUX verb have should not suddenly switch to have as a main verb.
- Drills should be conducted as rapidly as possibly so as to insure automaticity and to establish a system.
- Ignore all but gross errors of pronunciation when drilling for grammar practice.
- Use of shortcuts to keep the pace o drills at a maximum. Use hand motions, signal cards, notes, etc. to cue response. You are a choir director.
- Use normal English stress, intonation, and juncture patterns conscientiously.
- Drill material should always be meaningful. If the content words are not known, teach their meanings.
- Intersperse short periods of drill with very brief alternative activities to avoid fatigue and boredom.
- Introduce the drill in this way:
  - Focus (by writing on the board, for example)
  - Exemplify (by speaking model sentences)
  - Explain (if a simple grammatical explanation is needed)
  - Drill
- Don't stand in one place; move about the room standing next to as many different students as possible to spot check their production. Thus you will know who to give more practice to during individual drilling.
- Use the "backward buildup" technique for long and/or difficult patterns.
  - Tomorrow
  - In the cafeteria tomorrow
  - Will be eating in the cafeteria tomorrow

- Those boys will be eating in the cafeteria tomorrow.

- Arrange to present drills in the order of increasing complexity of student response. The question is: How much internal organization or decision making must the student do in order to make a response in this drill. Thus: imitation first, single-slot substitution next, then free response last.

FUNCTIONAL-NOTIONAL APPROACH

This method of language teaching is categorized along with others under the rubric of a communicative approach. The method stresses a means of organizing a language syllabus. The emphasis is on breaking down the global concept of language into units of analysis in terms of communicative situations in which they are used.

Notions are meaning elements that may be expressed through nouns, pronouns, verbs, prepositions, conjunctions, adjectives or adverbs. The use of particular notions depends on three major factors: a. the functions b. the elements in the situation, and c. the topic being discussed. A situation may affect variations of language such as the use of dialects, the formality or informality of the language and the mode of expression. Situation includes the following elements:

A. The persons taking part in the speech act
B. The place where the conversation occurs
C. The time the speech act is taking place
D. The topic or activity that is being discussed

Exponents are the language utterances or statements that stem from the function, the situation and the topic.

Code is the shared language of a community of speakers.

Code-switching is a change or switch in code during the speech act, which many theorists believe is purposeful behaviour to convey bonding, language prestige or other elements of interpersonal relations between the speakers.

FUNCTIONAL CATEGORIES OF LANGUAGE

Mary Finocchiaro has placed the functional categories under five headings as noted below:*personal, interpersonal, directive, referential,* and *imaginative.*

Personal = Clarifying or arranging one's ideas; expressing one's thoughts or feelings: love, joy, pleasure, happiness, surprise, likes, satisfaction, dislikes, disappointment, distress, pain, anger, anguish, fear, anxiety, sorrow, frustration, annoyance at missed opportunities, moral, intellectual and social concerns; and the everyday feelings of hunger, thirst, fatigue, sleepiness, cold, or warmth

Interpersonal = Enabling us to establish and maintain desirable social and working relationships: Enabling us to establish and maintain desirable social and working relationships:

- Greetings and leave takings
- Introducing people to others

- Identifying oneself to others
- Expressing joy at another's success
- Expressing concern for other people's welfare
- Extending and accepting invitations
- Refusing invitations politely or making alternative arrangements
- Making appointments for meetings
- Breaking appointments politely and arranging another mutually convenient time
- Apologizing
- Excusing oneself and accepting excuses for not meeting commitments
- Indicating agreement or disagreement
- Interrupting another speaker politely
- Changing an embarrassing subject
- Receiving visitors and paying visits to others
- Offering food or drinks and accepting or declining politely
- Sharing wishes, hopes, desires, problems
- Making promises and committing oneself to some action
- Complimenting someone
- Making excuses
- Expressing and acknowledging gratitude

Directive = Attempting to influence the actions of others; accepting or refusing direction:

- Making suggestions in which the speaker is included
- Making requests; making suggestions
- Refusing to accept a suggestion or a request but offering an alternative
- Persuading someone to change his point of view
- Requesting and granting permission
- Asking for help and responding to a plea for help
- Forbidding someone to do something; issuing a command
- Giving and responding to instructions
- Warning someone
- Discouraging someone from pursuing a course of action
- Establishing guidelines and deadlines for the completion of actions
- Asking for directions or instructions

Referential = talking or reporting about things, actions, events, or people in the environment in the past or in the future; talking *about* language (what is termed the metalinguistic function: = talking or reporting about things, actions, events, or people in the environment in the past or in the future; talking *about* language (what is termed the metalinguistic function:

- Identifying items or people in the classroom, the school the home, the community

- Asking for a description of someone or something
- Defining something or a language item or asking for a definition
- Paraphrasing, summarizing, or translating
- Explaining or asking for explanations of how something works
- Comparing or contrasting things
- Discussing possibilities, probabilities, or capabilities of doing something
- Requesting or reporting facts about events or actions
- Evaluating the results of an action or event

Imaginative = Discussions involving elements of creativity and artistic expression

- Discussing a poem, a story, a piece of music, a play, a painting, a film, a TV programme, etc.
- Expanding ideas suggested by other or by a piece of literature or reading material
- Creating rhymes, poetry, stories or plays
- Recombining familiar dialogs or passages creatively
- Suggesting original beginnings or endings to dialogs or stories
- Solving problems or mysteries

THINKING SKILLS AND ENGLISH LANGUAGE LEARNERS

English language learners should be asked critical thinking questions from all levels of Bloom's Taxonomy. Some of the tasks on the taxonomy are difficult for ELLs because they lack the language and vocabulary to work in English. However, teachers need to ask questions from all levels of the taxonomy that are age appropriate and at the English language level of the English language learners. Even very young children can work at the Synthesis and Evaluation levels.

Examples at each level below come from *Pa Lia's First Day* by Michelle Edwards. This book is written at a late second or early third grade level.

Level I: Knowledge.

This level of questioning is what is most frequently used when teaching ELLs, especially for students in pre-production and beginning production levels of English language acquisition. Responses to some of the questions can be made using yes/no or embedded questions. Pictures, drawings, and realia will help students give the correct answer. Responses to these questions are generally right in the text. Here are some questions and directions you might ask:

- What did Pa Lia's brother do on the way to school?
- Who pushed Pa Lia on the steps?
- What name did Stinky call Pa Lia?
- When did Pa Lia meet Calliope?

- What did Pa Lia do during Math Class?

Level II: Comprehension.

This level shows that the student has understood the facts and can interpret them. ESL/bilingual teachers use this level of questioning a lot. We ask students to compare, contrast, illustrate, and classify. We do this oral questions and graphic organizers such as Venn Diagrams and T-charts.

- Why did Pa Lia dawdle on the way to school?
- How will Pa Lia find her classroom?
- Why was Howie mean to Pa Lia?
- Why did Pa Lia get in trouble?
- Compare Calliope with Howie. Use the word bank.
- Make a drawing that shows how Pa Lia felt when she came in the classroom.
- Find a picture in the book that shows "Pa Lia felt like a teeny tiny minnow in a huge giant ocean".

Level III: Application.

Students are learning to solve problems by using previously learned facts in a different way. ELLs might need scaffolding and word banks to build, choose, construct, develop, organize, plan, select, solve, and identify.

- Why did Pa Lia send a note?
- How would you do if you needed to find your classroom on the first day of school?
- Can you list the ways you could make a new student feel welcome?
- Write a different ending to the story.
- What questions would you ask Stinky if you could talk to him?

Level IV: Analysis.

At this level students may not have enough vocabulary and language to express responses in English. The tasks at this level that English language learners will be able to complete with some teacher scaffolding are: classify, contrast, compare, categorize, sequence.

- How do we know Pa La felt nervous? Find the sentences in the story.
- Compare Pa Lia's feelings at the beginning of the story with her feelings at the end of the story.
- Sequence the following story sentences. What happened first?
- Look at the words in the word bank that describe people. Write the words that describe Pa Lia, Calliope, and Howie in the correct column
- Can you find four different feelings Pa Lia had during the story?
- How do you know that Pa Lia is the hero of the story?
- What do you think will happen next in this story?

Level V: Synthesis.

At this level students are compiling information together in a different way by combining elements in a new pattern or proposing alternative solutions.

ELLs will need teacher support and scaffolding to answer questions at level 5. Synthesis is particularly difficult for ELLs. Students may be able to choose, combine, create, design, develop, imagine, make up, predict, solve, and change.

- Pa Lia is a new student at school and she has no friends. How would you solve Pa Lia's problem?
- How would you change in this story?
- What happens if you do not tell the truth?
- Can you invent another character for the story?
- How would you change the story to create a different ending?
- How could you change the story? How else could Pa Lia make friends? Plan a party for Mrs. Hennessey's class.

Level VI: Evaluation.

Questions at this level of Bloom's taxonomy can be modified so that the langue is simplified but the task remains the same. English language learners can learn to give opinions, make judgements about the action in a story and evaluate the work of an author.

The vocabulary usually associated with evaluation may need to be simplified. Here are some questions ELLs would be able to answer with some scaffolding by the teacher.

- What do you think will happen if Pa Lia does not tell the truth.
- What didn't you like about the story? Why?
- Do you think Tou Ger was a good brother? Why or Why not?
- What is part of this book did you like best. Tell why you like it?
- Why did the Pa Lia decide to tell the truth?
- What would you do if you were Pa Lia and the teacher was angry with you?
- Read another story by Michelle Edwards. Do you like it better than "Pa Lia's First Day?"

CHALLENGES FOR ELLS IN READING

English language learners face many obstacles when reading literature in English. Most literature is culture bound. We expect students to have prior knowledge of literary genres such as fairy tales, myths, legends, and tall tales. If the teacher has not activated prior knowledge or built background information, knowing the vocabulary will not solve the problem. ELLs may be able to read the words but it doesn't mean they will understand the text. They are not aware of information that the author left unsaid; the information that "everyone knows."

Here are some specific challenges that ELLs face when learning to read material in English:

- An abundance of idioms and figurative language in English texts
- Density of unfamiliar vocabulary

- Use of homonyms and synonyms
- Grammar usage especially the "exceptions to the rules"
- Word order, sentence structure and syntax
- Difficult text structure with a topic sentence, supporting details and conclusion
- Unfamiliarity with the connotative and denotative meanings of words
- ELLs may not have practice in expressing an opinion about text.
- Use of regional U.S. dialects
- Fear of participation and interaction with mainstream students,
- Story themes and endings can be inexplicable
- Literary terms for story development are not understood
- Unfamiliarity with drawing conclusions, analyzing characters and predicting outcomes
- Imagery and symbolism in text are difficult.

CHALLENGES FOR ELLS IN MATHEMATICS

Mathematics is not just arithmetic. There are considerable challenges for English language learners in math. There are challenges for teachers of mathematics, too. We may find that our ELLs use a different processes to arrive at answers. Many teachers do not validate other systems and prior mathematical knowledge. Problem solving is not just language but a thought process. Students from other cultures may be more concerned with getting the correct response than with the process. They may not be able to justify their answers.

DIFFICULTIES THAT ELLS FACE WHEN LEARNING MATHEMATICS

- Formation of numbers varies from culture to culture
- Use of decimal point and comma vary from culture to culture
- Students have no experience with our measurement system, It is an abstract to them.
- Math is not spirally taught in many cultures. So students may not know a lot about geometry, for example.
- Many students have never seen or worked with manipulatives. They may not take a lesson using manipulatives seriously.
- Students learn math by rote memory.
- Math curricula in their countries may be primarily calculation.
- Word problems may not be introduced until much later.
- Estimating, rounding, and geometry are not often taught as early in other cultures.
- Mathematical terms do not always translate well.
- Mental math may be the norm. Students may not show work in addition, subtraction, multiplication and division or they may show work in a different way,

SPECIFIC CHALLENGES FOR ELLS IN SCIENCE

ELLs may lack of background knowledge in science. Our "hands-on" approach is different from what they are used to. Drawing conclusions on their own may be difficult for ELLs. In their own culture students may not have been trained to make guesses.

CHALLENGES THAT ELLS FACE WHEN STUDYING SCIENCE

- The vocabulary of science presents a huge difficulty. There are a special set of terms for the student to learn. Even simple words that the student may know, could have another meaning in science.
- Material is covered very fast
- Directions are often multistep and difficult.
- There are too many concepts explained on each page of a science text.
- Cooperative learning may not fit in with students experiences in learning.
- Visuals may be confusing and difficult to understand.
- Sentence structure is complex and the passive voice is used in textbooks.
- What was taught in class does not always match the assessment.
- ELLs are not used to science labs or equipment
- Students lack background in scientific method
- There is no standard form of delivery of information

CHALLENGES FOR ELLS IN SOCIAL STUDIES

Social studies and U.S. history provide the biggest challenge to ELLs in their content classes. They have very limited background knowledge to activate. ELLs lack prior knowledge of U.S. and U.S. history, geography, and current events needed. Many students will memorize information for a test, but it has no relevance for them so the information is quickly forgotten.

ELLs' difficulties when studying social studies.

- Use of higher level thinking skills for reading and writing.
- Lack of familiarity with historical terms, government processes, and vocabulary.
- Social Studies text contains complex sentences, passive voice, and extensive use of pronouns.
- ELLs may not be used to expressing their personal opinions.
- Nationalistic and cultural focus of maps.
- Concepts which do no exist in all cultures are difficult. This includes privacy, democratic processes, rights of citizens, free will.
- No concept of movement within the structure of a society.

- ELLs are seldom asked to contribute an alternate view that reflects conditions in other countries.
- Use in our schools of "timeline" teaching vs. learning history by "dynasty" or "period."
- Difficulty with understanding what is said by the teacher and being able to take notes.
- Amount of text covered and the ELLs' inability to tell what is important in the text and what is not important.

THE GRAMMAR -TRANSLATION METHOD:

This method, also known as the classical method, is one of the oldest or traditional methods of teaching English. In Europe it was used in the teaching of Latin and Greek for several centuries, and got introduced in India with the arrival of the British.

This method as Tickoo said: "came to English Language Teaching in most of Asia in general and India in particular with support in the long-established tradition of teaching classical languages in the United Kingdom. The system of education in the country served as a model for schools in most of its colonies. The psychological beliefs that prevailed then were (a) that classical languages with their intricate systems of grammar were capable of training human faculties including memory, and (b) that learning these languages was part of a truly liberal education. Teaching and learning primarily aimed at the ability to read full texts rather than to communicate orally in everyday situations". Thus, the above statement makes it clear that this method makes no provision for training in speech but lays stress on reading. Commenting on how this method operates in our schools and colleges, Bhatia and Bhatia assert:

"This method gives equal importance to grammar in the course in as much as the linguistic material presented for study is graded on a grammatical plan, and teaches the meaning of new English words, phrases and sentences, by means of word-by-word translation in the vernacular." They further add that: "the unit of speech or reading is not a sentence-a sentence comes last of all, first letters and words and then sentence."

This method, according to Pahuja, "has no psychological basis but has two suppositions: that a foreign language can easily be learnt through translation and that grammar is the soul of language." Criticizing this method, Rouse remarks that the aim of this method was "to know everything about something, rather than the thing itself."

Students found the method frustrating as they had to memorise words and rules. The use of 'L1' in the classroom prevented the learner from developing confidence to communicate in English. The learners found it very difficult to emancipate themselves from the clutches of their mother-tongue. They were unable to use English in their day-to-day communication. The excessive obsession with accuracy and competence in written rather than oral language inhibited learners who often preferred to remain silent rather than expose their ignorance.

The emphasis in this method is mainly on translation of English words, phrases, and passages into and from the mother-tongue of a learner. Tracing out the roots of this method Yardi observes: "Latin became very popular as the Roman Empire grew, and attained the status of an international language. It became the sole medium of instruction and remained so until after the middle ages. The emphasis in teaching Latin was, by and large, on formal grammar. This method grew out of this practice...".

J.B. Carroll, however, is of the view that this 'traditional approach' is of a comparatively recent origin. He states: "In the colonial days of America, language instruction seems to have included considerably more attention to oral aspects of language, even when the language was Latin, Greek or Hebrew. The 'traditional' approach then seems to have been developed to meet the needs of rapidly expanding popular education in the latter part of the 19th century. Before 1875, members of the elite classes learned foreign languages through individualised instruction by native instructors...".

The advocates of this method, as stated by Bhatia and Bhatia, assert that it is based on some sound principles such as:

- Foreign phraseology is best interpreted through translation.
- Foreign phraseology is best assimilated in the process of interpretation.
- The structure of foreign language can best be taught by comparing and contrasting it with that of mother-tongue; and this is best effected through translation."

A number of methods and techniques have evolved for the teaching of English and also other foreign languages in the recent past, yet grammar-translation method is still in use in many parts of India. This method dominated European and other foreign language teaching for nearly a hundred years (1840 to 1940), till the advent of structural linguistics.

The popularity of this method among generations of teachers in India can be related to factors that are universal. As we know, it maintains the mother-tongue of the learner as the reference particularly in the process of learning the second/foreign languages. Again it does not require special training or specialised skills on the part of the teacher. Its special appeal for teachers in India lies in the long established beliefs in the power of memory and its successful use in early learning of not only languages but other subjects as well.

H.E. Palmer catalogues the weaknesses of this method in the following words: "It is one which treats all languages as if they were dead, as if each consisted essentially of a collection of ancient documents to be deciphered and analysed... It is the one which categorically ignores all considerations of phonetics, pronunciations and acoustic image, and boldly places language on a foundation of alphabets, spellings and writing systems... It is the one which assumes translation to be the main or only procedure for the learning of vocabulary... It is the one which assumes that word and sentence structure is to be attained mainly or solely through the memorising of the so-called rules of grammar."

In spite of the weaknesses catalogued by Palmer, the method could best be put in use by discarding the overemphasis on the grammatical rules and by making a room for imparting training in the spoken aspects of English. The grammar-translation method in its modified form continues to be widely used in some parts of the world even today. In the mid-and late 19th century opposition to it gradually developed, and as a result of this it lost its hold in the domain of teaching of English.

THE DIRECT METHOD:

The direct method, sometimes also called as the 'reform' method, 'natural' method, 'psychological' method, 'phonetic' method, and 'anti-grammatical' method, was established in France and Germany around 1900, and introduced in India in the early 20th century as a reform which was needed in the methods of teaching English.

This was developed, as Rao has pointed out, "as a reaction against the grammar-translation method". The major assumptions of this method were in opposition to the grammar-translation method. Hence, it is considered as a reaction against the grammar-translation method with a distinct grammatical bias.

Again this method is a logical extension of the Natural method. It is also an offshoot of the Behaviourist school of psychology. It insists that the key to all language learning lies in association. It stresses the need for direct association between experience and expression in the foreign language. The aim is to enable the learner to think in foreign language and to cultivate an unerring language sense. It recognises that language sense has its roots in the spoken language and lays stress on the oral approach.

In the opinion of Diller this method has one basic rule: "no translation is allowed". In fact, this method receives its name from the fact that meaning is to be conveyed directly in the target language through the use of demonstration and visual aids, with no recourse to the students' native language.

For example, in a reading lesson to class V, a new word 'watch' occurs. If we associate it with its intermediate in the vernacular, *i.e.* 'Gharee', we are teaching the meaning indirectly; but if on the other hand, we associate the word with an actual 'watch' or with the picture of a watch, we are teaching the meaning directly.

If such a direct association is not possible, the teacher can explain the meaning of new words by giving synonyms, definitions, explanations, or by inference from the context. The same technique with a few modifications here and there, can be followed in teaching compositions-oral or written. Many new words can be added to the vocabulary of the learner without the intervention of the mother-tongue.

According to Bhatia and Bhatia, the main aim of teaching English by this method is to enable the learner: "to think in English and to discourage the practice of inwardly thinking in one's vernacular and then overtly translating the thought into the foreign language. He should be able to grasp what he hears or reads in English and should be able to express his thoughts and wishes directly and fluently so that in due course of time he obtains a real command over the language". The other significant assumption of this method according to Thirumalai is:

"Adult L2 learners can learn a second language in essentially the same manner as a child. Therefore, if possible, the teacher should try to create a natural learning environment within the classroom. Instead of explicit grammar instruction, the major emphasis is on communicating. Classes are carried out totally in the second language with absolutely no reliance on the first language or on any form of translation. The expectation is that through question-and-answer dialogues, the second language will gradually be acquired. Problems have arisen with such an approach because adults do not, in fact, learn exactly like children, and they express the need for explicit instruction in grammar and other aspects of the second language." Teaching of receptive skills (listening and reading) rather than teaching of productive skills (speaking and writing) was encouraged as the first step. Contrastive analysis of the native language of the learner with the target language was done. Teachers are required to have a good knowledge of phonetics of the language they teach, but they would use it to teach pronunciation and not phonetics. As this method uses conversation as the main tool in the teaching of a foreign language, the other tools are discussion and reading in the target language itself. Grammar is taught inductively.

W.F. Mackey points out the main characteristics of this method as: "there is an ample scope for the use of everyday vocabulary and structures; grammar is taught by creating situations through visual presentations. There is ample scope for extensive listening and imitation until form becomes automatic."

Thus, it becomes evident that there is almost no scope for the learners' mother-tongue. The method presupposes that a second language could be acquired as one acquires one's mother-tongue through its ample natural exposure.

Wilga Rivers comments on this method as: "A direct method class provided a clear contrast with the prevailing grammar-translation classes. The course began with the learning of the foreign words and phrases for objects and actions in the classroom. When these could be used readily and appropriately the learning moved to the common situations and settings of everyday life, the lesson often developing around specially constructed pictures of life in the country where the language was spoken. Where the meaning of words could not be made clear by concrete representations, the teacher resorted to miming, sketches or explanations in the foreign language but never supplied native-language translations.

From the beginning, the students were accustomed to hear complete and meaningful sentences which formed part of a simple discourse, often in the form of a question-answer interchange. Grammar was not taught explicitly and deductively as in the grammar-translation class but was learnt largely through practice. Students were encouraged to draw their own structural generalizations from what they had been learning by an inductive process. In this way, the study of grammar was kept at a functional level, being confined to those which were continually being used in speech. When grammar was taught more systematically, at a later stage, it was taught in a foreign language with the use of foreign language terminology."

From the aforesaid statement it becomes clear that this method discards the use of L1, even in teaching grammatical rules, favours the situational use of English, considers meaningful sentences at the core, teaches grammatical rules inductively, provides with ample opportunities to the students of using target language, takes care of the spoken aspects of the target language, and above all seeks gradual development of all, the basic linguistic skills viz-LSRW. According to William E. Bull "any given method is only as effective as its implementation". He further adds that "the superior teacher has regularly gotten superior results regardless of the method."

From the comments cited above it becomes evident that no method could be a complete one in itself. What makes it important is the man (the teacher) who does not allow the explanations in the students' native language creating English environment in the classroom. The main reason of the failure of this method in Indian context is perhaps the dearth of the expert teachers.

Therefore, the direct method considered better than the previous grammar-translation method, was not completely free from certain weaknesses either. For one thing the method is not all that direct, for only a limited number of words can be directly associated with their meanings or the objects they represent. Moreover, its main claim that it teaches a foreign language directly, and not through the mother-tongue, is only partly true.

Commenting on the limitations of this method Scott remarks: "The clever youngster thrives on the direct method by defeating it." Thus, the mother-tongue equivalents of words may not be used by the teacher but may be in the students' mind, and the student does not exclude them from his own mind.

Another limitation of this method in Verghese's opinion: "arises from its neglect of the language skills like writing and reading because of overemphasis on oral work. This method practically ignores the study of grammar, this is not desirable because the knowledge of grammar is useful to the students to correct errors and strengthen language habits." Wyatt also appears to be a critic of this method particularly in the Indian context. He observes that extreme followers of the direct method overlook a simple fact of human nature, of pupils' nature in particular. An Indian pupil cannot but utter in thought the vernacular equivalent of the new English word taught to him, because in associating the new English word with a familiar word in the vernacular, he is simply reinforcing the memory of the old friends. He Says: "The Direct method in all its rigour mistakes the end for the means, the goal for the path that leads to it -the direct association of words and phrases with their meanings is the eventual objective of language study and not a means. We cannot expect the pupil to make the association at the outset."

Thus in summing up it may be admitted that the direct method, in spite of its merits, did not make much progress because it neglected the facts mentioned above, and therefore, failed in the Indian contexts.

THE AUDIO-LINGUAL METHOD:

During the World War II, American soldiers had an urgent need to learn languages like-German, French, Chinese or Japanese to communicate effectively when posted in various countries. The Army Specialised Training Programme (ASTP) was established in 1942 by American linguists to meet this urgent need. 55 American Universities were involved in the programme by the beginning of 1943. This technique of teaching was initially called the 'Army Method' and was the first to be based on linguistic theory and behavioural psychology.

The objective of this programme, as stated by Richards Jack, C. and T.S. Rodgers, was for students "to attain conversational proficiency in variety of foreign languages."

Since this was not the goal of conventional foreign language courses in the US, new approaches were necessary. Leonard Bloomfield, a linguist at Yale, had already developed training programmes as a part of their linguistic research that were designed to give linguists and Anthropologists mastery of American-Indian languages and other languages they were studying. Textbooks did not exist for such languages. The technique which Bloomfield and his colleagues used was sometimes called as the 'informant method". Excellent results were achieved by this method.

The 'ASTP' lasted only two years but attracted considerable attention in the popular press and in the academic community. For the next ten years the army method and its suitability for use in regular language programmes were discussed. Charles Fries of the University of Michigan led the way in applying principles from structural linguistics in developing the method and for this reason, it has sometimes been referred as the 'Michigan Method'.

Later in its development, principles from behavioural psychology were incorporated. It was thought that the way to acquire the sentence patterns of the target language was through conditioning-helping learners to respond correctly to stimuli through shaping and reinforcement. Learners could overcome the habits of their native language and form the new habits required to be target language speakers.

The term 'Audiolingualism' was coined by Nelson Brooks in 1964, highlighting the basic belief of structuralism that: 'speech is primary'. Language is viewed as a set of structures. The behaviourist theory of learning was adopted. Language learning was assumed to involve a chain of stimulus-response-reinforcement; and it was believed that one learnt a language by acquiring a series of stimulus-response chain.

V. Saraswathi quotes the assumptions of this method stated by stern as follows:

- Foreign language learning is basically a mechanical process of habit formation.
- Language skills are learned effectively; if items of the foreign language are presented in the spoken form before the written form.
- Analogy provides a better foundation for foreign language learning than analysis.
- The meaning which the words of a language have for the native speaker can be learned only in a matrix of allusions to the culture of the people who speak that language."

The Audio-lingual method, according to Thirumalai, in some sense: "represents a return to the Direct Method, as its main goal is to develop native-like speaking ability in its learners. It is an extension as well as refinement of the direct method. Translation and reference to 'L1' are not permitted."

Underlying this method, he further adds that:

"L2 learning should be regarded as a mechanistic process of habit formation...Audio- lingual learning comprises dialogue memorization and pattern drills, thus, ensuring careful control of responses. None of the drills or patterns are to be explained, since knowledge of grammatical rules would only obstruct the mechanical formation of habits."

From the statements cited above it is evident that Audio-lingualism had its theoretical roots in the direct method; which was an extension of the Natural method. Again the audio-lingual method used exhaustively the linguistic structures identified in the descriptive analysis of the target language. It was skill oriented, with a practical emphasis on 'Oracy'.

This method provided 'contextualized' language practice in true-to-life situations including dialogue. Again, it provided a wide variety of activities to help maintain interest, and it made extensive use of visuals. It arranged for abundant practice although "the grammar based audiolingual approach moved cautiously from supposedly simple to more and more linguistically complex features, often without adequate consideration for what might be needed in everyday situations."

William Moulton has stated five important characteristics of this method as follows:

- Language is speech, not writing.
- A Language is a set of habits.
- Teach the language, not about the language.
- A language is what its native speakers say, not what someone thinks they ought to say; and
- Languages are different."

Examining each one of the five characteristics of this method, Wilga Rivers made the following recommendations with regard to Audio-lingualism:

- Learners' perceptions, motivation, and feelings should be taken into account.
- The emphasis should be shifted from linguistic form to communication in a socio-cultural context."

Thus, it becomes clear that this method emphasises teaching through oral presentation prior to written presentation. It believes in the fact that the children learn to speak before they learn to read or write. Thus, the teaching materials, that we prepare, should be based on the 'primacy of speech.' B.F. Skinner strongly believes that 'a language is a set of habits.' He further adds that "language is verbal behaviour."

Followers and supporters of this method were extremely influenced by its 'operant conditioning' theories. For them, the linguistic behaviour of the child can change as does its social behaviour through the process of habit forming. The kind of thinking introduced mimicry, memorization, and pattern drill into foreign language teaching.

Audio-lingual teachers consider that 'teaching through grammar-translation method is teaching about the language and not the language.' They give little attention to grammar. In this connection Moulton says:

"The real goal of instruction was an ability to talk the language and not to talk about it."

The statement cited above thus, makes it clear that the Audio-lingual method laid the practical emphasis on 'oral' practice of the language. Again, the assumption that 'a language is what its native speakers say' prompted the advocates of this method to prepare learning materials with expressions which student would hear around them in the country where the language is spoken. The teaching materials avoided prescriptive school grammars, passages from literary texts, and classics. Materials embodied with day-to-day experience were of prime importance for teaching. The increasing use of Audio-visual aids in second language teaching, according to Allen H.B. is based on the modern Audio-lingual theory which stresses on a 'listening-speaking-reading-writing sequence' in second language learning situations. The theory insists that 'learning to speak a language becomes easier, if the learner has enough training in comprehension.' Linguists and language teaching experts lay emphasis on planned listening experiences. Their main arguments are:

- Ear-training facilitates speaking. Articulation is dependent upon hearing sounds accurately...
- Concentration on one skill at a time facilitates learning by reducing the load on the student and by permitting the use of materials and techniques geared to the specific objectives and requirements of each skill.
- When students are required to speak from the outset, the likelihood of errors is increased... where listening comprehension precedes speaking, the students' initial experience includes more correct responses and more frequent positive reinforcement less comprehension, and more rapid development of confidence in his language learning ability.
- Prematurely listening to his own unauthenticated pronunciation, and to that 139 of other students, may interfere with the students' discrimination and retention of correct sounds".

Dr. Sharada Bhat has recorded the main strengths of this method as follows: "the teaching materials are more scientifically and systematically prepared than the one-author texts; it teaches a language in a graded manner; the motivation of the students is of a higher degree; the students enjoy learning the target language because the teaching materials are specially designed to interest the students avoiding boring passages from the classes".

Apart from these strengths, the Audio-lingual method was not completely free from its weaknesses and flaws. Behaviourist assumptions underlying this method have come under severe criticism. The importance given to achieve 'oral accuracy' only has prompted many linguists to question the very necessity of a teacher. Albert Valdman has criticized "the exaggerated emphasis on oral drilling" in this method.

Decanny has the following to say about mechanical drilling. He says:

"Drills are inherently unnatural, contrived examples of the use of language. Humanising these devices is left to the teacher. Unless the students are stimulated by variety, novelty, and a quick change of cues, they may be mouthing meaningless sentences and in this unwilling frame of mind no learning takes place."

In spite of the strong objection to the mechanical drilling, many pedagogues see some values in this method. In this regard K. Chastain writes: "to harvest these values the method must be made more responsive to the students' intellectual needs. The methods of drill and pattern have proved pedagogically very sound. Therefore, the language teacher should devise methods to make the drills more meaningful and interesting bringing in real communicative situations outside the classroom".

Thus, no Audio-lingual method can, however, be successful in the absence of a qualified, trained, inventive and resourceful teacher. Machines cannot replace teachers. The approach is and ought to be teacher-centred; that is to say, the aids require planned utilization by specially trained teachers. The high incidence of poorly qualified teachers only increases the waste of student time and public resources. Good teachers and good materials are an indispensable condition for the successful implementation of any scheme of teaching English as a second language in India.

The Bilingual Method:

This method was developed by Dr. C.J. Dodson. As the name suggests, the method makes use of two languages-the mother tongue and the target language. Hence, this can be considered as a combination of the direct method and the grammar-translation method. 'Selection, 'Gradation', 'Presentation', and 'Repetition' are the four cardinal principles of all language teaching methodology. This method has all the four principles in it. In the opinion of Dodson a good method should promote thinking in the language. According to him a new method should have the following features as:

- It must be simple. ii) It must strike a balance between the spoken and the written word, accuracy and fluency. iii) Constant revision of what is taught and learnt. iv) A new method must offer a new approach to the application of translation work. v) The method must give the teacher an opportunity to promote inter-communication between himself and the individual pupil. vi) The method must be sufficiently flexible to cope with various classroom conditions and the pupils' specific and general abilities."

The aims of this method as stated by Yardi are-to make the pupil fluent and accurate in the spoken and written words and to prepare the pupil in such a manner that he can achieve true bilingualism.

The main principles of the bilingual method as stated by Dr. Sharada Bhat are: Controlled use of the students' mother-tongue, the introduction of reading and writing early in the course of language learning and integration of writing and reading skills.

The advocates of this method believe that it is the wastage of time for recreating a situation while teaching a foreign language. They think that teaching-learning method is useful when mother-tongue equivalents are given to the pupil without duplicating the situation.

It differs from translation method in two respects. In the first case it is the teacher only who uses the mother-tongue to explain meaning. Furthermore, pupils are given a lot of practice in the drill of sentence patterns. Such practice is not provided in the translation method.

The Bilingual method was the reaction against the direct method. Dodson vehemently attacks the direct method in the following words:

"It is one of the tragedies at present being enacted in some emergent countries, where a major world language is being taught as a second language to young children by the direct method, that if this type of teaching were successful, which by all account it is not, the vernacular would disappear within a few generations. It is only possible to teach a second language by direct method techniques at the expense of the first language, and it is sheer hypocrisy to claim that the final aim of such teaching philosophies is bilingualism. Every aspect of the direct method teaching is directed towards keeping the two languages as far apart as possible, thus destroying the bridge which the learner must continuously cross to and fro if he wishes to be truly bilingual."

Dodson, thus, makes it clear that the excessive use of the direct method would result in disappearance of the vernacular in future. He was of the view that the direct method, operated at the expense of the first language, could not make the learner truly bilingual.

This method is not an independent new method with new concepts and models. It is, in fact, a happy synthesis of the best principles and features present in the other methods. It has modified the principles of other methods to overcome the objections and criticisms and to suit the objectives of the second language learning today. This idea was expressed by Carrol in the following words:

"But, then, in these highly advanced times it could hardly be expected that a new method would represent anything more than a new combination of procedures." The important contribution of this method is that it had made possible for the students to get both quantitative and qualitative acquisition of language skills.

The equipments necessary for the Bilingual method in Yardi's opinion are: a printed text of the situation to be learnt. This text ought not to be exceeding thirty sentences in length at the secondary level. The text has to be linguistically graded and made interesting to the learner. Each situation in the text should have a picture strip, not just one composite picture as in the usual textbook, representing the development of the content in the text-lesson. The intention in using the picture strip is not to help the learner acquire the sentence meaning but to retain it. Paucity of good teachers with excellent command of spoken and written English is the main difficulty in Yardi's opinion to introduce this method in the present Indian contexts.

To conclude in the words of Dr. H.N.L. Sastry this method is simple from the point of view of teaching and learning. That is why we see majority of teachers in Indian schools follow this method. The method increases the rate and amount of learning in the classroom and it creates better attitudes in the minds of students towards learning English. It also establishes rapport between the teacher and the taught.

6

Learning to Learn and Language Awareness

INTRODUCTION

Along with a greater recognition of adults' problem solving or cognitive abilities comes an awareness of their metacognitive skills. Metacognition is the term used for our ability to think about the way we learn or to reflect on the way we use language. These skills can be used to maximize the learning capabilities of adults, who may learn faster and better if they are consciously aware of the way they construct meaning for themselves.

In second language learning, this awareness is often extended to learning more about how language works, not just in terms of its grammar and structures, but in regard to its social functions as well. To foster and strengthen this awareness, many programmes involve learners in examining the role that literacy plays in their lives and in exploring the many ways that language can be used. The ability to think about language is often called "language awareness."

PERCEPTIONS OF LITERACY

The complex nature of literacy makes definitions difficult, and there is no consensus on what it means to be literate. There is even less agreement on what it means to be literate in a second language or in two or more languages simultaneously. To be sure, a number of descriptions of "being literate" have been proposed. These range from grade level equivalents to being able "to fulfill selfdetermined objectives as family and community members, citizens, job holders, and members of social, religious, or other associations..." The National Assessment of Educational Progress (NAEP) recognizes three distinct areas of knowledge and skills:

- Prose literacy understanding and using information from texts, such as newspapers, magazines, and books
- Document literacy locating and using information from documents, such as job application forms, bus schedules, maps, tables, and indexes
- Quantitative literacy applying numerical operations to information

contained in printed materials, such as checkbooks, menus, order forms, and advertisements.

This definition has also been adopted by the National Adult Literacy Survey (NALS) project.

Many Literacies

Although there is no universally accepted definition of literacy, there is a growing consensus that to be literate means different things in different situations or social contexts. Thus, a person may be perfectly literate in a college library but feel illiterate when confronted with immigration forms. Similarly, a person who has gone to school in a rural area may feel quite overwhelmed by the literacy demands of a factory job.

Given these complexities, defining ESL literacy as merely "the ability to read and write in English" appears simplistic and reductionist and fails to provide guidance for literacy education. Recognizing that literacy contains social, political, and cultural dimensions, the field has come to see literacy in the following two ways:

- As a plurality of literacies or "many literacies," shaped by social contexts and defined individually as well as collectively,
- As a continuum that grows and expands as a person gains experience with different types of literacies, rather than as a dichotomy or "great divide" between literate and illiterate.

When combined, these two perspectives show that nearly everyone who has grown up in a literate society will have experience with some form of literacy. The challenge for research then becomes to delineate these contexts and explore literacy uses within each. A second challenge will be to show to what extent literacy skills and practices transfer from one context to another and to determine whether there exists a threshold level that allows learners to access literacy independently in a variety of contexts.

The nature of ESL literacy is still more complex since it depends on literacy in two languages: the native language of the learner and English literacy. Since the degree of literacy in the first language can significantly influence the speed and depth of literacy development in the second language, the relationship between the two language systems needs to be taken into account. Since language and literacy are socially determined, ESL literacy is also influenced by two cultures: the learners' home culture and its literacy practices and the mainstream culture and its expectations of English literacy.

WORKING DEFINITIONS OF ADULT ESL LITERACY

Since no common definition of ESL literacy has been advanced, individual programmes can define literacy in their own terms. While some see this lack of consensus as a situation to be remedied, others consider it a healthy sign.

Clearly, any official determination of what counts as literacy would validate certain practices, perspectives, approaches, and outcomes and invalidate others. In the absence of a single definition, programmes are free to articulate their own views as to the nature of ESL literacy and the goals of ESL literacy education.

It appears that most programmes in the field have set the larger definition issue aside and have chosen instead to define literacy in two ways:

- By the learners they serve
- By the type of programme that they offer.

In many programmes, ESL literacy students are those who have less than three years of schooling in the home country and have difficulty progressing in a regular ESL class. This definition is not used in all programmes. In many workplace or family literacy programmes, for example, all students, even those who can read and write at intermediate levels of literacy, are classified as literacy students.

While there may be no agreement in the field on what ESL literacy is (similar to Supreme Court Justice Potter Stewart in his definition of pornography, many teachers say "they know it when they see it"), there is a growing consensus on what it is not.

From the perspective of practice, ESL literacy is "not" about

- Learning the alphabet and copying words, although these skills are useful when finding a pizza parlor in the phone book or writing down the name of a good dentist
- Phonics and decoding, although phonics is helpful when trying to pronounce the items on a menu in a Mexican restaurant
- Translating words from one language to another, although it may be fun to try to translate "Fahrvergnuegen" into Spanish
- Focusing on grammar, spelling, punctuation, and capitalization, although these skills are critical when writing a resume
- Reading paragraphs in a textbook and answering comprehension questions, although these skills are helpful when taking a reading test
- Memorizing vocabulary lists, although keeping personal "word banks" may make students feel knowledgeable
- Filling in workbook pages, although focused exercises can help students gain practice.

And finally, ESL literacy is "not just" about

- Power and politics, although it is important to understand the political aspects of language
- Functional literacy, although it helps to know how to read a paycheck
- Storytelling, although personal stories can enrich and enlighten the
- Individual learner.

While there is no one accepted definition of ESL literacy, ESL literacy *teaching* could be defined as supporting adults with little English and little formal education in their efforts to understand and use English in its many forms (oral and written, including prose, document, and quantitative literacy), in a variety of contexts (family, community, school, work), so that they can reach their fullest potential and achieve their own goals, whether these be personal, professional or academic.

Adult ESL Literacy Programmes

ESL literacy programmes can be defined as programmes that put a special emphasis on fostering the literacy skills and practices of adults who have limited proficiency in English. While most ESL literacy programmes teach only English literacy, others teach literacy in the mother tongue (or native language) as well. A number of programmes use both English and the mother tongue of the learners in their ESL literacy classrooms. Still others use only English in the classroom. ESL literacy programmes are highly diverse. They differ in size, from one-to-one tutoring to full classes. They differ in setting, from community colleges to local education agencies (LEAs) to community-based organizations (CBOs). The variety in programme contexts includes "generic" literacy, family literacy, workplace literacy, and community literacy, and the variety in funding sources includes federal, state, private, and combinations of these. Programmes also differ in their long term goals and educational orientations, along with the broader social goals they support. While some programmes are eclectic in their perspective on literacy (*e.g.*, seeking to combine traditional life skills with problem posing), others have a clearly defined literacy framework that guides classroom practice, staff development, and assessment.

Finally, programmes vary in the way they conceptualize learner-centeredness and the degree to which they share control of the programme. In most innovative programmes, learners are involved in deciding what they wanted to learn and how. To a much lesser extent, learners help make decisions about course goals and assessment. In some participatory programmes, learners are involved in the governance of the programme itself and help make decisions regarding programme direction and programme aims.

ADULT ESL LITERACY LEARNERS

Although there is no common definition of ESL literacy, there is some agreement as to the characteristics of ESL literacy learners. They tend to be adults who want to learn English and need to develop their reading and writing skills. Most have had only a few years of schooling. Some come from literate societies but have never been to school; others come from pre-literate societies where print is not in use. Still others may have some experience with reading but may not be familiar with the Roman alphabet. As literacy teachers have long known, those who have never been to school face challenges that are very different from those who have some basic knowledge of what reading and writing are all about. Conversely, learners who are literate in a non-Roman alphabet often acquire English literacy more quickly than learners who are not literate in any language. The programmes we studied served a wide range of learners, including those who have had fewer than three years of education and others who were quite literate in their mother tongues but had little literacy in English.

ESL literacy students often face special challenges. Refugees may be traumatized by years of warfare or political unrest in their home countries, and undocumented students may live in constant fear of being deported. Older learners may have vision or hearing problems that make listening and reading comprehension difficult. Others may have learning difficulties and may need a great deal of time before they acquire language and literacy in a second language. Literacy learners often have strong views of what language and literacy learning should be all about. To some learners, reading may mean reading aloud, writing may mean copying from the blackboard, and learning a language might mean memorizing grammar rules and studying vocabulary lists. Similarly, some students might resist the notion that learning literacy in their mother tongue will help them to learn English, especially if they see acquisition of English as their primary goal. Cognizant of divergent perspectives on literacy, some programmes have made learner discussions about language and literacy a part of their ESL literacy programme.

STRENGTHS OF ADULT ESL LITERACY /EARNERS

Increasingly, programmes have come to recognize that ESL literacy students, in spite of being classified as limited English proficient (LEP), bring a wealth of experience and background knowledge to the classroom. They have found that immigrant adults have a great deal of knowledge about "the real world," possess their own kind of strategic and communicative competence, have established strong social networks, and have proven problem solving abilities. These strengths are evidenced by the fact that most students have managed to secure housing, enroll their children in school, build strong families, access social services, and find jobs. As the experience with amnesty programmes has shown, thousands of ESL learners, classified as low-literate, have successfully filled out immigration papers and negotiated their way through the complex IRCA legalization process. Many successful ESL literacy programmes have harnessed the strengths of their learners and instituted models that involve these adults in programme decisions.

ACTIVE LEARNING METHODOLOGY

Active learning methodology is also a form of activity based learning. It makes all learners to participate in learning. In this method the students involve in reading, writing, speaking, drawing, sharing, expressing the skills and questioning individually and in groups. Active learning involves students in doing things and thinking about what they are doing.

According to Bonwell and Eison students must do more than just listen. They must read, write, discuss and solve problems. They must engage in higher-order thinking tasks. The tasks are analysis, synthesis and evaluation. Students like strategies promoting active learning than traditional lecture method. In active learning, the students are doing something including discovering, processing and applying information.

Many teaching strategies can be employed to actively engage students in the learning process. The activities in ALM improve skills in critical thinking, increase motivation and retention and interpersonal skills.

Active learning involves students directly and actively in the learning process. Instead of simply receiving information verbally and visually, the students are receiving and participating and doing. Active learning methodologies require that the student must find opportunities to meaningfully talk, listen, write and read.

MERITS:

(1) Students are involved in learning.
(2) More emphasis on developing students' skills.
(3) Students are involved in higher-order thinking (analysis, synthesis and Evaluation)
(4) They are engaged in reading, discussing and writing activities.

Active learning shifts the focus from the teacher to the student. Active learning derives from two basic assumptions:

(1) That learning is by nature an active endeavour and
(2) That different people learn in different ways.

EXTENSIVE READING

Extensive reading or reading for fluency involves reading of longer texts for pleasure. It is not meant for minute details. It is a fluency activity. The students can read on their own. This is called Rapid reading or Independent silent reading. The specific objectives of extensive reading are:

1. To understand the meaning as quickly as possible.
2. To increase passive vocabulary.
3. To develop taste for reading.
4. To develop the habit of reading for pleasure.
5. To concentrate upon subject matter.

The term extensive reading means to read silently and quickly. It helps to read without the help of the teacher. It trains the reader to understand the subject matter as quickly and efficiently as possible. It plays a vital role in the learning of second/foreign language. The students are made to read as much as possible. They are given choice and freedom to select the books of their choice. Reading has its own reward.

There are no follow up activities. The reading texts are within the linguistic competence of the reader. Students are permitted to read at their own pace. They choose when to read or where to read. This creates interest among the learners. So they learn to read faster without any disturbance.

STEPS INVOLVED IN EXTENSIVE READING

Introduction:

1. The teacher gives main hints of the passage,
2. He explains the difficult portions,

3. He deals with difficult areas of a language, II.) Silent Reading: The students should read silently and quickly.

In extensive reading, the readers must read silently and understand the matter. This would create interest among the readers. The students may not be interested in reading text books. Interesting magazines, newspaper, etc., may be recommended.

Advantages:

1. It helps in assimilation of ideas.
2. The class room is busy and active.
3. It increases vocabulary.
4. It prepares students for library reading.
5. Helps for individual method of study and self-education.
6. In extensive reading, a child practices what he has learnt.

STEPS IN TEACHING SUPPLEMENTARY READER

A supplementary reader gives students additional reading practice. They learn to read through reading. It develops the skill of silent reading. The students are able to guess the meanings of some words from the context. They grasp the central idea of the passage. It improves their vocabulary. They are able to understand the sequence of ideas and events. It extends reading experience. They consolidate the language learnt from the main reader. Finally the students enjoy reading. A supplementary reader usually contains stories. Later stages biographies and historical events are introduced. Supplementary reader contains long passages with structural and vocabulary items. The students are familiar with the vocabulary. There may be new words and they are not explained. Students guess the meaning of the new words. It has pictures to help the students.

Do's and Don'ts

1. The Supplementary reader is done in the class.
2. One full period is allotted for each lesson or story.
3. Allow students to read and understand as much as possible.

4. Do not read out the passage.
5. Do not explain the content.
6. No translation of any portion.
7. Use relevant pictures to help the students understand.

Teaching a Supplementary Reader

Supplementary reader lesson involves a story or a chapter of a long story or a chapter of a long novel.

- Introduce the passage shortly.
- A part of it is introduced to create interest among the students.
- Meanings for difficult words are not explained in detail. Mother tongue is used in translation. Black board is used to write the meanings.
- Pre-reading questions are presented on the black board.
- Students are asked to read silently.
- Group activities or discussions are followed to answer difficult passages. Different types of direct, local, factual and inferential questions are allowed. Make the students to speak in English while answering.
- Make students to retell the parts of the story or passage in English.
- Students are asked to write the answers at home.
- Select suitable passages for language study.

Teaching Continuous Writing

Writing is a productive skill which involves manipulating, structuring and communicating. Writing helps to strengthen the grasp of vocabulary. Appropriateness can be developed.

Writing involves

1. The ability to master the shapes of the alphabets. (Ortho Graphics)
2. Knowledge of the right combination of letters to form words. (spellings)
3. Skills in expressing oneself through the written piece.

PARAGRAPH

A paragraph consists of a topic sentence. It is followed by a number of related sentences. It usually ends in a concluding statement.

Paragraph:

1. Topic Sentence
2. Supporting Details
3. Closing sentence or Concluding statement

Name the Different Types of Paragraphs.

There are five types of paragraphs. They are

1. Definition

2. Sequence
3. Classification
4. Description
5. Compare and Contrast

What is a topic sentence ? It is the most important sentence in a paragraph. It sums up the whole idea of the para. It may come in the beginning, middle or at the end. It introduces the main idea of the para. What are supporting sentences ? Supporting sentences come after the topic sentence. They make up the body of a paragraph. They give details to develop and support the main idea of the paragraph. Supporting sentences may consist of facts, details and examples. What is a closing sentence ? A closing sentence is the last sentence of a paragraph. It restates the main idea of the paragraph.

Paragraph Writing

A paragraph is a number of sentences grouped together. It relates to one topic or a group of related sentences that develop a single point. What is the prewriting stage ? The prewriting stage needs careful thinking and organization of ideas before writing. There are six prewriting steps. They are:

1. Think carefully about what you are going to write.
2. Open your notebook.
3. Collect related facts.
4. Pen down your ideas.
5. Find the main idea.
6. Organise your facts and ideas (in a way that develops the main idea).

What is the writing stage ? Turning the ideas into sentences is called the writing stage. There7 are five steps involved in this. They are:

1. Open your notebook and word processor.
2. Write the Topic sentence, supporting sentence and closing sentence.
3. Write clear and simple sentences to express the meaning.
4. Focus on the main idea of the paragraph.
5. Use dictionary to find additional words.

What is the editing stage ? The editing stage is checking the paragraph for mistakes and correcting them.

1. Grammar and spelling
2. Style and organisation
3. Finalising paragraphs
   1. Grammar and Spelling:
      a. Check the spelling.
      b. Check the grammar.
      c. Reread the essay.
      d. Presence of subject in each sentence.
      e. Concord.

f. Check the verbs.
g. Meaning sentence.

2. Style and Organisation:
    1. Confirm the topic sentence.
    2. Confirm whether the supporting sentence focuses on the main idea.
    3. Confirm the closing sentence.
    4. Check all sentences focus on the main idea.
    5. It must be interesting.

3 Finalising Paragraph:

'The Publishing Stage' is when you produce a final copy of the paragraph to submit.

1. Make a paper copy.
2. Show the work to your teacher, parents.
3. Ask them for suggestion or hints to improve.

Name the different types of paragraphs and explain:

1. Definition
2. Sequence
3. Classification
4. Description; Compare and Contrast.

Definition Paragraph:

When writing a definition paragraph, you take an idea and explain what it is. It is defined as, It is a kind of .... Ex: A pest is defined as ...... A pest is a kind of ....

Sequence Paragraph:

Describing a series of events or a process in order is a sequence paragraph. This order is based on time.

Classification Paragraph

Grouping of things or ideas with specific categories is a classification para. Ex: Discussing two types of energy resources.

Description Paragraph

Describing about a person, place or thing. Even location of a place may be described. Related words: size, length, resembles, in, on, etc.,

Compare and Contrast

Writing about the similarities and differences between two or more people, places, things or ideas.

Ex: Compare two cars, two places.

USE OF ACTIVE LEARNING METHODS

Attitude is an important concept to understand human behaviour. It is defined as a complex mental state involving beliefs and feelings. Anastasi defines attitude as tendency to react in a certain way towards a designed class of stimuli. Attitude has been defined as a mental and neutral state of readiness, organised through experience, exerting a directive or dynamic influence upon the individual's response to all objects and situations with which it is related. People's attitudes towards their profession have an effect on their performance.

This case is also valid for the profession of teaching. According to Bradley, inadequate funds of schools, lack of parent and community support, and insufficient salaries are examples of those factors. Marchant added the role of experience to the factors influencing teachers' attitudes for their profession. Dodeen et al. found that female teachers have more positive attitude than male teachers. The attitude and expectation of society in general and of the family of the learner in particular affect how learning is viewed and how teaching is organised.

These attitudes and expectations vary from society to society and attempting to copy learning and teaching strategy from one society into another, without trying to adapt into the local conditions may not be successful. Studies have pointed out that teacher's negative personal and professional behaviour and poor social image of the teacher and teaching profession are serious factors responsible for teacher's low status.

Awanbor reported that teacher trainees had a negative attitude towards teachingn and those teacher trainees who had positive attitude towards teaching did so with strong reservation which range from the poor social image to the teaching profession, the comparatively poor financial remuneration for the teacher, to the general lack of encouragement by educational authorities.

The attitude of teachers comes to the fore as they reflect upon the language that they use in teaching. Consciously or unconsciously, their attitudes play a crucial role in language's "growth or decay, restoration or destruction". Their attitudes, too, as part of their cultural orientation, influence heavily their younger students. There has been a general agreement that the attitude of teachers towards teaching is significantly correlated with teaching success. In general, it may be concluded that there are indications that teacher's attitudes have a positive relation with success in teaching. Researchers identified many factors and situations that influence the development of attitudes are: type of schooling, the parental attitudes, and the attitude of friends, teachers, and siblings. The negative attitude of teachers has been documented in many studies. Another important factor is attitude or belief towards the subject. Callahan and Clark indicate that one can facilitate development of attitude by providing a conducive atmosphere and models. Development of understanding may enhance the development of attitudes just as value clarification, role playing, and discussion of dilemmas may enhance the development of values and morals. Teachers can have general attitudes towards students.

According to Brophy, general attitudes stem from the teacher's personality and definition of his role as a teacher. Many attitudes are the results of deliberately planned education and religious training and influences and propaganda. Person-oriented teachers are likely to enjoy their contacts with students and to hold generally favourable attitudes towards them. In contrast, introvert and withdrawn teachers may prefer to minimize social contacts with students and more likely to develop neutral or relatively negative attitudes towards them. Teachers' attitudes can affect teacher-student interaction. That is, once a teacher forms a particular attitude towards an individual student, the teacher is likely to begin to treat this student in individualised way. Thus, attitudes have the potential for affecting students and for functioning as self-fulfilling prophecies.

OBJECTIVE

To study attitude of English language teachers towards the use of active learning methods in teaching communicative English.

METHOD

Sample

The sample consisted of 23 English language teachers (All teachers at Bahir Dar University in Ethiopia.

Tool

A questionnaire developed by the researchers.

Method

Data analysis used percentages, frequencies and narrative description.

FINDINGS

Out of the 23 questionnaires distributed to the English language teachers, 20 were filled in and returned. The response rate was 86 per cent. Data on English language teachers' attitude towards the importance of active learning methods for communicative English language teaching revealed that 17(85 per cent) of the subjects were in favour of the idea that active learning methods can give students a sense of participation; while 3(15 per cent) were not in favour of this idea. With regard to the idea that active learning methods can integrate students' experiences, 14(70 per cent), and 6(30 per cent) respondents agreed and disagreed, respectively.

To the idea that active learning method creates desirable attitude towards communicative English language teaching, 13(65 per cent), and 7(35 per cent) of the English teachers responded agree and disagree, respectively. Moreover, to the item that students are engaged in reading, writing, listening, and speaking activities 15(75 per cent), and 5(25 per cent), responded agreed and disagreed, respectively. In summary, the great majority of the teachers had good attitude towards the significance of active learning method as it enables English language students to participate actively in English language classes, and integrate their learning experiences.

Therefore, the English language teacher respondents are in favour of utilisation of active learning methods to teach English language. The respondents were asked about students' learning experience in collaborative and supportive environment. It was found that 15(75 per cent), 4(20 per cent), and 1(5 per cent) English language teachers replied agree, undecided and disagree, respectively. From this, one can see that majority of the English language teachers have agreed with this idea. In the second item, the subjects were to respond as to how students identify, analyse, and resolve problems by using their previous experience. It was found that 12(60 per cent), 6(30 per cent), and 2(10 per cent) responded agree, undecided, and disagree, respectively. Thus, it seems to be true that students use their previous experience to identify, analyse, and resolve problems. Regarding the enhancement that the English language teachers provide for their students' motivation, it was found that 14(70 per cent), 5(25 per cent), and 1(5 per cent) replied agree, undecided, and disagree, respectively.

However, majority of the students responded that their English language teachers did not motivate them at all. Concerning whether students participate to learn sufficient content through active learning, it was found that 4(20 per cent), 5(25 per cent), and 11(55 per cent) of them responded agree, undecided, and disagree, respectively. Most of the English language teachers opined that students' participation to learn the content was not sufficient.

The English language teachers were also asked as to how far active learning method helps to classroom interaction. It was found that 13(65 per cent) agreed and 7(35 per cent) disagreed. Therefore, active learning method improves their classroom interaction. The fruitful support of active learning method utilisation becomes realised, only when equipments are available, class size is small, and the English language teachers has necessary training on active learning method utilisation.

CONCLUSION

The English teachers under study showed quite a positive attitude towards the utilisation of active learning methods. They were of the opinion that utilising active learning methods is crucial as it makes students participate in discussion, integrating their learning experiences, and raising their interest of learning English. Besides, teachers underlined the paramount significance of active learning as it helps them improve their English teaching methods. Though teachers showed positive attitude towards the utilisation of active learning methods, there were a number of factors hindering them from utilising the approach properly. These included lack of enough training and experience, inadequate budget meant for the purchase of instructional materials and the shortage of enough seats for the students. Since quality of education is a product of stable and solid leadership, sound and conducive polices, great concern and sustained commitments are vitally important. The reform of instructional practice in higher education must begin with faculty members' efforts. An excellent first step is to select strategies promoting active learning that one can feel comfortable with. Faculty developers can help, stimulate, and support faculty members' effort to change by highlighting the instructional importance of active learning in the newsletters and publications they distribute. Academic administrators can help these initiatives by recognising and rewarding excellent teaching in general and adoption of instructional innovations in particular. Comprehensive programmes to demonstrate this type of administrative commitment should address institutional employment policies and practices, the allocation of adequate resources for instructional development, and the development of strategic administrative action plans.

TEACHING AND LEARNING ENGLISH

Orissa, one of the states of the Union of India is situated in the east coast of India touching the Bay of Bengal in the east and bordering West Bengal on the north-east, Jharkhand on the north-west, Chhattisgarh on the south-west and Andhra Pradesh on the south. According to the 2001 Census, the total population of Orissa is 36,706,920 persons, comprising of 18,612,340 males and 18,094,580 females.

In recent years, due to consistent government support, Orissa has become a major centre for learning in eastern India. The Orissa government official web site lists1679 Degree colleges, 1112 Higher Secondary Schools, 6811 Secondary schools, 11, 510 Middle schools (Upper Primary schools) and 42, 824 Lakh formal primary schools, in the state. The medium of instruction for schools affiliated to the Board of Secondary Education (BSE) in Orissa is Oriya. In majority of the schools under BSE, English is taught from class III. Like other states in India, the teaching is carried out through the Grammar Translation Method (GTM) that puts stress on grammar and vocabulary. Generally, in these schools, the teaching process follows a system where the vernacular meanings of English words and phrases are given to the students and they learn it by rote. But, mostly it is seen that teachers themselves are not well-equipped to teach correct English pronunciation, speaking or reading skills to students. The reason being these teachers are the same people who have passed out from a similar educational system, where their exposure to ELT had been at the most basic level. Even trained graduate teachers who pass out from the Universities of Orissa are not exposed to phonetics or Standard English pronunciation as no university in the state teaches phonetics or spoken English during the graduate years. As most of the teachers themselves had limited exposure in mastering language skills, they complete their degree programme with average language proficiency and in turn follow similar strategies in teaching their students. Specialized English teachers with Diploma in ELT are quite few in number and hence a vicious circle is created in the teaching-learning process.

This scenario is not specific to Orissa but is seen in most other states of India. Gokak (1964) points out that "The foundational years for the teaching of English in schools are in the hands of teachers who neither know enough English nor are familiar with the latest and far-reaching developments in the pedagogy of English".

English is the medium of instruction in the schools affiliated to the Central Board of Secondary Education (CBSE), New Delhi, and to the Indian Council of Secondary Education (ICSE), New Delhi. These are the two central level boards that have schools affiliated to them throughout the country. But, interaction with the students, parents and teachers from some of these schools in Orissa, reveals that students get exposed to English language only for a few hours during the English classes, and for the rest of the classes, no real importance is placed on speaking and writing grammatically correct sentences. The students pass the secondary examination with English as a second language without getting real exposure to sound English teaching practices. As a result, even if they are able to cope with the English medium education at the Higher Secondary and under graduate level, their speaking and writing skills in English continue to remain inadequate. As pointed out by Tickoo (2004), the whole teaching-learning system could be stated to be at fault for this lack of English proficiency in our students, as they are taught by teachers who may not always be highly proficient in its use. The minimum qualification prescribed for English teachers by CBSE and ICSE and the Higher Secondary Boards of different states is a Post Graduate degree in the subject concerned, in addition to a Bachelor of Education (B.Ed.) degree. However, in many public schools in Orissa, Postgraduates without B.Ed. are teaching English in Higher Secondary classes, resulting in certain negative teaching outcomes, particularly in the language teaching process.

Most of the Higher Secondary Schools (Junior Colleges as they are known in Orissa) are affiliated to the Council of Higher Secondary Education (CHSE), Orissa. The Council has prescribed an English syllabus for 200 marks comprising some portions of Communicative English, vocabulary, grammar, essays, poems, short stories etc. for reading practice and for acquisition of the four basic language skills. The Communicative English course which claims to equip Higher Secondary students with the four language skills (listening, speaking reading and writing) does not achieve the targeted goals as the evaluation is done only on writing skills. In effect, the course is not much different from that of secondary schools. Both teachers and students tend to neglect the other language skills. As per students' own submission, they refer to Guidebooks and Key books widely available in the market, and manage to clear the examination. Moreover, the teachers who handle the higher Secondary syllabus of CHSE are not properly trained to teach Communicative English as most of them are postgraduates in English literature. Very few of them have the ELT background essential to teach the Communicative English syllabus.

In Orissa, avenues for higher technical education remained inadequate until the mid-nineteen fifties. Students depended upon other states for education in Engineering, Medicine and Management. The establishment of the University College of Engineering (UCE) in 1956, presently renamed as Veer Surendra Sai University of Technology (VSSUT) at Burla, followed by Regional Engineering College at Rourkela in 1961, (renamed National Institute of Technology, and designated as an institute of national importance) heralded the dawn of engineering studies in the state. Later on, the establishment of Orissa University of Agriculture and Technology (OUAT) at Bhubaneswar in 1965 became a milestone in promoting technical education in the state. Another Engineering College in the Government sector, Indira Gandhi Institute of Technology (IGIT) was started later in 1982 at Talcher, and Orissa Engineering College (OEC), the first of its kind in the private sector, came up in 1986 at Bhubaneswar, the capital city of Orissa. At present, there are more than hundred science and technology institutes in Orissa, including government funded and self-financing ones, out of which around ninety institutes are affiliated to the Biju Patnaik University of Technology (BPUT), which is the source University of this particular Research Study.

Department of Humanities and Social Sciences (HSS), which includes English as one of its major subjects, is an integral part of every technical institute in India. In most of these institutes, the HSS component has been made compulsory for all Bachelor of Technology (B. Tech) students. There are, however, big problems that go with this inclusion of the HSS component into the curriculum. English classes sometimes have a higher student–teacher ratio than engineering classes, varying between 50 and 100 students per class. Therefore, it is extremely difficult for the teacher to give special attention to each student in such big classes. Many Indian students also suffer from low confidence in their use of English, as English is not their mother-tongue. Other individuals and agencies have reported the lack of employability skills of the students quite frequently in the recent past. In the last few years, newspapers have repeatedly brought out reports about the un-employability of Indian engineering professionals in the global scenario. A *Times of India* (*Education Times* section) report dated 21 February 2008, states that, "As India rode the liberalization wave, the Indian youth, equipped with their inherent resourcefulness, intelligence, ambition and enterprise, were lapped up by Indian Inc and money-spinning MNCs... However, the past couple of years have witnessed a growing concern over the gradual erosion of the impeccable reputation of the Indian student... They are lacking in good communication skills and are deficient in analytical and process orientation skills." In 2007, MeritTrac, a Bangalore based skills assessment firm, conducted a study that found only 23 per cent of MBA students from tier two colleges were employable. Earlier that year, in another study, it had concluded that a staggering 74 percent of all engineering graduates were unemployable. MadanPadaki, Founder and CEO of MeritTrac says that, "A lot of our curriculum has been designed for rote learning, and hence, there is no scope for thinking." In addition, at a gathering of vice-chancellors during the 82nd annual meeting of the Association of Indian Universities, former President of India, Dr. APJ Abdul Kalam, asserted that only 25 per cent of graduating students were employable, and that students were lacking in areas such as technical knowledge, English proficiency and critical thinking.

Considering these adverse comments and criticism from the various stakeholders regarding the lack of adequate English proficiency among our students, it has become essential to conduct a needs assessment survey to bridge the gap existing between current ESP courses in engineering institutes of India and the expectations of an increasingly competitive industry. One of the factors that could aid the needs analysis of the learners in the first year of their engineering studies is an assessment of their English language competency gained during the Secondary or Higher Secondary levels. This assessment is to be done with students from both vernacular and English medium schools. As language acquisition related issues and problems are common for vernacular medium students throughout India, an analysis of the language ability of the students of Orissa is assumed to serve the purpose of all students.

Although researchers and educators agree that Indian engineering graduates are not proficient in English, few studies have been conducted to examine the procedures, measures and strategies of teaching and learning to improve engineering students' achievements in English. To the researcher's best knowledge all previous studies have focused on students' lack of English skills and the reasons for them. Not many studies have been conducted designed to explore the needs and requirements of students and thereby offer solutions towards improving their proficiency in English.

The engineering colleges of Orissa affiliated to BPUT, follow the Communicative English course and Business English or Professional English course for enhancing the language skills of engineering students at the undergraduate level. In most cases, it is either a two or a three-semester course, comprising of both theory and practical classes. In some deemed universities or colleges like NIT the colleges have the liberty to introduce it either in the first year (in either 1st 4th or 2nd semester) or in the second year (either in 3rd or semester) of the engineering programme. There are summative assessments for the two-credit theory papers and for the two-credit lab course, the performance of the students in the laboratory is assessed and credits recorded and forwarded to the University.

The goals and objectives of the course as noted in the syllabus are furnished below for better understanding:

- To develop listening, speaking, reading and writing skills.
- To cultivate the habit of reading newspapers, magazines and books to consolidate the skills already achieved.
- To familiarize the students with the sounds of English (Phonetics) in a nutshell.
- To provide adequate listening and speaking practice so that the learners can speak with ease, fluency and clarity in common everyday situations and on formal occasions.
- To be given practice to use grammar in meaningful contexts and perform functions like ordering; requesting, inviting etc. Similarly, the Business English course sets its objectives as the following:
- To prepare the students to handle various written communications like reports, letters etc.
- To make notes or summarize documents, organize meetings, prepare agenda, draft resolutions, write minutes of meetings, make oral presentations,
- To be familiar with the techniques of managerial communication for information sharing, making presentations, and taking part in meetings, interviews, and negotiations.
- Every college is supposed to provide a well-equipped Language Laboratory. Students are required to practice listening, speaking and writing skills in the practical or laboratory classes.
- Certain tasks/assignments are suggested to be taken up in the practical classes.

Taking into consideration the various objectives of the course it could be designed to be a part of the English for Academic Purposes (EAP), English for Specific Purposes (ESP) or English for Occupational Purposes (EOP), as the goals of these three dimensions of English learning do not differ much from each other. Long (2005), in this context states:

Instead of a one-size-fits-for-all approach, it is more defensible to view every course as involving specific purpose, the difference in each case being simply the precision with which it is possible to identify current or future uses of the L2. It varies from little or no precision in the case of most young children, to great precision in that of most adult learners.

The study covers the teaching-learning process of English language in government-funded institutions of engineering in Orissa along with self-financing colleges affiliated to BPUT. The course contents and credit system of government-funded institutes differ slightly from that of the colleges affiliated to BPUT. The target groups included students from different semesters, representing a cross-section of undergraduates. Colleges were selected based on year of establishment so that sampling of the statistical data was representative and objective. The target groups included learners from urban, semi-urban and rural areas of not only Orissa but also from other different parts of India like Bihar, West-Bengal, Jharkhand, Assam, other North-Eastern states and even from neighbouring countries like Nepal and Tibet, pursuing their undergraduate engineering studies in Orissa. The students are admitted according to their ranking in the Orissa Joint Entrance Examination (OJEE), which has various categories of listing according to caste and region. As a result, every college enrolls mixed ability students from different castes and regions.

Questionnaire survey among teachers and students of different semesters, discussion with teachers and focused interview involving students constitute the various tools for data collection. Other than recording comments and suggestions, objective information from questionnaires were analyzed by using statistical tools like SPSS software. The data collection was done personally, in classroom situations, by visiting the colleges and interacting with teachers, students and authorities concerned. A reliable interpretation of data based on questionnaire survey, observation and interaction with the respondents using triangulation method has been attempted. This researcher had been teaching Communicative and Business English courses in different engineering colleges of Orissa for around five years and is therefore quite familiar with the problems involved in the teaching-learning process.

ENGLISH LANGUAGE LEARNERS AND THE "HIDDEN CURRICULUM"

The goal of teachers of ELLs is to help interact with adults and peers in both formal and informal settings. English language learners need to be specifically taught social skills such as how to greet people, to give and receive compliments, to apologize, and to make polite requests. They need to know when to use their native language and when this is not appropriate. Students need to understand non-verbal language and proxemics. They need to be able to discover the appropriate voice tones, volumes, and language for different school settings.

The need for teaching socially and culturally appropriate language in social situations is evident every day in our classes. We have all had students who use the same language when speaking to a teacher that they would use when talking to a peer. I once had a beginning ESL student who had learned how to say "yeah, yeah, yeah" to friends during recess. He couldn't say or understand much else in English. Whenever I gave him directions, he would reply, "Yeah, yeah, yeah." I had a difficult time making him comprehend that this was inappropriate language for a child to use to an adult. I finally taught him to say, "Yes, Mrs. Haynes" but I needed to have a translator explain why "yeah, yeah, yeah" was unsuitable for the classroom.

The same thing occurs when a second language speaker swears in class. An exited ESL student in my school recently used an "x-rated" expression in his third grade classroom. The teacher was understandably distressed and required that the student write an apology for homework. Even more upsetting to the teacher was that the student's parents did not take the infraction of school rules seriously. I explained to her that swearing does not have the same "shock" value in a person's second language as it does in their first. So the parents were not "shocked" by their child's use of this language. What is considered "shocking" or inappropriate language for the classroom must sometimes be directly taught.

USE ROLE PLAYING TO TEACH GOOD MANNERS

I believe that teaching our ESL students what is considered good manners in the United States is very important. This is no way means that our ESL students are ill-mannered. Norms for social interchanges vary from culture to culture. What is expected of children also changes between cultures.

I spend a lot of time teaching students how to give and receive compliments, to thank someone for something, to answer the telephone, to ask directions, and to make small talk. Role playing, teacher modeling, peer modeling, and video are all good tools for teaching these social skills. Have students learn how to observe their peers for models of correct behaviour. Use real incidents that come up in your class. Have students practice saying "good morning" and "good-by" to their teachers and classmates right from the beginning. Encourage classroom teachers to set expectations for these behaviours.

Mainstream teachers need to receive special training so that they learn about some of the cultural differences in manners and behaviour. You don't want teachers to over-react when a student won't make eye contact or relates to other children by touching them all the time, or smiles at inappropriate times.

Teaching students appropriate times to use native language and English is a lesson I also cover in my ESL class. I have students brainstorm when it is appropriate to speak native language during the school day. I am looking for responses such as "before school," "lunchtime," "on the playground," "in the bathroom," or " in the hallway." Then we look for occasions during the instructional day that students might need to speak native language: To ask a peer for help; to explain something urgent or complicated to the teacher and to give or receive an explanation of material that isn't understood in English; We then look for circumstances when it would be impolite or inappropriate to speak native language. An example of this would be when someone is being left out because they don't speak the native language.

Many educators believe that English language learners will acquire socially appropriate behaviour and language simply by being with English-speaking natives. I don't think this should be left to chance.

ESL TEACHER AS CULTURAL BROKER

Understanding and interpreting the cultures of second language learners is an important part of the ESL/bilingual teachers' role. Helping classroom teachers to do this is even more of a challenge. Misinterpretations are bound to occur on both sides. Whenever a mainstream staff members thinks an ESL youngsters' behaviour seems unwarranted, bizarre, rude, or in some way unexpected, it's possible that this is a sign of cultural misunderstanding. And it is the ESL/bilingual professional who is called upon to unlock the cultural puzzle.

Can ESL/bilingual or classroom teachers learn all there is to know about the various cultures in your school? No, of course not!

Effective staff development courses are a way ESL/bilingual professionals can help mainstream staff members better interpret the cultures of the diverse student populations in your school. The objectives of a staff development workshop would be to give participants:

- An awareness of how much culture affects language acquisition and behaviour
- The discernment not to interpret the behaviour of others through the eyes of their own culture
- Insight into their own culture
- The tools to "unlock" cultural puzzles

Download these activities for your next staff inservice.

STATE YOUR POINT OF VIEW

Participants state their attitudes and beliefs about multiculturalism in the U.S. in a non-threatening way. This activity can easily be modified to meet the needs of individual groups or districts.

WHAT IS...?

See what the participants in your workshop know about ESL. There are two activities in this PDF file; one for ESL professionals and one for classroom teachers.

COMMUNICATION GAME

Most Americans who have not lived or gone to school in another country do not understand what it feels like to come to the United States and function in a strange school setting. Give workshop participants the experience of not being able to make themselves understood through this lively activity

STAND UP AND BE COUNTED

This is a demonstration of how we are all members of a minority at one time or another. At the end of this exercise, ask participants which items they were reluctant to stand up for and why. Discuss how it felt to be standing alone or with only a few other people. Of course, the items in this activity can be changed to meet the needs of your audience.

IS THE AMERICAN UGLY?

Adapted from the work of Hsu, an antropologist who spent half his life in China and half in the U.S, this activity will show participants how Americans are viewed from the outside. Hsu found Americans obsessed with privacy. However, we don't seem to value privacy to the French with our unfenced yards, open office doors and the windows of our homes facing the street. It all depends on who's looking.

CULTURAL QUIZ

This is a lively activity where participants develop cultural insights into the behaviour of second language learners in their classrooms. It is a favourite activity for staff inservice programmes. Divide participants into groups of three or four and provide each group with a cultural scenerio. Have groups discuss what they think is causing the problem in their scenerio and present their conclusions.

WHAT'S IN A GESTURE?

Gestures are an important element when exchanging ideas or information with people from other cultures. Learning how gestures can affect cross-cultural communication is another favourite with mainstream teachers.

MULTICULTURAL ME

This activity shows how we all identify with different groups at different times. Participants should write their names in the centre circle and then write five different groups with which they identify in the outside circles. Examples of the different kinds of groups that can be named are race, religion, gender, age, profession, language, town, neighbourhood, school, and beliefs. After the group has finished this activity, you might want to have them share when they felt proud to be a member of one of their groups and when it felt uncomfortable.

TRUTH OF STEREOTYP

South American culture is featured in this activity. Have your audience read the scenerios and decided if they agree or disagree.

TAKE THE ELEVATOR!

Have you ever heard anyone say "They're in the U.S. now, let them do it our way." This activity demonstrates how deeply ingrained our cultural behaviour is and how difficult it would be to change it.

EXPLORING PREJUDICE AND BIAS

Have participants in your workshop discover their own prejudices in a non-threatening environment. This activity provides an anonymous way for people to express themselves freely. The results will surprise you.

MYTHS OF SECOND LANGUAGE ACQUISITION

There are many misconceptions about how a second language is acquired. Address these myths with this short quiz. Some of the responses will surprise even the most savvy participants. This activity has been updated.

KEEP AN ARMS-LENGTH AWAY

Have you ever heard of the American "bubble?" Most Americans feel most comfortable when people keep an arms-length away during conversations. Try this out with this activity.

SECOND LANGUAGE SENSITIVITY

This is a dynamite activity for demonstrating to participants what it is like to sit in a classroom while someone lectures in an incomprehensible language.

BASIC INTERPERSONAL COMMUNICATION SKILLS

Experts such as Jim Cummins differentiate between social and academic language acquisition. Basic Interpersonal Communication Skills (BICS) are language skills needed in social situations. It is the day-to-day language needed to interact socially with other people.

English language learners (ELLs) employ BIC skills when they are on the playground, in the lunch room,on the school bus, at parties, playing sports and talking on the telephone. Social interactions are usually context embedded. They occur in a meaningful social context. They are not very demanding cognitively. The language required is not specialized. These language skills usually develop within six months to two years after arrival in the U.S.

Problems arise when teachers and administrators think that a child is proficient in a language when they demonstrate good social English.

COGNITIVE ACADEMIC LANGUAGE PROFICIENCY

CALP refers to formal academic learning. This includes listening, speaking, reading, and writing about subject area content material. This level of language learning is essential for students to succeed in school. Students need time and support to become proficient in academic areas. This usually takes from five to seven years. Recent research has shown that if a child has no prior schooling or has no support in native language development, it may take seven to ten years for ELLs to catch up to their peers.

Academic language acquisition isn't just the understanding of content area vocabulary. It includes skills such as comparing, classifying, synthesizing, evaluating, and inferring. Academic language tasks are context reduced. Information is read from a textbook or presented by the teacher. As a student gets older the context of academic tasks becomes more and more reduced.

The language also becomes more cognitively demanding. New ideas, concepts and language are presented to the students at the same time.

Jim Cummins also advances the theory that there is a common underlying proficiency (CUP) between two languages. Skills, ideas and concepts students learn in their first language will be transferred to the second language.

GIANTS STEPS WITH NONFICTION WRITING

A recent professional development programme in my district on the writing process prodded me to re-examine how I teach writing. I have been teaching process writing to English language learners (ELLs) over the past 20 years. (This is a method of teaching writing where the focus is on the process not on the product.) It was during this in-service programme, however, that I realized how many modifications I make to the writing process to meet the needs of my English language learners.

The biggest challenge when teaching writing to new learners of English is that many of them develop their text in their native language and then try to translate into English. This translated writing is full of inaccurate verb tenses and unintelligible sentences.

There are so many errors that editing becomes problematic for teachers. I feel strongly that it is better to help students avoid writing in English through the filter of their native language. In my experience, the problem is particularly evident when grade 3-6 students have developed writing skills in their first language and that language is very different from English.

For this reason, I don't have my students free write. (This is a writing technique in which students write without stopping and without worrying about correctness.) Why teach them to write incomprehensively? Nor do I encourage beginners to write in a journal, as this writing is also unstructured. One classroom teacher told me that she had students write every night in a journal at home. I could only imagine the results of that with English language learners. Their text would range from incoherent writing to work that has been overseen and overcorrected by parents. The writing would definitely be product oriented.

What problems do our students face when learning to write in English? First, their vocabulary is restricted and they limit themselves to words they know how to spell. As a result, they repeat the same words and phrases again and again. Their sentence structure is generally chaotic and grammar obscure. Let's examine the work of a 5th grade newcomer who wrote the following text in her mainstream classroom in response to the prompt: "If you were an animal, what animal would you like to be and why?"

"I like be eagle becas eagle birds king and he fly very up. They scard. When they baby, they take off they feather and they squek they claw. " Yimin,

How do we avoid the garbled writing that Yimin produced? I am convinced that English language learners write better if they begin with non-fiction reading and writing. Graphic organizers such as story maps, T-charts, and Venn diagrams help scaffold writing and provide students with language chunks that can be used in their text.

If topics are developed orally, non-fiction vocabulary expanded and charted, and correct sentence structure modeled, student writing will improve dramatically. One way to achieve this is to teach non-fiction writing during writing workshop and to modify writing process steps for beginning English language learners. The topics used during this lesson should be taken from the students' subject area content. I recommend the following steps:

PREWRITING

You will need to spend a lot of time in this stage with new learners of English.

- As a follow-up to non-fiction reading, brainstorm and chart facts about the topic in sentence form. Have them read the facts from your chart orally. Strengthen the link between oral and written language.
- Keep a running list of content vocabulary. Review and practice the vocabulary every day. Speak and write facts in full sentences.
- Use graphic organizers to help students arrange ideas. ELLs will usually find it difficult to go from phrases to comprehensible sentences so complete the organizer with sentences, not phrases. Your students may not value this strategy if they have not used organizers to write in their native language so you will need to insist on it.

WRITING

Have students practice writing from a story map, Venn diagram or other type of graphic organizer. Provide them with an organizer that you have written together on the non-fiction topic. This gives a beginning writer the language and structure that they need. Show clearly what should be covered in the writing and how it should be organized.

EDITING

Don't expect students who are not fluent in English to self-edit. They will not usually find their own mistakes. You will have to be more hands-on with the editing of non-native speakers and conference with them on a regular basis to discuss their works–in- progress. If you have your students peer-edit, they may be reluctant to share their work with native speakers. You may want to group beginners with more fluent native speakers. Give pairs a specific item to check. For example "Check the 's' at the end of a verb if you are talking about one other person." You may need to teach a mini-lesson about the item you want edited.

REVISING

English language learners will not remember what to revise unless changes are clearly marked on their papers. Instead of writing "Add more information here," write more specifically "Tell what eagles eat here." If students are a part of the editing process, the revisions will be more meaningful to them.

PUBLISHING

This is an important step. Help students develop a sense of audience by encouraging students to share their writing with classmates and family. Display work in the classroom and hallway or make classroom books.

I see my students take giant steps when non-fiction writing is introduced to beginners in writing workshop and steps are modified as shown above. Yimin wrote this piece on a forest animal in her ESL classroom.

"Eagle are carnivores. They live in forest. They eat small mammal, fish and snakes. They use eyes to see prey. They catch food with sharp talon. They are diurnal because they hunt in the day."

Yimin's non-fiction writing is comprehensible. The unit vocabulary has been correctly utilized, errors in grammar are easily identified and rectified and the sentence structure is accurate. She is now ready to try other types of writing.

DICTIONARY FOR LEARNERS

A dictionary is a collection of words in a specific language, often listed alphabetically, with definitions, etymologies, phonetics, pronunciations, and other information; or a book of words in one language with their equivalents in another, also known as a lexicon.According to Nielsen 2008 a dictionary may be regarded as a lexicographical product that is characterised by three significant features: (1) it has been prepared for one or more functions; (2) it contains data that have been selected for the purpose of fulfilling those functions; and (3) its lexicographic structures link and establish relationships between the data so that they can meet the needs of users and fulfil the functions of the dictionary.

In many languages, words can appear in many different forms, but only the undeclined or unconjugated form appears as the headword in most dictionaries. Dictionaries are most commonly found in the form of a book, but some newer dictionaries, like StarDict and the New Dictionary are dictionary software running on PDAs or computers. There are also many online dictionaries accessible via the Internet..

The oldest known dictionaries were Akkadian empire cuneiform tablets with bilingual Sumerian-Akkadian wordlists, discovered in Ebla (modern Syria) and dated roughly 2300 BCE.The early 2nd millennium BCE Urra=hubullu glossary is the canonical Babylonian version of such bilingual Sumerian wordlists.

A Chinese dictionary, the ca. 3rd century BCE Erya, was the earliest surviving monolingual dictionary, although some sources cite the ca. 800 BCE Shizhoupian as a "dictionary", modern scholarship considers it a calligraphic compendium of Chinese characters from Zhou dynasty bronzes. Philitas of Cos (fl. 4th century BCE) wrote a pioneering vocabulary Disorderly Words (ôáêôïé ãëöóóáé, Átaktoi glôssai) which explained the meanings of rare Homeric and other literary words, words from local dialects, and technical terms.Apollonius the Sophist (fl. 1st century CE) wrote the oldest surviving Homeric lexicon.

The first Sanskrit dictionary, the Amarakoœa, was written by Amara Sinha ca. 4th century CE. Written in verse, it listed around 10,000 words. According to the Nihon Shoki, the first Japanese dictionary was the long-lost 682 CE Niina glossary of Chinese characters. The oldest existing Japanese dictionary, the ca. 835 CE Tenrei Banshô Meigi, was also a glossary of written Chinese.

Arabic dictionaries were compiled between the 8th and 14th centuries CE, organizing words in rhyme order (by the last syllable), by alphabetical order of the radicals, or according to the alphabetical order of the first letter (the system used in modern European language dictionaries). The modern system was mainly used in specialist dictionaries, such as those of terms from the Qur'an and hadith, while most general use dictionaries, such as the Lisan al-'Arab and al-Qamus al-Muhit listed words in the alphabetical order of the radicals. The Qamus al-Muhit is the first handy dictionary in Arabic, which includes only words and their definitions, eliminating the supporting examples used in such dictionaries as the Lisan and the English Dictionary.

The earliest modern European dictionaries were bilingual dictionaries. The earliest in the English language were glossaries of French, Italian or Latin words along with definitions of the foreign words in English. An early non-alphabetical list of 8000 English words was the Elementarie.

The first purely English alphabetical dictionary was A Table Alphabeticall, written by English schoolteacher Robert Cawdrey in 1604. The only surviving copy is found at the Bodleian Library. Yet this early effort, as well as the many imitators which followed it, was seen as unreliable and nowhere near definitive.

Philip Stanhope, 4th Earl of Chesterfield was still lamenting in 1754, 150 years after Cawdrey's publication, that it is "a sort of disgrace to our nation, that hitherto we have had no... standard of our language; our dictionaries at present being more properly what our neighbours the Dutch and the Germans call theirs, word-books, than dictionaries in the superior sense of that title." It was not until Samuel Johnson's A Dictionary of the English Language that a truly noteworthy, reliable English Dictionary was deemed to have been produced, and the fact that today many people still mistakenly believe Johnson to have written the first English Dictionary is a testament to this legacy. By this stage, dictionaries had evolved to contain textual references for most words, and were arranged alphabetically, rather than by topic (a previously popular form of arrangement, which meant all animals would be grouped together, etc.). Johnson's masterwork could be judged as the first to bring all these elements together, creating the first 'modern' dictionary.

Johnson's Dictionary remained the English-language standard for over 150 years began writing and releasing the English Dictionary in short fascicles. It took nearly 50 years to finally complete the huge work, and they finally released the complete Dictionary.

It remains the most comprehensive and trusted English language dictionary to this day, with revisions and updates added by a dedicated team every three months. One of the main contributors to this modern day dictionary was an ex-army surgeon, William Chester Minor, a convicted murderer who was confined to an asylum for the criminally insane.

IMPORTANCE

IF YOU'RE A LAWYER

Judges quote from the dictionary all the time. It is well known that the U.S. Supreme Court and Justice Scalia in particular increasingly cite dictionaries in their decisions. Many different dictionaries get cited. There is no single best dictionary. While "Webster's" seems to be the most popular, several unrelated dictionaries can call themselves Webster's and Noah Webster's copyrights have long since expired. Other courts cite dictionaries as well.

So when preparing a brief, make sure that you look up key terms and refer to their definition. If a key term has multiple meanings, then use a thesaurus to find the correct unambiguous term.

A major part of legal research is sitting down in front of a search engine to find case law. Some of the user interfaces of major search tools for lawyers are difficult to use. If you don't use the exact words for the search, you will miss something or get too many documents.

A good dictionary lets you check the spelling of words before you launch a search. And a thesaurus lets you find synonyms and other related words. The full version of LookWAYup includes the option of generating a search of the FindLaw service, and can automatically search for synonyms, related words, and context terms.

IF YOU'RE A TEACHER

(this section adapted from the article *"How and Why Add LookWAYup to Hot Potatoes Exercises"*)

LookWAYup has a number of features that benefit the learner of English at several levels. Because it finds words in their natural habitat, it reduces them automatically to their dictionary form, through its extensive understanding of grammar. It is not easily fooled; "criteria" is changed to "criterion" and "aren't" to "be". Beyond correct inflected spellings, it also tolerates misspellings in words entered by the learner, particularly phonetic misspellings. For instance "emfasis" is changed to "emphasis" but the learner is told that this was an error. When it is not clear what the error was, LookWAYup provides several alternatives.

Where a word has several senses (and restricted-vocabulary words often do) the most likely sense is presented first, followed by all other meanings are in decreasing order of likelihood. Clicking on "More..." moves to a more detailed page with examples of usage and a thesaurus. "The satirists ridiculed the plans for a new opera house"

Synonyms include "laugh at" "make fun" "poke fun", that to ridicule is to mock, and that more specific verbs include satirize, debunk, and stultify. Clicking on "mock" similarly tells you that to mock is to treat with contempt, and that one can mock by ridiculing, teasing, or deriding. Licensed users of the full version would further find out that while people ridicule persons, things and activities, it is not unusual for things to mock persons.

The pedagogical advantages of adding LookWAYup to computer-assisted learning exercises are clear. Unlike a paper exercise where any one word can be the stumbling block to understanding, using LookWAYup provides the tools to overcome the difficulty, without embarassment to the learner.

The dictionary means that the teacher is not forced to analyse each word to see whether each learner is familiar with the use of this word in this context. The ability to use a slightly more advanced vocabulary without risk reinforces this vocabulary for those who have seen it and allows others to rapidly acquire the vocabulary, giving them the confidence to take on more challenging texts. The value of this risk-free uncertainty certainly depends on the cultural importance of embarassment for the learner.

The interaction that is possible with the text when LookWAYup is added means that the set of possible interactions between the learner and the learning materials is not resricted to what was predicted or prescribed by the teacher.

IF YOU'RE A STUDENT

How do you look up the spelling of a word when you don't know how it's spelled? This is where LookWAYup comes in. Unlike other online dictionaries, it fixes your spelling for you if you are reasonably close.

A thesaurus is a great tool if you are writing an essay. Teachers will always prefer writing where you vary the vocabulary. What does this mean? It means that you should not use the same word too many times in a row.

Start out your research on any paper with a dictionary. It will get you keywords, phrases, and synonyms that will help you formulate your searches using online databases and search engines.

It is good to have a dictionary handy when you are reading a document. If you're unsure of the meaning of a word in a document, you just highlight the word and launch LookWAYup and then you instantly find out what it means. You can have a LookWAYup window open and drag words onto it. This is particularly good if you are using software other than a browser. To be able to look up words while you are browsing, then just install the dictionary on your browser. It only takes a few seconds.

IF YOU'RE LEARNING ENGLISH

A dictionary is a great companion to stretch a small vocabulary. When you come across a word you're not familiar with, a dictionary helps you by defining the word and giving you examples of its use in a sentence. If you hear the word rather than reading it you may not be sure how to spell it. This is where a spelling-tolerant dictionary like LookWAYup can help: a reasonably close phonetic spelling is good enough. If you read the word, your may be faced with an irregular plural or participle. For instance, if you see the word "spoken" you need to look up the word "speak".

While you are looking up the word, you have an opportunity to learn a number of related words. The word may have several meanings. The more you learn English, the greater the number of secondary meanings you want to look up. These are usually in order of how commonly the sense is used. The better your English, the more senses you want to become familiar with. This will avoid confusion in the future as you start reading more complex documents. It is also useful to look up synomyms while you are there. Looking up synonyms is a good way of confirming that you have actually understood the word. Are the synonyms listed by the dictionary interchangeable in a sentence with the word you are looking up? If not, you may have the wrong sense of the word.

Another great tool for learning is "related terms". You can look up more general or more specific terms. Looking up more general terms is great for reading; it helps better understand the word but letting look at words that have slightly different meanings and understanding why they are not synonyms. Using LookWAYup to navigate through related words is also a great way to find the correct word. You can look up a similar or related word, or a general word, and by following the links you can find the right word. For instance if you are looking for a word that means to see something quickly, you can look up the word "see" then find more specific terms like "get a look" or its synonym "catch a glimpse". Another way of using a dictionary is to translate a term into your language. There are a number of online dictionaries, including LookWAYup, which will take a word in English and translate it into your language, or vice-versa. One of the features that is built into LookWAYup is that it associates the translation of the word with the sense of the word, that is to say it provides a full definition, examples, and thesaurus entries, not just "you give me a string of letters and I give you a string of letters". If you have an internet-enabled mobile phone, or a Palm or Blackberry, you can use LookWAYup anywhere, not just when you are sitting at a computer. If you see a word on a restaurant menu or an airport sign, simply type it into your mobile device and you will get an instant definition.

IF YOU'RE LEARNING ANOTHER LANGUAGE

An online dictionary is wonderful if you are learning a new language. If you don't know a language at all, then you have probably tried one of the many online translators; they take a page of foreign language that looks like complete gibberish and turn it into a page of English that is only mostly gibberish.

If you know the rudiments of the language, then you are better off reading it yourself with only a little help from an online dictionary for the words you're not sure of. The LookWAYup translation tools will do this. With the traditional "you give me a string of letters and I give you a string of letters" approach, you may be no further ahead. If it tells you "jouer" can mean "act", you do not know what sense of "act" is meant. LookWAYup plugs translation to the sense, with definition, examples, and thesaurus entries.

WHEN YOU'RE SURFING THE WEB

The web is a fine source of information, but first you have to ask it the right questions and then you have to understand the answer.

The first step (and also several of the middle steps) in finding information on the web is to create a good query for a search engine. This means making sure that you are using the right word, that it is correctly spelled, and you may want to add synonyms to broaden the search. This is something that LookWAYup can do automatically for a variety of search engines, using general engines like Google or specialized ones for case law or song lyrics.

WHEN SOMEONE USES A WORD YOU DON'T UNDERSTAND IN A MEETING

What do you do when you are sitting in a meeting and someone uses a word you don't know? Be the first one to admit your ignorance and ask the speaker, or hope that the word isn't important and risk missing the entire point?

If you have an internet-enabled mobile phone, or a Palm or Blackberry, you can use LookWAYup anywhere, not just when you are sitting at a computer.

It's very discreet if you want it to be, or you can look like you are studiously taking note of the important parts. Simply type it into your mobile device and you will get an instant definition. Even if your spelling is not quite right it should find it for you.

WHEN YOU'RE WRITING

A dictionary is an essential tool for writers. You have to make sure that words are spelled correctly. An automatic spell checker will find nothing wrong with a "two carrot diamond ring" or other homonyms, you need a dictionary to make sure you are correctly spelling the *right* word.

Editors will always tell you to vary your vocabulary. This means that you should not use the same word too many times in a row. When you see you are about to use the same word again, look it up in the thesaurus. If you're using LookWAYup, just drag the word to an open LookWAYup window. to see synonyms and related terms for a particular meaning of the word. You can then use some of the synonyms, or find more specific terms under "Examples" or other related terms if they fit the sentence.

TO AVOID LOOKING STUPID

Some people use fancy words to stifle open discussion, particularly in meetings. Or you may be new to a field and willing to learn, and for any word there's always a first time. Psychologists will tell you that one of the major motivators in life is to avoid looking stupid. *(So tell them they will look stupid unless they use it - Sales) (don't forget to remove this note - Sales)* If you actually are stupid, then no dictionary will help you. But if you're not, an online dictionary is a good way to quickly and discreetly bring yourself up to speed on the vocabulary that others are using. Put it on your wireless PDA or mobile phone.

7

Teaching and Learning Grammar in English Language

TEACHING AND LEARNING GRAMMAR

If you live in a country where English is the main language used, you may have discovered that many approaches to teaching English in schools tend to sideline the structure of the language. In fact, your first meeting with the notion of grammar is more likely to have been when you were studying a foreign language. This is not, of course, the same as learning the grammar of English, as languages differ in the way they work and in the terms we use to talk about them.

Consequently, if you are a native speaker of English, you may find that your knowledge of how English works is at best sketchy. This can be a particular problem for teachers of English as a foreign language because their students may sometimes know more about English grammar than an inexperienced teacher. This should not be too surprising since English language students study the structure of English in some detail. However, without the necessary background, the teacher will be at a disadvantage and may even find him/herself in an awkward situation when trying to explain a specific point of grammar.

Teachers of English need to have a good command of the grammar of English simply because our students expect to learn Standard English that will serve them in most situations. We need to remember that they are likely to be speaking to non-native as much as native speakers of English. This is not therefore a question of overly pedantic insistence on correct English, rather the emphasis is on a more pragmatic approach that ensures the English they use is not going to confuse the person they are writing or speaking to. Grammatical accuracy has recently become more important due to the rise in learners of English who need to communicate in writing. Currently, an increasing number of learners require English for Academic and Occupational Purposes (essay, dissertations and reports for example) to be as close to native-speaker competence as possible, so accuracy is a major consideration for them.

FOCUS OF ENGLISH GRAMMAR

Tense	Concerning time sequence
Person	Reference to people or things
Syntax	How parts relate to each other

USES OF ENGLISH GRAMMAR

An awareness of grammar or the structure of language can result in more efficient writing and speaking.

An understanding of the mechanics or workings of language is far more useful and more easily acquired than memorizing technical terms.

You can understand the mechanics of language by studying utterances and their:

audience – form – function

It is useful to be able to distinguish between the more grammatical items in a statement and those, which have a mainly lexical function.

The grammatical items are the working parts of the statement, whilst the lexical items carry content or meaning.

There is no absolute distinction between grammatical and lexical items. However, it is possible to think of a continuum, with lexis at one end and grammar at the other.

The study of English grammar study has developed over hundreds of years. The objective has generally been to find a set of rules which accurately and comprehensively define, describe, and explain the workings of the language.

In the past, grammar study was very prescriptive. Rules were laid down as to how English must be used. Many of these prescriptive rules were based on the rules of the Latin language, which historically had strong religious and cultural ties with English.

Latin was regarded as the perfect language and as such was used as a model for English. However, it was a blueprint which didn't fit, and the struggle to make it fit has left us with such prescriptive rules as 'Never end a sentence with a preposition'.

In the past, the study of grammar was thought to be a series of rules and regulations:

- Rules for writing good English
- Learning to analyse sentences grammatically

The most significant development this century has been the move towards a descriptive and functional approach to understanding of the workings of English. That is to say, the emphasis currently is on observing how the language is actually operating in practice. Changes are charted and variations noted, with a neutral attitude.

A language is best seen as a living organism, which is constantly in the process of evolution. The nature of its changes reflects and affects its users.

As Latin has been a dead language for hundreds of years, its imposition on English is at best interesting and at worst ludicrous.

Every language has a basic structure. This is composed of its essential grammatical features, which are its working parts. It also has more superficial features such as its vocabulary, which changes and develops in accordance with cultural and social phenomena.

IMPORTANCE OF FOCUSING ON GRAMMAR

- Without grammar, language doesn't exist.
- How can I feel confident about using grammar if I don't understand the rules?
- A solid knowledge of all the rules is necessary to speak a language well.
- The best way to learn a language is practice the correct usage.
- Good English means correct use of Grammar in English.
- Making mistakes reflect poor learning.

UNDERSTANDING ENGLISH GRAMMAR

Understanding English Grammar presents a linguistic introduction to the structure of English that is accessible to students who have had little or no opportunity to study the language.

- Familiarizes students with the essential structural characteristics of English.
- Features acccssible coverage of syntax, morphology, and phonology, as well as basic linguistic concepts.
- Includes numerous examples, exercises, and an indexed glossary.
- Is supported by an online instructor's manual

The latest and effective way to understand English grammar is based on reading textbooks and physical demonstrations. It can be done by teaching comprehension as a skill of the reader, which depends equally on the quality of the writing.

Good non-fiction and most good fiction start with good grammar. The reader does not need to know technical grammar; grammar is the responsibility of the writer. Traditional phonics is designed to TEACH READING. Literacy programme researchers and teachers consider writing and its accompanying grammar to be secondary.

The way in which teachers now teach writing is an example of how standards-based curriculum impact teachers.

Writing is primarily a group project in which self-expression is emphasized. Grammar is considered a restraint on expression. The opposite is true. The best way to teach English grammar is not as rigid rules.

In fact grammar gives writers great latitude in emphasis and emotion while giving clarity to the text for the reader. The parts of speech are mobile and interchangeable, one part often acting as if it were another. Sentences often contain phrases or clauses that act as a single part of speech. Grammar is not static; it slowly but constantly changes what is considered correct usage. The writer uses grammar like a symphony conductor uses the orchestra.

The education of children in home school should include grammar help, and the best way to teach English grammar is as a course with coverage of, and reference to, multiple parts of speech. Good grammar helps acceptance into higher education, and home schooled children can efficiently acquire good grammar through this book.

Grammar as a course is considered a necessity for all students.

An advanced artificial intelligence and grammar engine enable the detection and correction of language errors that may damage the image you want to project. The impressive proofreading abilities of the ever-improving spell checker and smart punctuation check will prevent you from getting embarrassed in case you are not sure about the nitty gritty aspects of the English language.

An English text correction features are coupled with its text enrichment database. The software algorithms constantly scan an endless number of texts, adding to the large variety of enrichment suggestions for synonyms, extra adjectives and adverbs that bring English text enhancement to a whole new level.

English text enhancement also builds on remarkable online English dictionary and thesaurus, which can be supplemented by an optional Multi-Language Translator, giving you immediate foreign language translations within any dictionary entry. This genuinely makes the software adaptable for international English users.

At its core, the term grammar refers to either the inherent structure of words and sentences (morphology and syntax respectively) in a language; or to the study and description of this structure, published as grammar rules in books about the language. Other approaches include more topics under the term grammar: orthography (spelling, punctuation and capitalization), semantics (word meanings), phonetics and phonology (sounds) and pragmatics (language use in context).

We unconsciously use grammar all the time when we use language for speaking, listening, reading and writing. If we want to improve our English language abilities, there is no escape from addressing grammar issues.

Grammar explains how the language should be structured, using various categories. Number refers to formation of singular and plural nouns and other parts of the sentence that have to agree with number (*e.g. child* Vs. *children*) whereas Gender, a category hardly existent in English, but alive in German, regards the differences between masculine and feminine or even neuter (*das Messer*, knife) nouns and how these affect other words in a properly phrased sentence.

Tense and aspect treat the formation of verbs, from the English *I write - She writes*; *We write - We are writing* distinctions, all the way to far more elaborate verb conjugation systems of other languages. A grammatical category or element never stands alone as it influences all other parts of the structural system of a language.

Grammar topics are usually sorted in books into word grammar and sentence grammar. Word grammar sections are further divided according to the different parts of speech - content words, containing verbs, nouns, adjective and adverbs; and structure words, containing determiners, pronouns, prepositions, conjunctions and interjections.

Sentence grammar relates to the construction of phrases, clauses and full sentences, all the way up to paragraphs and full texts.

ENGLISH GRAMMAR: THEN AND NOW

Nowadays, there are modern approaches to grammar, which bring it alive and relate it to our real life, outside of outdated grammar books containing endless lists of grammar rules.

The older prescriptive grammar approach, used to have students theoretically analyse sentences for correctness in literary and religious texts, as if they were training to become linguists.

This was based along the lines of the traditional approach to the instruction of ancient Latin and Greek, which were not even used in speech in the Middle-Ages onwards. The purpose was preserving the formal standard usage of these languages while treating grammar as a theorctically isolated area of study.

This is now supplemented by the descriptive approach that looks at how people actually use grammar in real life conversations and texts using modern living languages. It acknowledges language change and various styles as acceptable, resulting in more than one way of saying things. Pedagogical grammar for language learning purposes teaches only those grammar rules relevant to successful practical communication themes like shopping, looking for a job or opening up a business.

For example, the uses of the present perfect (*I have worked as...*) for indefinite past events or events going from past to present are geared towards speaking about former work experience either during a spoken job interview or in a written letter of job application.

Alternatively, perfect modal forms are used for a hypothetical discussion of alternative consequences to past actions (*could have done*) or the expression of regrets on what *may/should have been*.

Grammaris therefore now seen, not merely as theory, but as an enabling tool for authentic language practice. As some rules still need to be taught formally, a balanced combination of all the approaches is the solution for using grammar effectively.

For improving your English writing, It is not to be understood that grammar is less important today than how it may have been perceived before.

Whereas spoken language or literary dialogue may tolerate numerous grammar mistakes as part of a person or cultural group's individual style, written language of expository articles, business documents and of course academic texts must adhere to conventional grammar and style. Generally speaking, written language is more formal in both form and content than spoken language. Consequently, "She doesn't want to do nothing" (double negative) may qualify for informal coffee table chats, but will not for a written letter of complaint about a worker or service provider.

The conventional practice of avoiding double negatives in writing would therefore call for "She does not want to do anything."

RULES OF UNDERSTANDING

In order to understand and learn English Grammar you need to understand its basic rules which are described as follows:

Agreement

Agreement in a sentence refers to all of the parts of the sentence corroborating with each other.

For example, you wouldn't say "John have two pieces of toast and I has three." You would instead say, "John has two pieces of toast and I have three." The subjects and verbs need to be in agreement. Without sentence agreement you have all-out civil war in your sentence and no one knows what is going on. If your sentence parts don't agree with each other you will have to jump in and mediate, causing hard feelings all around.

Errors in agreement are the most common mistakes made in writings. To avoid this, just follow the simple rule: A singular subject requires a singular verb, and a plural subject requires a plural verb.

Wrong: Identification of these goods have been difficult.

Right: Identification of these goods has been difficult. ('Identification' is the subject here)

Wrong: The best way to keep your children happy are to give them enough responsibilities.

Right: The best way to keep your children happy is to give them enough responsibilities. (Use a singular verb if the subject is a phrase or clause)

Awkward: Neither John nor I am interested in this project.

Better: John is not interested in this project; nor am I. (If you write an awkward sentence, consider rewriting it)

Exception: Use a singular verb if a compound subject refers to the same person or thing.

Example: Milk and breads is a typical breakfast for many people.

Tense

Tense refers to time. Tense is used to show the relation between the action or state described by the verb and the time, which is reflected in the form of the verb. There are two basic tenses in English; the present tense and the past tense. The present is like the base form, although the third person singular adds -s. Regular verbs add -ed or -d to show the past tense, while irregular verbs change in many different ways, or not at all in some cases.

One of the forms which a verb takes by inflection or by adding auxiliary words, so as to indicate the time of the action or event signified; the modification which verbs undergo for the indication of time. What time is it in your sentence? Whatever time it is it should remain consistent throughout your whole piece of writing. If it was last week you are talking about, stay there.

Tenses in English Grammar are basically Verbs that can take various forms, depending on whether they refer to the present or the past, and on the temporal relationship of one event to another. These forms are the *tenses*.

Examples:

Every day we watch *television for an hour or two.* [simple present, here used for a routinely repeated action]

While I was watching *the news, the phone* rang.

Are *you* watching *the game on Saturday?* [present continuous, here used for the future]

You have been watching *too many thrillers.* [present perfect, denoting an action that has occurred in the past and continues to occur in the present. This tense causes particular difficulty for adult learners of English. It seems to have no equivalent in other languages, which instead have structures like "You are always watching too many thrillers" and "I am standing here since seven o'clock"]

Different linguists give these tenses different names; the names above are representative, but not definitive.

There are quite a few more tenses in English, but the above demonstrate the function of tense.

There are three tenses in writing, past tense, present tense and future tense. Here is an example of writing with mixed tenses: "Carrie wondered how she is going to finish in time, but Joe will help her." This sentence contains all three tenses, past in "wondered", present in "is" and future in "will

Here is an example of writing with mixed tenses:

Wrong: John wanted to know why Rebecca is sad, but she will not tell him.

Right: John wanted to know why Rebecca was sad, but she would not tell him.

Present tense, Past tense and Future Tense each has the following four forms. The examples below will help you understand that:

Past Tense

Simple Past – I spoke

The simple past expresses an action in the past taking place once, never, several times. It can also be used for actions taking place one after another or in the middle of another action.

Form of Simple Past

	Positive	Negative	Question
no differences	I spoke.	I did not speak.	Did I speak?

For irregular verbs, use the past form. For regular verbs, just add "ed".

Exceptions in Spelling when Adding 'ed'

Exceptions in spelling when adding *ed*	**Example**
after a final *e* only add *d*	love – loved
final consonant after a short, stressed vowel or *l* as final consonant after a vowel is doubled	admit – admitted travel – travelled
final *y* after a consonant becomes *i*	hurry – hurried

Use of Simple Past

- Action in the past taking place once, never or several times
  Example: He *visited* his parents every weekend.
- Actions in the past taking place one after the other
  Example: He *came* in, *took* off his coat and *sat* down.
- Action in the past taking place in the middle of another action
  Example: When I was having breakfast, the phone suddenly *rang*.
- If sentences type II (If I talked, ...)
  Example: If I *had* a lot of money, I would share it with you.

Signal Words of Simple Past

- Yesterday, 2 minutes ago, the other day, last Friday
- If-Satz Typ II (If I talked, ...)
  Past Continuous – I was speaking
  Past Perfect – I had spoken
  Past Perfect Continuous – I had been speaking

Present Tense

Simple Present – I speak

Simple present is also called present simple.

The simple present expresses an action in the present taking place once, never or several times. It is also used for actions that take place one after another and for actions that are set by a timetable or schedule. The simple present also expresses facts in the present.

Present Continuous – I am speaking
Present Perfect – I have spoken
Present Perfect Continuous – I have been speaking

Future Tense

Simple Future– I shall/ will speak

Form of will *Future*

	positive	negative	question
no differences	I will speak.	I will not speak.	Will I speak?

Use of will *Future*

- A spontaneous decision
  Example: Wait, I will help you.
- An opinion, hope, uncertainty or assumption regarding the future
  Example: He will probably come back tomorrow.
- A promise
  Example: I will not watch TV tonight.
- An action in the future that cannot be influenced
  Example: It will rain tomorrow.
- Conditional clauses type I
  Example: If I arrive late, I will call you.

Signal Words

- In a year, next …, tomorrow
- Vermutung: I think, probably, we might …, perhaps
  Future Continuous – I shall/ will be speaking
  Future Perfect – I shall/will have spoken
  Future Perfect Continuous – I shall/ will have been speaking

Double Negatives

Two negative words create a positive meaning, which may be just the opposite of what you have intended to convey.

Wrong: I don't have nothing to say.
Right: I don't have anything to say.
Wrong: Tom couldn't hardly believe what Jack said.
Right: Tom could hardly believe what Jack said.

Spelling

One of the most important things, and without it, you can kiss your credibility goodbye. Spell checkers are poor substitutes for knowing how to spell and can leave behind more errors than you realise. There are many different forms of words and your spell checker does not know which form you wanted to use.

For example, "When Mark washed they're care, he forgot too putt on the wax."

Run-On Sentences

A run-on sentence is one that is just too darned long! Not only is it too long, it is incorrect. Usually, a run-on sentence can be made into two or more sentences with a little punctuation and style. An example of a run-on sentence might be: "We walked over to the commissary to get something to eat but it was closed so we didn't know what to do so we kept walking until we saw a restaurant and decided to go in and get something to eat but Andrew didn't want to eat there so we kept going for another mile." This sentence could have gone on for another mile too! Break up the sentence into smaller, more coherent parts.

Punctuation

It is very important to know your punctuation, even if you never plan on using a semicolon for the rest of your life. The most important thing to learn is where to put your commas, a common mistake among writers. Commas are used to separate parts of sentences that stand alone, such as those that are parenthetical. For example "There were too many flowers, not that I minded, but they took up most of the room." Avoid using commas after conjunctions like "but" and "and."

Usage

If you are going to use a word, you really ought to know how to use it. Some writers think big words look impressive but actually the reverse is true if the word is used incorrectly. Words don't have to be big to be misused, consider its vs. it's. If you are going to use a word, you must know how to use it. Use simple words. Many people have the tendency to use big, difficult words while writing. Avoid fancy words and phrases when simpler ones convey the idea. Omit unnecessary words. A piece of writing, containing long words strung together in complex sentences, turns out to be poorly written and not impressive. You will have fewer chances for grammatical errors if you can cut a word out which can be cut out.

Stuffy: I will make modifications in the document.
Simple: I will change the document.

Capitalization

Words at the beginning of sentences aren't the only ones worthy of capital letters. Always capitalize proper names such as people and places. Titles of all kinds deserve capital letters and so do acronyms.

Point of View

The point of view refers to whoever is telling the story or "speaking." When you write a letter you are writing in "first person" which includes I, me, my, we and our. Second person writing occurs when we talk about you and yours and third person includes he, she, they and theirs. In third person writing, the author does not interject himself into the story.

Sentence Fragments

A sentence fragment is an incomplete sentence that does not include both noun and verb. An example of a sentence fragment might be, "Really dumb." Make sure your sentences reflect a complete thought unless you are writing dialog.

Wasted Words

A big no-no. Sometimes we throw in words just to round out our sentences, or we over-describe something, like, "The really ugly puke-green dress was hanging on the wall." Do we really need to point out that a puke-green dress was really ugly? Economize your words and you will have fewer chances for grammatical errors. There are several reasons why you might want to improve your understanding of the rules of grammar. For example:

- Without good grammar, clear communication is nearly impossible. Proper grammar keeps you from being misunderstood while expressing your thoughts and ideas.
- Writing and speaking correctly gives you the appearance of credibility. If you're attempting to build a reputation as an expert in your profession, this is extremely important.
- Other people consider good grammar to be a mark of intelligence and education. Don't allow strangers to form a negative impression of you based on your poor communication skills.

Unfortunately, there is no shortcut to learning English grammar. While there are many spelling and grammar check software programmes available, a computer can't fully grasp the intricacies of the English language. In some cases, a computer grammar check will even suggest incorrect alternatives when attempting to fix common errors.

Unfortunately, remembering all the rules can be a rather daunting task and consulting authoritative grammar handbooks becomes a necessity. Since many writers have difficulties with "run-on sentences," this post will address the topic of fused sentences and comma splices.

FUSED SENTENCES AND COMMA SPLICES

More commonly known as "run-on sentences," fused sentences and comma splices are independent clauses that are incorrectly joined. An independent clause is a group of words that can stand on its own as a sentence. When two independent clauses appear in the same sentence, they must be joined in one of the following ways:

- With a comma and a coordinating conjunction (and, but, or, nor, for, so, yet)
- With a semicolon (or occasionally a colon or a dash)

According to Strunk and White's The Elements of Style, there *is* an exception to the above grammar rule. It states that a comma is preferable when the clauses are very short and alike in form, or when the tone of the sentence is easy and conversational. They offer the following examples:

Man proposes, God disposes.

The gates swung apart, the bridge fell, the portcullis was drawn up.

I hardly knew him, he was so changed.

Fused Sentences

When there is no punctuation mark and no coordinating conjunction between independent clauses, the result is a fused sentence. The following is an example:

I would like to pursue a career in journalism I am taking a course in English Grammar and Composition.

Comma Splices

When independent clauses are joined by a comma without an accompanying coordinating conjunction, the result is a comma splice. The following are examples:

I would like to pursue a career in journalism, I am taking a course in English Grammar and Composition.

I would like to pursue a career in journalism, therefore, I am taking a course in English Grammar and Composition.

In the second example, "therefore" is a conjunctive adverb, not a coordinating conjunction. It must be preceded by a semicolon.

Correcting Fused Sentences and Comma Splices

- Use a comma and a coordinating conjunction (and, but, or, nor, for, so, yet). For example:

  I would like to pursue a career in journalism, and I am taking a course in English Grammar and Composition.
- Use a semicolon (or, if appropriate, a colon or a dash). A semicolon may be used alone; it can also be accompanied by a conjunctive adverb or transitional phrase. For example:

  I would like to pursue a career in journalism; I am taking a course in English Grammar and Composition.

I would like to pursue a career in journalism; therefore, I am taking a course in English Grammar and Composition.

- Make the clauses into separate sentences. For example:

  I would like to pursue a career in journalism. I am taking a course in English Grammar and Composition.

- Restructure the sentence. For example:

  As I would like to pursue a career in journalism, I am taking a course in English Grammar and Composition.

ROLE OF LINGUISTIC IN LITERATURE

In both the French and English instances the primary ideas of sex and time have become diluted by form-analogy and by extensions into the relational sphere, the concepts ostensibly indicated being now so vaguely delimited that it is rather the tyranny of usage than the need of their concrete expression that sways us in the selection of this or that form.

If the thinning out process continues long enough, we may eventually be left with a system of forms on our hands from which all the colour of life has vanished and which merely persist by inertia, duplicating each other's secondary, syntactic functions with endless prodigality. Hence, in part, the complex conjugational systems of so many languages, in which differences of form are attended by no assignable differences of function.

There must have been a time, for instance, though it antedates our earliest documentary evidence, when the type of tense formation represented by drove or sank differed in meaning, in however slightly nuanced a degree, from the type (killed, worked) which has now become established in English as the prevailing preterit formation, very much as we recognize a valuable distinction at present between both these types and the "perfect" (has driven, has killed) but may have ceased to do so at some point in the future.

Now form lives longer than its own conceptual content. Both are ceaselessly changing, but, on the whole, the form tends to linger on when the spirit has flown or changed its being. Irrational form, form for form's sake — however we term this tendency to hold on to formal distinctions once they have come to be — is as natural to the life of language as is the retention of modes of conduct that have long outlived the meaning they once had.

There is another powerful tendency which makes for a formal elaboration that does not strictly correspond to clear-cut conceptual differences. This is the tendency to construct schemes of classification into which all the concepts of language must be fitted.

Once we have made up our minds that all things are either definitely good or bad or definitely black or white, it is difficult to get into the frame of mind that recognizes that any particular thing may be both good and bad (in other words, indifferent) or both black and white (in other words, gray), still more difficult to realise that the good-bad or black-white categories may not apply at all. Language is in many respects as unreasonable and stubborn about its classifications as is such a mind. It must have its perfectly exclusive pigeon-holes and will tolerate no flying vagrants.

Any concept that asks for expression must submit to the classificatory rules of the game, just as there are statistical surveys in which even the most convinced atheist must perforce be labeled Catholic, Protestant, or Jew or get no hearing. In English we have made up our minds that all action must be conceived of in reference to three standard times. If, therefore, we desire to state a proposition that is as true to-morrow as it was yesterday, we have to pretend that the present moment may be elongated fore and aft so as to take in all eternity.

In French we know once for all that an object is masculine or feminine, whether it be living or not; just as in many American and East Asiatic languages it must be understood to belong to a certain form-category (say, ring-round, ball-round, long and slender, cylindrical, sheet-like, in mass like sugar) before it can be enumerated (*e.g.*, "two ball-class potatoes," "three sheetclass carpets") or even said to "be" or "be handled in a definite way" (thus, in the Athabaskan languages and in Yana, "to carry" or "throw" a pebble is quite another thing than to carry or throw a log, linguistically no less than in terms of muscular experience).

Such instances might be multiplied at will. It is almost as though at some period in the past the unconscious mind of the race had made a hasty inventory of experience, committed itself to a premature classification that allowed of no revision, and saddled the inheritors of its language with a science that they no longer quite believed in nor had the strength to overthrow.

Dogma, rigidly prescribed by tradition, stiffens into formalism. Linguistic categories make up a system of surviving dogma — dogma of the unconscious. They are often but half real as concepts; their life tends ever to languish away into form for form's sake. There is still a third cause for the rise of this non-significant form, or rather of non-significant differences of form. This is the mechanical operation of phonetic processes, which may bring about formal distinctions that have not and never had a corresponding functional distinction.

Much of the irregularity and general formal complexity of our declensional and conjugational systems is due to this process. The plural of hat is hats, the plural of self is selves. In the former case we have a true -s symbolizing plurality, in the latter a z-sound coupled with a change in the radical element of the word of f to v. Here we have not a falling together of forms that originally stood for fairly distinct concepts — as we saw was presumably the case with such parallel forms as drove and worked — but a merely mechanical manifolding of the same formal element without a corresponding growth of a new concept.

This type of form development, therefore, while of the greatest interest for the general history of language, does not directly concern us now in our effort to understand the nature of grammatical concepts and their tendency to degenerate into purely formal counters. We may now conveniently revise our first classification of concepts as expressed in language and suggest the following scheme:

- Basic (Concrete) Concepts (such as objects, actions, qualities): normally expressed by independent words or radical elements; involve no relation as such
- Derivational Concepts (less concrete, as a rule, than I, more so than III): normally expressed by affixing non-radical elements to radical elements or by inner modification of these; differ from type I in defining ideas that are irrelevant to the proposition as a whole but that give a radical element a particular increment of significance and that are thus inherently related in a specific way to concepts of type I
- Concrete Relational Concepts (still more abstract, yet not entirely devoid of a measure of concreteness): normally expressed by affixing non-radical elements to radical elements, but generally at a greater remove from these than is the case with elements of type II, or by inner modification of radical elements; differ fundamentally from type II in indicating or implying relations that transcend the particular word to which they are immediately attached, thus leading over to
- Pure Relational Concepts (purely abstract): normally expressed by affixing non-radical elements to radical elements (in which case these concepts are frequently intertwined with those of type III) or by their inner modification, by independent words, or by position; serve to relate the concrete elements of the proposition to each other, thus giving it definite syntactic form.

The nature of these four classes of concepts as regards their concreteness or their power to express syntactic relations may be thus symbolized:

I Basic Concepts
II Derivational Concepts
III Concrete Relational Concepts
IV Pure Relational Concepts

These schemes must not be worshipped as fetiches. In the actual work of analysis difficult problems frequently arise and we may well be in doubt as to how to group a given set of concepts. This is particularly apt to be the case in exotic languages, where we may be quite sure of the analysis of the words in a sentence and yet not succeed in acquiring that inner "feel" of its structure that enables us to tell infallibly what is "material content" and what is "relation."

Concepts of class I are essential to all speech, also concepts of class IV. Concepts II and III are both common, but not essential; particularly group III, which represents, in effect, a psychological and formal confusion of types II and IV or of types I and IV, is an avoidable class of concepts.

Logically there is an impassable gulf between I and IV, but the illogical, metaphorical genius of speech has wilfully spanned the gulf and set up a continuous gamut of concepts and forms that leads imperceptibly from the crudest of materialities ("house" or "John Smith") to the most subtle of relations. It is particularly significant that the unanalyzable independent word belongs in most cases to either group I or group IV, rather less commonly to II or III. It is possible for a concrete concept, represented by a simple word, to lose its material significance entirely and pass over directly into the relational sphere without at the same time losing its independence as a word.

This happens, for instance, in Chinese and Cambodgian when the verb "give" is used in an abstract sense as a mere symbol of the "indirect objective" relation (*e.g.*, Cambodgian "We make story this give all that person who have child," *i.e.*, "We have made this story *for* all those that have children").

There are, of course, also not a few instances of transitions between groups I and II and I and III, as well as of the less radical one between II and III. To the first of these transitions belongs that whole class of examples in which the independent word, after passing through the preliminary stage of functioning as the secondary or qualifying element in a compound, ends up by being a derivational affix pure and simple, yet without losing the memory of its former independence.

Such an element and concept is the full of teaspoonfull, which hovers psychologically between the status of an independent, radical concept (compare full) or of a subsidiary element in a compound (cf. brim-full) and that of a simple suffix (cf. dutiful) in which the primary concreteness is no longer felt. In general, the more highly synthetic our linguistic type, the more difficult and even arbitrary it becomes to distinguish groups I and II.

Not only is there a gradual loss of the concrete as we pass through from group I to group IV, there is also a constant fading away of the feeling of sensible reality within the main groups of linguistic concepts themselves. In many languages it becomes almost imperative, therefore, to make various sub-classifications, to segregate, for instance, the more concrete from the more abstract concepts of group II. Yet we must always beware of reading into such abstracter groups that purely formal, relational feeling that we can hardly help associating with certain of the abstracter concepts which, with us, fall in group III, unless, indeed, there is clear evidence to warrant such a reading in.

An example or two should make clear these all-important distinctions. In Nootka we have an unusually large number of derivational affixes (expressing concepts of group II). Some of these are quite material in content (*e.g.*, "in the house," "to dream of"), others, like an element denoting plurality and a diminutive affix, are far more abstract in content. The former type are more closely welded with the radical element than the latter, which can only be suffixed to formations that have the value of complete words. If, therefore, I wish to say "the small fires in the house" — and I can do this in one word — I must form the word "fire-in-the-house," to which elements corresponding to "small," our plural, and "the" are appended.

The element indicating the definiteness of reference that is implied in our "the" comes at the very end of the word. So far, so good. "Fire-in-thehouse-the" is an intelligible correlate of our "the housefire." But is the Nootka correlate of "the small fires in the house" the true equivalent of an English "the house-firelets"? By no means. First of all, the plural element precedes the diminutive in Nootka: "fire-in-thehouse-plural-small-the," in other words "the house-fireslet," which at once reveals the important fact that the plural concept is not as abstractly, as relationally, felt as in English. A more adequate rendering would be "the house-fire-several-let," in which, however, "several" is too gross a word, "-let" too choice an element ("small" again is too gross).

In truth we cannot carry over into English the inherent feeling of the Nootka word, which seems to hover somewhere between "the house-firelets" and "the house-fire-several-small." But what more than anything else cuts off all possibility of comparison between the English -s of "house-firelets" and the "-several-small" of the Nootka word is this, that in Nootka neither the plural nor the diminutive affix corresponds or refers to anything else in the sentence. In English "the house-firelets burn" (not "burns"), in Nootka neither verb, nor adjective, nor anything else in the proposition is in the least concerned with the plurality or the diminutiveness of the fire. Hence, while Nootka recognizes a cleavage between concrete and less concrete concepts within group II, the less concrete do not transcend the group and lead us into that abstracter air into which our plural -s carries us. But at any rate, the reader may object, it is something that the Nootka plural affix is set apart from the concreter group of affixes; and may not the Nootka diminutive have a slenderer, a more elusive content than our -let or -ling or the German -chen or -lein?

Can such a concept as that of plurality ever be classified with the more material concepts of group II? Indeed it can be. In Yana the third person of the verb makes no formal distinction between singular and plural. Nevertheless the plural concept can be, and nearly always is, expressed by the suffixing of an element (-ba-) to the radical element of the verb. "It burns in the east" is rendered by the verb ya-hau-si "burn-east-s." "They burn in the east" is ya-bahau-si.

Note that the plural affix immediately follows the radical element (*ya*-), disconnecting it from the local element (-hau-). It needs no labored argument to prove that the concept of plurality is here hardly less concrete than that of location "in the east," and that the Yana form corresponds in feeling not so much to our "They burn in the east" (ardunt oriente) as to a "Burn-severaleasts, it plurally burns in the east," an expression which we cannot adequately assimilate for lack of the necessary form-grooves into which to run it.

But can we go a step farther and dispose of the category of plurality as an utterly material idea, one that would make of "books" a "plural book," in which the "plural," like the "white" of "white book," falls contentedly into group I? Our "many books" and "several books" are obviously not cases in point. Even if we could say "many book" and "several book" (as we can say "many a book" and "each book"), the plural concept would still not emerge as clearly as it should for our argument; "many" and "several" are contaminated by certain notions of quantity or scale that are not essential to the idea of plurality itself. We must turn to central and eastern Asia for the type of expression we are seeking. In Tibetan, for instance, nga-s mi mthong "I-by man see, by me a man is seen, I see a man" may just as well be understood to mean "I see men," if there happens to be no reason to emphasize the fact of plurality.

If the fact is worth expressing, however, I can say nga-s mi rnams mthong "by me man plural see," where rnams is the perfect conceptual analogue of -s in books, divested of all relational strings. Rnams follows its noun as would any other attributive word — "man plural" (whether two or a million) like "man white." No need to bother about his plurality any more than about his whiteness unless we insist on the point.

What is true of the idea of plurality is naturally just as true of a great many other concepts. They do not necessarily belong where we who speak English are in the habit of putting them. They may be shifted towards I or towards IV, the two poles of linguistic expression. Nor dare we look down on the Nootka Indian and the Tibetan for their material attitude towards a concept which to us is abstract and relational, lest we invite the reproaches of the Frenchman who feels a subtlety of relation in femme blanche and homme blanc that he misses in the coarser-grained white woman and white man.

But the Bantu Negro, were he a philosopher, might go further and find it strange that we put in group II a category, the diminutive, which he strongly feels to belong to group III and which he uses, along with a number of other classificatory concepts, to relate his subjects and objects, attributes and predicates, as a Russian or a German handles his genders and, if possible, with an even greater finesse. It is because our conceptual scheme is a sliding scale rather than a philosophical analysis of experience that we cannot say in advance just where to put a given concept. We must dispense, in other words, with a well-ordered classification of categories. What boots it to put tense and mode here or number there when the next language one handles puts tense a peg "lower down" (towards I), mode and number a peg "higher up" (towards IV)? Nor is there much to be gained in a summary work of this kind from a general inventory of the types of concepts generally found in groups II, III, and IV. There are too many possibilities.

It would be interesting to show what are the most typical noun-forming and verb-forming elements of group II; how variously nouns may be classified (by gender; personal and non-personal; animate and inanimate; by form; common and proper); how the concept of number is elaborated (singular and plural; singular, dual, and plural; singular, dual, trial, and plural; single, distributive, and collective); what tense distinctions may be made in verb or noun (the "past," for instance, may be an indefinite past, immediate, remote, mythical, completed, prior); how delicately certain languages have developed the idea of "aspect" (momentaneous, durative, continuative, inceptive, cessative, durative-inceptive, iterative, momentaneous-iterative, durative-iterative, resultative, and still others); what modalities may be recognized (indicative, imperative, potential, dubitative, optative, negative, and a host of others); what distinctions of person are possible (is "we," for instance, conceived of as a plurality of "I" or is it as distinct from "I" as either is from "you" or "he"? — both attitudes are illustrated in language; moreover, does "we" include, you to whom I speak or not? — "inclusive" and "exclusive" forms); what may be the general scheme of orientation, the so-called demonstrative categories ("this" and "that" in an endless procession of nuances); how frequently the form ex-presses the source or nature of the speaker's knowledge (known by actual experience, by hearsay, by inference); how the syntactic relations may be expressed in the noun (subjective and objective; agentive, instrumental, and person affected; various types of "genitive" and indirect relations) and, correspo-ndingly, in the verb (active and passive; active and static; transitive and intransitive; impersonal, reflexive, reciprocal, indefinite as to object, and many other special limitations on the starting-point and end-point of the flow of activity).

These details, important as many of them are to an understanding of the "inner form" of language, yield in general significance to the more radical group-distinctions that we have set up. It is enough for the general reader to feel that language struggles towards two poles of linguistic expression — material content and relation — and that these poles tend to be connected by a long series of transitional concepts.

In dealing with words and their varying forms we have had to anticipate much that concerns the sentence as a whole. Every language has its special method or methods of binding words into a larger unity. The importance of these methods is apt to vary with the complexity of the individual word. The more synthetic the language, in other words, the more clearly the status of each word in the sentence is indicated by its own resources, the less need is there for looking beyond the word to the sentence as a whole.

The Latin agit "(he) acts" needs no outside help to establish its place in a proposition. Whether I say agit dominus "the master acts" or sic femina agit "thus the woman acts," the net result as to the syntactic feel of the agit is practically the same. It can only be a verb, the predicate of a proposition, and it can only be conceived as a statement of activity carried out by a person (or thing) other than you or me. It is not so with such a word as the English act. Act is a syntactic waif until we have defined its status in a proposition — one thing in "they act abominably," quite another in "that was a kindly act." The Latin sentence speaks with the assurance of its individual members; the English word needs the prompting of its fellows. Roughly speaking, to be sure.

And yet to say that a sufficiently elaborate word-structure compensates for external syntactic methods is perilously close to begging the question. The elements of the word are related to each other in a specific way and follow each other in a rigorously determined sequence. This is tantamount to saying that a word which consists of more than a radical element is a crystallization of a sentence or of some portion of a sentence, that a form like agit is roughly the psychological equivalent of a form like age is "act he."

Breaking down, then, the wall that separates word and sentence, we may ask: What, at last analysis, are the fundamental methods of relating word to word and element to element, in short, of passing from the isolated notions symbolized by each word and by each element to the unified proposition that corresponds to a thought? The answer is simple and is implied in the preceding remarks. The most fundamental and the most powerful of all relating methods is the method of order. Let us think of some more or less concrete idea, say a colour, and set down its symbol — red; of another concrete idea, say a person or object, setting down its symbol — dog; finally, of a third concrete idea, say an action, setting down its symbol — run.

It is hardly possible to set down these three symbols — red dog run — without relating them in some way, for example (the) red dog run(s). I am far from wishing to state that the proposition has always grown up in this analytic manner, merely that the very process of juxtaposing concept to concept, symbol to symbol, forces some kind of relational "feeling," if nothing else, upon us.

To certain syntactic adhesions we are very sensitive, for example, to the attributive relation of quality (red dog) or the subjective relation (dog run) or the objective relation (kill dog), to others we are more indifferent, for example, to the attributive relation of circumstance (to-day red dog run or red dog to-day run or red dog run to-day, all of which are equivalent propositions or propositions in embryo).

Words and elements, then, once they are listed in a certain order, tend not only to establish some kind of relation among themselves but are attracted to each other in greater or in less degree. It is presumably this very greater or less that ultimately leads to those firmly solidified groups of elements (radical element or elements plus one or more grammatical elements) that we have studied as complex words.

They are in all likelihood nothing but sequences that have shrunk together and away from other sequences or isolated elements in the flow of speech.

While they are fully alive, in other words, while they are functional at every point, they can keep themselves at a psychological distance from their neighbours. As they gradually lose much of their life, they fall back into the embrace of the sentence as a whole and the sequence of independent words regains the importance it had in part transferred to the crystallized groups of elements. Speech is thus constantly tightening and loosening its sequences. In its highly integrated forms (Latin, Eskimo) the "energy" of sequence is largely locked up in complex word formations, it becomes transformed into a kind of potential energy that may not be released for millennia. In its more analytic forms (Chinese, English). This energy is mobile, ready to hand for such service as we demand of it.

There can be little doubt that stress has frequently played a controlling influence in the formation of element-groups or complex words out of certain sequences in the sentence. Such an English word as withstand is merely an old sequence with stand, *i.e.,*, "against stand," in which the unstressed adverb was permanently drawn to the following verb and lost its independence as a significant element.

In the same way French futures of the type irai "(I) shall go" are but the resultants of a coalescence of originally independent words: ir a'i "to-go I-have," under the influence of a unifying accent. But stress has done more than articulate or unify sequences that in their own right imply a syntactic relation. Stress is the most natural means at our disposal to emphasize a linguistic contrast, to indicate the major element in a sequence. Hence we need not be surprised to find that accent too, no less than sequence, may serve as the unaided symbol of certain relations.

Such a contrast as that of g' between ("one who goes between") and to go between' may be of quite secondary origin in English, but there is every reason to believe that analogous distinctions have prevailed at all times in linguistic history. A sequence like see' man might imply some type of relation in which see qualifies the following word, hence "a seeing man" or "a seen (or visible) man," or is its predication, hence "the man sees" or "the man is seen," while a sequence like see man' might indicate that the accented word in some way limits the application of the first, say as direct object, hence "to see a man" or "(he) sees the man."

Such alternations of relation, as symbolized by varying stresses, are important and frequent in a number of languages. It is a somewhat venturesome and yet not an altogether unreasonable speculation that sees in word order and stress the primary methods for the expression of all syntactic relations and looks upon the present relational value of specific words and elements as but a secondary condition due to a transfer of values.

Thus, we may surmise that the Latin -m of words like feminam, dominum, and civem did not originally denote that "woman," "master," and "citizen" were objectively related to the verb of the proposition but indicated something far more concrete, that the objective relation was merely implied by the position or accent of the word (radical element) immediately preceding the -m, and that gradually, as its more concrete significance faded away, it took over a syntactic function that did not originally belong to it.

This sort of evolution by transfer is traceable in many instances. Thus, the of in an English phrase like "the law of the land" is now as colorless in content, as purely a relational indicator as the "genitive" suffix -is in the Latin lex urbis "the law of the city." We know, however, that it was originally an adverb of considerable concreteness of meaning, "away, moving from," and that the syntactic relation was originally expressed by the case form of the second noun.

As the case form lost its vitality, the adverb took over its function. If we are actually justified in assuming that the expression of all syntactic relations is ultimately traceable to these two unavoidable, dynamic features of speech — sequence and stress — an interesting thesis results: — All of the actual content of speech, its clusters of vocalic and consonantal sounds, is in origin limited to the concrete; relations were originally not expressed in outward form but were merely implied and articulated with the help of order and rhythm.

In other words, relations were intuitively felt and could only "leak out" with the help of dynamic factors that themselves move on an intuitional plane. There is a special method for the expression of relations that has been so often evolved in the history of language that we must glance at it for a moment. This is the method of "concord" or of like signaling. It is based on the same principle as the password or label.

All persons or objects that answer to the same countersign or that bear the same imprint are thereby stamped as somehow related. It makes little difference, once they are so stamped, where they are to be found or how they behave themselves. They are known to belong together. We are familiar with the principle of concord in Latin and Greek.

Many of us have been struck by such relentless rhymes as vidi illum bonum dominum "I saw that good master" or quarum dearum saevarum "of which stern goddesses." Not that sound-echo, whether in the form of rhyme or of alliteration is necessary to concord, though in its most typical and original forms concord is nearly always accompanied by sound repetition.

The essence of the principle is simply this, that words (elements) that belong together, particularly if they are syntactic equivalents or are related in like fashion to another word or element, are outwardly marked by the same or functionally equivalent affixes. The application of the principle varies considerably according to the genius of the particular language.

In Latin and Greek, for instance, there is concord between noun and qualifying word (adjective or demonstrative) as regards gender, number, and case, between verb and subject only as regards number, and no concord between verb and object. In Chinook there is a more far-reaching concord between noun, whether subject or object, and verb. Every noun is classified according to five categories — masculine, feminine, neuter, dual, and plural. "Woman" is feminine, "sand" is neuter, "table" is masculine.

If, therefore, I wish to say "The woman put the sand on the table," I must place in the verb certain class or gender prefixes that accord with corresponding noun prefixes. The sentence reads then, "The (fem.)-woman she (fem.)-it (neut.)-it (masc.)-on-put the (neut.)-sand the (masc.)-table." If "sand" is qualified as "much" and "table" as "large," these new ideas are expressed as abstract nouns, each with its inherent class-prefix ("much" is neuter or feminine, "large" is masculine) and with a possessive prefix referring to the qualified noun.

LANGUAGES AND ITS INFLUENCE

Languages, like cultures, are rarely sufficient unto themselves. The necessities of intercourse bring the speakers of one language into direct or indirect contact with those of neighbouring or culturally dominant languages. The intercourse may be friendly or hostile. It may move on the humdrum plane of business and trade relations or it may consist of a borrowing or interchange of spiritual goods — art, science, religion. It would be difficult to point to a completely isolated language or dialect, least of all among the primitive peoples. The tribe is often so small that intermarriages with alien tribes that speak other dialects or even totally unrelated languages are not uncommon. It may even be doubted whether intermarriage, intertribal trade, and general cultural interchanges are not of greater relative significance on primitive levels than on our own.

Whatever the degree or nature of contact between neighbouring peoples, it is generally sufficient to lead to some kind of linguistic interinfluencing. Frequently the influence runs heavily in one direction. The language of a people that is looked upon as a centre of culture is naturally far more likely to exert an appreciable influence on other languages spoken in its vicinity than to be influenced by them. Chinese has flooded the vocabularies of Corean, Japanese, and Annamite for centuries, but has received nothing in return.

In the Western Europe of medieval and modern times French has exercised a similar, though probably a less overwhelming, influence. English borrowed an immense number of words from the French of the Norman invaders, later also from the court French of Isle de France, appropriated a certain number of affixed elements of derivational value (*e.g.*, -ess of princess, -ard of drunkard, -ty of royalty), may have been somewhat stimulated in its general analytic drift by contact with French, and even allowed French to modify its phonetic pattern slightly (*e.g.*, initial v and j in words like veal and judge; in words of Anglo-Saxon origin v and j can only occur after vowels, *e.g.*, over, hedge). But English has exerted practically no influence on French. The simplest kind of influence that one language may exert on another is the "borrowing" of words. When there is cultural borrowing there is always the likelihood that the associated words may be borrowed too. When the early Germanic peoples of northern Europe first learned of wine-culture and of paved streets from their commercial or warlike contact with the Romans, it was only natural that they should adopt the Latin words for the strange beverage (vinum, English wine, German Wein) and the unfamiliar type of road (strata [via], English street, German Strasse).

Later, when Christianity was introduced into England, a number of associated words, such as bishop and angel, found their way into English. And so the process has continued uninterruptedly down to the present day, each cultural wave bringing to the language a new deposit of loanwords. The careful study of such loan-words constitutes an interesting commentary on the history of culture. One can almost estimate the role which various peoples have played in the development and spread of cultural ideas by taking note of the extent to which their vocabularies have filtered into those of other peoples.

When we realize that an educated Japanese can hardly frame a single literary sentence without the use of Chinese resources, that to this day Siamese and Burmese and Cambodgian bear the unmistakable imprint of dhism centuries ago, or that whether we argue for or against the teaching of Latin and Greek our argument is sure to be studded with words that have come to us from Rome and Athens, we get some inkling of what early Chinese culture and Buddhism and classical Mediterranean civilization have meant in the world's history.

There are just five languages that have had an overwhelming significance as carriers of culture. They are classical Chinese, Sanskrit, Arabic, Greek, and Latin. In comparison with these even such culturally important languages as Hebrew and French sink into a secondary position. It is a little disappointing to learn that the general cultural influence of English has so far been all but negligible. The English language itself is spreading because the English have colonized immense territories.

But there is nothing to show that it is anywhere entering into the lexical heart of other languages as French has coloured the English complexion or as Arabic has permeated Persian and Turkish. This fact alone is significant of the power of nationalism, cultural as well as political, during the last century. There are now psychological resistances to borrowing, or rather to new sources of borrowing that were not greatly alive in the Middle Ages or during the Renaissance. Are there resistances of a more intimate nature to the borrowing of words? It is generally assumed that the nature and extent of borrowing depend entirely on the historical facts of culture relation; that if German, for instance, has borrowed less copiously than English from Latin and French it is only because Germany has had less intimate relations than England with the culture spheres of classical Rome and France.

This is true to a considerable extent, but it is not the whole truth. We must not exaggerate the physical importance of the Norman invasion nor underrate the significance of the fact that Germany's central geographical position made it peculiarly sensitive to French influences all through the Middle Ages, to humanistic influences in the latter fifteenth and early sixteenth centuries, and again to the powerful French influences of the seventeenth and eighteenth centuries.

It seems very probable that the psychological attitude of the borrowing language itself towards linguistic material has much to do with its receptivity to foreign words. English has long been striving for the completely unified, unanalyzed word, regardless of whether it is monosyllabic or polysyllabic.

Such words as credible, certitude, intangible are entirely welcome in English because each represents a unitary, well-nuanced idea and because their formal analysis (cred-ible, certitude, in-tang-ible) is not a necessary act of the unconscious mind (cred-, cert-, and tang- have no real existence in English comparable to that of good- in goodness).

A word like intangible, once it is acclimated, is nearly as simple a psychological entity as any radical monosyllable (say vague, thin, grasp). In German, however, polysyllabic words strive to analyze themselves into significant elements. Hence vast numbers of French and Latin words, borrowed at the height of certain cultural influences, could not maintain themselves in the language.

Latin-German words like kredibel "credible" and French-German words like reussieren "to succeed" offered nothing that the unconscious mind could assimilate to its customary method of feeling and handling words. It is as though this unconscious mind said: "I am perfectly willing to accept *kredibel* if you will just tell me what you mean by *kred-*."

Hence German has generally found it easier to create new words out of its own resources, as the necessity for them arose. The psychological contrast between English and German as regards the treatment of foreign material is a contrast that may be studied in all parts of the world. The Athabaskan languages of America are spoken by peoples that have had astonishingly varied cultural contacts, yet nowhere do we find that an Athabaskan dialect has borrowed at all freely from a neighbouring language.

These languages have always found it easier to create new words by compounding afresh elements ready to hand. They have for this reason been highly resistant to receiving the linguistic impress of the external cultural experiences of their speakers. Cambodgian and Tibetan offer a highly instructive contrast in their reaction to Sanskrit influence.

Both are analytic languages, each totally different from the highlywrought, inflective language of India. Cambodgian is isolating, but, unlike Chinese, it contains many polysyllabic words whose etymological analysis does not matter. Like English, therefore, in its relation to French and Latin, it welcomed immense numbers of Sanskrit loan-words, many of which are in common use to-day.

There was no psychological resistance to them. Classical Tibetan literature was a slavish adaptation of Hindu Buddhist literature and nowhere has Buddhism implanted itself more firmly than in Tibet, yet it is strange how few Sanskrit words have found their way into the language. Tibetan was highly resistant to the polysyllabic words of Sanskrit because they could not automatically fall into significant syllables, as they should have in order to satisfy the Tibetan feeling for form. Tibetan was therefore driven to translating the great majority of these Sanskrit words into native equivalents.

The Tibetan craving for form was satisfied, though the literally translated foreign terms must often have done violence to genuine Tibetan idiom. Even the proper names of the Sanskrit originals were carefully translated, element for element, into Tibetan; *e.g.*, Suryagarbha "Sun-bosomed" was carefully Tibetanized into Nyi-mai snying-po "Sun-of heart-the, the heart (or essence) of the sun." The study of how a language reacts to the presence of foreign words — rejecting them, translating them, or freely accepting them — may throw much valuable light on its innate formal tendencies.

The borrowing of foreign words always entails their phonetic modification. There are sure to be foreign sounds or accentual peculiarities that do not fit the native phonetic habits. They are then so changed as to do as little violence as possible to these habits. Frequently we have phonetic compromises. Such an English word as the recently introduced camouflage, as now ordinarily pronounced, corresponds to the typical phonetic usage of neither English nor French. The aspirated k, the obscure vowel of the second syllable, the precise quality of the l and of the last a, and, above all, the strong accent on the first syllable, are all the results of unconscious assimilation to our English habits of pronunciation.

They differentiate our camouflage clearly from the same word as pronounced by the French. On the other hand, the long, heavy vowel in the third syllable and the final position of the "zh" sound (like z in azure) are distinctly un-English, just as, in Middle English, the initial j and v must have been felt at first as not strictly in accord with English usage, though the strangeness has worn off by now. In all four of these cases — initial j, initial v, final "zh," and unaccented a of father — English has not taken on a new sound but has merely extended the use of an old one.

Occasionally a new sound is introduced, but it is likely to melt away before long. In Chaucer's day the old Anglo-Saxon ü (written y) had long become unrounded to i, but a new set of ü-vowels had come in from the French (in such words as due, value, nature). The new ü did not long hold its own; it became diphthongized to iu and was amalgamated with the native iw of words like new and slew. Eventually this diphthong appears as yu, with change of stress — dew (from Anglo-Saxon deaw) like due (Chaucerian dü). Facts like these show how stubbornly a language resists radical tampering with its phonetic pattern.

Nevertheless, we know that languages do influence each other in phonetic respects, and that quite aside from the taking over of foreign sounds with borrowed words. One of the most curious facts that linguistics has to note is the occurrence of striking phonetic parallels in totally unrelated or very remotely related languages of a restricted geographical area. These parallels become especially impressive when they are seen contrastively from a wide phonetic perspective. Here are a few examples.

The Germanic languages as a whole have not developed nasalized vowels. Certain Upper German (Suabian) dialects, however, have now nasalized vowels in lieu of the older vowel + nasal consonant (n). Is it only accidental that these dialects are spoken in proximity to French, which makes abundant use of nasalized vowels?

Again, there are certain general phonetic features that mark off Dutch and Flemish in contrast, say, to North German and Scandinavian dialects. One of these is the presence of unaspirated voiceless stops (p, t, k), which have a precise, metallic quality reminiscent of the corresponding French sounds, but which contrast with the stronger, aspirated stops of English, North German, and Danish. Even if we assume that the unaspirated stops are more archaic, that they are the unmodified descendants of the old Germanic consonants, is it not perhaps a significant historical fact that the Dutch dialects, neighbours of French, were inhibited from modifying these consonants in accordance with what seems to have been a general Germanic phonetic drift?

Even more striking than these instances is the peculiar resemblance, in certain special phonetic respects, of Russian and other Slavic languages to the unrelated Ural-Altaic languages of the Volga region. The peculiar, dull vowel, for instance, known in Russian as "yeri" has Ural-Altaic analogues, but is entirely wanting in Germanic, Greek, Armenian, and IndoIranian, the nearest Indo-European congeners of Slavic. We may at least suspect that the Slavic vowel is not historically unconnected with its Ural-Altaic parallels. One of the most puzzling cases of phonetic parallelism is afforded by a large number of American Indian languages spoken west of the Rockies.

Even at the most radical estimate there are at least four totally unrelated linguistic stocks represented in the region from southern Alaska to central California. Nevertheless all, or practically all, the languages of this immense area have some important phonetic features in common.

Chief of these is the presence of a "glottalized" series of stopped consonants of very distinctive formation and of quite unusual acoustic effect. In the northern part of the area all the languages, whether related or not, also possess various voiceless l-sounds and a series of "velar" (backguttural) stopped consonants which are etymologically distinct from the ordinary k-series. It is difficult to believe that three such peculiar phonetic features as I have mentioned could have evolved independently in neighbouring groups of languages.

How are we to explain these and hundreds of similar phonetic convergences? In particular cases we may really be dealing with archaic similarities due to a genetic relationship that it is beyond our present power to demonstrate. But this interpretation will not get us far. It must be ruled entirely out of court, for instance, in two of the three European examples I have instanced; both nasalized vowels and the Slavic "yeri" are demonstrably of secondary origin in Indo-European. However we envisage the process in detail, we cannot avoid the inference that there is a tendency for speech sounds or certain distinctive manners of articulation to spread over a continuous area in somewhat the same way that elements of culture ray out from a geographical centre.

We may suppose that individual variations arising at linguistic borderlands — whether by the unconscious suggestive influence of foreign speech habits or by the actual transfer of foreign sounds into the speech of bilingual individuals — have gradually been incorporated into the phonetic drift of a language.

So long as its main phonetic concern is the preservation of its sound patterning, not of its sounds as such, there is really no reason why a language may not unconsciously assimilate foreign sounds that have succeeded in worming their way into its gamut of individual variations, provided always that these new variations (or reinforced old variations) are in the direction of the native drift.

A simple illustration will throw light on this conception. Let us suppose that two neighbouring and unrelated languages, A and B, each possess voiceless lsounds (compare Welsh ll). We surmise that this is not an accident. Perhaps comparative study reveals the fact that in language A the voiceless l-sounds correspond to a sibilant series in other related languages, that an old alternation s: sh has been shifted to the new alternation I (voiceless): s. Does it follows that the voiceless l of language B has had the same history?

Not in the least. Perhaps B has a strong tendency towards audible breath release at the end of a word, so that the final l, like a final vowel, was originally followed by a marked aspiration. Individuals perhaps tended to anticipate a little the voiceless release and to "unvoice" the latter part of the final l-sound (very much as the l of English words like felt tends to be partly voiceless in anticipation of the voicelessness of the t).

Yet this final l with its latent tendency to unvoicing might never have actually developed into a fully voiceless l had not the presence of voiceless l-sounds in A acted as an un- conscious stimulus or suggestive push towards a more radical change in the line of B's own drift. Once the final voiceless l emerged, its alternation in related words with medial voiced l is very likely to have led to its analogical spread. The result would be that both A and B have an important phonetic trait in common.

Eventually their phonetic systems, judged as mere assemblages of sounds, might even become completely assimilated to each other, though this is an extreme case hardly ever realized in practice. The highly significant thing about such phonetic interinfluencings is the strong tendency of each language to keep its phonetic pattern intact. So long as the respective alignments of the similar sounds is different, so long as they have differing "values" and "weights" in the unrelated languages, these languages cannot be said to have diverged materially from the line of their inherent drift. In phonetics, as in vocabulary, we must be careful not to exaggerate the importance of interlinguistic influences.

I have already pointed out in passing that English has taken over a certain number of morphological elements from French. English also uses a number of affixes that are derived from Latin and Greek. Some of these foreign elements, like the -ize of materialize or the -able of breakable, are even productive today. Such examples as these are hardly true evidences of a morphological influence exerted by one language on another.

Setting aside the fact that they belong to the sphere of derivational concepts and do not touch the central morphological problem of the expression of relational ideas, they have added nothing to the structural peculiarities of our language. English was already prepared for the relation of pity to piteous by such a native pair as luck and lucky; material and materialize merely swelled the ranks of a form pattern familiar from such instances as wide and widen.

In other words, the morphological influence exerted by foreign languages on English, if it is to be gauged by such examples as I have cited, is hardly different in kind from the mere borrowing of words. The introduction of the suffix -ize made hardly more difference to the essential build of the language than did the mere fact that it incorporated a given number of words.

8

Role of Language and Literature

The study of English language is gaining more and more significance and its inevitability is felt meticulously in the global contexts. The learning of English is inexorable in the present milieu as it has become the link language. However, the teachers and learners of English in India where students are the non-native learners of English face many problems related to teaching-learning of English. The teachers have to develop essential skills of students to teach them to express themselves in English in academic as well as real life contexts.

Along with the study of English language, study of English literature is also important. The English literature has a wide readership. Hence, study of this literature widens the literary spectrum of readers. Indian students are to be inspired to consider the study of English literature as significant as the study of English language. It is valuable even in language learning.

CULTURE AND LITERATURE

Most of the Indian universities prescribe the British, the American, and the Commonwealth literature. Except the Indian literature, the Indian students cannot easily understand the whole body of the British or the American or any other literature. These literatures contain various allusions, customs, manners, mythologies, and other details. They refer to various social, political, religious references. If the Indian students have to understand the foreign literature, they must know its context and background. They have to comprehend the lexical items in the text that carry the thematic or content meaning in the piece of literature. If they do not know the context, there is a possibility of ennui while studying literature. It is therefore the duty of the teachers of literature to make the study of English literature interesting and also sustain students' motive to seek an appropriate pleasure and knowledge which is usually found in studying literature. Consequently, it is indispensable to find out some creative techniques to teach English literature to the Indian students.

LITERATURE THROUGH TASK BASED METHOD

Among recent manifestation of Communicative Language Teaching, task based instruction has emerged as a major focal point of language teaching practice worldwide.

As the profession has continued to emphasize classroom interaction, learner-centered teaching, authenticity, and viewing the learner's own experience as important contributors to learning, task based interaction draws the attention of teachers and learners to task in the classroom.

Task based instruction is an approach that urges teachers, in their lesson and curriculum design, to focus on many of the communicative factors.

In order to accomplish a task, a learner needs to have sufficient organizational and illocutionary competence to convey intended meaning, strategic competence to compensate for unforeseen difficulties, and then all the tools of discourse, pragmatics, and even non-verbal communicative ability. It sounds quite clear that our major accountability as teachers of English as a Foreign Language is to assist our learners to reach their best potentials and to be eventually communicatively competent. But to do this successfully, we ought to go beyond the traditionally held views of mastering linguistic accuracy of form and structure because they do not definitely guarantee to be semantically, syntactically, and, above all, pragmatically competent'. It is believed that literature could serve this end.

OLD METHOD OF TEACHING ENGLISH

The English language teaching tradition has been subject to tremendous change, especially throughout the twentieth century. Perhaps more than any other discipline, this tradition has been practiced, in various adaptations, in language classrooms all around the world for centuries.

Kelly's (1969) informative survey of language teaching over "twenty-five centuries 'revealed interesting anecdotal accounts of foreign language instruction but few if any research-based language teaching methods.

As other languages began to be taught in educational institutions in the eighteenth and nineteenth centuries, the Classical Method was adopted as the chief means for teaching foreign languages.

Little thought was given at the time to teaching oral use of languages; after all, languages were not being taught primarily to learn oral/aural communication, but to learn for the sake of being "scholarly" or, in some instances, for gaining a reading proficiency in a foreign language. Since there was little if any theoretical research on second language acquisition in general, or on the acquisition of reading proficiency, foreign languages were taught as any other skill was taught.

NEW METHOD OF LANGUAGE TEACHING

Against the backdrop of the previous 19 centuries, a glance through the past century or so of language teaching gives us, ironically, a rather refreshingly interesting picture of varied interpretations of the "best" way to teach a foreign language. Perhaps beginning with Francois Gouin's (1880) Series Method, foreign language teaching underwent some revolutionary trends, all of which in one way or another came under the scrutiny of scientific (or observational) research.

As schools of thought have come and gone, so have language teaching trends waxed and waned in popularity. Historically, pedagogical innovation has been the beneficiary of the theoretical research, as witnessed by the influence of such research on trends in language teaching.

At the same time, language classrooms and their innovative teachers and students have been laboratories of research that have, in turn, informed theoretical stances as they have changed over time Task-based learning was first developed by Prabhu in Bangladore, southern India. Prabhu believed that students may learn more effectively when their minds are focused on the task, rather than on the language they are using

Nunan defines task as a piece of classroom work involving learners in a understanding, directing, producing or interacting way in the target language while the students' attention is focused on activating their grammatical knowledge in order to express meaning, and in which the aim is to express meaning rather than to manipulate form.

The task should also have a sense of wholeness, being able to stand alone as a communicative act in its own right with a beginning, middle and an end. The topics discussed in communicative and task-based environments arc generally topics of general interest to the learner.

Task-based learning involves those instructions in which classroom activities arc tasks similar to those which learners may engage in outside the second language classroom. Tasks may be complex, for example, creating a school newspaper or easier such as making a hotel reservation.

There are not many published examples of complete language programmes which claim that they arc totally based on formulations of task-based language teaching.

The literature contains mainly descriptions of examples of task-based activities. Breen makes a broad description of a task: A language learning task can be regarded as a springboard for learning work. In a broad sense, it is a structured plan for the provision of opportunities for the refinement of knowledge and capabilities entailed in a new language and its use during communication. Such a work plan will have its own particular objective, appropriate content which is to be worked upon, and a working procedure. A simple and brief exercise is a task, and also arc more complex and comprehensive Work plans.

Which require spontaneous communication of meaning or the solving of the problems? In learning and communicating? Any language test can be included within this spectrum of tasks. All materials designed for language teaching-through their particular organization of content and the working procedures they assume or propose for the learning of content- can be seen as compendia of tasks.

Brown (2001) assumes that in task-based instruction, the main concern is not the small pieces of language, but rather the practical purposes for which language must be used. And input for tasks may come from different sources such as speeches, conversations, narratives, public announcements, cartoon strips, interviews, oral descriptions, etc.

While in task-based instruction the focus is on communication, purpose and meaning, the goals are linguistics in nature. These goals are not in the traditional sense of just focusing on grammar or phonology, but they include preserving the centrality of functions like greeting, expressing opinions as well.

CHARACTERISTICS OF TASK-BASED INSTRUCTION

While proponents of Task-Based Instruction beliefs, according to Swan, there is a broad agreement on the following principles:

Instructed language learning should primarily involve natural or naturalistic language use, and the activities arc concerned with meaning rather than language. Instruction should favour learner centeredness rather than teacher control. Since purely naturalistic learning does not normally lead to target-like accuracy, involvement is necessary in order to foster the acquisition of formal linguistic elements while keeping the perceived advantages of a natural approach. This can be done best by providing opportunities for focus on the form, which will draw students' attention to linguistic elements as they arise incidentally in lessons whose prime focus is on meaning or communication. Communicative tasks are a particularly appropriate tool for such an approach. More formal pre or post-task language study may be useful. This may contribute to acquisition by leading or increasing noticing of formal features during communication. Traditional approaches arc ineffective and undesirable, especially where they involve passive formal instruction and practice separated from communicative work.

APPROACHES TO TEACHING LITERATURE

Having decided that integrating literature into the EFL syllabus is beneficial to the learners' linguistic development, we need to select an approach which best serves the needs of EFL learners and the syllabus. Carter and Long (1991) describe the rationale for the use of the three main approaches to the teaching of literature:

THE CULTURAL MODEL

This model represents the traditional approach to teaching literature. Such a model requires learners to explore and interpret the social, political, literary and historical context of a specific text. By using such a model to teach literature we not only reveal the universality of such thoughts and ideas but encourage learners to understand different cultures and ideologies in relation to their own. This model is largely rejected by those in TEFL since not only does it tend to be teacher-centred but there is little opportunity for extended language work.

THE LANGUAGE MODEL

The most common approach to literature in the EFL classroom is what Carter and Long (1991) refer to as the 'language-based approach'. Such an approach enables learners to access a text in a systematic and methodical way in order to exemplify specific linguistic features *e.g.* literal and figurative language, direct and indirect speech.

This approach lends itself well to the repertoire of strategies used in language teaching - cloze procedure, prediction exercises, jumbled sentences, summary writing, creative writing and role play - which all form part of the repertoire of EFL activities used by teachers to deconstruct literary texts in order to serve specific linguistic goals. Carter and McRae (1996) describe this model as taking a 'reductive' approach to literature. These activities are disconnected from the literary goals of the specific text in that they can be applied to any text. There is little engagement of the learner with the text other than for purely linguistic practice; literature is used in a rather purposeless and mechanistic way in order to provide for a series of language activities orchestrated by the teacher.

THE PERSONAL GROWTH MODEL

This model attempts to bridge the cultural model and the language model by focusing on the particular use of language in a text, as well as placing it in a specific cultural context. Learners are encouraged to express their opinions, feelings and opinions and make connections between their own personal and cultural experiences and those expressed in the text. Another aspect of this model is that it helps learners develop knowledge of ideas and language – content and formal schemata – through different themes and topics.

This function relates to theories of reading (Goodman, 1970) which emphasise the interaction of the reader with the text. As Cadorath and Harris point out "text itself has no meaning, it only provides direction for the reader to construct meaning from the reader's own experience". Thus, learning is said to take place when readers are able to interpret text and construct meaning on the basis of their own experience.

These three approaches to teaching literature differ in terms of their focus on the text: firstly, the text is seen as a cultural artefact; secondly, the text is used as a focus for grammatical and structural analysis; and thirdly, the text is the stimulus for personal growth activities.

What is needed is an approach to teaching literature in the EFL classroom which attempts to integrate these elements in a way that makes literature accessible to learners and beneficial for their linguistic development.

RATIONALE FOR AN INTEGRATED MODEL FOR TEACHING LITERATURE

According to Duff and Maley (1990), the main reasons for integrating these elements are linguistic, methodological and motivational. Linguistically, by using a wide range of authentic texts we introduce learners to a variety of types and difficulties of English language. Methodologically, literary discourse sensitises readers to the processes of reading *e.g.* the use of schema, strategies for intensive and extensive reading etc. And, lastly, motivationally, literary texts prioritise the enjoyment of reading since, as Short and Candlin assert (1986), 'if literature is worth teaching...then it seems axiomatic that it is the response to literature itself which is important'. Interpretation of texts by learners can bring about personal responses from readers by touching on significant and engaging themes.

An integrated model is a linguistic approach which utilises some of the strategies used in stylistic analysis, which explores texts, literary and non-literary, from the perspective of style and its relationship to content and form.

This involves the systematic and detailed analysis of the stylistic features of a text – vocabulary, structure, register etc. in order to find out 'not just what a text means, but also how it comes to mean what it does'.

This suggested model integrates linguistic description with interpretation of the text although for the benefit of the foreign language learners it is not as technical, rigourous or analytical as the stylistics approach. With the careful selection of the text, it can be adapted for all levels.

Stage 1: Preparation and Anticipation

This stage elicits learners' real or literary experience of the main themes and context of text.

Stage 2: Focusing

Learners experience the text by listening and or reading and focusing on specific content in the text.

Stage 3: Preliminary Response

Learners give their initial response to the text - spoken or written

Stage 4: Working at it - I

Focus is on comprehending the first level of meaning through intensive reading.

Stage 5: Working at it - II

Focus is on analysis of the text at a deeper level and exploring how the message is conveyed through overall structure and any special uses of language - rhythm, imagery, word choice etc.

Stage 6: Interpretation and Personal Response

The focus of this final step is on increasing understanding, enhancing enjoyment of the text and enabling learners to come to their own personal interpretation of the text. This is based on the rationale for the personal growth model.

CONCLUSION

There are many benefits to using literature in the EFL classroom. Apart from offering a distinct literary world which can widen learners' understanding of their own and other cultures, it can create opportunities for personal expression as well as reinforce learners' knowledge of lexical and grammatical structure. Moreover, an integrated approach to the use of literature offers learners strategies to analyse and interpret language in context in order to recognize not only how language is manipulated but also why.

An integrated approach to the use of literature in the language classroom offers foreign language learners the opportunity to develop not only their linguistic and communicative skills but their knowledge about language in all its discourse types. The use of literary texts in the language classroom can be a potentially powerful pedagogic tool.

PROGRESS IN LANGUAGE AND LITERATURE

It is held here that the model of evolution established in biology is also at least partially applicable to linguistic evolution. To describe linguistic change as evolutionary is, of course, in one way a metaphor, since the notion of evolution was first established in biology and has simply been transferred to linguistic study by analogy. The 'language instinct' certainly appeared in humans as a result of evolution, and bears all the hallmarks of having emerged through straightforward evolutionary processes.

As proof of this, we might notice, for instance, how-typically in biological evolution-the articulators used for human speech, such as tongue, teeth, nasal cavity and so on, had physical functions to do with eating and breathing before they developed secondary, speech-forming functions (cf. animals with tongues, teeth etc. but without speech); in biology, this process has been termed exaptation, and the term has recently been applied to linguistic evolution as well.

It may be permissible, however, to argue that historical linguistics is literally an evolutionary discipline, since the mechanisms of change with which the subject engages seem to work in evolutionary ways. Most notably, linguistic evolution seems to work through a 'blind watchmaker', or (using another frequent metaphor) through a 'hidden hand'. There remain, however, two important differences between biological and linguistic evolution. The first difference is one which is more apparent than real. Some early evolutionary biologists interpreted Darwin's theory to mean that there was an overall direction in evolution, in which more 'advanced' creatures succeeded more 'primitive' ones.

This view is no longer held in quite the same terms by modern evolutionists, although it remains part of the popular understanding of the theory; it is now felt by evolutionists that an amoeba (for instance) does a perfect job for the environment in which it exists, and in such an environment a human being (for instance) would not be nearly as efficient.

Dinosaurs were magnificent and complex creatures, comparable with many twentieth-century organisms, but the environment in which they lived changed and they became extinct. Much of the appeal of the modern ecology or 'green' movement lies in the way in which it has engaged with this notion of the 'equality of species'.

The older view of evolutionary progress had a certain vogue in the nineteenth century, correlating with contemporary ideas about the perfectibility of humankind, and it is therefore not surprising to find some nineteenth-and early-twentieth-century linguists extrapolating from this misunderstanding of Darwin's theories and introducing notions such as 'progress' or 'decay' into their linguistic speculations.

Thus O. Jespersen wrote in 1922 that in 'the evolution of languages the discarding of old flexions goes hand in hand with the development of simpler and more regular expedients that are rather less liable than the old ones to produce misunderstanding'. It is now generally held that linguistic evolution does not work in this way, however.

It is no longer believed by serious linguists that any language, at any point in its history, is any more or less 'primitive' or 'advanced' than any other; the language of the 'primitive' Bushmen is just as complex (or simple) in grammatical, phonological or lexical terms as the language of an 'advanced' European, and thus the adjectives complex and simple, difficult and easy are really inappropriate as neutral descriptors of natural languages. After all, many readers of this book may find Old English difficult-but the Anglo-Saxons, eleven hundred years ago, evidently did not. The second difference is a more significant one. In biological evolution, species diverge from each other so that it is possible to classify them as separate; they do not genetically come together again.

For example, the three orders of nature known as birds, insects and mammals undoubtedly share a common ancestor, a proto-form, which lived many thousands of millions of years ago; but it is possible to classify birds as a group separate from mammals and insects because all birds share a common ancestor which differs from the distinct common ancestors of mammals and insects. Languages do not behave precisely in this way. Present-Day English is a Germanic language, descended, like Present-Day German, Swedish, Dutch etc., from a common ancestor.

But English has also, during its history, taken on characteristics from non-Germanic languages with which it has come into contact, such as French. It is an important principle of biological classification ('cladistics') that separate orders, species etc. cannot overlap in evolutionary terms, and this distinction might be expressed notationally thus: (birds) (mammals) (insects).

However, languages cannot be separated in this way; were we to express the relationship between German, English and French using a similar notation we would arrive at a formula something as follows: (German (English) French). It follows from this formula that, unlike in biology, acquired characteristics in language can be inherited, for-for instance-English speakers can take on French vocabulary and integrate it into a system which can be then passed on to their successor language-users.

LINGUISTIC VARIATION AND CONSTRAINT

Corresponding in language to the minute mutations of biological evolution are linguistic variants. All living languages vary-the only ones which do not are dead ones, such as Latin, or formal ones, such as mathematical or logical notations. For instance, a single speaker can vary quite radically in the way he or she realises an individual linguistic item on different occasions-at its simplest, exemplified by the way in which many speakers of English have in their repertoire of usage two pronunciations of the stressed vowel in the item either, or different stress patterns for the word adult.

Most obviously, languages vary diatopically, that is, through geographical space, and we therefore distinguish between, for instance, Scottish and English accents or grammatical and lexical usage. However, variation can also arise within dialects or even individual linguistic repertoires because of such factors as age, social class and the level of formality adopted.

Such variation is a property of all natural languages, and it lies at the heart of linguistic change, for change depends on the availability of different choices. When a particular variant-innovation becomes adopted systematically by other speakers and used 'conventionally to communicate particular forms and meanings', it is possible to speak of linguistic change having taken place.

Since Weinreich et al. (1968), three stages in the operation of linguistic change have been generally distinguished by linguists: actuation, implementation and diffusion. A slightly modified version of this categorisation is adopted here: the potential for change, the triggering and implementation of change, the diffusion of change.

The potential for change exists in the particular linguistic choices made by particular language-users at a particular time; such choices may be compared with the constant process of biological mutation; it is constantly taking place, for it exists in the perpetual ebb and flow of linguistic variation. When linguists refer to linguistic change, they tend to refer to implementation and diffusion, that is, the systemic development.

Corresponding to natural selection in language are the constraints which govern communication within a given speech-community and therefore regulate the processes of implementation of change. These are the constraints of pragmatic interaction and of social setting; thus usage can only vary in so far as it remains broadly meaningful to the interlocutor, and there are powerful forces to do with social stigmatisation which constrain expression in other ways.

In pragmatic terms, it makes sense to use as little effort as possible to express meaning. However, this effort cannot be too little; the production of differentiated meaning is clearly a matter of speaker-hearer interaction, and the demands of communicative efficiency are such that a whole series of cues, not just one, must be offered to the hearer by the speaker. Languages need such redundancy, for no two speakers have the same usage, and to attempt to distinguish meaning on the basis of single cues would risk unintelligibility.

But if too much redundancy is maintained, or if the cues which are chosen are contradictory (*e.g.* an intended statement is expressed with intonation appropriate to a question), the system undergoes pressure. Such an opposition correlates with functionalist views of language, in which a 'principle of least effort' is balanced against a 'principle of maintaining intelligibility'. Notions such as these are well established in the literature.

A key notion in this context is that of variational space. Variation is possible because individual linguistic items occupy fairly broad slots in the langue within which they are situated, and their realisations in parole can therefore vary quite widely. Variational space is relevant to all levels of language. Thus, for example, the realisations of the vowel-phoneme produced by seventy-six different speakers in terms of recorded sound-frequencies.

These speakers all considered that they were producing the 'same' sound; but the records show that, although there are clearly defined limits for these realisations, there was nevertheless considerable phonological space within which they could take place.

This variation is not inefficiency, but communicatively necessary. Any two speakers will have, to a greater or lesser extent and as the result of slight physiological and social differences, a differing set of realisations for a particular phoneme, and it is therefore important for communicative purposes for each speaker to have a fairly wide tolerance of others' usages.

Similarly, in grammar, formal and informal usages can exist side by side within the same variational space, for instance isn't and is not occupy the same slots in the sentences That isn't right and That is not right, and, although one usage is more formal than the other, there are situations when either is suitable. Other sources of variation in grammar are to do with stress, and with analogy. The most obvious examples of analogous usage are produced by children acquiring linguistic skills.

When children say mouses for mice, or singed for sang, or mines (cf. yours, hers, his) for mine they have observed certain regularities in language and have extrapolated by analogy to regularise historically inherited forms which seem to them irregular.

A similar process is found in 'non-standard' English spoken by adults; thus foots for 'feet', a common usage in children's speech, has been recorded in adult language by dialectologists in (for instance) Present-Day East Suffolk, buyed for 'bought' in Present-Day Devon, and *badder* for 'worse' in Present-Day Cumberland.

All such examples, of course, are commonplace in those varieties of speech which are comparatively unconstrained by the pressures of formal and normative education. It is the custom of modern parents and teachers to correct such analogical creations and for adult users of such forms to suffer social stigmatisation; but, with reference to earlier times, before prescriptive norms of language became established; it is easy to conceive of a situation where analogical reorganisations would have been widely imitated.

Thus, Present-Day English those, a form entirely acceptable in the modern prestigious language, arose in the late Middle Ages through analogy: a prototypically plural inflection was added to earlier tho (from Old English þa), and the resulting form has been accepted into Present-Day English prescribed usage. The new, analogically produced form those seems to have been favoured in the standard language because it corresponds to an ancient contrastive usage ('ablaut'), whereby front vowels correlated with nearness (thus *these*) and back vowels with distance (thus *those*).

On the other hand Present-Day English yous ('you' pl.), a more recent analogical creation found in many varieties of the language, providing speakers with a potentially useful singular/plural distinction in the paradigm for the second-person pronoun and correlating with other grammatical markers such as the form of the verb *to be,* has not been so accepted; it appeared after the emergence of prescriptive norms, and has thus been stigmatised.

As for the lexicon, it is a proven fact that words mean different things in different contexts, and therefore have a fairly broad variational space. For instance, the expression to let the cat out of the bag has both a literal and a metaphorical significance: literally, a feline is liberated, but metaphorically, a truth (usually unwelcome) has been revealed, and this metaphorical usage would seem-in my own variety, at any rate-to be now more commonplace. Another source of variation is to do with linguistic register: thus, two words may denote the same referent-for example, begin and commence-but have very different connotations (in this example, to do with levels of formality).

This second example shows what happens when two words from different language-families-here, Germanic (begin) and Romance (commence)-are brought together within the same language: the two words, because first heard in different (and socially charged) circumstances, develop different connotations. A similar example is the contrast between destroy and break up.

Yet another kind of variation is demonstrated by the difference in connotation of the words ordure and shit; the usage of these words in Present-Day English exemplifies the contrast between technical and taboo usage (cf. the colloquial expression the shit hit the fan, beside a potentially more formal if less likely. The ordure hit the fan). Ordure and shit refer to the same natural object, but they plainly have developed distinct connotations. It should have become clear how such variation within variational space corresponds to the mutations of biological evolution; and, as in biological evolution, these linguistic mutations are constrained by the setting in which they exist. The main constraint on (phonological, grammatical, lexicological) variational space within a given variety of a language relates to the systemic properties of language in general.

Thus, for instance, analogical change in the history of a language may proceed further than the rest of the system requires, so further regulation becomes necessary. If language is systematic, then the rules of language are interconnected, and change in one can be assumed to have implications for others.

Space can be 'squeezed', that is, variables may start to overlap with each other to an unacceptable extent, introducing loss of information content and subsequent reorganisation; or space can be 'expanded', leading to an excess of redundancy. The interaction between variation and systemic constraints will be returned to frequently in subsequent chapters.

CONTACT BETWEEN LINGUISTIC SYSTEMS

The attentive reader will have noticed a flaw in the argument as presented in the previous section. If variation is constrained by a system, and that system reacts therapeutically, then there will in theory come a point in time when the system reaches an optimum position where all elements of which the system consists are in stasis; the variational spaces for each linguistic item will be stable, and the potential for the implementation of linguistic change will not be realised.

In such a situation, and given the existence of the mechanisms of linguistic evolution sketched so far, change should cease to occur. However, it is a matter of observation that no living language is unchanging. It is therefore necessary to distinguish a third factor in the operation of linguistic change: contact. Contact is most obviously manifested linguistically in the changing lexicon, when words are borrowed into English from other languages, but it can be more subtle: not only words, but also grammatical structures and even sounds can be transferred between languages, or from variety to variety within a language, for all sorts of reasons (*e.g.* for reasons of social prestige).

Moreover, the effects of linguistic contact need not be simply a matter of transference of forms; languages or varieties can affect each other in more subtle ways. Contact is a crucial factor in linguistic change because no language or variety of language exists in a vacuum. Speech-communities come into contact with other speech-communities in all sorts of situations, and the subsequent interaction between these communities causes linguistic change.

Some languages and varieties of language certainly change more slowly than others, and the reasons for the variable speeds of linguistic change are easy to determine, through the observation of extralinguistic correspondences. Languages such as Icelandic and Lithuanian have changed slowly over time because they are spoken by relatively homogeneous speech-communities which are comparatively isolated-either by geography or by historical hostility-from the groups of people around them. Thus rural varieties of English tend to change slowly in comparison with their urban counterparts not only because people in the countryside have fewer folk to interact with, but also because those folk who are there interact more closely.

In all these cases, there are strong social ties between the users of these languages or varieties, necessary in communities where the environment is hostile or where a strong communal sense is necessary for the efficient functioning of society. In urban settings, such limited change is demonstrated by those who stick closely to one social group without interacting greatly with those outside their immediate circle (*e.g.* the core members of certain urban 'gangs', who sustain their linguistic norms through exceptionally strong social ties).

Other languages, or varieties of language, change more quickly, and here, too, the social correspondences are well attested. Change is peculiarly liable to occur when large-scale immigration, invasion or social revolution takes place; it also tends to happen more quickly in towns, where large numbers of people, many with quite distinct linguistic systems, interact with each other. The term used to describe the social relationships between such folk is 'weakly tied', that is, having comparatively loose social ties with those around them.

Typically, a person with weak social ties will be 'class-mobile', attempting to leave one class and enter another, or feeling uneasily poised between one social group and another. It is an interesting fact that the modern discipline of dialectology/sociolinguistics has tended to move away from the study of strongly tied individuals (*e.g.* the notorious NORMS, 'non-mobile older rural males' who have preserved traditional usage because their language tends not to change, reflecting their tight social networks) towards weakly tied persons whose language, because it is liable to show a wider range of variation, exemplifies the processes of linguistic change discussed above.

There is a parallel in biological theory for 'variable-speed' evolution in language: so-called 'punctuationism', which, to put it crudely, holds that evolution takes place more quickly at some periods than at others. Some who have written on these matters have unfairly taken the work of the punctuationists to represent a rejection of Darwinian theory.

However, it has been shown quite conclusively that punctuationism, or more properly the 'theory of punctuated equilibrium', can be comfortably accommodated within the Darwinian paradigm; Dawkins points out that to take punctuationism as a rejection of Darwinian theory 'is as if the discovery that the Earth is not a perfect sphere but a slightly flattened spheroid were given banner treatment under the headline: The three mechanisms of linguistic change distinguished above-variation, systemic regulation, contact-are not to be taken as totally separate causes of the phenomenon; rather, they interact in complex and, except in the most general terms, practically unpredictable ways to produce dynamic change in the history of a given language. To sum up the argument so far: new variants are produced, and are imitated through contact; but they are constrained by the changing intra- and extralinguistic systems of which they are a part. The description of change given above might be considered somewhat mechanical, but it can easily be restated in more human terms. Human beings are social creatures, and not simply transmitters (speakers) or receivers (hearers); they are both.

When humans speak, they are not only producing sounds and grammar and vocabulary; they are also monitoring what they and others say by listening, and evaluating the communicative efficiency of their speech for the purposes for which it is being used: communicative purposes which are not only to do with the conveying and receiving of information, but also to do with such matters as signalling the social circumstances of the interaction taking place.

And what humans hear is constantly being monitored, that is, compared with their earlier experience as speakers and hearers. In any given speech-community there may be broad agreement as to the prototypical core-value of a given linguistic item, but, when speech-communities interact with each other, the overlap will not be exact, and this 'rough fit' is the source of linguistic variation.

Such individual microlinguistic events, the choices of individual speakers, can (although they need not) develop into those macrolinguistic events which we term 'linguistic change'. This principle of monitoring, or feedback as it is sometimes called, is crucial to an understanding of language-change. Individual and group-usages are all systems which overlap to a greater or lesser extent, each system consisting of a range of allowable variation-variation which can be found at every linguistic level. The range of allowable variation within any individual system makes up the 'givens' from which each new utterance proceeds: the linguistic input to a new speech-act. Givens may be considered to be either inherited or borrowed; speakers use variants which are native to their own variety, or they select variants which are available to them through contact with other varieties or even with other languages. This process whereby givens are transmitted is not of course genetic, for there does not seem to be any genetic transmission of language-specific features.

Rather, the process comes about through immersion in a particular speech-community. The truth of this argument is indicated, for example, by the fact that children of immigrants often adopt not their parents' language or variety but that of their peers in the same age-group. Linguistic givens exist at every level of language-lexicon, grammar, graphology, phonology-and in all they exist as the set of inherited and borrowed choices. They provide the language-setting from which any particular linguistic choice made at a particular time must proceed.

TREES AND WAVES

The last section concluded with a reference to the notions of inheritance and borrowing, and these notions are central to the historical study of language. Two descriptive models have traditionally been used to illustrate the processes of inheritance and borrowing respectively: the tree model and the wave model.

Both models derive from nineteenth-century scholarship, and stem from comparisons with what were (and in some quarters still are) perceived to be more 'mature' sciences: the tree model relates to the phylogenetic tree used in evolutionary biology, and the wave model relates to theories of action and reaction developed for the discipline of physics.

At one time the two models were seen as mutually exclusive, but most linguists since the end of the nineteenth century have considered them to be complementary. These models are relevant in both micro- and macrolinguistic contexts. According to the tree model, children attempt to reproduce the language of their parents; according to the wave model, children borrow linguistic features from their peers.

These models are also relevant on a macro-linguistic scale: languages descend from earlier ancestors (thus French and Spanish descend from Latin), or they borrow from neighbouring languages (thus Finnish, a non-Indo-European language, contains many Indo-European lexical items borrowed from Swedish).

Bibliography

Arthur A. Macdonell: *A History of Sanskrit Literature*, Kaveri Books, Delhi, 2015.

Arvind Krishna Mehrotra: *A Concise History of Indian Literature in English*, Permanent Black Publication, Delhi, 2013.

B.K. Patel: *A Critical History of English Literature*, Mangalam Publishers, Delhi, 2012.

Bimala Churn Law: *A History of Pali Literature*, Indica Books, Delhi, 2000.

C. Jagannath: *A Critical Assessment of Romantic Literature*, Swastik Publications, Delhi, 2011.

Chenchiah and Bhujanga: *A History of Telugu Literature*, AES Publication, Delhi, 2003.

D.K. Patnaik: *A Background to the Study of English Literature*, Swastik Publications, Delhi, 2012.

Daniel Reed and Tim Horton: *A Critical View of the Significance of Various Periods in English Literature*, Dominant Publication, Delhi, 2010.

Donald V. Bodeen: *A Critical Study on Life and Works of Sir Walter Scott : The Restless Dynamism in Life and Literature (2 Vols-Set)*, Dominant Publication, Delhi, 2008.

F.E.Keay: *A History Of Hindi Literature*, Rupa Publication, Delhi, 2003.

George Saintsbury: *A Short History of English Literature (2 Vols-Set)*, Atlantic Publication, Delhi, 2005.

George Saintsbury: *A Short History of English Literature (Vols 1 to 2 Set)*, Radha Publication, Delhi, 2008.

James B. Apple: *A Stairway Taken by the Lucid : Tsong Kha Pa's Study of Noble Beings (Sata-Pitaka Series: Indo-Asian Literatures: Vol. 643)*, Aditya Prakashan, Delhi, 2013.

John Dowson: *A Classical Dictionary of Hindu Mythology and Religion : Geography, History and Literature*, D.K. Printworld, Delhi, 2005.

John Dowson: *A Classical Dictionary of Hindu Mythology and Religion Geography History and Literature*, Satguru Publications, Delhi, 2008.

John Dowson: *A Classical Dictionary of Hindu Mythology and Religion Geography, History, and Literature*, Asian Educational Services, Delhi, 2004.

John Dowson: *A Classical Dictionary of India : Geography History Literature Sanskrit Religion and Mythology*, Sankalp Prakashan, Delhi, 2011.

John Garrett: *A Classical Dictionary of India : Illustrative of the Mythology, Philosophy, Literature, Antiquities, Arts, Manners, Customs and c. of the Hindus*, D K Printworld, Delhi, 2006.

K. Krishna Murthy: *A Dictionary of Buddhist Literature and Literary Personalities*, Sundeep Prakashan, Delhi, 1994.

K.M. Jan and Shabnam Firdaus: *A Guide to English Literature*, Atlantic Publication, Delhi, 2003.

Laurie Magnus: *A Dictionary of European Literature : Designed as a Companion to English Studies*, Cosmo Publication, Delhi, 2006.

M.L. Wadekar and Sweta Prajapati: *A Survey of Sanskrit Stotra Literature*, Bharatiya Kala Prakashan, Delhi, 2013.

Prasanna Kumar Acharya: *A Dictionary of Hindu Architecture : Treating of Sanskrit Architectural Terms with Illustrative Quotations from Silpasastras, General Literature and Archaeological Records.. Vol. I*, Munshiram Manoharlal, Delhi, 1995.

Ram Babu Saksena: *A History of Urdu Literature*, Cosmo Publication, Delhi, 2002.

Suraj Vashishth: *A Handbook of Buddhism: Art, Architecture, Literature and Philosophy*, Cyber Tech Publication, Delhi, 2009.

T. K. Krishna Menon: *A Primer of Malayalam Literature*, AES Publication, Delhi, 2001.

Thummapudi Bharathi: *A History of Telugu Dalit Literature*, Kalpaz Publication, Delhi, 2008.

Tim Horton: *A Critical Guide to the Life and Literature of Mark Twain, Vol. I and II*, Dominant Publication, Delhi, 2009.

W.T. Brande and Rev. George W. Cox: *A Dictionary of Science, Literature and Art (3 Vols-Set)*, Komal Publication, Delhi, 2000.

Yajanveer Dahiya: *A Critical Appreciation of Austerity in Ancient Indian Literature*, Eastern Book Linkers, Delhi, 2003.

Index